URBANISM:
IMPORTED OR EXPORTED?

URBANISM: IMPORTED OR EXPORTED?

EDITED BY

Joe Nasr and Mercedes Volait

First published in Great Britain in 2003 by
WILEY-ACADEMY
a division of
John Wiley & Sons Ltd, The Atrium, Southern Gate,
Chichester, West Sussex PO19 8SQ, England

Telephone (+44) 1243 779777

Email (for orders and customer service enquiries): cs-books@wiley.co.uk

Visit our Home Page on www.wileyeurope.com or www.wiley.com

This publication is designed to provide accurate and authoritative information in regard to the subject matter covered. It is sold on the understanding
that the Publisher is not engaged in rendering professional services. If professional advice or other expert assistance is required, the services of a
competent professional should be sought.

Other Wiley Editorial Offices
John Wiley & Sons Inc., 111 River Street, Hoboken, NJ 07030, USA
Jossey-Bass, 989 Market Street, San Francisco, CA 94103–1741, USA
Wiley-VCH Verlag GmbH, Boschstr. 12, D–69469 Weinheim, Germany
John Wiley & Sons Australia Ltd, 33 Park Road, Milton, Queensland
4064, Australia
John Wiley & Sons (Asia) Pte Ltd, 2 Clementi Loop #02–01,
Jin Xing Distripark, Singapore 129809
John Wiley & Sons Canada Ltd, 22 Worcester Road, Etobicoke,
Ontario, Canada M9W 1L1

ISBN 0470851600

Cover design: Artmedia Press Ltd, London
Typeset by Florence Production Ltd, Stoodleigh, Devon, UK
Printed and bound by TJ International Ltd, Padstow, Cornwall, UK

This book is printed on acid-free paper responsibly manufactured from
sustainable forestry, in which at least three trees are planted for each one
used for paper production.

CONTENTS

PREFACE

Using a dozen examples from around the world and from the past two centuries, this book explores the transfers of models that seek to shape urban environments, largely from the perspective of those who import them instead of those who export them, thus placing the multitude of local actors inside rather than on the margins of the fabrication of urban spaces. The book emerged from the observation by a few young researchers who are at its origin, that they shared a sense of unease with the content, the methods as well as the tone of much recent literature dealing with the formation of modern cities, particularly in 'developing countries': a feeling that it often did not adequately convey the complexity of power relations and flows in this formation. In particular, the local elements are under-represented in many recent studies, and where they are present they are often dealt with as recipients of actions rather than as actors. In reaction to this, a project was assembled one paper at a time to illustrate the variety of ways in which local and foreign actors and concepts have interacted, particularly since the advent of global colonialism and since its demise and replacement by a loosely defined postcolonial period.

In order to examine these matters, these researchers organized a seminar from 20 to 22 December 1998, with close to thirty participants. Presenters included both younger and established scholars, including Anthony King who delivered the keynote lecture. The eighteen papers presented were distributed in advance to all the participants, allowing the seminar to be devoted to discussing the papers, identifying the broader themes and common points across them, and bringing out conclusions of broader implications. Five papers from that seminar were published first as a special issue of the journal *City and Society*.[1] Most of the remaining papers – plus three later additions – would form the basis for this book.

The seminar and book were limited to cases dating from the nineteenth and twentieth centuries to concentrate on the 'modern'/industrial period, an era of accelerated diffusion of Western ideas around the world, parallel to the expansion of several imperial powers (and the decline of some others). Moreover, more than half the papers dealt with cities and countries located in the Middle East (broadly defined) and the Mediterranean basin, as considerable debate and implementation of urbanistic and architectural models born in Europe took place in that region, given the geographic proximity.

Nevertheless, in order to place these cases in the larger context of the international diffusion of Western techniques and doctrines so as to ensure the broader applicability of the arguments made here, contributions that deal with Asia, Latin America, Africa and Europe itself were also included.[2] While the papers are historical in nature, several of them bring new perspectives to current issues such as the globalization phenomenon.

The researchers whose original initiative led to this undertaking are Joe Nasr, Fuad Malkawi, Fassil Zewdou, Rula Sadik and Mercedes Volait (the first three were at the University of Pennsylvania at the time). The project was launched at the 1996 conference of the International Planning History Society (IPHS) in Thessaloniki. It was thus placed under the aegis of the IPHS; several of its members – including its past president, Stephen Ward – took part in the Beirut seminar. While this was essentially a closed seminar, some other interested individuals were invited. Most participants were affiliated with, or had studied in, French or US universities; so incidentally this project sought to integrate the knowledge of the subject in the French- and English-language literatures.

Joe Nasr and Mercedes Volait were the organizers of the Beirut seminar – and continued as the editors for the book. The institutional sponsors for the seminar were: the Center for Behavioral Research (CBR) at the American University of Beirut; the Centre d'études et de recherches sur le Moyen-Orient contemporain (CERMOC), Beirut; and the Centre d'études et de recherches sur l'urbanisation du Monde Arabe (URBAMA), Tours. France's Centre National de la Recherche Scientifique (CNRS) provided vital complementary funding. Key commitments to the project came from Samir Khalaf (CBR), Pierre-Robert Baduel (URBAMA), Eric Huybrechts and Elisabeth Picard (both formerly at CERMOC). The support staff at the three institutions permitted the seminar to take place smoothly.

Many of those present in Beirut have remained a steady source of encouragement and wisdom in the years since, particularly Jens Hanssen, Anthony King and Stephen Ward. Our authors deserve our congratulations simply for remaining patient with us as we have brought the project to very slow fruition. We wish to thank Sharon Nagy for enabling us to maintain the momentum by agreeing to edit the papers that went into *City and Society*. We also appreciate the contribution made by the three other founders of the project (Fuad, Fassil and Rula) who could not continue with us. We recognize as well Eric Verdeil and Taoufik Souami, who were inspired by the project to set up research programs of their own. Other individuals have provided us with advice or other backing at different stages of the project as it went from concept to seminar to book, and include Ray Bromley, Jeff Cody, Will Glover, June Komisar, Pauline Lavagne, Seymour Mandelbaum, Alan Middleton and Anthony Sutcliffe. The many who hosted Joe's many visits to Paris allowed us to have the countless face-to-face meetings that proved essential to develop both seminar and book.

The working relationship with the professionals at Wiley has been excellent,
including Abigail Grater, Mariangela Palazzi-Williams, Colin Howarth and
Caroline Ellerby.

Finally, we offer our personal thanks to those nearest to us for enabling
us to pursue this activity year after year – above all Louise and Thérèse, our
local supporters.

Joe Nasr and Mercedes Volait
2002

Notes

1. The title of that issue matches the one for this book: 'Urbanism: Imported/
    Exported', vol. 12, no. 1 (2000): 147 pp, and was guest-edited by Sharon Nagy, one
    of the participants in the seminar. The five papers in that issue are summarized
    in the introductory chapter of this book.
2. As a result of these different origins, the papers use terms from a range of original
    languages. Consequently, no attempt has been made at forcing a standard trans-
    literation across the papers. Similarly, different writing styles and methods of
    expressions coexist in this book.

INTRODUCTION: TRANSPORTING PLANNING

Joe Nasr and Mercedes Volait

ON PLACING THE PERIPHERY AT THE CENTER

This book seeks to explore the complex nature of modern urbanism (broadly understood)[1] since the nineteenth century, by emphasizing the modes of diffusion[2] and implementation of its models away from their place of origin, primarily in the countries of the Mediterranean basin. The project is rooted in the observation that much has been written in the past couple of decades, from a variety of perspectives, on the transfer of ideas on the built environment, and more particularly on the history of colonial and postcolonial city planning and architecture. The literature has generally approached these topics from the angle of either the transfer of city-building concepts from the 'center' to the 'periphery', or the invention of concepts in the periphery by those originating from the center, to fulfill a number of explicit and implicit aims. These aims received special attention and, consequently, the local handling of these processes has tended to be largely neglected. Here, we propose a shift in perspective, 'placing the periphery at the center' of attention.

Our objective is certainly not to ignore the exporters of ideas and their motives – nor for that matter to replace one paradigm with another. Rather, this endeavor shifts the spotlight to the importers of ideas and their local realities, incorporating their interactions with the exporters. By expanding the field of observation in urban research, this enlarges our comprehension of the cultures, processes and agents at work in the production of the city, and of the identity of its inhabitants. In doing so, we acknowledge certain antecedents and parallels to the approach we call for here. These include, among others: histories of 'common folks', which have shifted historical writings away from their obsession with great people, landmark events and grand movements; the 'subaltern' literature, which has brought to light the stories of those on the lowest rungs (and thus the most silent and invisible) in a society; analyses of urban planning models and techniques and their flows, networks, exchanges and adaptations; and the emergence of an understanding of 'planning cultures' and of a milieu of professionals who shape the urban environment.

Reacting against an image of locals that, at its extreme, regards them as impotent, passive and guileless recipients of concepts foreign to their cultures and as spectators observing physical and spatial changes that they neither control nor understand, we posit that locals often played active roles in helping shape the choice, adaptation and realization of the planning and architectural ideas. This does not imply that importing consisted simply of blind mimicry of the West. In addition to seeking to partake in the global modernization project, local actors (autochthons and settlers, the elite and non-elite, majority and minority groups) have used the elaboration of plans to address their own urban concerns and ambitions. So the local demands and aspirations of stakeholders of varying origins (indigenous and other) could actually form, in part, the basis for the plans that were put forward by outside planners.

Consequently, the book examines how particular techniques and concepts of urban intervention developed in some 'Western' (chiefly European) countries in the past two centuries and projected as modern, were then introduced in several types of situations: within those countries (with ideas transmitted from one city – typically the capital – to the rest of the nation), into other Western countries (with several known examples, from the spread of Haussmannism to the Garden City, to the more recent New Urbanism), and into non-Western countries (in both non-colonial and colonial settings). The transfer of these concepts and techniques, whether it consisted of processes of importation, exportation or (most frequently) a mixture of the two, could be coercive or voluntary. While different power relations defined each setting and bore certain implications for the basis on which the diffusion occurred, across all these possible relations (developed below), the transmission involved dynamic interactions that were not unidirectional. Taking into account that highly differentiated historical and spatial frameworks (going beyond colonial and Mediterranean cases) are being considered here, the book seeks to study comparatively the processes through which modern principles of urbanism have arisen and evolved away from their spheres of origin – acknowledging all the complexity the latter concept entails.

The point of view adopted in this book explains why colonialism was intentionally left out of its title. This is not to de-emphasize the place of the colonial experience, nor to underrate its importance as a productive and destructive force. Rather, it is based on three beliefs. First, colonial urbanism can be placed among a number of experiences where certain power relations interact with the built environment; consequently, it bears some parallels with non-colonial urban settings and should not be studied in isolation. Second, even in the extreme imbalance of power that colonialism represents, those whom one may believe to be voiceless and powerless still have some capacity to impact their built environment through the appropriation of production means, adaptation of models, setting of priorities, uses of space and so on – and through an instrument that is often under-recognized: inaction. Third, the aspirations of some of the (more or less) colonized may coincide – in various ways and on a range of occasions – with the objectives of the colonizers (change, living standards, 'modernity', 'development' . . .) or the interventions they adopt to achieve them (the boulevard, the sewer, zoning regulations . . .). Ultimately, the entire city-building process is revealed as much more elaborate than is often portrayed in the literature on colonial and postcolonial urbanism. In particular, urbanistic and architectural dissemination appears to be a phenomenon the channels, mechanisms and effects of which are far more varied than has been generally documented previously; it is part of an infinitely complex dialectic between center and periphery.

This book (and, we hope, future research) will seek to evaluate, among others, the following claims:

* planning and architectural discourse can be shaped by domestic realities (such as economic and social structures and political intents) as much as by the experience of professional planners (whether indigenous or foreign);
* a lack of planning or the thwarting of the implementation of plans can represent as much of a local choice as the successful introduction of foreign urbanistic precepts;
* rather than solely non-contextual foreign implants, the plans of outside planners are often influenced by, if not specific responses to, the priorities and expectations of actors from the host cities on the periphery, not just where local actors commissioned them but even where the planners may appear to be omnipotent and independent;
* while some outside planners and designers arrive in a foreign city with a collection of predetermined planning ideas, they often leave with their conception of planning having evolved as a result of their experience there, including their interaction with locals;
* the locals include a great variety of stakeholders and actors, ranging from the elite (who may have acted not only as willing participants in the colonizing process and the resulting urbanism, but even as catalysts for urbanistic changes) to the weakest members of society (who may nevertheless find ways to appropriate what is handed to them, though their contribution can frequently be difficult to recognize);
* in some cases, non-indigenous protagonists can be counted as locals when they (and sometimes several generations of their family) have been raised in that city or country; on the other hand, autochthons who have spent a portion (or all) of their professional career overseas may not be considered as locals upon their return; one can also identify go-betweens, advisors, mediators, who have their feet planted firmly in particular places and act as channels to the world at large; indeed, these and other

observations may lead in turn to rethinking how 'local' and 'foreign' are defined;

* the importing of Western ideas into some non-colonial situations may have been just as strong as the introduction that took place in neighboring and contemporary colonial situations; this and other remarks can put into question how much the transmission of modern urbanism should be linked to colonial arrangements, and whether principles based on domination, segregation, insertion and other urbanistic impositions of power should be associated solely with actors who are external to local cultures.

Changes in urban form, architecture, spaces, physical patterns, functions and so on will thus be shown to be generated by agents and forces both local and national/global. This broadens the discussion of how the transfers of ideas and techniques take place, in this case focusing on the activities and actors that shape built environments. The book aims to strengthen this line of questioning and test the validity of the stated hypotheses, while defining a set of issues that can be the object of future scholarly investigations concerning the relation of the locals to foreign planners, planning principles and processes of city building. It helps redress the neglect of the local element found in much of the relevant literature.

Across the wide range of cases described below, one can note a high degree of complexity in the ways models of urbanism are imported and exported. Depending on the local context, the *Zeitgeist*, the balance of power and other factors, these different types of urbanistic exchanges can result in contradictory relations between actors, structures, objectives and, consequently, urban forms. The call for papers for a recent conference on 'urban geopolitics' summarizes well many of the points we are making here:

> Urban space is the result of actions by multiple political, economic and social decision-makers and by citizens who are more or less mobilized and organized for the defense of their living environment. Motivated by divergent interests over frequently conflicting stakes, these urban actors function in a balance of power that is generally unequal. All of them develop varied strategies of appropriation of space, for occupying and defending the territory as for conquering power under its multiple forms . . . The proposing and opposing forces mesh with and confront each other; alternatives are put forward. A territorial mosaic, often complicated, submitted to subdivision and resubdivision, serves as a frame for the play of actors and as a springboard for their action strategies.[3]

COMPLEXITY AND CONTRADICTION IN URBANISM

The book is limited to cases dating from the nineteenth and twentieth centuries in order to concentrate on the 'modern'/industrial period, an era of accelerated transfer of Western ideas around the world, parallel to the expansion of several colonial powers (and the decline of some). Moreover, the focus is on the Middle East and the Mediterranean basin, as considerable debate and implementation of urbanistic and architectural models born in Europe took place there, given the geographic proximity. Consequently, more than half the papers deal with cities and countries located in that region. Nevertheless, in order to place these cases in the larger context of international diffusion of Western techniques and doctrines so as to ensure the broader applicability of the arguments made here, contributions that deal with Asia, Latin America, North America and Europe itself have also been included. Besides, the relation of the center to the periphery is a relevant question even within and amongst Western countries themselves.

Over the course of the exploration of the issues raised by this project's line of questioning, four main themes emerged as central. After a chapter by Anthony King that helps ground the book within the broader literature, the twelve case studies were grouped according to these four themes. This section outlines briefly the way every article (plus each of the five articles published in the *City and Society* special issue, since we conceived these as an integral part of this project) contributes to each theme, although most papers touch on several themes simultaneously. Common to all the papers is a central problem that King had defined in his introduction to that special issue: 'How, in a variety of political conditions, does a local, indigenous population respond to, modify, control or domesticate the urban development strategies of an external authority or power, be it a colonial state, a powerful commercial interest, or simply a firm of planning consultants?'[4]

Domesticating modernity: the latest models

Achieving or resisting modernity (no matter how defined) is an overarching objective for many of the actions taken by individuals and institutions, whether indigenous or exogenous. It underlies what is sought by those who hold power and resources, but also forms part of the motives of those who may contest them. Wishing to be modern – or to make others modern – often leads one to look other people and places for practices that can transform one's environment, or that of others. Newer practices thus serve as models that are imported and more or less adapted to local needs and conditions. While there may be a multitude of actors, interests and visions, the importation/exportation circuits are often relatively straightforward, with the origin and destination of a particular concept definable by a simple pair such as 'local client and foreign expert'. However, in other instances the circuits are more elaborate, so a single arrow cannot adequately represent the impacts of one source on one receptor. An analysis of the flows of models and the intermediaries in these flows frequently brings out the complexity in urbanistic exchanges.

Models can be introduced in one place first, then rapidly diffused across other urban landscapes in a given country or even across those of a number of countries in a given region. In Stephen Ward's chapter, we see several examples of this process spreading in both directions between Western Europe and North America.[5] A series of models can be proposed and often implemented, in succession or simultaneously, sometimes withstanding shifts in actors and institutions in power; the century-long history of Cairo's trans- formations outlined in Mercedes Volait's chapter makes clear how often mismatches could be found, at different points in time, between who held power in that city and what models were imposed there.

In other cases, later models represent a drastic shift in approach relative to the earlier ones. Brenda Yeoh's paper in *City and Society* tells the story of such a reversal in attitude – and consequently in interventions – towards the older forms of worker housing in Singapore.[6] The importing of a model can be indirect, passing from a source to a colonizer then to a colonized. The timing and means of introduction of exogenous models vary, from the colony (or the hinterland) being used as a 'laboratory' for new urbanistic approaches, to the periphery absorbing planning models after they have been developed in the center, to the colonial practice generating 'return effects' (*effets de retour*) once the expert goes back to the mother country with fresh experience.[7] Carola Hein's chapter shows how the Japanese adapted European planning ideas and introduced them simultaneously at home and in their colonies, through an elaborate set of exchanges between the two spaces, often using the same intermediaries. Ultimately, the interplay of ideas of urbanism, in conjunction with the complexity in the power relationships, can be no less than bewildering.

City-building, state-building and nation-building

State-building and nation-building are two goals that often get wrapped up in discourses of modernity. The relationship between these on one hand, and different models of city-building on the other, is worthy of special attention. Building a new state and creating a national identity for the first time (or once again) often leads those who gain power to accompany this effort (more or less explicitly) by new built environments. Indeed, over time the city- building effort can contribute to establishing a transformed relationship between the new state and its new citizens. Sharon Nagy's article in *City and Society* shows how this can be an explicit aim of the state in its placement of priority on civic intervention, while making clear that talking of 'the State' as a monolith hides the variety of public stakeholders, the multiplicity of their motives, and the inequality among them as actors upon the city.[8] In fact, competing interest groups – public, quasi-public, private – can come to bear on the shaping of the new environments of a recent nation-state, even in totalitarian settings.

Ironically, in creating new national settings, those in power may draw on the expertise of international figures, as Alexandra Yerolympos describes in the new Balkan states at the start of the twentieth century, in cities such as Thessaloniki. However, the process of nation-building can lead to the local contesting of the legitimacy of the roles of 'foreign' experts. The tale told by Alaa El-Habashi proposes explanations for why the role of European members in an expert committee in Egypt came to be contested by some of their Arab colleagues under the mantle of an emerging nationalism, caught between personal and professional interests, and looks at the definition of foreign and native in a multicultural setting such as the world of experts involved in the care for historic buildings in pre-Nasser Cairo. Yet, building a new state, creating a new national identity and setting up new built environments are not necessarily very articulated processes, as Roland Strobel shows in the paradoxical struggle between local architects and their Soviet interlocutors over a national aesthetic for the young East Germany half a century ago, whereby the latter pressed for an architecture that was recognizably 'German', against the internationalist approach to design initially maintained by the former.

Negotiating space: powerful 'subjects'

The two previous points indicate how the shaping of built environments, and particularly urban ones, is a very dynamic process, subject to constant tension, contestation, subversion and discussion – in other words, negotiation. A wide range of actors take part in this process (or attempt to do so). The ways in which these multiple actors, with their manifold individual and collective interests and visions, negotiate urban space, reveals power relations that can be highly variegated. The conflicts in interests and visions manifest themselves in the realization of some projects, the alteration of some plans and the blockage of some proposals. The divergence in visions can thus frequently explain the difficulties a particular effort may encounter, as illustrated vividly by Sibel Zandi-Sayek's article in *City and Society* on the multiparty struggle over whether and how to transform the waterfront in late Ottoman Izmir.[9] The conflicts in urbanistic visions can be tied to broader, more fundamental contrasts in outlook regarding society itself, and regarding the identities of those who inhabit the urban environments; in the same journal, Sherry McKay brought this to light in the differences in conceptions (and conceivers) of 'Mediterraneanism' in architecture in pre-independence Algeria.[10]

Two types of power relationships warrant particular scrutiny, as the balance of power within them may not prove to be what it seems at first glance. The first type of relationship is between those who control the shaping of urban space and those who are subject to this control. The former may, by necessity if not by choice, interpret and use a combination of imported and native models, with the articulation between the two determining the outcome of their interventions. In his *City and Society* paper, John Archer shows the succession of attempts, two centuries ago, to transform Calcutta by different Englishmen over the years, and the outcome of these attempts in the context of different interests of both colonizers and colonized.[11]

While the latter may often be assumed to be powerless, in fact they can hold multiple means for molding, influencing or utilizing their environment. They can hence help shape both newly created built form as well as emerging institutions. May Davie delineates how the Beiruti, specifically the local elite, received and impacted the creation of a new urban pattern, imposed by the Ottomans then the French authorities. Meanwhile, Nora Lafi shows how the new 'municipality', as a new type of organization in Libya in the second half of the nineteenth century, was based on older forms of governance and came about through a mixture of provincial players and representatives of the central authorities in Istanbul.

Throughout this book, it becomes apparent that the choices available to the 'subjects' can be ever shifting, given the frequently mercurial articulation between, on one hand, their own priorities and beliefs and, on the other hand, the pressures exerted by those who hold sway over them. This discussion on the relationship between governor and governed is relevant to non-colonial situations as well – even to the dynamics between center and periphery within the same country. It is for this reason that we included in this collection Joe Nasr's paper on how the takeover by the French national government of urban planning powers within France itself in the 1940s came to conform to the existing priorities of the local actors traditionally in control of cities.

Foreign experts, local professionals

The second type of relationship that requires special attention is among those professionals who, by training and practice, shape human settlements, and more precisely the relation between those reared locally and those brought in from outside (the city, country or region). The most obvious example is where an established master arrives from afar and comes into contact with indigenous professionals; but even in such a case the relationship may be subtle. The foreign expert's approach may evolve as a result of this mediation. Sometimes the expert's influence comes through being used as a figurehead for the local experts who have their own agendas, rather than through generating that agenda for them. The activity of the foreign invitees can help reinforce the formation of a local expertise. Indeed, the invitations themselves may originate from indigenous sources; Alicia Novick's paper on the succession of Europeans who came to Buenos Aires in the first half of the twentieth century[12] illustrates well the processes by which foreigners become invited foreign experts – an under-researched question in planning history. In other situations, interventions by foreigners may limit local capacity to intervene, and may be subject to great resistance from indigenous professionals. Eric Verdeil's tale of the travails of two notable French experts in Lebanon during the reformist period of the late 1950s and early 1960s echoes El-Habashi's in this regard, but shows how the presence and success of resistance by native professionals to foreign interventions may depend on the ability of the foreigner to integrate him- or herself into the local urbanistic culture.

The relationship between these parties is always complex, even where expatriate and native experts appear to function as coequal colleagues. Distinctions between the categories of foreign and local are in fact blurred in the case of some professionals, who may use to their advantage the ambiguity in their identities (their transnationality, their peripherality, their regional origin), whether in gaining work contracts or in having smoother interactions with their clients. Ray Bromley thus concludes with the story of Constantinos Doxiadis, perhaps the best-known personality within this book, yet one whose role in the annals of urbanism is not clearly understood; he is shown to have been able to build a significant reputation within his lifetime by knowing how to utilize his liminal position between multiple worlds – though this liminality likely explains his limited impact, over the long term, on the shaping of human settlements.

POSITIONALITIES

In his opening comments to this volume, King aptly recalls that the ways a topic might be framed change drastically over time, due to shifts in the dominant paradigms used by the academic community – and, one may add, to the personal evolving concerns and experiences of the scholars themselves. Thus a major drive in the development of urban planning history may have been, in its early decades, to assess 'the (socially progressive) effectiveness of planning' and to 'explain the socially positive or negative outcomes of planning decisions', to quote again King's piece.

As we have already indicated, the present book originates from a distinct concern: a wish to understand the formation of modern cities, especially in the 'periphery', in their full sociocultural and political complexities. One such aspect concerns, in particular, the local dimension of this dynamic, that is the varied ways in which 'local' elements (people, plans, practices, situations, etc.), interacting with 'foreign' ones, may have influenced, shaped and subverted the creation and use of their built environment, however paradoxical or dissonant the forces and flows at work could appear. This seemed to be a rather under-represented aspect in most of the relevant recent literature, due to the main focus on the major figures, forms and places of Western planning, either at home or overseas, and to the accent on the exporting side of the picture. This accent has shed light in particular on the multiple dimensions of the European colonial project as applied in space. Yet these studies tell us very little about the implementation of the schemes, the ways in which the intentions were (or not) translated concretely on the ground, and more generally the construction of the so-called colonial city through the interventions of those who effectively put it together on a day-to-day basis.

The approach proposed here also emerged from our unease with the essentializing categories still much in use in urban research despite the criticism they have been subjected to. The 'Arab city', discussed by Janet Abu-Lughod,[13] is a case in point, but the same can be said of the 'Mediterranean city' or the 'colonial city', and so on. The latter notion of colonial city covers a diversity of practices and realities that have not been adequately accounted for: the accent tends to remain on the larger scenographic compositions and other plans emanating from the central authorities and conquering powers at the expense of the subdivisions laid out by construction firms, new towns erected by mining corporations, clusters initiated by religious congregations, projects built by obscure entrepreneurs, etc. In other words, the ordinary fabric of the colonial city, or a substantial portion of it at least.

Our approach is moreover rooted in a clear cautioning against broad generalizations and globalizing interpretations, such as those based on over-simplified forms of the Foucauldian rhetoric – realities seen and explained through the 'unique' prism of disciplinary powers, framing devices and controlling strategies, specifically in imperial contexts. Such a warning is perhaps most important when these analyses are made by relying substantially on secondary, single-sourced, one-sided and ultimately incomplete evidence. In fact, a significant part of the literature on colonial urbanism has been written based on strictly metropolitan sources, rather than being (also) based on local archival material. The use of such a limited grounding carries inherently certain biases, filters the light shed on the city-building process through a fragmentary prism, and brings about an unnecessarily partial understanding of urban formation. As a result, while much is known about all the subtleties of the colonial enterprise seen from the metropolitan side – including the marked responsiveness to local history and culture that clearly distinguishes colonial urbanism as a particular version of modern urbanism, according to Gwendolyn Wright[14] – the local facets of the story are all but ignored.

The epistemological posture we have chosen to adopt advocates a more extensive and cross-checked documentation of the situations under scrutiny, the consideration of a large spectrum of explanatory factors, the inclusion of a sphere of stakeholders that is as all-encompassing as appropriate in the particular situation, and an eventual indetermination in the possible interpretations. The need to enlarge the focus is by no means new. If we stay in the field of colonial urbanism, Robert Ross and Gerard Telkamp, for example, were already led in 1985 to state, on the basis of a series of case studies, that '[e]ven in a colonial capital, the imperial power was not the prime mover of everything'.[15] Nor was colonial domination the only channel for transmitting and transforming Western (or Western-looking) forms and doctrines.

More generally, our concern for the local mediations of (Western in origin) planning, in all their complexities, and the ways we suggest to explore them, have clear connections with current developments in many fields of history, besides urban planning history itself. In the domain of area studies, for example, emphasis on the local aspects of any phenomenon studied – 'history from within' – has long been central to the discipline. Within Ottoman studies, to choose a period and region that is well represented in this book, a growing body of literature is available on the indigenous forms and processes of Westernization and modernization that developed throughout the Empire from the early nineteenth century, within the framework of the large reformist movement known as the *Tanzîmāt*; their effects and translations in the city-building sphere are indeed starting to receive attention.[16] Africanists interested in colonial urban history have been led to question the very existence of a 'White City' (which in fact almost never materialized as such); they have also pointed out the cultural hybridization processes at work within the indigenous inhabitants of towns founded by colonists, due to their interactions with the norms, forms and various populations in these towns.[17] In other instances, the contribution of the local elite to the very building of so-called 'colonial cities' – and later to their transformation – has been, or is being, documented,[18] showing in particular the important role of some intermediary groups (religious or ethnic minorities, for example) in the process. That such cities could bring together – with more or less 'overlapping territories' – plural societies, multiple identities and 'intertwined histories', is well captured in Edward Said's autobiographical account of his youth in pre-Second World War Cairo.[19]

Another obvious connection with our project certainly lies in the recent rediscovery of the 'actors', and the ways they can affect their own history, beyond social, political or economical global determinants. This can be framed within the broader (re)emergence of the individual in the social sciences, and gets reflected in the current concerns of 'micro-history' for individuals and small groups of actors, notably those belonging to subaltern or marginal communities.[20] The interest in agency, in reaction to sole structural explanations, has thus developed not so much through investigating big names and major personalities, but by focusing on ordinary people and obscure individuals, on 'the people without history', and their capacity to react, resist, contest, adapt.[21] Indeed, it can be argued that all citizens are worth considering in this respect.[22]

Without sensitivity towards agency and modest protagonists, most of the local professionals, city fathers, activists or real-estate developers evoked in the following pages would probably never have emerged from anonymity. Our goal is certainly neither to denigrate large trends, structural frameworks and broad movements, nor for that matter to deny the importance of big names and major personalities (as attested by the presence of a Blumenfeld, Doxiadis, Ecochard and Le Corbusier in this collection). Rather it is to anchor the latter within the multitude of other actors who enabled, promoted, hindered and otherwise impacted their designs, plans and actions, and to populate, flesh out, 'give a face' to the former.[23] In this way 'both people who claim history as their own and the people to whom history has been denied emerge as participants in the same historical trajectory'.[24] Ultimately, structure and agency are not contrasted, but complexified and integrated.[25]

The related issues of reception and appropriation have in the same way a decisive influence on how to look at the situations and phenomena discussed in the volume. 'Contemporary urban forms are as much a product of assimilation and adaptation, as they are of hybridization and resistance'[26] – collaboration is hence as likely to occur as confrontation. 'Existing local (and political) circumstances shape the process of appropriation. In a common field of action, there are always local varietals'. As the reception and espousal of ideas is typically based on a partial, selective understanding or interpretation, the translation process is always active rather than passive, the form, mechanisms, extent and causation of translation vary, and 'translation is selectively tuned to some melodies but not others'.[27] There is thus no inevitability about the adoption process: ideas, 'however foreign in the first instance, quickly take a national form. If they cannot be nationalized in this way, they soon fade away and cease to exercise any influence'.[28]

To refer more specifically to planning history, this endeavor is also very much the product of a long-established but accelerating attention devoted by planning historians to the issues of international diffusion of ideas and practices, and of transnational and transregional cross-influences in their domain of research.[29] As Ward has highlighted, these are in no way a simple byproduct of the current globalization paradigm but rather the result of a significant historical phenomenon: the extensive international flows and exchanges that have been going on since the nineteenth century in the field of planning.[30] Since Anthony Sutcliffe's pioneering book *Towards the Planned City*,[31] a large volume of work has explored how 'learning from other countries'[32] by planners takes place, in varied geographical settings and historical contexts, allowing ultimately the construction by Ward of a typology for the diffusion of planning, based on the 'power relationship between the countries originating and receiving planning models'.[33] Building on such works, this book offers a panel of little-known cases and largely unpublished material that could help in further elaborating the typology, eventually modifying and enriching it, and hopefully bettering our understanding of these dynamics.

Finally, we should acknowledge that this enterprise is the result of the specific personal experiences and biographies of its authors. In fact most of us are of mixed origins, have access to more than one language, have undertaken Atlantic or other crossings, and have been living in different countries and even continents within distinct cultures. This certainly cannot be a negligible factor in the way we have framed our questioning. Would our questions have been the same without the specific sensitivity (oversensitivity?) to issues such as plurality, multiplicity, complexity, hybridization, brought out by our own singular identities? Probably not. As with all narratives, ours have potential biases that needed to be transparent.

METHODOLOGICAL CHOICES AND CHALLENGES

In his introduction to the papers in *City and Society*, King had already identified briefly a number of methodological questions that arise when one considers 'the tension between imported and exported ideas of urban form' and 'the local, indigenous contribution to urban planning practices introduced at the instance of external or foreign powers':

> What evidence exists, in different contexts, regarding the extent of indigenous or exogenous inputs? And does operating with such a binary model exclude searching for the presence or absence of contributions from other, third or fourth parties? . . . Is evidence of local contributions to be found in the space, built form, or architectural culture of the city itself, or in archival texts? If the latter, by whom are they produced, in what form and what language, and under what political or cultural conditions? And for us, as researchers and scholars, how accessible is this evidence to our scrutiny? What linguistic skills, ideological or theoretical presuppositions will be brought to bear in the reading of particular texts?[34]

These and other methodological challenges faced by researchers of urbanism are developed in this section.

The most basic challenge in undertaking research along the lines that we suggest here – particularly in postcolonial settings – is certainly the difficulty in locating the type of evidence that would be needed in such research. The reasons for this difficulty are often manifold. Solid, comprehensive archives that are pertinent to the subject, time and place may be lacking, and those that do exist may not be maintained adequately. A tradition of certain types of archival collections being held (such as individual papers of ordinary professionals involved in local urban planning) may be absent. Where sufficient evidence exists in a former colony, the material may be split between the archives of the new nation and those of the former colonizers, and in many a case they may be dispersed between holdings of the authorities in the locality itself (often meager) and ones at the national level, which entails (expensive) multi-site research, commonly in two or more languages.[35] This

may encourage the researcher to focus on the most easily accessible sources
– resulting in incomplete and biased findings. The challenge is multiplied if
one chooses as the object of research the flows of urbanistic concepts and
techniques themselves,[36] or the networks of professionals who channel these
concepts and techniques.

Where relevant archives are available, they may emphasize certain power
relationships while others remain unaccounted for. Thus by relying on court
records and other mechanisms of justice or dispute resolution, the voices of
some of the locals who would otherwise remain absent can be heard; however,
these would be their voices at times of conflict only, since the way these
individuals operate in non-conflictual situations would not be illuminated.
This implies a built-in bent towards antagonistic settings in research, to the
detriment of the ordinary negotiated resolutions that take place quietly on
a daily basis.

More generally, the difficulty of providing a voice to the voiceless – which
does not mean powerless – in the past is an ever-present challenge for open-
minded historians. In the specific context of an understanding of the
city-building process, the challenge lies in how to access indigenous viewpoints and figure out the priorities, motivations and approaches of local actors
in this process. For instance, how does one tease out the endogenous inputs
from sources that pertain to exogenous plans, given that extensive documentation of such inputs typically does not exist (if one finds any at all)?
Ultimately, this can mean that an interpretation has to be based on evidence
that other historians may find quite marginal, given the fragmentary nature
of the documentation on indigenous roles. Conclusions may thus be necessarily hesitant; yet this is still preferred to making what appears to be
well-grounded claims, but ones based on a highly biased and incomplete set
of records.

Indeed, the richest sources one might find may be those about (and
collected by) the urbanistic exporters; these can be useful to understand not
only the exporters themselves,[37] but those locally who invite them in, cooperate with them, modify their plans, protest their problems, block their
actions . . . Yet, despite the wealth of information that such sources may
yield, there can be dangers in an over-reliance on the archives of the
exporters. The latter are generally not only researched more than the others
involved in localized city-building, but are, especially the most established
ones, often written up biographically with their experience, life story,
contacts, etc. acting as focal points in the undertaking of the research, as
leading threads in the description of the urbanistic process, as mirrors
reflecting the reception of their ideas and actions by local protagonists.
Hence, even when they are analyzed under critical light for their insensi-
tivity, imposition or ignorance in dealing with the local context, this is
achieved by placing them at the center of attention, as lightning rods, as the

examples of Michel Ecochard and Father Lebret make clear in Verdeil's paper. When the autochthons are given voice, the foreign messengers often channel their voices. In fact, it is the archives of the latter that are frequently most readily available when attempting deliberately to assess the roles and reactions of the former, which involves a necessary filtering mechanism. The more important and difficult challenge for urban researchers thus lies in figuring out not simply how to make sense of the filtering but how to identify and use a greater range of sources to avoid the filtering itself.

The statements made so far in this section run the danger of reinforcing the local/foreign dichotomy, with all the risks this entails. Furthermore, by focusing our attention on the local, there can be a tendency to take the specific to be an instance of the general. It is certainly not our intention here to essentialize or reify the 'locals'. Rather we would point to the necessity – but difficulty – of differentiating into multiple types of locals, indeed of being able to personalize the locals, with their characteristic spheres of action, logics, motivations and relations to other local individuals and groups, which may be conflicted, contradictory, ambivalent, subtle, multifaceted. In a sense, it may be ultimately desirable to think in terms of the singular rather than the local.[38]

A more concrete challenge when seeking to give greater consideration to locals in urbanistic research is that, even when one finds records of the reactions and contributions of a local stakeholder to actions by non-locals, it is only certain locals who are likely to be heard, namely those who have a more or less ample opportunity and ability to interact with the outsiders. These may be elite, intelligentsia, 'city fathers', professional bodies and others. Indeed, one could perhaps talk of varying degrees of voicelessness. Even elites are not all equal; they vary in their level of access to power, of interest in urbanism, of connection to foreign experts and ideas. Here, the efforts by those who have been attempting to piece together subaltern histories can provide models for how this challenge can be met. Subaltern histories are inherently tough to construct; for the same reason placing subalterns within planning histories is a formidable but essential task.

In order to write a history of city building, to be able to contextualize this process and explain how it came about and how it evolved in the way it did, it is usually necessary to write a history of the flows of actors and ideas. This means investigating, for instance, not only the planners who were sent abroad to study but also the places they visited, the contacts they made, the lectures they heard, the journals they subscribed to. A channel for transfers that requires a particular focus is the educational route. Among planners in many countries, professional training abroad is fairly common.[39] A set of planning principles and doctrines – such as civic design taught at the University of Liverpool in the 1920s and 1930s, or new urbanism at certain US universities today – is thus brought back home and eventually transferred elsewhere afterwards, through international consultancies and other commissions. When a planning education is available (or pursued) locally, its curriculum may have been established by foreign professionals or through cooperation with foreign academic institutions.[40] Particular knowledge and practices are thus transmitted to several generations of graduates. The making of these specific professional and technical cultures in planning deserves attention.[41] This web of learning and teaching may be difficult enough to reconstruct within Western countries – it is even more challenging in poorer countries with less developed documentary traditions. In fact, ethnographic approaches can be better suited than histories based on archives/written sources to piece together the web of interactions that make up such complex stories of city building.[42] Yet ethnographies of flows are exceptionally hard to do, and are harder when focused on the little-known local planners.

In some regions like the Middle East or North Africa, the picture can be even more complex to assemble, as city-building histories can be understood only through urbanistic flows *across* the region, in addition to the customary ones between a country and its neighbors, ones between a former colony and its 'mother country', and the general, global ideas floating around internationally at that time. The importance of urbanistic flows across the Middle East is derived from the extent to which Arab planners, architects, builders and so on have customarily worked in other countries in their region. These intraregional flows, carrying practices across national boundaries, are often not easy to capture and hence may be greatly underestimated. So for instance, largely unexamined are the 'return effects' from the practices of designers who originated in non-oil-producing countries (Jordan, Lebanon, Palestine, Egypt) and had worked in various oil countries of the Arabian Gulf, on the architecture of their home country. Yet those who practice across a region represent only a partial enlargement of scale; at a higher scale of complexity is of course the global practitioner. While decades ago there were only a handful of planners and architects who had a genuinely global practice, the consideration of the global scale within the practice as well as education[43] of urban professionals has become increasingly essential – and is exceptionally complicated.

Ultimately, what we are suggesting here is a need to fashion approaches to developing histories of urbanism that 'can recognize the city as a fragmented or discontinuous domain', to use Archer's words.[44] Yet this is rife with difficulties, as we have been stating, particularly given the uneven availability of sources of knowledge on the various fragments of the city. 'The emphasis on the fractal character of urban life nonetheless carries with it the possibility of recreating the deficiencies of earlier paradigms in contemporary urban discourse. Specifically, ideas, concepts, material goods, and power are essentialized by a discourse which represents these concepts as discrete particles moving through the interstices of global space.'[45]

Moreover, when writing up a piece of planning history, a dilemma typically exists as to what type of narrative to construct. Generally it is already a challenge to figure out whether to focus on telling stories of places or of actors. When one overlays on this a concern for not only silent actors but also forgotten places, the challenge is necessarily heightened. The quandary goes beyond these two foci as history-writing choices: it can be important to consider which regulations, procedures, instruments, players, declarations, images, financial flows, stylistic repertoires and so on each actor faces or uses in each place. When relating such city-building histories, one must confront the question of how to portray these complex scenes in all their nuances without getting lost in the array of details.

We are aware that we are emphasizing here places that become the way they are because they are mixing bowls, the result of a high level of 'hybridization' of sources, of 'adaptation' of models, of 'regurgitation' of images, of 'corruption' of ideals. We acknowledge that other places may be less prone to absorbing a multitude of sources, models, images and ideals. Nevertheless, it is evident that no city is an island – now or in the past – and no actors (local or not) live in a cocoon. So we would argue that, even in less obviously crossbred places, it is necessary to ensure that the range of influences that come to bear on the city-building process, and the transformations in these influences as they become reality, is appropriately covered. In fact, in such instances, identifying influences, influencers and influencees may be subtler. Therefore, detecting these traces is no less important but can be a more arduous venture.

So far, we have not differentiated among the mass of influences on the production of urban space. Of course all factors are not equal, and new light can be shed on some of the key factors if the call is heeded for a fuller consideration of actors and a more complex grasp of flows. A broader comprehension of power, and a better grounding of this in the city, can emerge. The State (or states) can be contextualized within the production of urban place and space. As King asserts in his paper, the role of nations in this production can be endowed with both more *and* less importance. Ultimately, the meaning and relevance of the classic conceptual pair agency/structure can be reappraised. Are power, state and nation – to stay for now with the influences we have identified here – factors of agency in the generation of urbanism, or are they structural factors that define the setting in which agency operates? It is evident that developing an analytical framework to comprehend the production of urban patterns becomes a formidable task when seeking to flesh out this understanding fully rather than settling for an interpretive glimpse into select corners of this framework, leaving other corners in the shadow.

The issue of power deserves further observation. We are calling in this book for the possibility of adopting similar approaches to analyze the production of urban forms in a variety of power-relation settings. These settings range from oppressive colonialism to the association of countries through non-colonial arrangements, or even to political conditions within a single country. The basis for urban transformations (such as modernizing strategies) or for resistance to such transformations (such as inertia[46] from local property owners) may be in common across all these cases, but the power relations obviously differ in fundamental ways. What is a researcher to do in the face of such a dilemma? This is a thorny question, and one that can be fraught with controversy. The decision to include in our collection a chapter dealing with the relationship between two French provincial cities and central authorities (very much an intentional inclusion) was, for instance, the subject of some strong debate. Another example of questions raised by the choice of a particular research topic can be found in Dipesh Chakrabarty's *Provincializing Europe,* where, as the title suggests, the Eurocentrism in postcolonial historiography is contested.[47] That said, it is obvious that assessing concurrently settings where differences in power relations are very uneven does indeed present a challenge that calls for a high level of sensitivity on the part of researchers.

If power needs further consideration, it is also certainly necessary to return to the question of colonialism, given its centrality to the issues discussed here. Indeed, after deliberately choosing to avoid placing the colonial at the center of our *problématique*, it must be brought back at some point and recognized as a construct of essential relevance to it. Colonialism has been a very important context in which importing *and* exporting of urbanistic elements have taken place. At what point must it be resituated within this discussion, and how should its specificities be recognized? One must therefore ponder the ways in which colonialism in general, and colonial urbanism in particular, are pertinent to our thesis as distinct concepts and historical phenomena. While colonialism is an identifiable relationship of subjects, ideas, structures and agents, our claims in this book about importation and exportation in urbanism have a context-driven dynamism that can modify the colonial relationships. How has this connection evolved over time? How have locals engaged questions of urbanism within various colonial contexts? How should researchers address these different forms of engagement by locals?[48] These are some of the tough questions raised by the shift in frame of reference proposed here for urbanism in colonial (as well as post-, quasi- and pseudo-colonial) settings.[49]

Hovering above all discussions of the intentions of colonizers, of the motivations of locals, of globalizing trends,[50] of planning interventions and so on, is the issue of modernity. The will to modernize and to become modern cannot be separated easily, and both are part of a desire to move towards a better place in life and in space. The latter are indeed fundamental, normative elements of modernity; the interventions undertaken to achieve these objectives have had a very mixed record, on several levels. Furthermore, the studies in this book have made it clear that modernity is not monolithic, that one can talk of modernities, distinct yet interlinked.[51] If so, how does one eke out particular modernities,[52] or how alternatively can one disaggregate the main elements of modernity? In examining elements such as, say, improved public health, how can a researcher dissect the normative modernizing intentions from the results? Can – and should – one question the epistemological basis for the norms while holding on to the norms themselves? These are among the many difficult questions when modernity, and modernizing urban planning and architecture, are considered through the prism of the local and the individual.[53]

Conversely, the 'invention' of heritage and the processes of 'patrimonialization' – in other words, how existing built areas come to be seen as 'historic' and what happens to them as a result of this perception and labeling mechanism – are worthy of close examination. Indeed, unbuilt areas are by no means the sole field of action in planning. Whether they are already considered to be historic or are on their way to becoming so, how (more or less) older districts are dealt with through the course of city building and in planning practice is an essential issue. The means of marking certain urban fabrics (and not others) with particular designations, their representations as conveyed through conservation schemes or preservation campaigns, the myriad spatial translations of these (from heavy remodeling to extensive protection) – all are worth considering historically and comparatively.[54] How the most ancient parts of cities are handled is interesting; yet equally compelling are cases as divergent as the colonial architecture of the 1930s in the Mediterranean, the Western European city centers rebuilt after war devastation in the 1950s, or the housing blocks of the 1970s in Eastern Europe. Also worth scrutinizing are the personalities and politics of organizations – from a Casamémoire (Morocco) or AMO Ouro Preto (Brazil) locally, to an IASTE or DOCOMOMO globally[55] – that are formed to take on such zones, whether through study, lobbying, legislation or other means.

In this section we have repeatedly made reference not just to what and how to research but also to those undertaking the research. Indeed, one can raise a number of questions related to the nature and positionality of the researchers themselves. We will focus on two aspects here. The first is the identity, and particularly the nationality, of the researcher. Does the researcher belong to the 'communities' being studied? More pointedly, is he or she local or foreign? The point here is not to enter into an identitarian quagmire, mirroring the substantial questions raised by some of the papers in this book and echoing decades-old debates in anthropology and elsewhere about researchers' relationship to the communities researched. Rather it is appropriate to recognize that there are certain differences that come from being a 'local' researcher as opposed to a 'foreign' one. Generally there are some advantages and disadvantages to each. For foreign researchers there are frequently problems that come from the limitations inherent in entering a culture that is originally foreign. Language constraints, for instance, can result in a very partial access to sources, in missing out on subtleties in the relations between actors, in histories that concentrate on elites and bypass other groups and individuals with whom they cannot communicate.[56] King ponders the impacts of these limitations in the self-referential first pages of his chapter. On the other hand, being an outsider can also offer multiple assets to the researcher, from a greater openness by the person interviewed, to a higher ability by the researcher to break from local conventions.

A second aspect on which we will dwell here is the capacity of the researcher to consider honestly and wholly the strategies of autochthons and the nature of their actions. The dare to the analyst is thus in being able to state: locals may *not* be totally innocent, nor thoroughly oppressed, nor entirely powerless. Furthermore, they may be filled with class considerations, with religious biases, with vanity,[57] whether they belong to the elites or the hoi polloi. Moreover, they may have brought about some of the changes in urban patterns that may be viewed today (by us) in negative terms. A double challenge hence emerges. For local researchers, the most significant problem may be an absence of detachment, derived from being 'native' themselves. For foreign researchers, it may be one of legitimacy, related to the ability – as an outsider – to portray candidly, warts and all, the city-building process and the society in which it takes place. The difficulty would come here from the sway on research of what has come to be labeled 'political correctness': '*you* cannot say that, only *I* can!'

We have thus returned to a binomial view, in terms of local/foreign in this instance. In the same vein, the title of this book presents us with a question about urbanism and how it is generated, but it does so in binary terms. It is essential to go beyond this dualistic model of importation and exportation. Ultimately, the methodological question with which we would close this section has to be: How can a researcher develop a more complex vision of city building that integrates all the intermediaries, the modifiers, the transnational world citizens, the 'supra-local'[58] stakeholders, the itinerant freelancers, the detours, the filters, the merger of influences, etc.?

PERSPECTIVES FOR PLANNING: TOWARDS CHANGED HISTORIES OF URBANISM

This broadened interest and complexified understanding would have multiple historiographic consequences. It would alter the terrain for historians of urbanism, whether they are architectural historians, historical geographers, urban morphologists, urban historians or planning historians. We will conclude with some thoughts about what transformations may occur in planning history through this changed vision.

A shift would necessarily take place, from a history of urban planning to a history of city-building. This would entail more attention to the construction of the city, beyond its conception and planning – and where the diverse domains of planned intervention are studied, an emphasis on the implementation of plans and its modalities emerges as necessary. One could further talk of a history of appropriation of urban spaces and practices through planning. Planning history is already partly a history of flows of planning ideas, but we are suggesting a need for it to become more systematically and deeply so. It would look more explicitly at the various roles of the keys to the dissemination that takes place: people, mechanisms, power relations.

We have already greatly emphasized the necessity of attempting a history of many actors (including silent ones) and many places (including ignored ones) in planning – thus, more fully inclusive planning histories. In effect this would modify the object of study. It would eventually result in a more comprehensive history of interests, strategies, actions, coalitions, etc. in planning. The basis for writing planning histories would have to change, that is: all stakeholders in the city and its construction would have to be viewed as agents of some sort, rather than treating just a select few as 'actors'.

Some of the methodological implications of such changes have been detailed above. Planning histories would have to be put together out of more varied sources, so as to tell more varied stories. This would reject neither the classic sources used in planning history nor the attention to the role of the standard personalities in planning history, but would place these within broader arrays of tools for, and subjects of, historical research on planning. As King details, such histories would draw on the strengths (and seek to avoid the limitations) of a range of other historical approaches, from the subaltern to the world-systems literatures.

In particular, precolonial, colonial and postcolonial planning histories may need to be reinvented, notably by reconsidering the separation itself into these three categories and their isolation from what has been presumed to be non-colonial planning histories. All these stories can therefore be envisioned as pieces of a history of how 'an increasingly large body of professional knowledge and set of techniques', as well as a cadre of 'technicians of a general order': came to be constituted – out of Europe and other Western countries, 'but also including a fund of local knowledges and expertise elsewhere'.[59]

NOTES

1. We realize that both 'modern' and 'urbanism' will be understood in a number of ways by different readers, depending on their disciplinary, linguistic and even generational profile. We will not attempt here to provide a definition of either term. We expect that our usage will become clear when reading through the rest of this Introduction.

2. We are aware that 'diffusion' and 'dissemination' are terms that have been criticized by some historians of ideas and others because they leave out the local agency and originality from the process. They become shorthand that denies the force as well as the normativity with which a concept is applied. For example, the ideas of the French Revolution can be viewed as the starting point and ideals that travel around the world and change everything, somehow, by 'diffusion'. That said, we are not ready to give up on these terms, or others for that matter. We have chosen to use them almost interchangeably with 'transfer', 'transmission', etc. We are clearly not ignoring the complexity and selectivity in such processes – in fact, these are at the very heart of the argument of this book. Thanks to Jens Hanssen for stressing the sensitivity of this terminology.

3. 'Pourquoi un colloque de géopolitique urbaine?,' in call for papers for International Conference on Urban Geopolitics, Libreville, Gabon, 6–10 May 2003. Our translation.

4. Anthony King (2000) 'Introductory comments: The dialectics of dual development', *City and Society*, Vol. 12, No. 1, p. 9.

5. As these shifts in winds of influence take place, other countries stand aside but manage to capture the winds blowing from multiple directions. These turning influences were the subject of a discussion around sources for twentieth-century Brazilian urbanism between Adauto Lucio Cardoso and Margareth da Silva Pereira on the H-Urban listserv, in September 2000.

6. Brenda Yeoh (2000) 'From colonial neglect to post-independence heritage: The housing landscape in the central area of Singapore', *City and Society*, Vol. 12, No. 1, pp. 103–24. Yeoh focuses on a particular type of housing form, the shophouse. In the 1960s and 1970s, when the imperatives of nation building and the need for rapid development dictated the planning agenda, a 'demolish-and-rebuild' philosophy prevailed, excising much of the shophouse fabric to make way for high-rise complexes with modern amenities. From the 1980s onwards, the revalorization of the historic past as both an asset for tourism and a means to rediscover the roots of the city has reversed the redevelopment juggernaut, with the surviving shophouse areas being conserved as Historic Districts and Ethnic Quarters. It is this shift, as part of the reinvention of the 'housing question' in Singapore, that is the subject of the paper.

7. On the impact of the Moroccan colonial experience on the French, see Hélène Vacher (1997) *Projection coloniale et ville rationalisée: Le rôle de l'espace colonial dans la constitution de l'urbanisme en France, 1900–1931*, Aalborg, Denmark: Aalborg University Press. This impact should not be confused with the broader set of influences of colonialism on European and other Western cities. For the latter, see for example Felix Driver and David Gilbert (eds) (1999) *Imperial Cities: Landscape, Display and Identity*, Studies in Imperialism, Manchester and New York: Manchester University Press.

8. Sharon Nagy (2000) 'Dressing up Downtown: Urban development and government public image in Qatar', *City and Society*, Vol. 12, No. 1, pp. 125–47. Nagy's paper examines the ways in which the use of foreign planning and building agents and concepts can satisfy the objectives of local actors. It analyzes how local authorities used choice elements from two master plans commissioned from Western planning firms but never formally approved, to inform their planning decisions and to shape the capital of Doha and life therein. One effect has been the extension of state influence into domestic spheres in ways unprecedented in Qatar. As a result, the visibility and high profile of the urban design and building projects successfully undertaken by the state have situated it as a prominent actor in the

aesthetic and spatial presentation of Doha; at the same time, the paper shows how some statal actors gained from this process at the expense of other statal actors.

9. Sibel Zandi-Sayek (2000) 'Struggles over the shore: Building the quay of Izmir, 1867–1875', *City and Society*, Vol. 12, No. 1, pp. 55–78. This paper analyzes the debates around the making of the new harbor facilities in Izmir, one of the most cosmopolitan seaports of the Ottoman Empire, to which various Ottoman subjects – Armenians, Jews, Muslims and Orthodox Greeks – joined by colonies of foreign merchants from numerous origins gravitated in search of economic opportunity. From its early conception through its implementation, the project was to face important legal and financial difficulties as well as the Smyrneans' and foreigners' diverging visions in matters of public interest and municipal politics. The paper focuses on questions of the drawing of public and private boundaries, the look of the new quays and adjacent spaces, the use of these spaces and the meaning ascribed to them.

10. Sherry McKay (2000) 'Mediterraneanism: The politics of architectural production in Algiers during the 1930s', *City and Society*, Vol. 12, No. 1, pp. 79–102. Throughout the 1920s and 1930s a growing number of architects working in Algeria urged a regionalist approach to design. However, there were competing frames of reference, one to a specifically Algerian architecture and another to a more inclusive Mediterranean one. The paper compares both the strategies under-taken in the forging of an Algerian and a Mediterranean architecture, and the rhetoric developed in its support. McKay investigated the politics of the inven-tion of regionalism, and the fraught relationship between regionalism and the universalist aspirations of modernism, particularly in a contested colonial terrain.

11. John Archer (2000) '*Paras*, palaces, pathogens: Frameworks for the growth of Calcutta, 1800–1850', *City and Society*, Vol. 12, No. 1, pp. 19–54. During the first decades of British presence in Calcutta, four different models, imported in close succession, articulated the British response to changing circumstances, both local and remote: the mercantile 'City of Palaces', the British Imperial Seat, the site for a healthy and hence economically productive population, and the pathogenic urban environment to be freed from its diseases – medical and social. These models engaged in a complex spatial negotiation with a number of indigenous models that derived from Bengali practices, notably the structuring around *paras* (clusters of houses organized along the characteristics common to the residents) and around marketplaces established for specific commodities. Archer's paper describes how, in colonial Calcutta, contiguous and sometimes overlapping spaces were fashioned and articulated according to quite distinct and even antithetical manners, based on how these models were reacted to: negotiation, disregard, conflict.

12. On European planning experts in Latin America, see also Arturo Almandoz (1997) *Urbanismo Europeo en Caracas (1870–1940),* Caracas: Fundarte, Equinoccio, Ediciones de la Universidad Simón Bolívar; and Arturo Almandoz (ed.) (2002) *Planning Latin America's Capital Cities 1850–1950,* London: Spon.

13. Janet Abu-Lughod (1987) 'The Islamic city: Historic myth, Islamic essence and contemporary relevance', *International Journal of Middle East Studies*, No. 19, pp. 155–76.

14. Gwendolyn Wright (1991) *The Politics of Design in French Colonial Urbanism,* Chicago, IL: University of Chicago Press. European architecture in the Middle East followed a somewhat similar pattern; see Catherine Bruant, Sylviane Leprun and Mercedes Volait (guest eds) (1996) 'Figures de l'orientalisme en architecture',

special issue of *Revue du Monde musulman et de la Méditerranée*, No. 73/74, 391 pp.

15. Robert Ross and Gerard J. Telkamp (eds) (1985) *Colonial Cities: Essays on Urbanism in a Colonial Context*, Dordrecht, The Netherlands: Martinus Nijhoff Publishers, p. 5.

16. See Hans Chr. Korsholm Nielsen and Jakob Skovgaard-Petersen (eds) (2001) *Middle Eastern Cities 1900–1950: Public Spaces and Public Spheres in Transformation*, Proceedings of the Danish Institute in Damascus, I, Damascus: Danish Institute; and Jens Hanssen, Thomas Philipp and Stefan Weber (eds) (2002) *The Empire in the City: Arab Provincial Capitals in the Late Ottoman Empire*, BTS 88, Beirut: Orient Institute.

17. Catherine Coquery-Vidrovitch (1983) 'La ville coloniale, "lieu de colonisation" et métissage culturel', *Afrique contemporaine*, 4ème trimestre special issue, pp. 11–22; and other works by the same author.

18. See, for example, recent literature on: Calcutta [Pierre Couté (1996) 'Calcutta: An imperial trading counter', *Le Courrier du CNRS*, No. 82, May, pp. 196–8]; Tunis [Christophe Giudice (2002) 'La construction de Tunis, "ville européenne", et ses acteurs de 1860 à 1945', *Correspondances*, No. 70, March-April, pp. 11–17, on line at www.irmcmaghreb.org/corres/index.htm]; Cairo [Mercedes Volait *et al.* (2003) 'Héliopolis Création et assimilation d'une ville européenne en Egypte au XXe siècle', in Denise Turrel (ed.) *Villes rattachées, villes reconfigurées, XVIe–XXe siècles*, Collection 'Perspectives histouriques', Tours: Presses universitaires François-Rabelais, pp 335–66; Ceylon/Sri Lanka [Nihal Perera (1998) *Society and Space: Colonialism, Nationalism, and Postcolonial Identity in Sri Lanka*, Boulder, CO: Westview Press].

19. Edward W. Said (1999) *Out of Place: A Memoir*, London: Granta.

20. Giovanni Levi (1991) 'On microhistory', in Peter Burke (ed.) *New Perspectives on Historical Writing*, Cambridge: Polity Press, pp. 93–113.

21. See, for example, Wayne Te Brake (1998) *Shaping History: Ordinary People in European Politics, 1500–1700*, Berkeley and Los Angeles, CA: University of California Press.

22. Isabelle Berry and Agnès Deboulet (eds) (2000) *Les compétences des citadins dans le Monde arabe: penser, faire et transformer la ville*, Paris: Karthala.

23. One of the best-known stories of twentieth-century planning led by invited for-eigners is Chandigarh, founded as capital of Punjab, India. A new book brings to light the role of local planners, architects and bureaucrats in its creation and adap-tation: Vikramaditya Prakash (2002) *Chandigarh's Le Corbusier: The Struggle for Modernity in Postcolonial India*, Seattle, WA: University of Washington Press. Note, however, the emphasis placed in the title on the famous foreigner.

24. Eric R. Wolf (1982) *Europe and the People without History*, Berkeley, CA: University of California Press, p. 23, quoted in Brenda S. A. Yeoh (1996) *Contesting Space: Power Relations and the Urban Built Environment in Colonial Singapore*, Kuala Lumpur: Oxford University Press, p. 312.

25. See the introductions to: Harvey Molotch *et al.* (2000) 'History repeats itself, but how?: City character, urban tradition, and the accomplishment of place', *American Sociological Review*, Vol. 65, pp. 791–823; and Joe Nasr (1996) 'Beirut/Berlin: Choices in planning for the suture of two divided cities', *Journal of Planning Education and Research*, Vol. 16, No. 1, Fall, pp. 27–40.

26. Frank Spaulding (1998) 'The politics of planning Islamabad: An anthropological reading of the master plan of a new capital', unpublished paper presented to the seminar 'Imported and Exported Urbanism?', Beirut, December 1998, p. 4.

27. Harry M. Marks, 'Social politics across the Great Pond: A summary of Daniel T. Rodgers, *Atlantic Crossings*', posted on the H-Urban listserv, 10 October 1999.

28. Anthony Sutcliffe (1998) 'Modern urban planning and international transfer', in *The History of International Exchange of Planning Systems*, proceedings of the third conference of the International Planning Historical Society, Tokyo: City Planning Institute of Japan/Planning History Group, pp. 10–11. For an example of a failed transfer, see the case of the Bata Shoe Company's factory towns in the US. Eric J. Jenkins (1997) 'Bata colonies: Modern global architecture and urban planning', in *Building as a Political Act*, proceedings of the 1997 ACSA International Conference, Berlin, June, Washington DC: Association of Collegiate Schools of Architecture, pp. 199–202.

29. See, for example, Stephen V. Ward (2002) *Planning the Twentieth-Century City: The Advanced Capitalist World*, Chichester: Wiley; Peter Hall (2002) *Cities of Tomorrow: An Intellectual History of Urban Planning and Design in the Twentieth Century*, 3rd edn, Oxford: Blackwell; Anthony King (1995) *The Bungalow: The Production of a Global Culture*, 2nd edn, Oxford: Oxford University Press; and the above-cited Proceedings of the third conference of the International Planning Historical Society. These issues are now interesting a larger spectrum of disciplines; in particular, researchers in historical sociology and cultural history have recently devoted attention to the extensive and complex exchanges between certain professionals, especially progressive proponents of social reform, and the associated emergence of institutions; see especially Christian Topalov (ed.) (1999) *Laboratoires du Nouveau Siècle: La nébuleuse réformatrice et ses réseaux en France, 1880–1914*, Paris: Editions de l'Ecole des Hautes Etudes en Sciences Sociales; Daniel Rodgers (1998) *Atlantic Crossings: Social Politics in a Progressive Age*, Cambridge, MA and London: Belknap Press; and *Contemporary European History*, special issue on 'Municipal Connections: Co-operation, Links and Transfers among European Cities in the Twentieth Century', guest ed. Pierre-Yves Saunier, Vol. 11, No. 4, 2002.

Considerations of intellectual, economic, cultural and other circuits across national and regional borders have been increasing as *explicit* research areas in general. We can mention that, within a year of the writing of this paper alone, *The Journal of Transatlantic Studies* and *Global Networks: A Journal of Transnational Affairs* are being started, and several scholarly meetings were or are being organized, including: a conference on Transcultural Architecture in Latin America (9–11 November 2001, London); Transatlantic Studies Conference (8–11 July 2002, Dundee, Scotland); a Seascapes, Littoral Cultures and Trans-Oceanic Exchanges Conference (13–15 February 2003, Washington DC); a conference on Globalization, Diasporic Thinking and Transnationalism (6–7 March 2003, Hempsted, NY); and a conference on Mediterranean Studies: Identities and Tensions (19–21 June 2003, Beirut). (From the latter's call for papers: 'The Mediterranean is a geographic, cultural, and historical construct: a circuit of states linked by fragments of shared social and cultural history, and fractured by cultural and political differences. . . . By focusing on a region where borderlands intersect – a littoral zone traversed by shifting geographic and political boundaries – scholars aim to enliven their work on eras and areas where imposed political or academic taxonomies collapse'.)

30. Stephen V. Ward (1999) 'The international diffusion of planning: A review and a Canadian case study', *International Planning Studies*, Vol. 4, No. 1, pp. 53–77.

31. Anthony Sutcliffe (1981) *Towards the planned city: Germany, Britain, the United States and France 1780–1914*, Comparative Studies in Social and Economic History, No. 3, Oxford: Basil Blackwell.

32. Ian Masser and Richard Williams (eds) (1986) *Learning from Other Countries: The Cross-National Dimension in Urban Policy-Making*, Norwich: Geo Books.

33. Stephen V. Ward (2000) 'Re-examining the international diffusion of planning', in Robert Freestone (ed.) *Urban Planning in a Changing World: The Twentieth-Century Experience*, London: Spon, pp. 40–60. Ward provides a brief summary of the typology in his chapter in this book.

34. King, *City and Society*, op. cit., p. 8.

35. To do proper research according to the terms we define here may necessitate a valiant and determined effort. An example currently under way is a dissertation by a young French scholar, Pauline Lavagne d'Ortigue, on the factory towns built and managed by the Anglo-Iranian Oil Company (AIOC) in the first half of the twentieth century. She is learning that it is essential: to explore the holdings of the former half-statal corporation in the UK; to locate material scattered between the Iranian national archives, national oil company and several ministries; to track down the records of the pertinent municipalities and regional authorities in southern Iran where the company had operated (finding it difficult to assemble materials since these administrations had been nascent at the time of the AIOC); to look for the remaining material evidence of these towns in Khuzistan, a region with one of the harshest climates in Iran; as well as to try to track down descendants of those who had been involved in the planning and construction of these towns – all of this as a foreigner in both Iran and the UK. The results of this research appear to be very rich, but not many a scholar would have had the resolve and multiple capabilities to undertake such a bold project.

36. An example of a book on the dissemination of a concept is Stephen Ward (1992) *The Garden City: Past, Present and Future*, Studies in History, Planning and the Environment, No. 15, London: Spon. For one on the spread and use of a technique, see Ian Masser and Harlan J. Onsrud (1993) *Diffusion and Use of Geographic Information Technologies*, Dordrecht, The Netherlands, and Boston: Kluwer Academic.

37. Some rich studies of the work of planning specialists originating from particular countries – and covering well beyond the select 'leading experts' – have been published over the past few years. These include: Jeffrey W. Cody (ed.) (2003) *Exporting American Architecture 1870–2000*, London: Spon; and Robert Home (1997) *Of Planting and Planning: The Making of British Colonial Cities*, London: Spon.

38. In a review of David Prochaska's *Making Algeria French: Colonialism in Bône, 1870–1920* (Cambridge and New York: Cambridge University Press, and Paris: Edition de la Maison des Sciences de l'Homme, 1990), Zeynep Çelik praises the book for 'inserting personal accounts and family stories of settlers and native Algerians into his arguments based on archival documents. The academic style is deliberately disrupted by this human touch, which helps the reader understand the colonial system from an individual's point of view'. Zeynep Çelik (1997) 'French colonial cities', *Design Book Review*, No. 29/30, p. 55.

39. On the education of planners abroad, see Bishwapriya Sanyal (ed.) *Breaking the Boundaries: A One-World Approach to Planning Education*, New York: Plenum Press.

40. For instance, the University of Pennsylvania was instrumental in setting up one of the most established planning programs in the eastern Mediterranean, at the Middle East Technical University. More recently, American and European planning programs and teachers were granted major support from Western and multilateral development agencies to help 'reform' the teaching of urban planning in formerly communist countries in the early 1990s.

41. Two research activities are currently examining the nature and constitution of planning cultures: a francophone one, led by Taoufik Souami, on 'Cultures et milieux urbanistiques dans le Sud de la Méditerranée', and an anglophone one, led by Bish Sanyal, on 'Comparative Planning Cultures'. See also Eric Verdeil (ed.) (forthcoming) *Cultures professionnelles des urbanistes au Moyen-Orient*, Cahiers du CERMOC, Beirut: CERMOC.

42. One example is Fuad K. Malkawi (1996) 'Hidden Structures: An Ethnographic Account of the Planning of Greater Amman', PhD. dissertation, University of Pennsylvania, Philadelphia.

43. We will cite here three illustrations of the growing recognition of this development. In the mid-1990s, the Association of Collegiate Schools of Planning created a Global Planning Educators Interest Group. On 29–30 January 1999, the University of Arizona held a 'Symposium on the Globalization of Architecture, Planning, and Landscape Architecture'. The International Division of the American Planning Association recently published a report on *International Careers in Urban Planning*, ed. Sarah Bowen and Christina Delius, New York: International Division of APA, December 2001.

44. Archer, *City and Society*, op. cit., p. 19.

45. Spaulding, op. cit., p. 3.

46. On inertia, see Robert A. Dodgshon (1998) *Society in Time and Space: A Geographical Perspective on Change*, Cambridge and New York: Cambridge University Press.

47. Dipesh Chakrabarty (2000) *Provincializing Europe: Postcolonial Thought and Historical Difference*, Princeton Studies in Culture/Power/History, Princeton, NJ, and Oxford: Princeton University Press.

48. It should be noted that *whether* researchers address the locals' engagement in particular places may depend on the weight of the West's imperialism there. Dilip K. Basu observed an interesting dichotomy between studies on East Asia, on the one hand, and those on south and southeast Asia on the other. 'While the former emphasize the indigenous structures, hierarchies or networks in a systematic fashion, underplaying the colonial/semi-colonial factor, colonialism is the main motor of analysis in the latter.' 'Perspectives on the colonial port city in Asia,' in Dilip K. Basu (1985) *The Rise and Growth of the Colonial Port Cities in Asia*, Lanham, MD: University Press of America, p. xx.

49. This paragraph was based on points raised in a discussion with Fassil Zewdou.

50. Globalization is of course another inescapable concept in relation to the issues on which we are touching. We have chosen not to delve into this imponderable here, partly because Anthony King gives it some consideration in Chapter 1 of this book. See also Peter Marcuse and Ronald van Kempen (eds) *Globalizing Cities: A New Spatial Order?*, London and Cambridge: Blackwell Publishers; and Hemalata C. Dandekar (ed.) (1998) *City Space + Globalization: An International Perspective*, Proceedings of an International Symposium, Ann Arbor, MI: University of Michigan.

51. An example of a study that takes on directly the question of modernity and urbanism is 'Modernity in the Shadow of the Minaret: Paris and the Mediterranean City, 1830–1900', currently under way by Seth Graebner, based at Washington University at St Louis. By focusing simultaneously on Paris and three cities Graebner considers to have been antithetical to it in different ways (Algiers, Cairo and Marseilles), he seeks to 'show how alterations in the urban fabric of each of these cities influenced changes in the others, and how these interactions engendered the development of a consciousness of modernity', thus 'reorienting dichotomies of colonial centers and margins'. From the research proposal, 2002.

52. Even modernist architecture was adapted to the American context when it was adopted from the 1930s onwards. 'Such vernacular or place-specific divergences from the universalist orthodoxy of modernism often came under harsh attack as sentimental or backward. Yet it is the specifics of place, like the specific nature of any other problem, that defines a pragmatic response. This approach can incorporate the possibilities of change as well as the desire for familiarity.' Gwendolyn Wright (1996) 'Modernism and the specifics of place', in Patricia Yeager (ed.) *The Geography of Identity*, Ann Arbor, MI: The University of Michigan Press, p. 332.

53. This paragraph was based on points raised in a discussion with Will Glover. The final phrase echoes the title of Daniel Miller (ed.) (1995) *Worlds Apart: Modernity through the Prism of the Local,* London and New York: Routledge.

54. A research program currently running, led by Mercedes Volait, seeks to examine these questions: 'Patrimoines partagés: savoirs et savoir-faire appliqués au patrimoine architectural et urbain des XIXe-XXe siècles en Méditerranée.' See www.patrimoinespartages.org.

55. IASTE: International Association for the Study of Traditional Environments. DOCOMOMO: DOcumentation and COnservation of buildings, sites and neighborhoods of the MOdern MOvement.

56. An upcoming special journal issue is meant to tackle this problem expressly. It seeks to 'critically examine the hegemony of colonial languages within postcolonial studies, and . . . investigate how postcolonial theory might be enriched, critiqued, nuanced, or exposed through the perspectives of non-colonial (indigenous or "lesser taught") languages. . . . What "blind spots" are revealed in postcolonial theory from the perspective of texts or traditions not in a colonizer's language?' From Call for papers, *Comparative Studies of South Asia, Africa, and the Middle East*, posted by Michael Benton, English Department, Illinois State University, on H-Urban listserv, 25 March 2002.

57. On the global skyscraper race, see Anthony King (1996) 'Worlds in the city: Manhattan transfer and the ascendance of spectacular space', *Planning Perspectives*, Vol. 11, No. 2, April, pp. 97–114.

58. Jens Hanssen proposes this subtle but significant variant on the transnational to suggest a category of individuals who operate on a level that regularly reaches out beyond the local, yet who are strongly anchored in the local context and whose power is largely derived from it.

59. King, *City and Society*, op. cit., p. 8. The phrase to which he refers in single quotes comes from Paul Rabinow (1989) *French Modern: Norms and Forms of the Social Environment,* Cambridge, MA: MIT Press.

CHAPTER 1

WRITING TRANSNATIONAL PLANNING HISTORIES

Anthony D. King
State University of New York at Binghamton

POSITIONALITY AND THE CULTURAL POLITICS OF WRITING

I am prompted by the title of the conference on which this book is based to start this chapter in a confessional mode by commenting on two items I wrote more than twentyfive years ago: *Colonial Urban Development*, a book published in 1976,[1] and 'Exporting planning: The colonial and neo-colonial experience', an article first published in 1977.[2]

Whatever other issues the book addressed, it was certainly about my (re)discovery not only of a phenomenon called 'culture' but rather of a particular kind of 'colonial' culture and spatial environment that was somehow 'almost the same, *but not* quite'[3] British. In the late 1960s, traces of this culture and environment (and in places the social and behavioral practices that went with it) could still be identified and experienced in certain postcolonial settings, such as the diplomatic enclave in New Delhi or various Indian hill stations. This was also a consciously political study, as was made clear at the start.[4] While it focused on analyzing the urban spaces and built environments of the colonial British, it studiously avoided addressing in any but the most superficial way, and only where essential for the argument, the social and cultural production of the 'Indian'[5] built environment, let alone the indigenous 'Indian' contribution to the construction and use of colonial space.

While the study might well be faulted because of this last factor, there were at least two reasons for this decision. One stemmed from my inadequate understanding of the social, political and cultural construction of 'Indian' space, including the lack of an adequate linguistic command of either Hindi or Urdu. More important, however, and not least in the context of what were to become the nationalist, anti-foreign(er) diatribes of early pre-Bharatiya Janata Party (Jan Sangh) politics of the late 1960s, was that I was hyperconscious of the fact that, while I felt politically and culturally entitled to speak and write about British colonial space, I was neither competent nor entitled to speak on behalf of or represent indigenous Indian perspectives. This was also an outcome of what I saw at the time as the privileged 'aid' conditions under which I had spent five years in India between 1965 and 1970.[6]

The book was also intended to be a 'cultural critique':[7] first, through a process of defamiliarization – of making the familiar strange – to make explicit the social and cultural values underlying what can be called 'English land-scape tastes'[8] and especially their economic, social, ideological and political underpinnings; and second, of a certain tradition in urban studies and urban history I was familiar with in Britain prior to going to India. This I would describe as a state-centric[9] Victorian studies framework, a style of analysis restricted both in historical time and national (or perhaps Western) space, prevalent in both the UK and the US well into the early 1970s, if not later. It was also, to use Gayatri Spivak's term, no doubt partly inspired by 'colonial guilt'. And though this term (and the mode of enquiry associated with it) did not come into general circulation in the humanities for another decade, it was also meant to be read as a postcolonial critique of the nature of urban space in Delhi, despite the somewhat ambivalent positionality referred to above.

A similar yet at the same time somewhat different rationale motivated the writing of the paper on 'Exporting planning'. As is evident from the only slightly veiled sense of exasperation at the start of the paper, it was written as much as a critique of what I felt to be a Eurocentric, or perhaps Euro-American perspective, of the first 'International Planning History Conference' held in London in September 1977, as for any other reason.[10] In that context, the positionality of the article was also postcolonial (in regard to the metro-pole). Like Spivak's reading of *Jane Eyre,* imperialism is always the unspoken subtext of the narrative. In Derridean terms, imperialism and colonialism have always been the constitutive absence of the metropolitan (planning) presence.[11]

In case the reader is wondering about the purpose of these seemingly self-indulgent comments,[12] I should explain my purpose in making them. I want, first, to draw attention to ourselves, as researchers and writers, and what we are doing; to examine the place and positionality of the author in the text. I want to know the economic, social, spatial and especially the political condi-tions in which knowledge is produced and the influences and constraints exercised on its production. I am arguing, therefore, not just for a sociology but also for a history and geography of knowledge production. From where, by whom and when is knowledge produced and for what purposes?

Second, I want to draw attention to the vast changes that have taken place over the last two decades in the theoretical and historical paradigms and presuppositions with which we now operate. For example, the way we might have framed a topic in 1976 would be totally different in 2000, and will be even more so in 2020 when our aim – or aspiration – is to address a more 'global' readership.

Third, I want to recognize the enormous number of empirical and theoretical studies related to our field of urban and planning history that have been produced over the last two-and-a-half decades. Robert Home's 1997 study on *The Making of British Colonial Cities*[13] is a good illustration here. While drawing selectively for his theoretical insights on the various ideas of Fernand Braudel, Michel Foucault, John Friedmann and others, some two-thirds (around 350) of Home's 550 references were published in the twenty years before the publication of the book (and a third in the preceding ten years).

WHAT, AND WHO, IS 'THE LOCAL'?

In the context of 'importing planning' and the need 'to redress the neglect of the local element in much of the literature', we can, of course, also ask how many of these 350 sources actually represent, to the satisfaction of the localities and people represented, 'the local element'. Scanning Home's bibliography in order to identify those references with non-Anglo-Saxon names would be a futile exercise. Though 'local' scholars may well have the linguistic competence not exhibited by scholars from the metropole, this is less important than their political and cultural positionality. What is more significant, as I have spelt out elsewhere,[14] is the question of the resources and time needed to undertake the research, as well as access to the necessary archives. Brenda Yeoh, Mariam Dossal and others have also pointed to the difficulty of accessing indigenous viewpoints.[15] The presence or absence of a usable archive is clearly a major influence on the outcome. In other words, some sources have their own story to tell even if one actively endeavors to read against the text. This is one instance of the cultural politics of representation and writing that is central to my argument here.

A further question, however, refers to the general theoretical framework within which we understand the practices of 'exporting and importing planning', especially with regard to our particular focus on the influence of 'the local'. In her study of colonial Singapore, Brenda Yeoh argues that the city 'has to be treated on its own terms' and shows how different elements of the urban landscape become invested with different meanings and purposes, placing explanation on 'the practical nature of everyday life' as lived within the colonial city. The colonial urban landscape is 'a terrain of discipline and resistance' involving both colonialists and colonized groups where the colonized 'must be seen as knowledgeable skilled agents with some awareness of the struggle for control, not just as passive recipients of colonial rule'. In Singapore, the 'Chinese laboring classes participated in the production of social spaces'.[16]

More recently, in his study of urban and spatial developments in post-colonial 'New Order Indonesia' under Suharto (1966–98), Abidin Kusno has suggested that in placing emphasis on the relations between the East and the West, on the postcolonizer and postcolonized, what has often been overlooked is the substantial role of historical subjects who are not quite 'the other' but are also not entirely 'the same. Those who live side by side within the region are also important in constituting postcolonial identities'.[17] This might also be an appropriate place to recognize the productive metaphor of Edward Said, who writes of 'overlapping territories, intertwined histories'.[18]

Yet while the studies of Yeoh, Kusno, Said and others are excellent examples of how the 'contribution of the local' might be illuminated, what in the longer term is our ultimate purpose in giving recognition to this 'local'? Who exactly constitutes this 'local' from a regional, ethnic, gendered or class position? And what is the wider significance of what we are addressing here? We have, of course, perhaps given a voice to those previously denied one. We have recognized, possibly even constructed an identity previously denied, but in the interests of whom or what? Planning, whether exported or imported, or the result of both processes, does not exist in or of itself. The real outcome of planning decisions depends on their interpretation and implementation.

We can interpret planning as inevitably part of a larger (or even a smaller) agenda; it replaces one form of social and spatial order, constructed on the basis of one set of power relations, with another, inflected as each of these is with someone's prevailing 'norms and forms'.[19] The test for the (socially progressive) effectiveness of planning is whether the results conform to the wishes of the majority of the people affected by it. As Kusno shows, 'post-colonial' urban-planning policies in Jakarta under the 'local' authority of Sukarno and Suharto did not replace the colonial inequities introduced by the ('non-local') Dutch colonizers, but in effect confirmed and exacerbated them.[20] In circumstances such as these, therefore, 'local' and 'non-local' are on their own neither necessary nor sufficient variables to explain the socially positive or negative outcomes of planning decisions. The conditions under which the introduction of planning can take place can be both colonial or non-colonial, they can be totally autochthonous and they can also be seen as dependent. Let me offer two or three hypotheses.

THE NATIONAL AND THE TRANSNATIONAL

In referring in the title of this article to transnational planning, the intention is to focus on the production of space as the outcome of transnational processes, 'processes that take place between nations but also transcend them'.[21] If we think of this phrase in relation to planning, what it highlights is not merely the transfer and transplantation in the contemporary era of ideologies and practices between various nation-states (virtually 200 of them in the 1990s) but also the unforeseen and possibly incidental, innovatory processes and practices that emerge as a result of such a transfer. And as planning is in most if not all cases initiated at the level of the local state (though usually legislated at the national level), the process of transplantation also draws our attention to the mutually reciprocal way in which the nation-state is itself constructed.

For example, a combination of historical, cultural, social and spatial practices are brought together in a particular territory by a particular set of people (agents) and social and political institutions to construct from out of the 'imagined community' of the nation,[22] the city, town or any other kind of settlement. Simultaneously, however, or possibly later, the nation-state further develops its own identity through a 'national' tradition of planning (and a national tradition of literature, music or law). In this context, urban planning becomes on the one hand a step towards the social construction of 'the nation' (that is, the people) and on the other a step towards the strengthening of the idea of the state.

This issue also draws our attention to a point made by Mohammad Bamyeh in his account of the development and spread over the last two centuries of the (Eurocentric) idea of the nation-state as the dominant form of governance worldwide.[23] With the rise of the state as the standard form of governance, standard structures of domination and models of political behavior have been created, and urban planning is a major example.

In the multiple processes, therefore, by which a state acquires its identity as a state, as a *particular* state and as a *modern* state, it represents itself in space, marking its boundaries so to speak, inscribing itself urbanistically onto its own territory. The state represents itself spatially and architecturally, as well as discursively and textually through the relevant forms of state apparatus – government, law courts, administrative and professional practices, schools and universities – and through particular 'norms and forms'. In the process, these norms and forms act as disciplining parameters – socializing mechanisms for the minds and bodies of its citizens. We are disciplined to drive on the left- or right-hand side of the road; we embody cultural attitudes to phenomena labeled (dependent on our location) 'wilderness', 'countryside', 'environment' and so on. As part of a system of control or indeed the absence of such a system, the national as well as the local state (the county, municipality or city administration) establish a distinct urban identity. The social, spatial and architectural dimensions constructing this identity then become critical in investing national and urban subjects with their own sense of both civic and national state identities, whether as Muscovite, Cairene and Parisian or Russian, Egyptian and French men or women.

However, with regard to the introduction of planning under the conditions of colonialism, 'transnational planning' is strictly speaking an inappropriate term since we are clearly not discussing 'neutral' transnational relations taking place across, or in relation to, two or more independent and equal states. But are we in searching for 'the local' in fact helping the construction of proto-national or proto-local identities? There are two levels to this: first, in identifying the 'local' element in importing planning, whether this refers to the manner in which space is appropriated and used, codes and regulations ignored or interpreted, or territory symbolically marked; and second in the act of 'writing', interpreting and representing, historically, the development of that proto-national or proto-local space (as is the case in the articles in this volume). As all knowledge is both politically positioned and dialectically produced, that is, produced in relation (or reaction) to previous accounts, or indeed the absence of these, we may even be celebrating the construction of proto-national space. If this is the case, which local identities – ethnic, regional, religious, class, gender, occupational, political and cultural – are being included or excluded in the process?[24]

What is being suggested here, therefore, is that this concern with 'putting the record straight', of identifying the local in the production of space and especially the production of place in the context of the 'export and import' of planning, is essentially about transforming the identities of cities as well as citizens. It is also about acknowledging those populations, whether they are indigenous ethnicities, professions, workers, women, children or the physically or economically marginalized, whose presence has previously been excluded, unrepresented and usually unrecognized in colonial or other types of cities.[25]

The next section examines this important question of city identity in the context of contemporary understandings of the social and spatial world and the theoretical ways in which we try to understand it. It is not just the many new empirical studies in planning history that have changed our views in the last twenty-five years. We should also acknowledge the growth in what can be described as 'macro theories', the object of which is to explain economic, political, social, cultural and spatial transformations in the modern world: competing or complementary theories of postmodernism, of the world system, of globalization, transnationalism, postcolonial theory and criticism, and no doubt others. Addressing some of these theories may reveal the significance and importance of identity, both in the contemporary as well as the future twenty-first-century city. What I believe we will discover is that these theories are lacking in the attention they give to the local and historically specific, not just in relation to the 'global condition' of contemporary capitalism but rather in regard to the impending global urban condition. I will refer briefly to only four of them: world-systems perspectives and theories of globalization, postcolonialism and postmodernism. Rather than speaking to them directly, however, I will first address the issues which any theoretical framework must accommodate in dealing with the writing of the 'transnational space' of planning history.

Framing Identities in Space – in the World and of the World

Our primary interest here is in 'the diffusion of modern urbanism', both in relation to the rapid growth of urbanization and to the 'urbanization of capital'[26] (though this phrase does not capture or encompass all that urbanization implies). The adoption, modification or rejection of ideas and practices of urban planning[27] between different nation-states, whether in colonial or non-colonial situations, requires a framework for spatial analysis that extends beyond a single, or even two or three nation-states and also acknowledges the uneven distributions of power between them. We need a model for understanding transnational economic and political processes in which some nation-states, at different points in history, exercise some hegemonic influence within the system of states or territories as a whole, for example the dominant influence of the Dutch in the seventeenth century, the British in the nineteenth century, and the US or Soviet Union in the twentieth century.

However, we also need a framework that, while acknowledging these economic and political processes, also recognizes the social and cultural dimensions of urban life and the way these together bring about spatial and material changes. For example, in relation to increased processes of urbanization, these might include the adoption of new communications technologies (such as steam power, railways, telecommunications), the redistribution of local resources, the transformation (or introduction) of social and political institutions with the concomitant introduction of new (or modified) building types and forms of spatial organization in the urban fabric.[28]

Recognizing that these processes need to be seen as part of 'intertwined histories, overlapping territories', such a framework also needs to acknowledge the nature, scale and degree of local influences. This requires sensitivity to issues of historical and geographical difference, to the importance of human as well as social agency, and not least to the time- and place-specific exchange of ideas and technologies that are transferred by means of human agency from one part of the world to another. In a context where social and political power is inequitably distributed, as in colonial situations, we need to be conscious not simply of 'resistances' to the implementation of colonial 'norms and forms' but also of processes of accommodation as well as 'cultural translation' in specific colonial situations.[29]

Finally, we need a framework that recognizes the role of existing spatial, built or even remembered environments in the formation of identity, whether at the level of the individual, the community, the city or the nation-state. Parts of this identity may develop from socially progressive planning policies that make housing, education and social amenities available to all, irrespective of background. Other parts, however, may result from the unintended (and sometimes intended) social consequences of particular spatial and perceived environments that help to reinforce ethnicized, classed, racialized, aged, gendered and other place-specific subjectivities. Obvious examples here are the role of spatial segregation in contributing to the construction of race and class-consciousness, or the nature of and access to public space in the construction of gendered and sexualized subjects. We also need to know how such subjectivities become politically mobilized at particular moments in history, whether via demonstrations, social movements or riots. Much more needs to be understood about how material and spatial environments help to construct human subjectivity.[30]

MACRO THEORIES AND THEIR LIMITATIONS

What macro-theoretical ideas are available to help our understanding of 'transnational space'? Consider first the **world-systems perspective**. While we need not accept all the different dimensions this offers, we might nonetheless take note of some of Wallerstein's assumptions:

> The modern world-system took the form of a capitalist world-economy that had its genesis in the long sixteenth century and . . . involved the transformation of a particular redistributive or tributary mode of production, that of feudal Europe . . . into a qualitatively different social system. Since that time, the capitalist world-economy has geographically expanded to cover the globe and manifested a cyclical pattern including technological advance, industrialization, proletarianization and the emergence of structured political resistance to the system – a process that is still going on today.[31]

Though a framework along these lines would suggest that the diffusion of modern urbanism can be related to the expansion of the capitalist world-economy, and that particular 'cores' generate powerful political, economic and ideological influences (presumably including the ideologies and practices of planning), not much can be gleaned here of the way in which culturally different forms of capitalism work in different cultures and spaces. As Ashcroft *et al.* suggest, world-systems theory:

> does not explain, nor is it interested in, human subjectivity, the politics of colonization, the continued dominance of certain discursive forms of imperial rhetoric, nor the particular and abiding material consequences of colonialism in individual societies. It offers no place for individual agency, nor is it concerned with the local dynamics of cultural change, nor even with the operation of 'societies', all these things being subsidiary to the broad structural forces of the world system.[32]

Ashcroft *et al.*'s critique is characteristic of the rapidly burgeoning field of **postcolonial theory and criticism**, which since the mid-1980s has brought important new perspectives to a wide range of disciplines. It also has much to offer historical studies in urban planning. The best of postcolonial criticism is an oppositional form of knowledge that critiques Eurocentric conceptions of the world. In 'provincializing Europe', to quote Chakrabarty,[33] it demands a 'rethinking of the very terms by which knowledge has been constructed'.[34] Applied in the realm of the urban, postcolonial criticism – by foregrounding indigenous developments – is a liberating form of discourse.

However, a serious criticism has been the confinement – until relatively recently – of this particular academic perspective, supposedly addressing 'the effects of colonization on cultures and societies', primarily to the realm of texts, that is, 'draw(ing) deliberate attention to the profound and inescapable effects of colonization on literary production; anthropological accounts; historical records; administrative and scientific writing',[35] in a clinically distanced and separate way from critical postcolonial studies in urbanism, architecture, planning and the built environment more generally.[36]

Postmodernism will not be discussed at any length here, even though this is a paradigm that, at least in its most popular manifestations, unlike those above, both addresses as well as represents itself in spatial and architectural form. One reason for keeping the discussion here brief is that Eurocentrically defined characteristics of what is referred to as 'postmodernity' – irony, pastiche, the mixing of different histories, intertextuality, fragmentation, incoherence, cultural gaps and clashes, the destruction of 'pre-modern' cultures – all supposedly characteristics of our 'postmodern times' in Europe and North America according to Harvey,[37] were features typical of colonial societies, cultures and environments on the so-called global periphery (in Calcutta, Cairo or Rio) decades, if not centuries, before they appeared in Europe or the US.

How did the local inhabitants of Bombay read the text of the 'modern' city in the 1870s, or British colonialists that of the village settlements of the Gujaratis at the same time?[38] In a more formal architectural and planning sense, as the work of Gwen Wright, Tom Metcalf, Mark Crinson, Abidin Kusno[39] and others has shown, postmodernism understood as a deliberate practice of hybridization (the mixing of different histories and cultures), as a conscious transcultural intertextuality, was a sophisticated practice of colonial architecture and urban design long before the emergence of the term 'modern movement'. In this context we might say that the social, economic and cultural characteristics of postmodernism preceded rather than succeeded those of the so-called 'modernism'.

If the focus here is on the question of identity, of constructing and maintaining individual as well as collective identities in relation to others, theories of **globalization** (defined by Robertson as 'the increasing consciousness of the world as a whole') also have something to offer. Robertson suggests that

> [T]he contemporary concern with civilizational, societal (as well as ethnic) uniqueness – as expressed via such motifs as identity, tradition and indigenization

– largely rests on globally diffused ideas. In an increasingly globalized world . . . there is an exacerbation of civilizational, societal and ethnic self-consciousness. Identity, tradition and indigenization only make sense *contextually*.[40]

While Robertson is correct in stating that identities are established contextually (though the context is too often seen as the system of states), it is only in a very general sense that the increased concern with identity and tradition is an outcome of 'globalization', which is a rather indiscriminate way of referring to 'the world as a whole'. Identities are usually constructed in relation to much more specific, smaller, historical, social and spatial contexts.

Towards more Micro Theorizations?

The problem with many of these theories of social, political and spatial change in the modern world is that they conceive of social and spatial units that are often too large to be relevant for understanding identities, or places, at the local level, whether city, settlement, neighborhood or dwelling. While nationality, ethnicity, class, religion, region, caste, descent, health, kinship, race, gender, occupation, age – the categories dependent on where people live – are all factors that contribute to the making of the multiple identities of people, spaces far smaller than the state, region or city are mobilized in identity construction. Various spaces, at different scales, take on identities invested in them by their inhabitants: not just cities but villages and neighborhoods; not just villages but markets and festivals; not just streets but plots, enclaves and vehicles; not just dwellings but rooms and clothes.[41]

This is a scale where current conceptual language and transnational theorizations are seriously underdeveloped. How do we address the spatial construction of identity at a local 'micro' level in a world increasingly characterized by mobility and interactive cultural flows? For example, recent essays discuss transnationalism and migrancy as phenomena that create fluid and multiple identities that cross multiple racial, national and ethnic lines. Transmigrants move between a family network abroad and back home, maintaining many different racial, national and ethnic identities.[42] In this way, people express their resistance to the global political and economic situations that engulf them, and at the same time may also immerse themselves within these situations.

This is why it is difficult to actually speak about 'the local'. Arjun Appadurai defines 'locality' as a 'non-spatial term . . . a complex phenomenological quality . . . constituted by a series of links between the sense of social immediacy, the technologies of interactivity and the relativity of contexts'. He distinguishes it from 'neighborhood' as 'existing social forms in which locality, as a dimension of value, is variably realized'.[43]

In addition to the transnational, we also need to recognize the transurban, transurbanity, even transurbanization. We need to rethink, in terms of contemporary communications, the real connectivities in the intercity system. Continuing processes of hybridization take place at scales smaller than the city, not least the suburb, block, apartment or individual dwelling. Chinese-American scholar Wei Li, writing on the 'anatomy of a new ethnic settlement in Los Angeles', coined the term 'Chinese ethnoburb'.[44] If this sounds unfamiliar, remember that just over a century ago (1895) when the term 'suburbia' gradually came into use, no one had heard of it either. In 2025, will anyone raise an eyebrow to learn of the 'globurbs' (transmigrant housing of people from all over the world) around Paris, London or New York?

Nor have we developed a way to conceptualize the transnationalization of the dwelling, that is, the transcultural adaptation of residential and building forms out of their native habitus. What we might refer to as 'cut and paste' forms of shelter are cut from the history, society and mode of production in one society and culture and pasted into those of another, albeit usually with a fair amount of editing in the process.[45] Native English-speakers could stick to their Latin roots and refer to transdomification, or the transculturization of dwelling form. With regard to the recent extensive introduction of the European villa into Istanbul and Beijing, I am tempted to speak of an international process of 'villafication'.[46] Given its diversity, the twenty-first-century metropolis, just as that of the recent and more distant past, will need to generate a much more diverse set of theorizations before we can begin to interpret and understand it.

ACKNOWLEDGEMENTS

My many thanks to Joe Nasr and Mercedes Volait for their helpful suggestions in editing the earlier versions of this paper, and also to Abidin Kusno for some initial comments. Further thoughts on this topic are published in Anthony D King (2000) 'Introductory comments: The dialectics of dual development', *City and Society* 12, 1, pp. 5–18.

NOTES

1. Anthony D. King (1976) *Colonial Urban Development: Culture, Social Power and Environment*, London and Boston: Routledge & Kegan Paul.
2. Anthony D. King (1977) 'Exporting planning: The colonial and neo-colonial experience', *Urbanism Past and Present*, 5, Winter, pp. 12–22. A revised version of this article appeared in Gordon Cherry (1980) (ed.) *Shaping an Urban World: Planning in the 20th Century*, London: Mansell, pp. 203–26, and a further revised version (perhaps significantly) retitled 'Incorporating the periphery (2): Urban planning in the colonies', can be found in Anthony D. King (1990) *Urbanism,*

Colonialism and the World-Economy: Cultural and Spatial Foundations of the World Urban System, London and New York: Routledge, pp. 44–67.

3. Homi K. Bhabha (1994) 'Of mimicry and man: The ambivalence of colonial discourse', in *The Location of Culture*, London and New York: Routledge, p. 86.

4. 'In the past there have been many cases in which the orientations of a "colonial anthropology" have been used to study non-Western and relatively small-scale communities (Asad, 1973). In an attempt to redress the balance, this book uses the orientations of a Western and relatively small-scale anthropology to study the colonial community itself" (Anthony D. King (1976) *Colonial Urban Development: Culture, Social Power and Environment*, London and Boston: Routledge & Kegan Paul, p. xvi; see also p. 288).' The title referred to is Talal Asad (1973) *Anthropology and the Colonial Encounter*, London: Ithaca Press.

5. The 'scare quotes' here are necessary to acknowledge the variety of religious, caste, class, geographical, temporal and other variables entailed in discussing what is only a unity when categorized as 'Other'.

6. For reference to the 'absence of the Indian contribution', see Sidartha Raychaudhuri (2001) 'Colonialism, indigenous elites, and the transformation of cities in the non-Western world: Ahmedabad (Western India) 1890–1947', *Modern Asian Studies*, 35, 3, pp. 677–726.

7. This is the message of George E. Marcus and Michael J. Fischer (1986) *Anthropology as Cultural Critique: An Experimental Moment in the Human Sciences*, Chicago: University of Chicago Press.

8. This phrase is from David Lowenthal and Hugh C. Prince (1965) 'English land-scape tastes', *Geographical Review*, 55, 186–122.

9. See Peter Taylor (1996) 'Embedded statism and the social sciences: opening up to new spaces', *Environment and Planning A*, 28, 11, pp. 1917–28.

10. The particular disciplinary specialization of planning history in the UK had begun in 1974.

11. Gayatri C. Spivak (1985) 'Three women's texts and a critique of imperialism', *Critical Inquiry*, 12, 1, pp. 243–61. Alicia Novick's chapter addresses similar issues.

12. For readers interested in the further genealogy of these ideas, it is necessary to state that, on returning from five years working at the Indian Institute of Technology in Delhi between 1965 and 1970, on the payroll of the Ministry of Overseas Development under the then Labour government and financed through the Colombo Plan, I first held a two-year Fellowship at the University of Leicester at the suggestion of H.J. Dyos, holder of the first (personal) Chair of Urban History in the UK, and editor of *The Victorian City* (London and Boston: Routledge & Kegan Paul, 2 vols., 1972). I was also informally connected with the Development Planning Unit (DPU) of University College London. The latter had developed (1970) out of the Tropical Architecture Studies Unit, established in 1955 at the Architectural Association School of Architecture, London, by the late Professor Otto Koenigsberger, a refugee from Nazi Germany and previously (until the late 1940s) planning consultant to the Government of Mysore in India. The DPU was, and still is, an international center of planning education with students originating from all over the world.

13. Robert Home (1997) *Of Planting and Planning: The Making of British Colonial Cities*, London: Spon.

14. See Anthony D. King (1992) 'Rethinking colonialism: An epilogue', in Nezar AlSayyad (ed.) *Forms of Dominance. On the Architecture and Urbanism of the Colonial Enterprise*, Aldershot: Avebury, pp. 339–55.

15. Brenda S.A. Yeoh (1996) *Contesting Space: Power Relations and the Urban Built Environment in Colonial Singapore,* Oxford: Oxford University Press; Mariam Dossal (1991) *Imperial Designs and Indian Realities: The Planning of Bombay City 1855–1875,* Delhi: Oxford University Press.
16. Yeoh, op. cit., pp. 9–11.
17. Abidin Kusno (2000) *Behind the Postcolonial: Architecture, Urban Space and Political Cultures in Indonesia,* London and New York: Routledge.
18. Edward Said (1994) *Culture and Imperialism*, London: Vintage.
19. Paul Rabinow (1989) *French Modern. Norms and Forms of the Social Environment,* Cambridge, Mass.: MIT Press.
20. See Kusno, op. cit.
21. Sarah J. Mahler (1998) 'Theoretical and empirical contributions toward a research agenda for transnationalism', in Michael P. Smith and Luis Eduardo Guarnizo (1998) *Transnationalism from Below. Comparative Urban and Community Research*, vol. 6, New Brunswick: Transaction Publishers, p. 66.
22. I cite here the phrase of Benedict Anderson (1983) *Imagined Communities: Reflections on the Origin and Spread of Nationalism,* London: Verso.
23. Mohammed Bamyeh (2000) *The End of Globalization*, Minneapolis: University of Minnesota Press.
24. This is a question addressed by Lawrence Vale in *Architecture, Power, and National Identity* (New Haven and London: Yale University Press, 1992). Kusno has also drawn attention, in Yeoh's account, to her neglect of other ethnic/cultural subjects in the plural society of Singapore, the Indian and Malay (personal communication).
25. On these issues see Leonie Sandercock (1995) *Towards Cosmopolis: Planning for Multicultural Cities*, Cambridge, Mass.: MIT Press; Doreen Massey and P. Jess (eds) (1995) *A Place in the World? Places, Cultures, Globalization,* Oxford: Oxford University Press.
26. David Harvey (1985) *The Urbanization of Capital: Studies in the History and Theory of Capitalist Urbanization,* Baltimore, MD: The Johns Hopkins University Press.
27. I use this phrase in a modern sense to refer to the formal practice of planning including, for example, the control of land uses, the establishing and implementation of codes, the directing of urban development and so on rather than the management of settlement systems according to well-defined cultural traditions.
28. On this issue, see Stephen Graham and Simon Marvin (2001) *Splintering Urbanism: Networked Infrastructures, Technological Mobilities and the Urban Condition,* London and New York: Routledge.
29. The interstitial space of 'accommodation' between 'colonial domination' and 'indigenous resistance' is well addressed by Garth Myers in his account of Ajit Singh's architecture in colonial Zanzibar. See Garth Myers (1999) 'Colonial discourse and Africa's colonized middle: Ajit Singh's architecture', *Historical Geography*, 27, pp. 27–55.
30. For a discussion of the Jakarta kampong in the construction of Indonesian subjectivities, see Kusno, op. cit.
31. Immanuel Wallerstein (1980) *The Modern World System II. Mercantilism and the Consolidation of the European World-Economy 1600–1750,* New York, San Francisco and London: Academic Press, pp. 7–8.
32. Bill Ashcroft, Gareth Griffiths and Helen Tiffin (1998) *Postcolonial Studies: The Key Concepts*, London and New York: Routledge, p. 280. In fairness to world-system proponents, we might note that while acknowledging this critique, it should

14
—

also be said that Ashcroft *et al.* pay virtually no attention to the role of place, space, architecture or the built environment in the construction of 'human subjectivity', 'individual societies', 'individual agency' or, indeed, the 'world system' and the identities associated with each.

33. Dipesh Chakrabarty (1992) 'Postcoloniality and the artifice of history: Who speaks for "Indian" pasts?', *Representations*, 37, Winter, pp. 1–27.

34. P. Mongia (1995) 'Introduction' to *Contemporary Postcolonial Theory: A Reader*, London: Edward Arnold, p. 2.

35. Ashcroft *et al.*, op. cit., pp. 186 and 192.

36. A genealogy of the development of postcolonial theory and criticism in the humanities, its connection to earlier studies of colonialism in the social sciences, and the significance of spatial, architectural and urban geographical studies to the field is discussed in Anthony D. King (1999) 'Cultures and spaces of postcolonial knowledges', in M. Domosh, S. Pile and N. Thrift (eds) *Handbook of Cultural Geography*, London, Thousand Oaks, New Delhi: Sage, pp. 381–98. See also G.B. Nalbantoglu and C.T. Wong (1996) *Postcolonial Space(s)*, New York: Princeton University Press.

37. David Harvey (1989) *The Condition of Postmodernity*, Oxford: Blackwell.

38. See Anthony D. King (1995), 'The times and spaces of modernity: (Or who needs "postmodernism"?)', in Mike Featherstone, Scott Lash and Roland Robertson (eds) *Global Modernities*, Newbury Park and London: Sage, pp. 108–23.

39. Gwendolyn Wright (1991) *The Politics of Design in French Colonial Urbanism*, Chicago: University of Chicago Press; Thomas J. Metcalf (1989) *An Imperial Vision: Indian Architecture and Britain's Raj*, Berkeley, CA: University of California Press; Mark Crinson (1996) *Empire Building*, London and New York: Routledge; Abidin Kusno, op. cit.

40. Roland Robertson (1992) *Globalization: Social Theory and Global Culture*, Thousand Oaks, CA, London and Delhi: Sage, p. 130.

41. For a creative approach to this question, see Christopher Breward (1999) 'Sartorial spectacle: clothing and masculine identities in the imperial city, 1860–1914', in Felix Driver and David Gilbert (eds) *Imperial Cities: Landscape, Display, Identity*, Manchester: Manchester University Press, pp. 239–53.

42. See note 20.

43. Arjun Appadurai (1996) 'The production of locality', in *Modernity at Large: Cultural Dimensions of Globalization*, Minneapolis: University of Minnesota Press, 1996, p. 178.

44. Wei Li (1998) 'Anatomy of a new ethnic settlement: The ethnoburb in Los Angeles', *Urban Studies*, 35, 3, pp. 470–501.

45. What better example than the bungalow?

46. See Anthony D. King (2000) 'Suburb/ethnoburb/globurb: the construction of transnational space in Asia', in World Academy for Local Democracy (WALD) *Global Flows/Local Fissures: Urban Antagonisms Revisited*, Istanbul: World Academy for Local Democracy.

PART I

THE LATEST MODELS

CHAPTER 2

MAKING CAIRO MODERN (1870–1950): MULTIPLE MODELS FOR A 'EUROPEAN-STYLE' URBANISM

Mercedes Volait

CNRS/URBAMA, University of Tours

Across the cities of the Arab world, Cairo represents an early case of strong expansion and radical transformation in urban space that did not coincide with European colonization. Instead, this was inscribed within an endogenous reform process that emerged in the Ottoman province of Egypt from the first decades of the nineteenth century, helped by the arrival of a new dynasty – the Khedivial dynasty – that would remain in power until 1952.

Spurred on by its founder, Muhammad ʿAlî (who ruled from 1805 to 1848), and pursued by his successors, this reform process was certainly dependent on the *Tanzîmāt* reforms being conducted by the Ottoman imperial authority at around the same time, though by no means was it simply a byproduct of these reforms. While both movements shared identical reference models (from Europe) and analogous political foundations (reassertion of the central authority in the case of the 'Sublime Porte', and reinforcement of the autonomy from Istanbul in the Egyptian province), they also differed in many respects. The early orientations of the Egyptian modernization project were rather specific: besides building up a modern army and bureaucracy (as in Istanbul), priority was given to developing the cultivated lands of the country and to setting up an ambitious industrialization program, while the Ottoman project was more institutional and legal in nature.

From the beginning, Egypt's independent (even competing) modernization project was indeed to generate serious (eventually military) conflicts with Istanbul. However, from the 1830s the Egyptian rulers managed to pursue their own policies with only limited reference to the wishes of the Ottoman sultan,[1] as demonstrated by their resistance to apply the *Tanzîmāt* itself (the first reformed Ottoman legal code issued by 'The Noble Rescript' of 1839) and its later adoption in a modified version.[2]

At the urban planning level, the autonomy of the Egyptian process was reflected in the rhythm and the extent of the (firstly administrative) reforms. As early as 1834 (thus some years before Istanbul itself was outfitted with a similar institution),[3] an agency was created in the city of Alexandria (then experiencing a tremendous population growth above 10 per cent per annum)[4] to regulate the increase in construction. The official title of this 'Commission of Ornament', as the British termed it, was the *Commissione di Ornato* (with varied designations in Arabic sources, among them *maglîs al-ûrnâtû*). Such a label was borrowed from the commissions set up in Italy from 1807 during the Napoleonic occupation, based on the model of the *Commission des Arts* during the French Revolution.

However, the Alexandrian *Ornato* had an entirely different composition and function since its membership included government officials and representatives of the foreign communities (instead of artists and architects, as in the French and Italian precedents), and its powers were not limited to advice.[5] As such, it was therefore also the product of Egyptian realities: an autocratic tradition and a centralizing process combined with the constraints of the Capitulary privileges.[6] This case is not unique, though: while regularly seeking European expertise for his many Western-influenced reforms, Muhammad ʿAlî is also known, as a general rule, to have modified such advice, adapting it to fit the needs of his country[7] – a pattern that was to last for some time to come.

In 1843, in Cairo, a similar council, known in the records as *maglîs tanzîm al-mahrûsa* or *maglîs al-ûrnâtû*, saw the light, and was entrusted with 'the beautification of the city as well as the improvement and straightening of its streets, similarly to what was done in Alexandria'.[8] At the time, the *Ornato* had already implemented significant operations (the relocation of cemeteries, the cutting of new streets through the old fabric, the creation of a monumental esplanade and of regular subdivisions) in Alexandria,[9] and most of these were reproduced in Cairo. Other interventions reflected a more direct French influence, for example the opening in 1846 of the 'New Street' through-road, the path of which picked up exactly that of an unrealized project conceived half a century earlier by engineers from the Expedition of Bonaparte in Egypt (1798–1801).[10] (Fig. 1) These early achievements clearly show the diversity and cross-breeding of the models used in Cairo in matters of urban improvement, and the variety of circuits, sometimes indirect, that they managed to follow.

As a whole, the planning history of modern Cairo appears to have followed rather paradoxical or unexpected paths, at least when compared to that of other cities of the 'periphery'. In order to pinpoint them, this article will consider the main developments that shaped the physical appearance of the city along European lines – before Americanism was to take command in the late 1940s. These developments occurred during three distinct political situations: the reign of khedive Ismâʿîl (1863–79), the British occupation (1882–1922) and the so-called 'Liberal Age' (1922–52).

The great works carried out from 1868 onwards, partly modeled after the Parisian example, represent a first major shift in the development of the city.

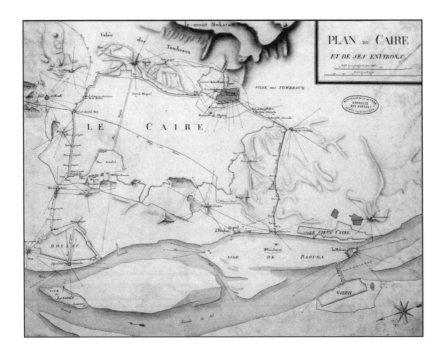

Figure 1. *Plan du Caire avec ses environs immédiats avec les ouvrages construits ou projetés par les ingénieurs géographes français en 1799 (Source: Vincennes, Service historique de l'Armée de Terre)*

They were undertaken under the initiative of Ismâ'îl, a man known for his will to prove that his 'country was no longer part of Africa, but belonged to Europe'. Within less than a decade, new quarters were created at the edge of the old city, new gardens and promenades were laid out, streets were cut through the old fabric and a vast spa was built south of the city.[11] These improvements, far more significant than anything implemented in Istanbul at the time, resulted in the irreversible shift of the city's center.

After 1882, the colonial authorities maintained as their priority the growth of agricultural resources, pursuing the policy of developing the irrigation infra-structure adopted by the first viceroys at the scale of the entire territory. However, in strong contrast with previous khedivial policies, British rule in Egypt was also characterized by a disengagement of the State from matters of urban planning.[12] The only significant public intervention at the time was the implementation of a sewer and drainage system (1907–1915) in Cairo. The other large urban planning operations dating from that period were all due to private initiative (both local and foreign), for example the subdivisions of Garden-City and Koubbeh Gardens, the garden suburb of Maʿâdi, or the new town of Heliopolis. The urban expansion of Cairo thus continued over the course of the colonial period and testifies to the vigor of its real estate and construction markets at the time, yet the 'public authorities' were no longer the client and consequently held no control over this expansion.[13]

It was not until it gained independence, granted unilaterally to Egypt in 1922, that the state began to regain the initiative by affirming its will to master and accompany the urbanistic development of Cairo. This new orientation manifested itself as early as 1923, for example in the construction of many public facilities, and was followed by the elaboration of a comprehensive town plan by an Egyptian planner who had been trained in Britain.[14] The first of its kind, this plan was only partially and belatedly realized, nevertheless it certainly contributed to the development of postwar Cairo.

While the formation of modern Cairo thus predates the British colonization of Egypt, and while the latter does not constitute its most impressive episode as far as public action is concerned – in contrast to what was to take place during the 'Liberal Age' – it is, however, in direct reference to various European models, and under European know-how (whether of European expatriates or of Egyptian professionals trained in Europe), that the urban planning of the Egyptian capital was to be conceived and conducted. The early borrowings from such models throughout the period in question here hence make modern Cairo an interesting case of 'European-style' urbanism, an urbanism resulting from an endogenous policy of importation and appropriation of European-born forms and technics rather than from an exportation of these via colonial dominance.

This is not to infer, though, that colonial-type procedures and technics were not occasionally put into use. Just as paradoxical is the observation that the French urbanistic tradition would fundamentally remain the necessary reference point over the course of the British occupation, and that British aesthetics would assert themselves after, instead of before, 1922. If such an urbanism was originally imposed 'from above', there is evidence that it may have been perceived by different local groups as an opportunity rather than a constraint; moreover, with time, local actors who contributed to its diffusion tended to diversify. Given the present, quite fragmentary knowledge on the subject,[15] this is at least what emerges from an examination of the large operations proposed or conducted in pre-colonial, colonial and postcolonial Cairo.

KHEDIVIAL CAIRO: A PRINCELY 'URBANISM' OF FRENCH INSPIRATION?

While khedive Ismâʿîl expressed an interest in embellishing Cairo as early as 1863,[16] it is after his visit to the Paris Universal Exhibition in June 1867

that this 'architectural fanatic'[17] is known to have resolved to 'transform the
Egyptian capital following the example of Paris'.[18] This sojourn also provided
Ismâ'îl the opportunity to meet with the famous Prefect of the Seine
Department, Baron Haussmann, and for visits to projects already in progress
around Paris. Later on, Ismâ'îl would also consult with the Parisian architect Hector Horeau (1801–72),[19] and in 1869 he even considered inviting
Haussmann, along with the architect Jacques Drevet (1832–1900), to Cairo,
'in order to haussmannize'[20] the city. However, to conclude that the khedivial endeavor amounted only to a 'haussmannization' – as his contemporaries
liked to point out – seems excessive, since it was the extension of the city
to encompass its nearby territory which made up the principal element of
the enterprise, rather than simply the restructuring of the existing built areas.

A logic of urban extension

The creation in several steps of new quarters adjacent to the city on its entire
western flank (over 200 hectares were urbanized in five years)[21] indeed represents the most evident legacy of the modernizing/Europeanizing ambitions
of the viceroy. The Azbakiyya quarter was the first project to get under way,[22]
on the site of a former lake that had been drained in 1848 and transformed
into a park. (Fig. 2) A smaller park was maintained in the center, redesigned
as an undulating octagonal garden; it was bordered on the north by a subdivision of attached residential constructions holding commercial arcades along
the streets, and on the south and east by ministries and large entertainment
buildings, including an opera, a circus, a French theater and a grand hotel,
most of which were erected within the span of a few months in 1869.[23]

To this nucleus of a new recreational and business center was attached a
second new quarter, a luxurious residential area (*quartier de plaisance*)
intended to be rich in vegetation. Named Ismâ'îliyya, in homage to its
founder, this would replace, and partly follow, the old alignments of orchards.
The street network was thus made up of an orthogonal grid attached to a
star-shaped pattern, both centered on a circular square. The streets defined
substantially sized blocks (with plots ranging from 2000 to over 5000 square
meters) that were to be reserved for the construction of large town houses
surrounded by gardens. The exception was the central block, which was
intended to hold a racecourse, the only public facility on the initial program
for this area. For a Parisian passing through in 1879, this suburban quarter
was clearly a remake of Passy (an affluent, new Parisian suburb at the time)
and the surroundings of the Bois de Boulogne.[24]

The plans and execution of Azbakiyya and Ismâ'îliyya were actually the
work of two French engineers, Jean-Antoine Cordier bey (1810–73) and his
nephew and assistant Alphonse Delort de Gléon (1843–99).[25] The son and
partner of a renowned hydraulic engineer responsible for the early water
supply of many provincial towns in France, Cordier bey had started his career

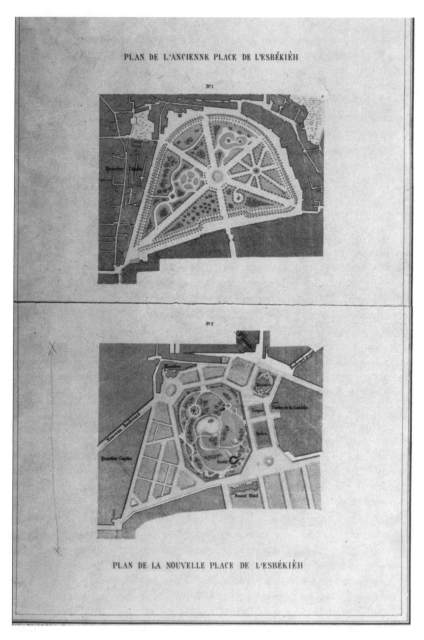

Figure 2. *Plan de l'ancienne et de la nouvelle place de l'Esbékieh (Source: Linant de Bellefonds Mémoire sur les principaux travaux d'utilité publique exécutés en Egypte depuis la plus haute Antiquité jusqu'à nos jours, Paris: Arthus-Bertrand, 1872–73, pl. 9)*

in Egypt by conceiving with his father and then managing alone a project for Alexandria's water distribution, before being awarded the concession for a similar operation in Cairo in 1865.[26] So it was that Ismâ'îl turned to the head of a private enterprise (Société des Eaux du Caire), which though lacking specific competence in matters of urban planning had much experience and knowledge of Egypt, for his projects.

Starting in 1871, the complementary formation of Azbakiyya and Ismâ'îliyya continued southward with the development of two further, exclusively residential subdivisions, the Bâb-al-Lûq and Chaykh Rihân (or Nasriyya) quarters, both of which again had different morphologies. (Fig. 3) The Bâb-al-Lûq plan centered on a large, elongated esplanade at the intersection of two diagonal roads. It featured a somewhat denser site pattern than Ismâ'îliyya, with plots of 400 to 3000 square meters. Nasriyya was a simple orthogonal grid, a portion of which contained still narrower plots of 50 to 300 square meters. In contrast to the Azbakiyya/Ismâ'îliyya ensemble, both Bâb-al-Lûq and Nasriyya were partially sited atop old suburbs, thus requiring some demolition prior to their implementation.[27]

Once again, the construction of the new quarters was orchestrated by a French engineer, Pierre-Louis Grand (1839–1918), but this time under the supervision of Cairo's *Ornato* Council. A former employee of the Société des Eaux du Caire since 1868, in 1871 Grand replaced Cordier and Delort de Gléon as the director of a new Administration de la Voirie, created that year under the aegis of the *Ornato* to implement the new quarters. Since the Council was by then headed by the architect Husayn Fahmî (replaced by the engineer 'Alî Fahmî in 1872), this move can be interpreted as a wish to regain some sort of local as well as 'public' control on the works in progress. However, Grand was appointed head of the Council in 1873 and his subaltern position to an Egyptian official was consequently to be rather short-lived.[28]

A strong hierarchy emerges from the totality of these suburban creations. There is a gradation from Azbakiyya to Nasriyya, in the sense of an increasing functional specialization (from mixed use to the purely residential), of an impoverishment of the planning design (from a monumental ordering to a simple gridded pattern), and of a shrinkage of plot sizes – an early instance of '"zoning" before zoning'?[29]

Particularly unexpected was the means by which the plots were allocated. With the exception of Azbakiyya, the buildable land of which was offered for sale, the land was granted for free but with certain conditions: the obligation to build, within a year and a half, and at a set minimum cost, a two-storey house on a property fenced off according to stated specifications.[30] This granting of free land was frequently used by the French in Algeria, yet was of colonial rather than French, and certainly not Parisian, inspiration. However, contemporaneous Parisian operations were indeed used as a reference for other aspects of the adopted procedure.[31]

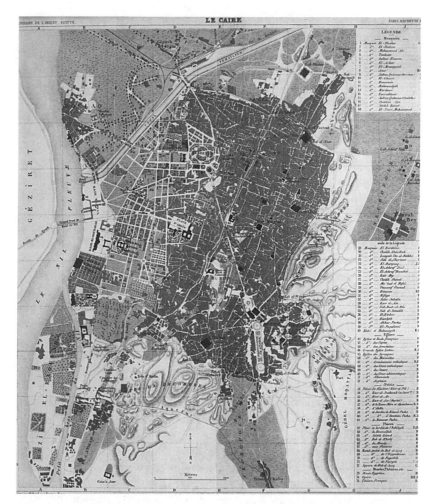

Figure 3. *L. Thuillier, Map of Cairo, 1883 (Source: Cairo, Institut français d'archéologie orientale)*

This concession system presented obvious advantages, both political and legal. On the political level, a strong stimulus to demand would hasten the transformation of Cairo's urban landscape, and this in turn would represent a powerful 'message' of the ruler's potency, addressed as much to the European world as to his own subjects. On the legal level, it could palliate the absence of appropriate legislation by imposing building restrictions through the concession acts.[32]

The system eventually proved successful, but was not without some initial setbacks. For example, up until 1872, there were few requests, particularly for plots at Ismâ'îliyya; moreover, some of the grantees were not able to respect the contractual conditions and consequently had to give up their concessions.[33] However, from this date onwards there was a wave of petitions for all the new quarters, and although a full assessment has yet to be carried out, indications are that a significant proportion of the petitioners did manage to secure a proper ownership title based on constructions that conformed to the stipulated conditions.[34]

From the sociological perspective, at first glance these petitioners made up a public that varied depending on the quarters, but that corresponded closely to the functional and formal hierarchy mentioned above. From the documentation that has been gathered so far, several categories emerge. In Ismâ'îliyya the concessionaires were primarily European nationals (part of the quarter had been explicitly reserved for Europeans),[35] but also members of 'older minorities' (Armenian and Syrian officials, Jewish bankers, Greek merchants and so on) together with other prominent members of the viceregal household (most often of Turkish origin). The most common link among them seemed to be their close relations to, if not official positions at, the khedivial court.

In Bâb-al-Lûq, as in Nasriyya, the petitioners were exclusively 'Egyptian' – Ottoman subjects with clearly identifiable names of autochthonous origin, either Copts or Muslims.[36] The largest plots were taken by 'beys' and, to a lesser extent, 'pachas', along with religious men or heads of guilds, and the medium-sized plots were granted largely to 'effendis', a title given to learned men who were generally employed as civil servants. Finally, the narrowest plots were requested by untitled individuals.[37]

It is possible to attach multiple interpretations to the noteworthy participation of the local élite as well as the middle classes in the construction of the new quarters of Cairo (the attractiveness of the model, or an aspiration for change, or more prosaically a pure speculative strategy). Irrespective of the interpretation, though, this new urban form put in place a segregation system that was both ethnic and social, again reflecting the colonial environment.

Gardens and promenades

The second chapter of Cairo's khedivial enterprise pertained to landscaping, and consisted of an ambitious program of botanical gardens, pleasure grounds and promenades on the outskirts of the city (around 350 hectares).[38] As early as December 1867, Ismâ'îl had demanded to see plans of Parisian gardens.[39] In addition to the undulating garden of Azbakiyya, embellished with a rockery, cascade, miscellaneous kiosks and ornamental structures, this led to the creation of an immense public botanical park (60 hectares) on the island of Gazîra (containing a wide variety of exotic species, a meandering artificial river, numerous kiosks, a menagerie of African animals and an aquarium) and of a series of shaded promenades (one of which led to the Pyramids). Numerous gardens were also laid out within the properties of the khedive, including that of the Gîza Palace on the left bank of the Nile, today the site of the city's zoo, and where a small footbridge designed by Gustave Eiffel – an exact replica of the one he conceived for the Buttes-Chaumont park in Paris – still survives.[40]

The above were largely the works of European landscape architects and gardeners, several of whom (such as the French Pierre Barillet-Deschamps and the Belgian Gustave Delchevalerie) had in the past collaborated with Adolphe Alphand (Haussmann's chief landscape designer and, later, successor), and had been recruited since 1868 through the intervention of Haussmann himself.[41] It is certainly in this domain that the Parisian reference in the khedivial projects is most direct and most evident.

The city 'slit open'

The opening of new routes through the city was the last of the proposed khedivial works in Cairo to be set in motion – after some trial and error. According to a khedivial order of 7 June 1869, the key parts of the project (five new streets) had in effect already been decreed.[42] Nevertheless, in November 1869 Ismâ'îl took advantage of a visit to Cairo by Horeau, on the occasion of the inauguration ceremonies of the Suez Canal, to solicit ideas from him regarding these final khedivial works. Soon after, Horeau submitted to Ismâ'îl a general plan of street openings proposing long diagonals across all of the old quarters; however, this generated sharp opposition due to the extent of the necessary demolitions. According to Horeau:

> Of all the ideas that I expressed in Cairo, this was the one where I encountered the most adversaries, and certainly the most potent ones. What, I was told, you want to Haussmannize Cairo? . . . Is it not vandalism to wish to make into a European city the Oriental city par excellence?

His chief opponent was indeed a man of importance, since he was no less than Ismâ'îl's foreign minister, the Armenian Nubar Pacha (1825–99), who 'love[d] his old Cairo right down to its ruins'.[43] In fact, in February 1870 Nubar requested (from French archeologist Auguste Salzmann (1824–72)) a note regarding the conservation and restoration of Cairo's 'Arab monuments', which he hastened to submit to the khedive. As a result, Ismâ'îl entrusted Salzmann with watching over the structures for a period of three years, as well as creating a museum.[44] But within the immediate entourage of the khedive there were also a number of genuine supporters of the proposals. One such supporter was the engineer 'Alî Mubârak (1823–93), who at the time held various ministerial portfolios, including that of public works, and who was later to describe a project prepared by his own staff that appeared even more ambitious than that proposed by Horeau.[45]

Neither of the above projects was implemented, and instead a compromise solution was reached. The new roadways that were eventually cut through the old neighborhoods in fact added up to just over 4 kilometers, and essentially consisted of two long streets, monumental in nature, starting at the Azbakiyya: one towards the train station (Clot-bey Street, begun in 1870) and the other towards the Citadel, the seat of khedivial power (Muhammad ʿAlî Street, begun in 1872). Their paths are particularly revealing. They suggest, first of all, that while local preservationists did in fact manage to get their voices heard, the ruler was not about to give up entirely on the reform of traffic movement through the old city fabric. The localization of the roadways also demonstrates the primary motivation for such works: to facilitate the crossing of the old city by an exclusive public – the 'users' of the railway station, the Azbakiyya quarter and the Citadel.

The way in which the two new roads were implemented is just as significant. To ensure that they were bordered with uniform arcades along their entire length, set guidelines were imposed on the facades of the new wayside constructions rather demanding a complete architectural project. In practice, the guidelines were inconsistently – if at all – respected, and the wished-for regularity only partially materialized. (Fig. 4) It is difficult to understand, then, how the Rue de Rivoli is so often cited as the model for the two roads (the use of an Algerian example such as Bab-Azoun Street would have been more appropriate), and even more so considering that contrary to the rules of formal composition prevalent in France at the time, Clot-bey and Muhammad ʿAlî streets are far from perfectly rectilinear: the former is broken past its midway point so as not to tear up a property of the Coptic Patriarchate, while the latter bends at one end in order to spare one of the most ancient and admired of Cairo's mosques, indeed producing an impressive architectonic effect.[46]

Compared with other works undertaken at the time, the khedivial reforms thus appear to be of secondary importance, linked chiefly to circulation imperatives that did not include the objective of remodeling the city around a renewed historical center, as had been the case in Paris. In this respect again, and though sharing the same source of urbanistic inspiration (from mid-eighteenth-century France), the Cairo reforms remain quite different from their Haussmannian counterparts.[47]

Although numerous French professionals were involved in, and Parisian projects without doubt directly inspired certain khedivial initiatives, it may be that the French reference for the embellishments of Ismâʿîl can be found in the colonial transformation of Algerian cities as much as in those of Haussmannian Paris. Indeed, many of the French engineers active in Egypt had previous experience in Algeria. An interesting example is Barthélemy Gallice (1790–1863), who also taught at the French military school where Egyptian engineers including Mubârak, Husayn and ʿAlî Fahmî were trained – another possible bias via which French colonial urbanism in Algeria may have reached Egypt.[48] However, one also wonders whether, of the Paris visited in 1867, it was in fact the Universal Exhibition – this new urban scenography

28

Figure 4.
Muhammad
'Alî Street in
the early
1880s,
showing the
irregular
arcades
(Private
collection)

with an emphasis on entertainment – that made the greatest, most vivid impression on Ismâ'îl. The importance he granted to buildings that were festive and recreational in nature, their concentration in Azbakiyya, the way they were staged, the rapidity of their execution – all these facts corroborate the hypothesis, hence opening up even further the range of models of reference, revisited locally, of khedivial Cairo.

'HAUSSMANNIZATION' AND 'GARDEN CITIES' IN BRITISH TIMES

The princely 'urbanism' described above was succeeded after 1882 by a more modest urban policy. Having gained control over Egypt due to the latter's financial insolvency,[49] the British authorities gave priority to the continued reduction of the Egyptian debt. To this end, they worked as much on drastically reducing public expenditures that were not immediately productive as on increasing national, particularly agricultural, resources.[50] Planning and equipping the cities (as well as improving sanitary conditions and public education), now considered to be too costly and financially unrewarding in the short term, was thus sacrificed in favor of the development of the water, road and rail infrastructure. That the colonial authorities brought in from India the best irrigation specialists from 1883, yet retained the services of French engineer Pierre-Louis Grand as chief of the Towns and Buildings Department until 1897, is a clear indication of what was now the prime concern. Even more eloquent were the terms used in 1899 to refuse the necessary funds to pave Cairo's streets. The entrusted authorities judged that

> the maintenance of Cairo streets holds only secondary importance, and it is necessary above all to devote the available funds to the improvement of the various services that would result immediately in increasing the arable lands of the country.[51]

Yet the existence of such a project to pave the streets of Cairo – one of the first initiatives of the engineer Arnold H. Perry, the English successor to Grand – also shows that the choices made at the top were not necessarily adhered to by the entire colonial hierarchy.

'Reforming' and 'sanitizing' the city

It appears, then, that the deficiency in the funds made available to the technical services of Cairo did not mean that the British agents in charge abandoned all interventionist desires. An examination of their projects indicates that the remodeling of Cairo's older quarters 'in conformity with hygienic and traffic requirements' was a central concern, particularly during Perry's administration (1897–1910).[52] The first move was to accelerate the decreeing of building lines for the progressive widening or rectification of any public street or road in the city, in application of the so-called *Tanẓîm* (or Alignment) Law of 1881.[53] By October 1890, the work was completed: about 1200 detailed plans fixed such lines for each Cairo street and portion of government-owned land within the city.[54] The *Tanẓîm* Law was made applicable to foreign residents of Egypt in 1887 and expanded in 1889.[55]

In 1902, the cost of rectifying and widening the entire street network was estimated, paired with cutting four new streets and opening up the 350 blind alleys identified in the 'native quarters'. This led to a new demand for special credits to enable the expropriation of 64 hectares of built-up lands required by such an initiative. Without the credits, Perry argued, given the currently available funds and 'assuming a constant budget, Cairo may expect to be "Haussmannised" or endowed with proper thoroughfares in 145 years'.[56] The request was once again rejected, and Perry managed to secure a progressive increase of the expropriation credits only over the course of the following decade, which meant pursuing the widening and straightening of the road network at a more sustained pace.

Still, the city's road network remained quite unsatisfactory for the officials concerned. In 1911, Perry's successor produced a table showing the percentage of the total area in each Cairo district occupied by roads. The result was an average of 23 per cent, reaching as low as 11 per cent in congested districts such as Bûlâq, even though 'the rules of town-planning *in general* do not admit a lower percentage than 30 for road areas [emphasis added]'.[57] In order to remedy the 'existing unsanitary and undesirable conditions of most quarters of the town', and to reach the minimum 30 per cent coverage, it was calculated that 230 hectares would have to be expropriated. But this represented a considerable expenditure. One proposed solution was to amend the 1906 Expropriation Law, so as to make improvement schemes pay for themselves via 'betterment'.[58] However, the public acquisition of additional property for purposes of resale after betterment did not become available by law until 1931.[59]

A second proposal was to elaborate new building regulations so as to prevent at least the plotting out of new building areas with narrow roads.[60] Planning and development of private estates at the time was yet to be subjected to any street or building regulations. The *Tanzîm* Law applied only to existing public streets, in built areas or in public subdivisions. In unbuilt areas, estate owners and land development companies were thus free to set their own – generally low – standards, and public action was thus limited to the direct development of government-owned land, the legal basis for imposing specific restrictions in such areas being to incorporate them in the deeds of sale of the individual plots.[61] Though a draft was prepared 'in accordance with the best practice of the day as regards distribution of space and hygiene',[62] a new Building Act was not to be issued before 1940 (Law n°52/1940). The British justification for their inability to pass new legislation was the alleged blocking of other European powers whose sanction was necessary for any new law that affected their nationals in Egypt, by virtue of the Capitulations.[63]

Nevertheless, and although the impact on the ground has yet to be fully evaluated,[64] it was during the British occupation and through the initiative of English engineers that the 'Haussmannization' of Cairo came to be envisioned. Besides the projected transformation of the road system, work on the ambitious sanitary network that got under way in 1907 is another indicator of such a trend.[65] Here, again, comparison with the Haussmannian undertaking is compelling; the Parisian sanitary network, constructed on the initiative of this famous prefect, is now considered his most essential legacy as well as one of the key elements of his strategy of urban intervention.[66]

A more general observation was offered by the British urban planner W.H. McLean (1877–1967)[67] at the end of twenty years of service in the Middle East, primarily in Egypt (from 1913 to 1926):

> The most striking feature about all the town-planning work [done in the region under British rule] is the fact that the planning and execution of the improvement and redevelopment of built areas has been in progress for over a generation, whereas the planning of unbuilt areas there is comparatively recent, while in England it is the reverse order.

This was due to the great resistance encountered in any urban renewal project and the lack of a legal basis for it in the latter.[68] In this sense, Cairo was not exceptional, yet this is surprising relative to other colonial situations. It is true that, from Algeria under French dominion to the Indian territories of the British Empire, colonization was the occasion of urban planning experiments, but it also frequently resulted in the transfer of metropolitan forms and concepts. In Egypt it appears that the British rarely sought to impose or promote the urbanistic ideas and practices they had developed at home, most notably the booming Garden City movement of the period (in Britain and elsewhere), and the extensions of Cairo implemented at the turn of the century offer another illustration of this.

Domesticating the Garden City

Almost all of Cairo's suburban developments under British rule (from the Garden-City suburb, designed in 1906, to the famous satellite town of Heliopolis, started the following year), resulted from the initiatives of land development companies, without any control from the authorities, for the reasons already mentioned above. Such companies flourished in Egypt between 1904 and 1908, some of them using European capital. From the beginning of the century, Egypt in fact distinguished itself as an interesting place for investment. And with the British presence perceived as a guarantee of political stability for the country, and of its engagement in liberal economics, European capital continued to flow in on a massive scale.

About one-tenth of this incoming capital went into land and real estate development, in which Belgian investors played a dominant role,[69] particularly in the creation of Heliopolis (thanks to financier Edouard Empain) and the residential quarter of Koubbeh Gardens (an operation of a subsidiary of the Heliopolis company, founded in 1908). Other projects attracted mixed capital, such as the garden suburb of Maʿâdi (by the Egyptian Delta Land and Investment Co., a product of two companies holding rail concessions in Egypt, one of them funded with British capital and the other with local funds). Yet other ventures resulted from purely local investments, such as the subdivisions on the left bank of the Nile in Gîza and on the island of Rawda (500 hectares developed by the Zervudachi brothers, Alexandrian entrepreneurs of Greek origin),[70] or the Garden-City suburb by Charles Bacos, another wealthy merchant and landowner from Alexandria (but of Syrian origin) through his Nile Land and Agricultural Co., formed in 1904.[71]

The latter is an interesting example of the local interpretation of a Garden City. Situated along the riverside, on land abutting the areas developed under Ismâ'îl, Bacos' estate (28 hectares) was initially planned for exclusively residential purposes. It was laid out in a plan designed in May 1906 by a local land surveyor (Joseph Lamba, also of Syrian origin) and was intended to be picturesque, featuring a systematic curving of the road network. (Fig. 5) Such a fantasy was probably meant to attract a well-off public looking for more than the usual grid-pattern environment. However, the undulating streets represented the sole originality of the adopted design. The area was classically divided into 272 building plots, without a center and with no community facilities, taking the profit-maximizing approach.

The plots (averaging 800 to 900 square meters) were offered for sale as unbuilt land. However, Bacos himself reserved twelve of them, for which he commissioned a French architect, Walter-André Destailleur (1867–1940), who came from a well-established dynasty of professionals specializing in architec-

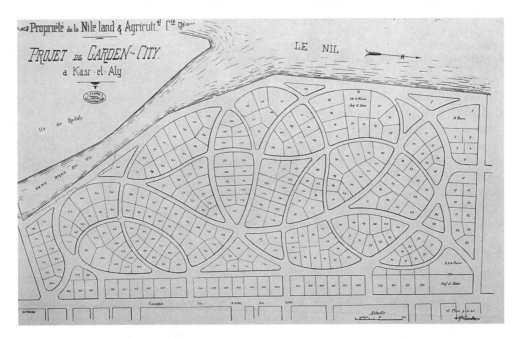

Figure 5. *Initial subdivision of Garden-City, dated 9 May 1906 (author's collection)*

ture for the upper classes (châteaux, resorts and *hôtels particuliers*), to design apartment buildings as well as his own mansion (on the best spot), all on a quite opulent scale.[72] In order to achieve homogeneity of the whole estate, Bacos resorted to the usual method of incorporating restrictions in the deeds of sale for the individual plots. The main restrictions were that the built-up area should not exceed two-thirds of the plot's total area, that the house should be set back from the street by at least two meters, that it should not exceed 18 meters in height, and that the fencing on the street should not be plain.[73]

Bacos' enterprise proved quite successful in the initial stages: during 1906 alone he managed to sell more than half of the overall site. However, in 1907, Egypt's financial crash[74] rendered the remainder unsaleable for many years, and his company was unable to distribute dividends after 1906. Bacos himself may have experienced financial difficulties if not bankruptcy, since Destailleur's upmarket designs were apparently not executed. Yet some of the earliest of the estate's buildings were clearly French-inspired, for example the neo-Haussmannian apartment blocks completed before the First World War or the exuberant Art-Deco villas and flats of the next decade, while others had an obvious Italian flavor, starting with the impressive Italianate palace built in 1908.[75] (Fig. 6) In its planning standards, function, social aims and aesthetics, this dense speculative development was thus very far from a replica of the British Garden City.

Figure 6. *Charles Beyerlé's palace at Garden-City, by architect Carlo Prampolini (ca 1908) (from The American Architect – London, Royal Institute of British Architects Library, Photographs collection)*

The same could be said for Koubbeh Gardens (44 hectares), a very similar development though with more generous open spaces, probably because of the lower cost of land in an area further away from downtown Cairo. Here, specific regulations limited the built-up area to between one-third and one-half of the plot's total area, and setbacks were to be six meters; a portion of the estate was also reserved for commercial and industrial buildings.[76]

No less rhetorical were the 'Garden Cities' built at Heliopolis in 1909–10: the term was in this case applied to what could be described as dense tenements consisting of two- to three-storey apartment buildings with balcony access, arranged in parallel rows.[77] (Fig. 7 and Fig. 8) As a whole, Heliopolis (240 hectares had been built up by 1922) far from conformed to the Garden City ideals of Howard and Unwin. It was certainly self-contained, greenery played an essential role, and its layout has also been regarded as presenting some affinity with Letchworth's plan.[78] However, the arrangement of the buildings at block level used a rigid rather than a picturesque layout, the densities were much higher than those advocated by the British movement, and along the wide boulevards were numerous monumental apartment blocks with arcades (some with rather Parisian massing blended with Moorish or even Indo-Saracenic style facades), bearing little reference to the cottage architecture of the British Garden City. Though rather distinctive, the townscape of Heliopolis was certainly closer to the 'grand designs' in the Beaux-Arts manner than to the sense of intimate space that relates to nature at work in the British prototype.

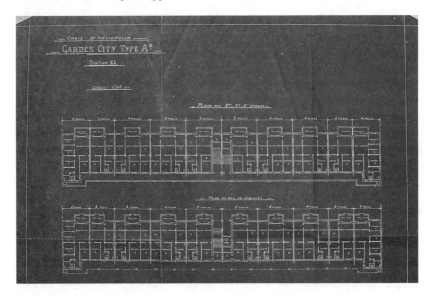

Figure 7. A Heliopolis' "garden-city" built circa 1921, plan (Cairo, Archives of the Heliopolis Oases Company)

The sole undertaking in which the imprint of the British concept is most obvious in Cairo, one that offers the 'appearance of a veritable "Garden City"',[79] is the suburb of Maʿâdi. (Fig. 9) The site on which it was to be built (located south of Cairo on a desert-like plateau overlooking the Nile) was acquired in 1905 and developed the following year using a pattern that may have taken its inspiration from the plan for the new city of Khartoum that had been conceived by two British engineers in 1898. The idea of creating a garden suburb at the Maʿâdi site is attributed to Felix Suarès (1843–1906), a local financier of remote Spanish origin, well known for his anticipatory vision particularly in matters of urban development.[80] The (largely British) managers of the company formed to implement the plan opted for a sub-division into lots of 1000 square meters each, so as to obtain a maximum density of 'four houses per acre' (10 per hectare). They also insisted that individual dwellings did not exceed 15 meters in height and were widely spaced apart. Finally, they required that property borders be marked with hedges rather than masonry or iron fencing. An extensive planting program was begun in parallel with the construction; this would ensure that the town was protected from the desert sand (with a belt of eucalyptus and casuarina trees), and that all of the streets would eventually be tree-lined. The choice of species was therefore carefully based as much on their capacity to provide shade as on the duration and color of their blossoming.

The members of the small British colony in Cairo were immediately attracted to what Maʿâdi had to offer, and were the first to acquire properties in

Figure 8. *A Heliopolis' "garden-city" built circa 1921, elevation (Photo by the author)*

the area (often buying four adjacent plots to increase the size of their gardens).[81] They made the project into a success, and a sort of long-term British enclave within Cairo. Hence, Maʿâdi constituted the implementation of the colonial period that showed the closest affinity to British planning principles – though in terms of land tenure the project was classically based on private ownership of the plots and not on cooperative land ownership.

In summary, during the period of colonial domination of Cairo, public interventions were limited and centered on the remodeling of existing quarters, while private initiatives for undertaking urban extensions flourished. Generally speaking, a relatively weak penetration of British urban planning concepts characterized this period, in contrast to what was occurring in other territories of the British Empire.[82]

THE URBAN PLANNING ERA

The situation that would prevail during the subsequent 'Liberal Age' represents an almost diametric opposite to the above. The general tendency in Egyptian urban development was to consist of expanding statal interventionism, an increased emphasis on controlling urban extensions, and an intensification of references to British practices. This turnaround was essentially due to the new political context opened up by Independence in 1922. However, this by no means ended British interference; in fact the final evacuation of all British troops from Egyptian soil did not take place until 1956. Still, as regards domestic matters, the margin of Egyptian authorities was significantly widened: in addition to its parliamentary system, in 1922 the country also restored its financial autonomy.[83] Having regained full control of public expenditure, the new government gave priority to those fields that until then had been sacrificed, prominent among which was urban planning.

Towards a Town Plan

In Cairo, the change was first reflected in 1923, starting with the execution of an ambitious program of improvements: the cutting of new arteries across the old quarters (including al-Azhar and al-Gaysh Streets, both completed in 1929), the systematic widening of a major thoroughfare (Khalîg Street), the disengaging of several historic mosques (among them, that of Ibn Tûlûn in 1925–26), and the undertaking of large public facilities (starting with the Parliament, the new seat of the Mixed Courts, the Qasr al-Ayni hospital and school of medicine, and the Cairo University campus).[84]

Next, public interventionism manifested itself in a will to plan the evolution of the city and to control its expansion. The first step was the setting up in 1929 of a central planning body, the *Tanzîm* Higher Advisory Council, which had as its mandate the coordination of the activities of the various

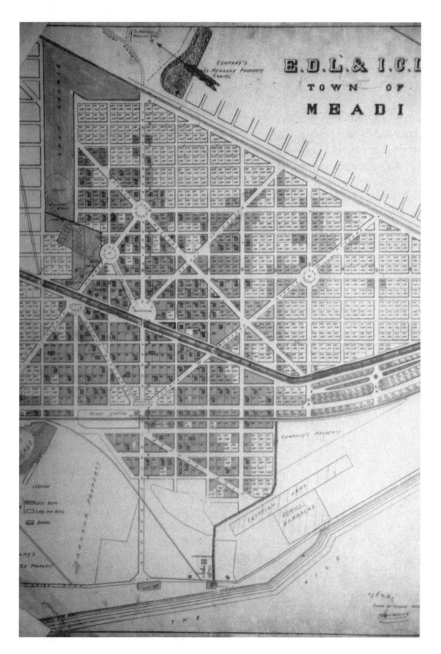

Figure 9. *Plan of Ma'âdi, dated August 1929 (private collection)*

departments in charge of 'municipal affairs' (or 'civic activities' according to the expression used at the time). Due to the absence of an autonomous municipal structure (until 1949), Cairo was at the time directly governed through departments that functioned independently of each other, including the *Tanzîm* (exercising most of the usual functions of a municipality), 'City Police', 'Public Health', 'Main Drainage' and 'State Buildings'.[85] The new, much-needed central body, made up of the heads of these departments and independent experts who met about ten times a year, was also to advise on all projects of city improvement and embellishment.[86]

The next step was to begin negotiations with the large development companies in order to lead them, in the absence of a set of general regulations, to adopt provisions that better conformed to 'modern Town Planning lines' in their future developments. 'To ensure for a large area of Cairo of the future the full play of modern ideals with regard to planning, zoning and other general civic amenities,' the new body looked to the company in charge of Heliopolis. Though Heliopolis was still regarded as 'the most remarkable and important enterprise in modern town development that had been undertaken in Egypt,' its initial regulations were nevertheless seen as rather out-of-date as well. Criticism was specifically directed to 'the inadequate provision of public gardens and interior open spaces, over-concentration of buildings in many areas, unrestricted and irregular heights of blocks of flats and defective

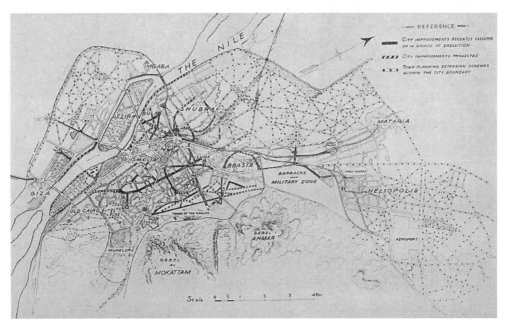

Figure 10. Mahbûb's Town Plan (By permission of The British Library, PP. 1092.K)

zoning.'[87] After several years of negotiations, agreement was finally reached in 1931. Rather sophisticated, the new regulations for the company's undeveloped estate required, among other things, that 48 per cent of the area be surrendered for roads, parks and playgrounds.[88]

The new planning approach eventually – and importantly – resulted in the elaboration of a general town plan for Cairo's improvement and extension, following the undertaking of a 'comprehensive survey' of the city. (Fig. 10) Prepared under the supervision of Mahmûd Sabrî Mahbûb (an English-trained engineer, and member of the Royal Town Planning Institute since 1924), the plan proposed, in addition to further modifications of the existing street pattern, two city extension schemes over the agricultural areas to the north and west of the city.[89] On the northern periphery, the plan predominantly included the layout of main arterial connections. On the left bank it was more detailed since the pertinent lands constituted a single property that could easily be acquired by the State. The plan proposed the creation of a new residential district (680 hectares) here, organized around a vast central park and surrounded by a park belt.[90] Submitted in 1930 to the *Tanzîm* Higher Advisory Council then to the Council of Ministers, this particular chapter of the overall town plan was approved in September 1932.[91]

Reform of the city and working-class housing

Simultaneously, the State took action on the regulatory front. In 1931, as mentioned earlier, it reformed the Expropriation Law of 1906 – despite the alleged obstacle presented by the Capitulations, which were not abolished until 1937. The new law permitted the public acquisition of both large zones bordering newly created streets and roads (for resale under building restrictions), as well as whole areas for replanning.[92] It thus opened up a new field in which the authorities could intervene: the replanning and reconstruction of slum areas. The first tentative scheme to be considered applied to the Bûlâq district (200 hectares). The master plan was to transform it into a 'modern commercial and good class residential area' – in the very words of Mahbûb – given its prime location along the Nile and close proximity to the city center. To achieve such an aim, the plan proposed the demolition of almost all the existing sites and buildings (except for mosques and churches), the fixing of a new road pattern (the provision for streets, squares, gardens and open spaces amounting to about 40 per cent of the whole area), and complete reconstruction adhering to 'proper architectural and sanitary regulations'.

Rehousing the majority of the 140,000 residents to be affected by the reconstruction plan, most of whom had only modest incomes, was also addressed. A preliminary survey determined that a significant number of Bûlâq's inhabitants worked in government workshops (for the state railway, National Printing Department, arsenal and so on), the relocation of which on the outskirts of Cairo had already been planned or was under way. These workmen could be rehoused in the vicinity of the new sites, where cheap land was available for housing schemes. As for the remaining population, as a first step the project included a housing scheme, to be located across the Nile from Bûlâq, which could accommodate 5000 workmen's families.

The financial aspect of the whole scheme was also carefully considered. Rough estimates demonstrated that although the project would involve heavy public investment, this could be largely balanced out by the prospective values of the sites that would be created, based upon their use for the erection of many-storeyed blocks of mixed commercial and residential buildings.[93]

Deferred implementations

These initial developments in the planning-oriented approach took place in Egypt, as elsewhere, under regimes that were authoritarian (the government led by Muhammad Mahmûd – 1928–29) – or even despotic (the cabinet of Ismâ'îl Sidqî – 1930–33). These regimes advocated a general policy of 'renewal and reform' (*siyasat al-tagdîd wa al-îslâh*) as an essential requisite to resume the full sovereignty of the country;[94] in strong contrast, a much more popular (especially in rural areas) nationalistic attitude regarded internal reforms as secondary to solving the question of Anglo-Egyptian relations. It could be argued, then, that for these so-called minority governments (since they were based on political parties that held a weak electoral base), the urban component of their reform agenda was also instrumental in attempting to woo urban voters in the face of a rural population that overwhelmingly favored the nationalists.[95]

While the proposals were numerous, the realization of such plans was more limited. The most noteworthy advances remained those at the institutional and regulatory levels. Indeed, the Sidqî cabinet was succeeded by transitional governments that did not last long enough to set up large-scale operations. With the return to power of the nationalists in 1936 (they had earlier been in command from 1924 to 1928), the 'reform of the Egyptian countryside' began to take precedence.[96] Such an orientation was actually quite logical in a country where the rural population still made up around three-quarters of all inhabitants, but it was also undoubtedly a proper reward to this population for its partisan backing. For the duration of the Second World War, the construction sector was largely paralyzed, and it was only after the war that two of the principal proposals of the Mahbûb plan could be implemented: the urban extension on the left bank of the Nile and the building of the 'workmen's housing scheme'.

The client for the new extension was not the Public Works ministry, however, as had initially been envisioned. In fact, in 1944 the ministry of *Waqfs* (religious endowments), as owner of the properties concerned, announced its intention to appropriate the idea of erecting a new district. The ministry's chief engineer, the architect Mahmûd Ryâd (1905–?), was entrusted with the task of establishing a design for the new district. Thus, the conception of the main urban planning operation of the postwar era in Cairo in the end fell to an Egyptian engineer, again one trained in England.[97] While maintaining the element of a vast central open area, Ryâd's design certainly differed from that of Mahbûb, yet it still bore the mark of contemporary British urban planning, as reflected in the semi-circular streets, large parkways and U-shaped quadrangles of houses around a central green. (Fig. 11) Open for sale since 1948, the plots in this new quarter, which was advertised as an 'international model city, combining the beauty of Vienna with the elegance of Paris,' would not find any buyers until after 1955.[98] Now known as Muhandisîn, this has become one of the more fashionable districts of Cairo.

As for the design of the housing estate for workers, this was finally erected between 1947 and 1950 on the site originally assigned to it (1100 units built on 140 hectares). (Fig. 12) Its design was the work of 'Alî al-Malîgî Massa'ûd (1898–?), an engineer who had also been trained in England and who was at the time the chief urban planner for the Administration of Municipalities and Local Commissions at the Ministry of Public Health.[99] The British influence also manifested itself again here in the type of housing, layout forms and in the play of materials on the facades to give variety, but without reference to the most contemporary applications of the British movement. Apparently out of concern for adapting to the local context, the project adopted the by-then-discredited model of the back-to-back two-storey row

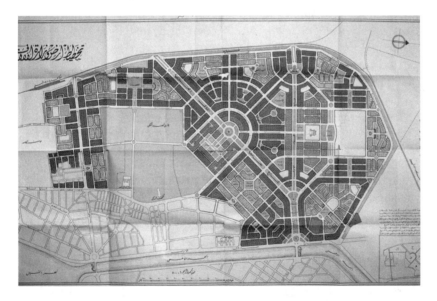

Figure 11. *Ryâd's plan for the urban extension on the west bank of the Nile, 1948 (Author's collection)*

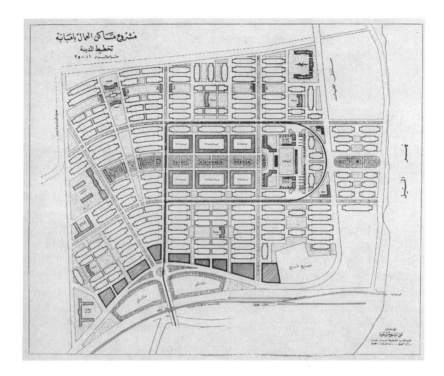

Figure 12a. Massaʿûd's workmen housing scheme in ʿImbâba: general plan (from Magalla al-ʿimâra, 5/6, 1947, author's collection)

housing, as well as densities that were higher than those advocated at the time (140 residents per acre rather than the maximum 100 called for in England by the Dudley Report).[100]

The late implementation of the above two examples aside, they indeed suggest that it was during the period of liberation from British tutelage that reference to English urban planning imposed itself most strongly in Egypt, and it was Egyptian urban planners who in the end proved to be its most propitious agents. Interestingly enough, in the 1950s Egyptian planners were already exporting their skills to almost all of the countries in the region, from Algeria to the Arab Gulf.[101]

CONCLUSION

To summarize, the picture is thus far more complex than may have been expected. It centers on a double irony. Indeed, the penetration of European (in particular French and British) urban planning models in Cairo, including

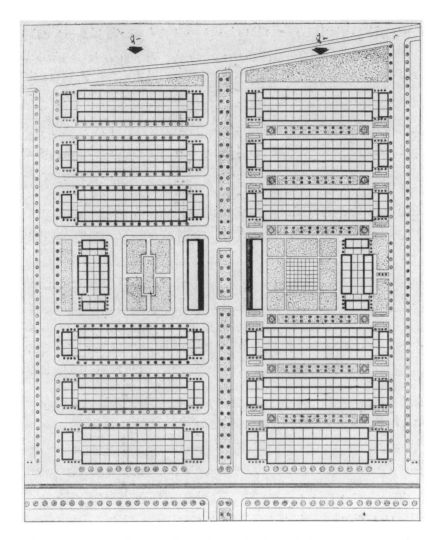

Figure 12b. Massa'ûd's workmen housing scheme in 'Imbâba: layout of the rows (from Magalla al-'imâra, 5/6, 1947, author's collection)

during the colonial episode, came about largely due to local actors, whether rulers, property developers or the professionals themselves. Moreover, one of the main obstacles such a Europeanization had to overcome was European inertia, if not opposition, since it necessarily affected the privileged status granted to European nationals in Egypt by the Capitulory system. A number of conclusions can be drawn from the proposed account and analysis. One may choose to question the supposed synchronization between colonization,

Westernization and urbanization, and beyond, the coincidence between cultural hegemony and political domination. On another level, the narrative can contribute to the growing debate surrounding the endurance of projected designs over the longer term.

In terms of the international diffusion of planning, and in reference to Ward's recent typology, the pattern here appears to be one of 'selective borrowing' (although this type of diffusion has generally been recognized as occurring among Western countries).[102] Several of the examples above suggest that educational and professional ties probably acted as determinant channels in this process. Thus the results far from conformed to the original reference models: because the game was mastered locally, the importation (for which the desired international image of the Egyptian capital acted as a powerful drive) led to the elaboration and development of all sorts of cross-breeding and hybridizing, to complex tinkering with the various models, both in their metropolitan (home) and colonial (overseas) variants. In fact it appears that, from the stock of possible models, Cairo's 'builders' (*édiles*) tapped into those which best suited their ambitions and concerns of the moment (or, more prosaically, those that were most accessible to them) – even if on occasion they had to resort to arrangements that had become anachronistic in their sphere of origin, yet were viewed as satisfactory for the Egyptian context. It is, then, the concrete mechanisms of these systems of selective appropriation and of domestication that, from now on, we should be able to better comprehend.

NOTES

1. See Afaf Lutfi al-Sayyid Marsot (1984) *Egypt in the Reign of Muhammad 'Alî,* Cambridge: Cambridge University Press; Fred Lawson (1992) *The Social Origins of Egyptian Expansionism during the Muhammad 'Alî Period,* New York: Columbia University Press; and for a new assessment see Khaled Fahmy (1998) 'The era of Muhammad 'Alî Pasha', in M.W. Daly (ed.) *Modern Egypt,* Cambridge: Cambridge University Press, Vol. 2, pp. 139–79.

2. See Joan Wucher King (1984) *Historical Dictionary of Egypt,* London: The Scarecrow Press, pp. 604–05.

3. For a detailed study of early municipal organization and building regulations in Istanbul (with a documentary appendix), see Stéphane Yerasimos (1989) 'Réglementation urbaine et municipale (1839–1869)', in Alain Borie et al., *L'occidentalisation d'Istanbul au XIXe siècle,* Paris: École d'Architecture de Paris-La Défense, pp. 1–97.

4. Between 1821 and 1848, its population increased from 12,000 to 104,000 inhabitants; see Michael Reimer (1997) *Colonial Bridgehead, Government and Society in Alexandria (1807–1882),* Cairo: The American University in Cairo Press, pp. 89–90.

5. For its Italo-French inspiration, see G. Romanelli (1980) 'La Commissione d'Ornato: da Napoleone al Lombardo-Veneto', in P. Morachiello and Georges

Teyssot (eds) *Le Macchine Imperfette*, Rome: Officina, pp. 129–45. For its actual organization and working, see Reimer, op. cit., pp. 73–6.

6. By virtue of the Capitulations (a series of legal concessions originally made by the Ottoman sultan to various European powers, starting in the sixteenth century), nationals of these countries enjoyed a privileged status in Egypt, including virtual freedom from all local law and tax exemption. Approval of their consulates was thus necessary for any new measure that might affect the status quo – hence the presence of consular delegates in the *Ornato*.

7. When, in 1847, a French expert suggested, for example, the establishment of a parliament modeled on the French system in order to secure more adequate performance of the government machinery, and to control it in an efficient way, his proposal was typically turned down as being unsuitable for Egypt at the time; see Raouf Abbas Hamed (1995) 'The *Siyasatname* and the institutionalization of central administration under Muhammad 'Alî', in Nelly Hanna (ed.) *The State and its Servants, Administration in Egypt from Ottoman Times to the Present,* Cairo: The American University in Cairo Press, pp. 75–87.

8. Khedivial order of 30 December 1843, cited in Helmy Ahmed Chalabi (1987) *Al-hukm al-mahallî wa al-magâlis al-baladiyya fî misr* [Local Government and Municipal Councils in Egypt], Cairo: 'Alam al-kitab, p. 35.

9. Reimer, op. cit., pp. 123–35.

10. Plan du Caire avec ses environs immédiats avec les ouvrages construits ou projetés par les ingénieurs géographes français en 1799 (Service historique de l'Armée de Terre, Vincennes, 6. C. 19). I wish to thank P. Tsakopoulos for making me aware of this document.

11. For this spa, see Elke Pflugradt (1996) 'La cité thermale d'Helwan en Egypte et son fondateur, Wilhelm Reil-bey', in Catherine Bruant, Sylviane Leprun and Mercedes Volait (eds) *Figures de l'orientalisme en architecture,* Special Issue of *Revue du Monde musulman et de la Méditerranée,* 73/74, pp. 259–80.

12. As I have tried to demonstrate in Mercedes Volait (1993) *Architectes et archi- tectures de l'Egypte moderne (1820–1950), Emergence et constitution d'une expertise technique locale,* Doctoral dissertation, Université de Provence, chapter 5 passim. It has to be recalled, among other things, that this late British posses- sion was not meant to be a settler colony.

13. Due to shortcomings of the available legal tools, see below.

14. Presented by its author in Mahmoud Sabry Mahboub (1934/35) 'Cairo, some notes on its history, characteristics and town plan', *Journal of the Town Planning Institute* XXI, pp. 288–302.

15. A much neglected field of research, the planning history of modern Cairo is still strongly dependent on secondary sources, due to difficult access to primary sources. A notable – though recent – exception is the period of Ismâ'îl, thanks both to H. Rivlin's pioneering work of indexing the Cairo National Archives (here- after CNA) foreign language collections (including the so-called '*Asr Ismâ'il*' series, a collection of papers, mostly in French, from the private cabinet of the khedive; see Helen Rivlin (1970) *The Dâr al-Wathâ'iq in 'Abdîn Palace at Cairo as a Source for the Study of the Modernization of Egypt in the 19th Century,* Leyden: Brill, pp. 74–98), and to the personnal in-depth knowledge of Egyptian scholars regarding the unclassified archive resources for this period. I am particularly indebted to Khaled Fahmy and Mohamed Aboul Amayem for drawing my atten- tion to unpublished material used for this paper. For an architectural portrait of modern Cairo, see Cynthia Myntti (1999) *Paris Along the Nile: Architecture in Cairo from the Belle Epoque,* Cairo: The American University in Cairo Press; and

46

Ghislaine Alleaume and Mercedes Volait (2002) 'The age of transition: the nineteenth and twentieth centuries', in A. Raymond (ed.) *The Glory of Cairo: An Illustrated History*, Cairo: The American University in Cairo Press, pp. 361–464.

16. Mirrit Boutros Ghali (1983) *Mémoires de Nubar Pacha,* Beirut: Librairie du Liban, p. 211.

17. In the words of Gabriel Charmes in *Revue des Deux Mondes,* 1879, p. 776.

18. Gustave Delchevalerie (1897) *Le parc public de L'Ezbékieh au Caire,* Gand: Annoot-Braeckman, p. 5.

19. Pierre Larousse (1874) *Dictionnaire universel du XIX° siècle,* Paris: Administration du grand dictionnaire universel, Vol. IX, p. 391.

20. Handwritten note by Drevet, dated 19 March 1892 (Paris, private collection).

21. Figure given in ʿAlî Pacha Mubârak (1969) in *Al-khitat al-tawfîqiyya al-gadîda li-misr al-qâhira* [New Guide to the Districts Ruled by Tawfiq], Cairo: Al-hayya al-misriyya al-ʿâmma lil-kitâb, 2nd edn (1st edn 1888–89), Vol. I, p. 207. This is a well-informed source given the high official positions of this engineer, though equally biased for the very same reason.

22. According to an estimate of works to be carried out on the area, dated 12 March 1868 in CNA, *ʿAsr Ismâʿîl* series, file no 82/4.

23. Volait, op. cit., pp. 154–6, and for a detailed description of the quarter in 1873, Léon Hugonnet (1882) *En Egypte.* Paris: Calmann Lévy, pp. 280–320.

24. Gabriel Charmes (1880) *Cinq mois au Caire et dans la Basse-Egypte,* Cairo: Jules Barbier, p. 58.

25. Pierre Giffard (1883) *Les Français en Egypte*, Paris: Victor Havard, pp. 67 and 69; CNA, *ʿAsr Ismâʿîl* series, file nos 81/1 and 79/3.

26. The conception and execution of which were entrusted in turn to Delort de Gléon in 1869; on these men, see Marie-Laure Crosnier Leconte and Mercedes Volait (1998a) *L'Egypte d'un architecte: Ambroise Baudry (1838–1906)*, Paris: Somogy, pp. 59–61.

27. According to the records on these three extensions, in the files of another CNA series, entitled *Muhâfaza Misr, Mahâfiz* sub-series (boxes 1871 to 1876).

28. On Grand's career, see *Résumé des travaux de la Société des Ingénieurs civils de France*, 1918, p. 38 and CNA, *Muhâfaza Misr* series, *Mahâfiz* sub-series, box 1873; on H. Fahmî and ʿA. Fahmî, both of whom trained in France, see Volait, op. cit., pp. 90–94.

29. See Richard Dennis (2000) '"Zoning" before zoning: the regulation of apartment housing in early twentieth century Winnipeg and Toronto', *Planning Perspectives*, 15, no. 3, pp. 267–99.

30. Conditions listed in the official engagement that petitioners were asked to sign to obtain a plot. The earliest engagements in the records go back to 1869 (CNA, *ʿAsr Ismâʿîl* series, file no. 79/3); the system seems to have been in force until 1876, when the decision was made to sell the remaining ungranted plots (Cairo's Governor order, dated 3 January 1876, in CNA, *Muhâfaza Misr* series, *Mahâfiz* subseries, box 1870).

31. The type of fencing imposed at Ismâʿîliyya – 'une partie maçonnée surmontée d'une grille en bois ou en fer, pleine ou à jour' (CNA, *Muhâfaza Misr* series, *Mahâfiz* subseries, box 1873) – is exactly the same as that being used at the time for new avenues of western Paris.

32. The *Ornato*'s regulations mainly concerned building lines in built areas, with some clauses governing frontage projections; see Volait, op. cit., pp. 120 and 206–7.

33. Various examples in CNA, *ʿAsr Ismâʿîl* series, file no. 79/3 and *Muhâfaza Misr* series, *Mahâfiz* subseries, boxes 1871–6.

34. According to the petitions kept in the files of CNA, *Muhâfaza Misr* series, *Mahâfiz* subseries, boxes 1871–1876. Since these files seem to contain only part of the petitions presented, an evaluation is still out of reach. Equally premature is the drawing of an accurate picture of ownership actually achieved (by obtaining a *hugga*, i.e. the deed delivered by an Islamic court after approval both from Cairo's governor and from the khedive on the grounds of compliance with the stipulated conditions), but examples of such approvals can also be extracted from the same files.

35. A letter dated 19 November 1871 referring to a plot in Ismâ'îliyya describes it as being located 'in the portion of the quarter bestowed by His Majesty to the Europeans' (CNA, *Muhâfaza Misr* series, *Mahâfiz* subseries, box 1872B).

36. For problems of national definition, see Fréderic Abecassis and Anne Le Gall-Kazazian (1992) 'L'identité au miroir du droit: le statut des personnes en Égypte (fin XIXe-milieu XXe siècle)', *Egypte-Monde Arabe*, 11, pp. 11–38.

37. According to the data provided by the petitions themselves (CNA, *Muhâfaza Misr* series, *Mahâfiz* subseries, boxes 1871–1876).

38. Gustave Delchevalerie (1899) *Les Promenades et les Jardins du Caire*, Chaumes, p. 45.

39. CNA, *'Asr Ismâ'îl* series, file no. 62/1.

40. Marie-Laure Crosnier Leconte and Mercedes Volait (1998b) 'Les architectes français ou la tentation de l'Egypte', in Jean-Marcel Humbert (ed.) *France-Egypte, dialogues de deux civilisations*, Paris: AFAA/Gallimard/Paris-Musées, pp. 102–115.

41. CNA, *'Asr Ismâ'îl* series, file no. 39/22.

42. Amîn Samî (1936) *Taqwîm al-Nîl* [The Nile Almanach], Cairo: Matba 'Dâr al-Kutub al-Misriyya bil-Qâhira, Vol. III, p. 813.

43. Hector Horeau (c.1870) *L'avenir du Caire au point de vue de l'édilité et de la civilisation*, Paris, pp. 10–12.

44. CNA, *'Asr Ismâ'îl* series, file no. 7/2. For this founding episode and European pressure on the issue of preservationism during the next decade, see Crosnier Leconte and Volait (1998a) op. cit., pp. 100–2.

45. See Mubârak, op. cit., Vol. I, p. 210; Vol. III, pp. 253–54 and 353; Vol. IX, p. 142; and the tentative map reconstructed in Janet Abu-Lughod (1971) *Cairo*, Princeton, NJ: Princeton University Press, p. 110 on the basis of these descriptions.

46. Michael Darin and Mercedes Volait (1993) *La percée exportée: le cas du Caire*, Paris: LAREE/Plan Urbain.

47. For a stimulating critical view on the so-called 'Haussmannian model', see Michael Darin (1995) 'L'art de la percée: les boulevards d'Haussmann', in André Lortie (ed.) *Paris s'exporte, Modèles d'architecture ou Architectures modèles*, Paris: Picard, pp. 197–204.

48. See Volait, op. cit., pp. 52–53 and 209.

49. Ismâ'îl's modernizing ambitions had led him to borrow impressive amounts from British and French bankers; by 1875 he proved unable to meet the interest payments. The following year, an international control over the country's finances was imposed by France and Britain, followed by Ismâ'îl's forced dismissal in 1879 to be replaced by his son Tawfîq. Political unrest due to the resentment of the general population against the increasing presence of the British and French in the economy and administration of the country was to bring about the British occupation of Egypt in 1882.

50. Robert Tignor (1966) *Modernization and British Colonial Rule in Egypt, 1882–1914*, Princeton, NJ: Princeton University Press, p. 214.

51. Interview with William E. Garstin, Under-Secretary of State for Public Works, in *La Bourse Égyptienne*, 11 November 1899.

52. Ministry of Public Works (1912) *Report on the Department of Towns and State Buildings for 1910*, Cairo: National Printing Department, p. 16.

53. Issued on 12 March 1881 as the '*Règlement sur le service du Tanzîm*', this law was meant to coordinate all previous regulations governing construction and to reorganize the old *Ornato* Councils, now named *Tanzîm* services; see Soubhi bey Ghali (1897) *Tanzim ou voirie urbaine en Égypte*. Paris: Delagrave, p. 11.

54. See successive issues of Gouvernement Égyptien (1886–1890) *Bulletin des Lois et décrets*. Cairo: Imprimerie Nationale. The oldest existing alignment plans all bear the date of 1882 (Cairo Governorate Archive Department: unclassified maps) but there are references to older ones; see Ministère des Travaux Publics (1882) *Compte rendu de l'exercice 1881–82*. Cairo: Imprimerie Nationale, pp. 71–72.

55. Soubhi bey Ghali, op. cit., pp. 10–11; Mahboub, op. cit., p. 289. The law of 1889 is regarded as having partly followed French and Belgian legislation (Ministry of Public Works (1912), op. cit., p. 17). It is worth noting that, as far as French legislation is concerned, the law actually drew on rather old regulations (particularly a Parisian bylaw of 1796 and the Alignment Act of 16 September 1807) rather than on the latest ones.

56. Public Works Ministry (1903) *Report on the Administration of the Public Works Department in Egypt for 1902*. Cairo: National Printing Department, pp. 296–98 and 311–14.

57. Ministry of Public Works (1913) *Report of the Ministry of Public Works for the Year 1911*, Cairo: Government Press, pp. 355 and 454.

58. Ibid., pp. 30 and 355.

59. Mahboub, op. cit., p. 292.

60. Ministry of Public Works (1913) op. cit., pp. 355–56.

61. See Mahboub, op. cit., pp. 288–302.

62. Ministry of Public Works (1912) op. cit., p. 15.

63. A rather rhetorical argument if we are to believe a critical observer, who considered that the Capitulations formed above all 'a convenient cloak of ample folds to conceal official short-comings'; John M. Robertson (ed.) (1908) *Letters From an Egyptian to an English Politician on the Affairs of Egypt,* London: Routledge, p. 106.

64. References to newly widened streets in the 'native quarters' can be found in the annual reports of the Ministry of Public Works; see for example Ministry of Public Works (1914) *Report of the Ministry of Public Works for the Year 1912*, Cairo: Government Press, p. 12. However, there is no evaluation of how many (and which) streets were actually rectified under British rule.

65. On this scheme, which met strong criticism both in Egypt (where it was seen as too limited) and in Britain (where it was considered too ambitious) see Volait, op. cit., pp. 402–22.

66. See Pierre Pinon (1991) 'Les réseaux techniques: de l'eau salubre, limpide et fraîche . . . et des égouts', in Jean Des Cars and Pierre Pinon (eds) *Paris-Haussmann*, Paris: Picard/Pavillon de l'Arsenal, pp. 150–61.

67. For biographical data on this planner, see Robert Home (1990) 'British colonial town planning in the Middle East: the work of W. H. McLean', *Planning History*, XII, no. 1, pp. 4–9.

68. William H. McLean (1930) *Regional and Town Planning in Principle and Practice*, London: Lockwood & Son, pp. 71 and 122.

69. See Charles Issawi (1947) *Egypt: An Economic and Social Analysis*, London: Oxford University Press; Henri de Saint-Omer (1907) *Les entreprises belges en Egypte*, Brussels: G. Piquart.

70. Involved in all kinds of banking and financial operations among which land enterprises, their firm was particularly prosperous at the time, see Wright, Arnold (ed.) (1909) *Twentieth Century Impressions of Egypt*, London: Lloyd's Greater Britain Publishing Cy, p. 440.

71. On the early history of this company, see P. Taylor (1911) *African World Egyptian Companies Manual*, London, p. 59.

72. Bacos' instructions to Destailleur give an idea of the kind of high-class building he had in mind. For one plot, for example, his specifications were for a building with one apartment of about 300 square meters each floor, containing six bedrooms, two drawing rooms and a dining room, with ceilings not less than four meters. The designs for his own house reveal a luxurious French-Renaissance style mansion (Archives Nationales [hereafter AN], Paris, CP, 536 AP/70, no. 105 and nos 82–94). On the Destailleurs, see Pauline Prevost-Marcilhacy (1995) *Les Rothschild, bâtisseurs et mécènes*, Paris: Flammarion, p. 564.

73. Contrat-type pour l'acquisition de terrains à Garden-City, in AN, Paris, CP, 536 AP/70, no.16. The original metalwork fencing can still be seen today in most of Garden-City's streets.

74. A 'market's correction' after a decade of intense speculation, also due to a world slump; see Issawi, op. cit., p. 31.

75. A Palace in Cairo, *The American Architect*, 9 February 1910, no. 1781, pp. 69–71, and plates. Commissioned by a German banker, a few years after completion the palace was acquired by Sarag al-Din Chahin Pacha, a wealthy Egyptian landowner.

76. Mahboub, op. cit., p. 298.

77. Robert Ilbert (1981) *Héliopolis, genèse d'une ville (1905–1922)*, Marseille: CNRS, p. 82.

78. Ibid., p. 77.

79. Mahboub, op. cit., p. 298.

80. Samir Raafat (1994) *Maadi 1904–1962, Society and History in a Cairo Suburb*, Cairo: The Palm Press, pp. 11–18 ; Pflugradt, op. cit., pp. 268–69.

81. Raafat, op. cit., pp. 23–4.

82. As evidenced in Robert Home (1997) *Of Planting and Planning: The Making of British Colonial Cities*, London: E & FN Spon.

83. See Arthur Goldschmidt (1990) *Modern Egypt, The Formation of a Nation-State*, Cairo: The American University in Cairo Press, ch. 6 *passim*.

84. For these undertakings see Volait, op. cit., pp. 455–69.

85. Sirry Hussein (1933) 'City and town development: Egypt's municipal systems', *The Manchester Guradian Commercial*, 25 March, p. 12. On Cairo's special status regarding municipal affairs, see also Abu-Lughod, op. cit., pp. 147–50.

86. See the ministerial decree dated 23 July 1929, creating the *Tanzîm* Higher Advisory Council in *Journal officiel du Gouvernement égyptien*, no. 67, pp. 3–4.

87. Quoted from Mahboub, op. cit., p. 296.

88. Règlement pour la création et le développement de nouveaux quartiers dans le périmètre du domaine d'Héliopolis, dated 1 March 1931, in *Journal officiel du Gouvernement égyptien*, no. 45, pp. 4–9.

89. For a detailed analysis of this plan, see Mercedes Volait (2001) 'Town planning schemes for Cairo conceived by Egyptian planners in the "Liberal Experiment" period', in Hans Chr. Nielsen and Jakob Skovgaard-Petersen (eds) *Middle Eastern Cities 1900–1950: Public Spaces and Public Spheres in Transformation*, Aarhus: Aarhus University Press, pp. 44–71.

90. Mahboub, op. cit., p. 298 and plate VI.

91. Ministry of Public Works (1939) *Annual Report of the Ministry of Public Works for 1930/31*, Cairo: National Printing Press, p. 120; *al-Musawwar*, no. 413 of 9 September 1932.

92. Law no. 94 of 15 June 1931, *Journal officiel du Gouvernement égyptien*, no. 65 (no. extraordinaire).

93. Mahboub, op. cit., pp. 300–2 and plate VII.

94. Muhammad Mahmûd (1929) *La dictature libératrice*, Alexandria: Alexandria Printing Press, p. 197.

95. See Afarf Lutfi al-Sayyid Marsot (1977) *Egypt's Liberal Experiment: 1922–1936*, Berkeley, CA: University of California Press, pp. 118–19.

96. For the evolutions of public concern regarding social housing in Egypt, see Mercedes Volait (1995) 'Réforme sociale et habitat populaire: acteurs et formes (1848–1946)', in Alain Roussillon (ed.) *Entre réforme sociale et mouvement national: identité et modernisation en Egypte (1882–1962)*, Cairo: CEDEJ, pp. 379–409.

97. Ryâd had followed the famous course in Civic Design at the University of Liverpool, at a time when Patrick Abercrombie taught there. See Volait (1993), op. cit., pp. 487–90.

98. Ibid., pp. 595–97.

99. Massa'ûd had been sent to England in 1924 through the Educational Missions Abroad program to specialize in Town Planning. After working one year at the Town Planning Department of the Ministry of Health in London, he spent three further years in a similar structure in Iraq, after which he was admitted as a member of the Royal Town Planning Institute; ibid., p. 530.

100. Ibid., pp. 588–91 and The Earl of Dudley (1944) *The Design of Dwellings*, London: HMSO, p. 23.

101. Tawfîq 'Abd al-Gawwâd (1989) *Misr al-'imâra fil-qarn al-'ishrîn* [Egyptian Architecture in the Twentieth Century], Cairo: The Anglo-Egyptian Bookshop, pp. 160 and 165–67.

102. Stephen Ward (2000) 'Re-examining the international diffusion of planning', in Robert Freestone (ed.) *Urban Planning in a Changing World: The Twentieth Century Experience*, London: Spon, pp. 40–60.

CHAPTER 3

THE TRANSFORMATION OF PLANNING IDEAS IN JAPAN AND ITS COLONIES

Carola Hein

Bryn Mawr College

Japan's role in the transmission of planning ideas is multifaceted. Since the mid-nineteenth century, the country has imported architectural and urban design concepts and techniques, particularly from Europe and the US, and appropriated them to its own needs. During the same period, Japan also exported planning methods to the Asian neighbors it colonized, where it combined Western imports with Japanese practices. This exchange and transformation occurred at a time when Japan and its global role were rapidly changing, and these developments influenced the degree of implementation and transformation of foreign models as well as the possibility of exports.

Starting with the Meiji Restoration in 1868, Japan's political and economic system evolved from a secluded island nation with a feudal organization and a strict social hierarchy, to a militaristic colonial power, and finally to a democratic and industrialized country. Modern urban planning, developed over decades in the West in response to industrialization and urbanization, entered Japan simultaneously with the country's overall modernization and transformation. Planning was seen as a means to ensure the most important elements for economic development: establishing infrastructure and industrial sites, but also creating government and business centers. The Japanese planning profession developed slowly through a small group of specialists who worked primarily in governmental positions. These new planning experts concentrated on two specific tasks: adapting selected cities and areas to the modernization of the country, and creating a Japanese planning system.

The role and interests of the planning profession in Japan have changed over the last century and a half. In the early Meiji years, Western models were eagerly imported. Japanese planners transported their freshly acquired knowledge to the newly gained colonies, where military power allowed them to implement ideas based on this knowledge, sometimes before establishing these ideas at home. On their return to Japan, they often tried to re-import their colonial experience; rapid realization rarely ensued, but the seeds for later innovation were planted.

As Japan established itself on the international stage in the early twentieth century, and as it developed its own planning system as a mixture of local traditions and foreign ideas, planners became more selective in their choice of Western models since the innovations had to respond to the particularities of Japanese urban form and organization. Traditional land ownership and distribution patterns proved very resistant to change. Sudden disasters, such as the Great Kanto Earthquake of 1923, required rapid and particular responses, which the Western concepts *per se* did not provide. Military defeat in the Second World War again modified Japanese society and the country's relationship with Western and Asian countries. Japan lost its colonies, the many urban plans it had laid out for Manchuria or other Asian nations were therefore rendered obsolete, and the occupation forces became a new player in postwar reconstruction within Japan itself.[1] Since the 1960s, the economic boom has further changed Japan's global position and its role as a recipient and distributor of planning concepts.

Amid this larger theme of Japan's position in the international exchange of planning ideas,[2] this article focuses on the role of foreign and Japanese planning experts in the development of modern Japanese planning from the Meiji Restoration to the early postwar era. It uses the year 1919, which saw the adoption of the Japanese City Planning Law, as a dividing point for two periods. The first period, from 1868 to 1919, largely coincided with the Meiji era and the establishment of Japanese planning practice. The second phase, from 1919 to the early post-Second World War period, is characterized by the confirmation of new planning tools.[3] Using terms coined by Stephen Ward, the first phase is characterized by 'selective borrowing', or an eagerness on the part of the Japanese to try out foreign concepts through widespread borrowing and erratic application. The second phase is typical of 'synthetic innovation', described by Ward as not just an adaptation but a synthesizing with other ideas and practices leading to further innovation.[4]

During the first phase, foreign models shaped the country's organization in fields such as education, politics and law enforcement. The Japanese government specifically invited Europeans and Americans to build, plan and teach in Japan,[5] and other specialists went to Japan on their own initiative. The input of these experts, whose work was closely modeled on foreign examples, was often not appropriate for the special Japanese context, as demonstrated by examples such as the Ginza brick district designed by Thomas J. Waters and the new government district projected for Tokyo by Böckmann and Ende.

The Japanese government also sent selected individuals and members of the ministries to Europe and the US. This group of students included such well-known names as army doctor Mori Ōgai and future mayor of Osaka, Seki

Hajime, both of whom were to become major influences in the creation of a Japanese planning system. Their findings from abroad, transmitted through committees and legal texts to the planning community in Japan, directly influenced the development of Japanese planning techniques and laws in areas such as zone expropriation, building lines and land readjustment. Over the years, experience determined whether these methods were properly adapted to the Japanese urban culture or whether they were discontinued.

Though the planners had a deep understanding of Japanese practice, their study of European and American planning methods and culture often remained superficial. They rarely applied the imported ideas in their original form; instead, they mixed them with traditional Japanese practice or transformed them to suit Japanese lifestyles. This resulted in hybrid forms of architecture and planning,[6] as well as cultural practices in general, which often led to criticism from foreign visitors to Japan regarding the transformations in the built environment during the Meiji period. However, this criticism, just as their intervention in Japan, reveals a lack of understanding of the particular needs and the cultural and historic background of the country. This first phase is thus characterized as a period of trial and error.

During the second phase, once Japanese planning practice had been established, the government granted less authority to foreigners. Internationally recognized specialists, such as Charles Beard, former director of the New York Bureau of Municipal Research and an internationally renowned figure in scientific urban management, and Bruno Taut, a leading European modernist and author of numerous public housing complexes, could no longer find eager listeners. Yet important Japanese individuals also found it difficult to influence planning. The laws and other tools they had helped create had to prove their value and show that they could hold up against landowners and established interests. Even powerful leaders such as Gotō Shinpei, an administrator at home and in the colonies who served at different times as the first president of the South Manchuria Railway, then head of the Public Health Department at the Ministry of the Interior, Home Minister and Mayor of Tokyo, did not always manage to implement their ideas.

At the time, Japanese specialists used criteria such as applicability and importance in selecting models and documents from Western countries. Specific works were singled out and discussed in Japanese journals, and selected foreign articles and books were translated. As a result, some Japanese specialists, for example Kyoto professor of urban planning Nishiyama Uzō, and long-time chief of Tokyo planning Ishikawa Hideaki, became influential figures in the transmission of Western concepts, and their interpretations of foreign works became references for generations of planners to come.

After focusing on the Japanese archipelago in the first part of this chapter, the second part demonstrates that Japanese planners were not only importing planning concepts but were simultaneously experimenting with urban planning ideas and techniques in several of its East Asian colonies, practicing – to use Ward's term – 'authoritarian imposition' of their practice.[7] Japan thus exported its Western-influenced evolving planning practices to Taiwan, Korea, China and Manchuria, functioning as a transformer and interpreter along the way.

The colonial period can also be broken into two phases. The first phase saw the implementation of numerous advanced planning techniques in the colonies, which provided an important testing ground for planners and architects. For example, building laws and land readjustment were tested in the colonies before they existed or were applied in mainland Japan.

The colonial experience was not limited to the export of planning ideas from Japan but also provided a way to import (or re-import) such ideas into Japan itself. European and American techniques and concepts had reached China and Russia before the Japanese colonization, and the Japanese occupants learned from the planning laws and design forms that already existed in cities in this part of northeastern Asia as they colonized them. For example, when the Japanese took over Dairen (built as Dalny by Russia between 1899 and 1904), they inherited a plan for a monumental city and decided to continue and improve on this design. The ambitious scale and design of the project was to set a precedent for later visionary urban planning.[8] Qingdao, organized as Tsingtau under German control since 1897, is another instance of this importing of planning ideas via the colonies. When the Japanese took over the city in 1914, they examined and maintained the building laws, thereby gaining first-hand knowledge of applied German planning legislation.[9]

After 1919, the colonies continued in their role as important training grounds. Colonial planners could create plans of a huge scope and demonstrate what they had learned from international discussions. Many of them later occupied important positions in Japanese planning before, during and after the Second World War. Whereas comprehensive urban projects had failed in Japan, the implementation of these in the colonies suddenly appeared possible. The Japanese desire for comprehensive planning and three-dimensional design was exemplified in the project for Datong (or Daidô in Japanese), which was the work of a group of architect-planners including Takayama Eika, a future planning educator. However, the colonial period was far too short to realize such plans. In addition, Japanese land laws and ownership patterns at the time were resistant to change, and it was therefore not until decades later that many of the ideas developed in the colonies during the period were applied in Japan.

This article showcases the role of planners in the import and export of planning concepts through two periods in the development of modern Japanese planning, analyzes their impact on design forms (as seen in visionary drawings and realizations) as well as on planning methods and techniques, and assesses the implementation and application of the concepts they introduced. Finally, it compares the role of the planner in the Japanese context with that of its Western counterpart, and addresses the issue of ideology in the importing and exporting of urban planning.

WESTERN SOURCES AND JAPANESE TRADITIONS: THE IMPORT OF PLANNING CONCEPTS INTO JAPAN

Western practice influenced Japanese urban planning for many decades, with the understanding of the European or American models typically colored by the source of the transmission. This section concentrates on the role of individuals in the creation of a Japanese planning tradition and examines the introduction of Western planning ideas by foreigners and the insights gained by the Japanese during their studies abroad. It also analyzes how planning ideas were translated and findings applied. It is through this process that specifically Japanese planning tools began to take shape.

Generalized imitating and borrowing from the West: 1868 to 1919

Japan's isolation ended in the middle of the nineteenth century as a result of pressure from the US. European nations had turned many East Asian countries into colonies and with the US they controlled Japan through the so-called 'unequal treaties'. To achieve a position equal to that of the leading powers, Japan's new elites embarked on a path towards rapid industrialization. They transformed the political system into a parliamentary democracy and reinvented the former shogun capital, Edo, as the nation's new capital, Tokyo, a metropolis that was meant to rival those of leading European centers. To gain acceptance in the West, Japan tried to integrate the culture, techniques and formal languages of Europe and the US into its cityscapes, and architectural and urban design types derived from the European tradition flourished in major Japanese cities. However, one of the most profound changes of the Meiji period was the establishment of private land ownership as the basis for a land taxation system.[10]

Whereas the European countries and North America could build upon a long tradition of architectural and urban forms with common roots, Japan had a very different – though equally strong – tradition. The European tradition of classical forms as a reflection of political and economic power had no parallel in Japan. Public places comparable to the monumental squares of European cities, where highly decorated buildings faced the street, did not exist in Japan, where public buildings were often secluded from public space by high walls and meeting places were informal spaces often located at bridge-heads. Even the overall city form differed from that of Western metropolises. While most continental European cities possessed a radio-concentric street pattern based on fortification walls surrounding the medieval city, traditional Japanese cities are better characterized as a patchwork of neighborhoods where large-scale developments for military aristocracy coexisted with small-scale developments for ordinary townsfolk. The multiple-storey buildings and urban apartments typical in many European cities contrasted with tiny, low-rise row houses in Edo Japan. Furthermore, in Japan the position of the architect was not yet established, due to the late introduction of architecture as a profession, and a two-dimensional approach to urban form dominated. Given these fundamental differences between Japanese and European or American cities, when 'planners' finally began to emerge they had to consciously select and adapt Western models to Japanese needs.

IMPORT BY FOREIGN PLANNERS

The images of Western cities that were first to reach Japan often came from European surveyors, builders and architects, some of whom had worked in colonial towns and quarters in other East Asian countries and elsewhere. Urban planning based on a unified streetscape and separation of traffic, typical of many European cities, was implemented in Japan for the first time in Tokyo's Ginza district. The plan emerged after a fire destroyed nearly 3000 houses in the area in 1872. Under the authority of the English engineer Thomas J. Waters, the central street and part of the surrounding neighborhood were rebuilt with brick architecture on a comprehensive scheme. (Fig. 1) The Ginza district was traditionally the city's central area for common citizens; located close to the Western settlement of Tsukiji in Tokyo and the Shinbashi Station, from which trains left for the Yokohama settlement, it was an important site, and a redevelopment following the newly imported design principles thus seemed appropriate.

A new entry to the city could be created here as a strong urban statement. Brick buildings and a boulevard with partitions between footpaths and car-riageways, as well as arcades, gaslighting and roadside trees appeared for the first time in Japan. The project, which was designed to provide a Western-style metropolitan boulevard for Tokyo, reflected similar projects in neigh-boring East Asian colonies and the emerging awareness of famous European streets, such as Regent Street in London and Rue de Rivoli in Paris. However, the Ginza project was not merely an aesthetic statement designed to put Tokyo in line with Western metropolises, but was also conceived to improve the city's resistance to fire, a frequent occurrence in Edo/Tokyo. While streets were widened and some blocks rearranged and replotted, the urban layout of the

area was largely maintained since modern planning tools such as land readjustment were yet to be established. But the project was far from successful
as Tokyoites perceived the buildings as expensive, damp and lacking protection against earthquakes. Many of the buildings lay empty for years, the project
was ended in 1877 and it remained limited to the Ginza area.[11]

The Ginza project was the first and last attempt to transform Tokyo into
a metropolis that aesthetically resembled major European cities. The area was
destroyed by earthquake in 1923 – proving the critics right – and by war in
1945, and the original planning attempts vanished in the typically chaotic
Japanese cityscape[12] (though a number of later interventions, such as wider
streets and fire-proof buildings, addressed public safety concerns). The need
for a uniform architectural streetscape had no historical roots in Japan and,
while it was tried once, it did not leave a lasting impact on the country.

Although other comprehensive urban design projects were proposed for
Tokyo, these were never constructed. The most famous is the proposal by the
Berlin office of Böckmann and Ende for a government district and a central
train station, and major infrastructure improvements in the Hibiya area of the
city. New ministries and other administrative buildings had to be built for
the Meiji government. To demonstrate the new parliamentary system and the
transformations that Japan had undergone, the government wanted public
buildings of Western character that would be integrated into a larger district.
This, at least, was the conviction of the man responsible for this project,

Figure 1. Brick buildings along the boulevard in Tokyo's Ginza area, 1873
*Source: Kanagawa Prefectural Museum of Cultural History (reproduced in Tokyo,
La ville moderne, 1870–1996, Exhibition catalogue)*

Minister of External Affairs Inoue Kaoru. Given the French tradition of monumental architecture and the transformation of Paris under Haussmann,
France seemed an obvious choice as a model for the project. However, Inoue
instead asked the young German Reich for advice. Like Japan, Germany was
a newcomer among the established powers. It had recently gained status as a
major European power, and the ongoing redesign of its capital city, Berlin,
could be used as a model for the transformation of Japan's capital, Tokyo.

In 1886, responding to a request from the Japanese government, Wilhelm
Böckmann, one of the office partners and a founding member of the German
architectural magazine *Deutsche Bauzeitung*, elaborated a proposal for several
major boulevards that would connect various ministries and public institutions in Tokyo. (Fig. 2) Large streets were also to connect the new parliament
and the imperial palace to the projected central station, in front of which
would be erected major representative buildings.[13] Such a large-scale, long-
term monumental project did not relate to the concrete need for the rapid
creation of a modern infrastructure, government buildings and company headquarters, and the necessity to respect the existing patterns of land ownership
and division. Nor did it acknowledge the lack of a Japanese tradition of urban
representation. Although the German designers realized some buildings, the
project had only a restricted impact on Japanese cities. Designed by Western
architects who largely ignored the cultural, socioeconomic and political background of Japan, this grand schemes was never implemented, even though it
corresponded to the desire to transform Tokyo into a capital city that could
function as a political and economic center of power.

Under pressure from the Ministry of Home Affairs, the project for a government district was dropped in favor of the First Plan for Urban Improvement
of Tokyo (1889). Developed with the participation of government officials,
military officers and members of the Tokyo Prefectural Assembly, which
centered on the Urban Improvement Committee (chaired by Akimasa
Yoshikawa, Vice-Minister of Home Affairs), this plan tried to address the
overall transformation of the city.[14] (Fig. 3) While in scale similar to the
transformation of Paris under Haussmann, the main concern in Tokyo was
the amelioration of the roads and parks rather than the creation of urban
beauty inherent in the Paris plan.

So the Meiji government, or rather some of its members, examined the
possibility of transforming its capital city into a design copy of Western
metropolises. However, the government quickly realized that urban design was
not the solution to its modernization needs and that the design, provided by
foreign planners were not integrated within Japanese traditions of patchwork
development. Meanwhile, planning specialists had begun to emerge within the
Japanese administration. These specialists tended to be interested in Western
urban planning techniques rather than Western urban design. Many individuals had gained insight into foreign planning practices during their studies

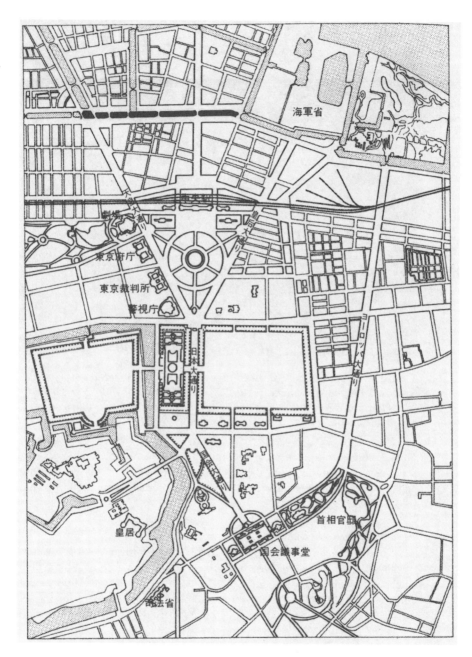

Figure 2. Böckmann and Ende, proposal for a government center in Hibiya, 1886
Source: Ishida Yorifusa, Nihon kindai toshi keikaku no hyakunen (Tokyo, Jichitai
kenkyûsha, 1992), p. 45

Figure 3. First Plan for Urban Improvement of Tokyo, 1889
Source: Ishizuka Hiromichi, Ishida Yorifusa (eds.), Tokyo: Urban Growth
and Planning 1868–1988 (Tokyo: Center for Urban Studies, Tokyo
Metropolitan University, 1988)

abroad, concentrating on technical and administrative topics. They also had
a better understanding than the foreigners of the needs of the transforming
Japanese cities and particularly the necessity to create appropriate planning
tools.

IMPORT BY JAPANESE PLANNERS
The Japanese government undertook the study of foreign countries systematically. In 1871, the Iwakura mission, a group with forty-eight members
including leading government officials, left Japan to tour Europe and
America.[15] In the field of architecture and planning, members of the mission
were particularly impressed by the transformation of Paris from a chaotic
medieval city to a modern metropolis with a widespread infrastructure
network. This experience, together with the results brought back by several
Japanese planners after their stay in Europe or the US, strongly influenced
Japanese planning concepts and law, and was partially reflected in imitations
and adaptations of the built environment in the West.

In addition to these shorter exploratory missions, the government sent members of Japanese ministries and young individuals, over the course of the late nineteenth century, to various European countries and America to study select fields, including the emerging urban planning discipline. Numerous Japanese acquired profound knowledge of the most advanced Western planning discussions via intensive reading of Western literature. Mori Ōgai is one such example. Mainly known in the West for his novels *The Dancer* and *Wild Geese*, Ōgai studied in Germany from 1884 to 1888. Together with the hygienist Nakahama Tôichiro, who lived in Germany from 1885 to 1889, he was interested in discussions of public health and hygiene, and he strongly influenced the creation of a building code in Japan. As Ishida Yorifusa has shown, he even translated passages of German texts and included them in his proposals for Japanese building laws.[16] Other influential Japanese planners included Yamaguchi Hanroku, author of an extension plan for Osaka in 1889, and Seki Hajime, the initiator of the Midosuji-Boulevard, Osaka's main axis,[17] who studied in France and Belgium, respectively. But their knowledge of Europe was superficial and, as a result, some concepts were misunderstood, wrongly chosen or incompletely applied.

It should be noted that the inclusion of new ideas into Japanese laws did not necessarily mean they were implemented. Urban planning techniques that were successful in Germany, France and other European countries did not work as well in Japan, and some laws were rarely applied due to resistance from landowners and lack of popular support. Following is a review of some examples of European planning techniques, including zone expropriation, building lines and land readjustment that the Japanese studied and introduced into planning in Japan.

The Iwakura mission (see above) praised the Paris transformation under Haussmann, which used a form of zone expropriation. Called 'chōkashūyō' in Japanese, this technique consisted of expropriations in connection to and alongside newly built streets. The method was adopted in the 1888 urban improvement plan, following the strong support of several well-known Japanese planners.[18] However, due to the resistance of the Ministry of the Interior with regard to the high costs involved, it was rarely applied.[19] The 1919 urban planning law contained 'chōkashūyō' as a clearly formulated system, but even in the 1920s this technique did not gain recognition, despite the support of several major influences in planning. Gotō Shinpei and Ikeda Hiroshi, head of urban planning under Shinpei (both authors of the 1919 urban and building laws), promoted zone expropriation without success. Later (1926–37), Seki Hajime was forced to use a different technique – the definition of so-called aesthetic districts – to create Midosuji Boulevard in Osaka.

Another major tool of early Japanese planning were building lines. Introduced in their original German version in lectures by the Prussian police captain Wilhelm Hoehn between April 1885 and March 1886, these aimed at creating setbacks relative to the street line, delimiting the land to be built on. In 1913, while working on a draft of a new building ordinance for Tokyo, the Architectural Institute of Japan (Kenchiku Gakkai) took up the idea in its English or French usage of 'street line as building frontage'. The same view was shared by architects from the Research Committee for Urban Planning (Toshi keikaku Chōsakai), established in 1918, which was responsible for the preparation of the Town Planning and the Urban Building Acts of 1919. Instead of delimiting a line beyond the street line, this became a tool for them to deal with parts jutting out of buildings. Although specialists such as Ikeda Hiroshi or Seki Hajime understood the German form of the building line, the architect Kataoka Yasuo, a student of the influential British-trained architect and professor Tatsuno Kingo,[20] took the lead among architects of the Research Committee and promoted the English version of the building line. Its introduction into the Japanese building law in 1919 provided a means for the densification of Japanese inner-city areas after they were destroyed by fire or other disasters. The law allowed for a separation of the two lines. It also stated that the existence of a passageway delimited by two parallel building lines on an official plan gave the owner the right to build on a plot that was accessed by it, even if the corresponding street was never built.[21] This offers a particularly interesting example of Japanese planners making clever use of Western planning instruments.

The most important tool of Japanese urban planning was, and still is, land readjustment, a technique of unifying and redistributing land. (Fig. 4) The sources of this system are multiple. The most important root, especially for land readjustment in suburban areas, was the traditional Japanese arable land readjustment (*denku kairyō*, or *kōchi seiri*). Early implementation of urban land readjustment can be found in the first years of the 1890s, even before the Arable Land Readjustment Act (Koochi seiri hō), based on the model of German arable land readjustment Acts, was put in place in 1899. This Act was revised in 1909 as it did not take into account the specific needs of irrigation, and many provisions of this later Act were applied in similar fashion to the urban land readjustment system provided in the Town Planning Act of 1919. The Japanese planners were aware of the preparatory works for the Lex Adickes, a German planning law of 1902.[22] An 1893 bill of the German law, although it had been rejected by the German parliament, was translated into Japanese. But Japanese planners examined it primarily for the excess condemnation system (*chōkashūyō*) and not in regard to land readjustment. In fact, the overall system of Japanese land readjustment for suburban areas resembled the 1902 Lex Adickes because both shared their roots. The Japanese land readjustment system was based on the farmland rearrangement technique that had existed since the Meiji period and had been defined in the 1899 Arable Land Readjustment Act; indeed, the German arable land readjustment Acts on which the Japanese Act had been based were also roots of the Lex Adickes.[23]

Japanese planners thus studied and then adapted foreign planning tools for local usage. They quickly drew on and abandoned urban design concerns using their knowledge to create tools that were appropriate for the transformation of the rapidly changing Japanese cities, the creation of a modern metropolis and the adoption of the building and planning laws of 1919.

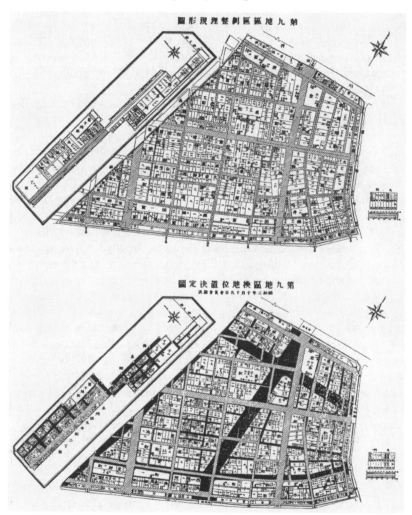

Figure 4. Illustration of the technique of land readjustment
Source: Ishida Yorifusa, *Nihon kindai toshi keikaku no hyakunen* (Tokyo, Jichitai kenkyûsha, 1992), p. 165

Selective borrowing: 1919 to 1945

With the adoption of the Town Planning Law and the Building Law for Urban Areas in 1919, the basis for planning in Japan was established, and foreign models therefore became less important. The government no longer invited Westerners to participate in projects for Japanese cities, and Western critiques were often rejected, though on specific occasions advice was requested from individual planners. For example, Ishikawa Hideaki, a major figure in the urban planning of Nagoya and later of Tokyo, consulted Raymond Unwin on his Nagoya plan during his trip to Europe in 1923.[24] And Fukuda Shigeyoshi, author of the visionary New Tokyo Plan of 1918, met Fritz Schumacher on a trip to Hamburg and discussed, among other topics, the rebuilding of Tokyo after the Kanto Earthquake.[25]

Although they had become more selective, Japanese planners nonetheless remained very aware of ideas from elsewhere that might be applicable to their country. The Garden City movement is one example of this. As in most other cases, only some of the design forms associated with the Garden City were applied in Japan, and the major social and economic ideas that were inherent in the British concept were lost. However, founded in 1923, the city of Denenchōfu with its unique urban form of three radials reaching out from the station cut by half-circle roads, is one example of the direct application of the Garden City concept in Japan,[26] yet it remained an exception.

The test case for the new planning law came in 1923, when the Kanto Earthquake destroyed large parts of Tokyo and Yokohama. The hopes of planners for a comprehensive reconstruction or a complete transformation of the city rapidly dissolved due to the urgent nature of the necessary rebuilding. The Beaux-Arts-trained Nakamura Junpei, for example, felt that the proposals being made were inadequate, particularly in regard to the third dimension of the city and the relation between streets and buildings. He prepared a monumental rebuilding proposal, knowing full well that his design did not stand any chance of being realized since it required preparation time and huge finances, public support and legal tools that were simply not available after the earthquake. Furthermore, the opposition of landowners to large-scale changes led to the rejection of comprehensive planning and urban design.[27]

Even less grandiose comprehensive projects prepared by major public figures did not succeed. Gotō Shinpei took up ideas expressed by Fukuda Shigeyoshi and expanded his project to areas left untouched by the earthquake. Despite his powerful position and the support of the internationally renowned former head of the New York Bureau of Municipal Research, Charles Beard, Gotō Shinpei's proposal was not accepted. Instead, land readjustment provided a tool that could be used to widen streets when needed and where possible. Of 3000 hectares designated for land readjustment, about 2000 hectares were so treated between 1923 and 1930. Land readjustment, by regrouping and redividing the land, reduced the size of the plots[28] but permitted landowners to maintain their land close to its original site. The tool allowed interventions in specific sites and concentrated on the creation of major public infrastructures without interfering with design issues, establishing land readjustment as the main tool of Japanese urban planning.

Through the 1930s, Japanese planners continued to study Western examples, especially the recently established regional studies, greenbelt planning and neighborhood design. Initially established in the period before the Second World War to ameliorate the quality of urban life, these concepts – greenbelt planning in particular – were at the time used for military purposes. Following the air defense laws of 1937 and 1941, only projects of military importance could be realized, and some imported planning ideas fell within this category.

Japan's awareness of foreign publications is evident in the acceptance and diffusion of Gottfried Feder's book *Die neue Stadt* (The New City).[29] Based on a lengthy survey of existing cities, Feder listed all the institutions necessary for a small town and created a guidebook for city planning. Based on this very technical study, he proposed urban housing for 20,000 inhabitants divided into nine autonomous units and surrounded by agricultural areas. The institutions necessary for daily life were listed in detail, ready to be used as an introduction to city building. Feder wanted this technical project to be connected with the art of city planning, as shown in the subtitle of his book, *Versuch der Begründung einer neuen Stadtplanungskunst aus der sozialen Struktur der Bevölkerung* (Essay on the Creation of a New Art of City Planning, Based on the Social Structure of its Inhabitants). However, the aesthetic part of this project and the reference to medieval forms were not appropriate to Japan.

The technical aspects of the book nevertheless captured the attention of Japanese planners. Published in January 1939, it was already on the shelves of the administrative library of the city of Tokyo by 1 June that year. It cannot be assumed that *The New City* was read and understood by all planners, but it provoked enough interest to be partially translated by the Tokyo Chamber of Industry and Commerce (Shōkōkaigisho) by March 1942. At about the same time, several Japanese planners commented on the text in a number of different articles. Itō Goro, officer at the building police section of the Metropolitan Police Board in Tokyo, mentions it in his articles on Nazi Germany.[30] And other major planners who introduced and discussed the text included Ishikawa Hideaki, who referred to it in 1943, and Nishiyama Uzō, who examined it in his study of the 'life units'.[31] *The New City* is still a major reference in the Japanese urban planning textbooks of today,[32] in contrast to Germany, where research on Feder primarily concentrates on his role as an early supporter of Hitler and his function in the Nazi party.

Whereas Feder's book became a central reference for many Japanese planners, the urban design proposals of a foreign specialist, such as the German architect Bruno Taut, found less support because they were too strongly oriented towards architectural issues.[33] Taut, who was revered in Germany as one of the founders of the Modern Movement and the author of numerous widely publicized modernist housing estates, lived in Japan from 1933 to 1936. In April 1934 he published an article in the fourth edition of the Japanese magazine *Kaizō*, in which he strongly criticized Japanese urban planning and claimed to be the only person in Japan competent in that field. Taut's strongly voiced criticism of modern Japanese urban planning was considered arrogant and provoked critical responses by Ishikawa Hideaki as well as Kaneiwa Den'ichi, a civil engineer and planner also prominent in the Communist Party. Hideaki responded to Taut's criticism by mentioning the German planner's unrealistic visions published in *Der Weg zur Alpinen Architektur*.[34] The use of Taut's expressionist drawings of the 1920s to discredit his opinion on urban planning in Japan illustrates conceptual differences between Germany and Japan. German architects in the early 1920s, a time of major unemployment, were producing architectural visions that foretold new design ideas and a new society. Such visionary proposals were less current in Japan. In his comments, Nishiyama Uzō notes that Taut's description of urban planning as a part of the architectural profession was rejected by Japanese planners who considered urban planning to be closer to engineering and industrial needs.[35]

The interpretation of the works of Feder and Taut largely depended on the analysis of a handful of planners, who commented and wrote about the Western texts and examples. Through their commentaries in planning magazines, major figures in the development of Japanese urban planning, such as Nishiyama Uzō and Ishikawa Hideaki, framed the understanding and interpretation of foreign planners and urban planning practice abroad. Japan thus deliberately chose to open itself to Western techniques and culture. Individual planners were instrumental in creating a planning system that was adapted to the country's particular conditions, and generally promoted pragmatic planning techniques that could be rapidly applied on a case-by-case basis without the need for a comprehensive long-term plan.

It is striking that the powerful individual planners of the early period, some of whom like Gotō Shinpei and Seki Hajime held important municipal positions, could not implement their ideas in a way that autocratic planners in the West were able to. Although they were politically connected, they could not realize the strong symbolic statements made by their Western counterparts. There was no political or public support for comprehensive plans, the necessary finances were unattainable, and Japan did not have a tradition of monumental planning. The Japanese planners were administrators first; they acted as mediators in the transmission of planning ideas and left it up to the larger planning community to use the tools they helped create.

PLANNING IN THE COLONIES[36]

Leading Japanese planners, deeply involved in the creation of a Japanese planning system, were thus aware of foreign planning concepts and their potentials and limits. Inside Japan, however, they were confronted with local traditions and often did not have the power to use the legal tools they created to fully implement their ideas. The situation was different in the colonies, where administrators had military power behind them. Almost simultaneously with the import of planning ideas from the West, Japan had the occasion to apply (or at least to propose) the newly obtained knowledge to its colonies and occupied territories in Asia.

Japanese colonialism differed in several ways from Western colonial practice, as documented in Gwendolyn Wright's *The Politics of Design in French Colonial Urbanism* and Paul Rabinow's *French Modern*.[37] In contrast to European governments, and especially the French who had centuries of experience with colonial practice and tried to export their culture and tradition through social technology, architecture and urban planning, Japan did not have a tradition of colonization other than that of Hokkaido (1873–83), which was primarily a settlement colony.[38] As mentioned earlier, the nation also lacked a strong history of translating political power into the built environment through urban planning, a European tradition visible in the design of many colonial cities. As a result, the question of which architectural or urban forms to use in the colonies remained open.

The Japanese colonial design is striking in the sense that – apart from a major shrine that was erected in all occupied cities as a sign of the Japanese Shinto belief – there was no particular national form that expressed the Japanese position as colonizer. While the Japanese imposed forms imported from the West, they also brought with them the tools they had recently developed, particularly land readjustment. As with the Japanese import of Western ideas in the Meiji period, when architectural types and urban design forms were rejected while planning techniques were included in emerging Japanese planning, once the colonization ended, architectural forms imposed by the Japanese colonizer were rejected while postcolonial administrations maintained some of the planning methods imposed by the Japanese.

'Authoritarian imposition' of newly developed techniques

The Japanese approach to colonization and planning in the colonies differed from place to place.[39] In the early phase of Japanese colonization, the Japanese aimed at good local administration, exporting up-to-date town planning concepts that were not even in use in the mother country. The Japanese administration considered its oldest colonies, Taiwan (1895–1945) and Korea

(1910–45), as places in which to demonstrate its achievements and its capacity as a colonial power. For many planners, the colonial experience was an important intermediary step in their careers, and the colonies allowed them to refine and test their ideas as well as prepared them for their later work on the mainland. Gotō Shinpei, for example, was head of the Taiwan Public Welfare Department from 1898 to 1906 and president of the South Manchuria Railway before he participated in the elaboration of the building and planning laws of 1919 and influenced the rebuilding after the 1923 Great Kanto Earthquake.

Numerous innovative planning concepts were created and applied first in the colonies. For example, the Provisional Taiwan Buildings Code was enacted in 1895, and the Taiwan Housing Regulation came into force in 1900 and was amended in 1912.[40] The land readjustment technique had been implemented in the colonies in the 1930s, although without the consultation or compensation of the landowners. Despite its colonial origin, Taiwan and South Korea maintained this technique after the Second World War and applied especially from the 1960s onwards since, as Natacha Aveline has shown,[41] it was the most appropriate tool to deal with population growth. The smooth integration of this planning technique differs sharply from the postcolonial rejection of architectural and urban forms.

In regard to design, the Japanese planners tried to act like the Western colonizers who had left their mark on the urban landscape of the occupied cities: the English in Hong Kong, the French from the Bay of Guanghzhou to

Figure 5. *The Government General building in Seoul, before its recent demolition (Photo by Fujimori Terunobu)*

Yunnan, and the Russians in Manchurian cities like Harbin or Dalian. Similar to the German intervention in Qingdao, the Japanese created a monumental Government General building in the axis of a large boulevard in Seoul. (Fig. 5) Erected on the former site of the main palace gates, the monument of the new government stood in front of the traditional seat of power. Its architectural form, however, was Western, and did not symbolize the Japanese colonizer. Despite its German style, the Government General building in Seoul was torn down in 1997 because it was a symbol of the Japanese occupation.[42] Thus pure technical interventions that could not be traced so easily to the occupier had a greater chance of being integrated into the respective local urban planning.

Unrealized dreams of grand-scale imposition: the Manchurian example

By 1919, the Japanese had developed a technical town-planning instrument that would determine much of the urban development in Japan, a method that left little room for comprehensive, grand-scale proposals. Individual planners nonetheless continued to be aware of ongoing discussions in Europe and America, and developed visionary projects for citywide master plans, using the colonies as a frame for projects that had no chance of realization at home. The projects were initiated after the Japanese had consolidated their planning knowledge at home and in some of the colonies, and established land readjustment as the main planning tool. The following section focuses on the colonization of Manchuria, where Japanese planners tried out their knowledge of Western-style, large-scale, long-term planning projects, and provides an account of their knowledge of Western concepts and their interpretation of the theories they borrowed.

The Japanese put a lot of energy into city planning in Manchuria. Following the example of Dairen, where the Japanese planners continued the original Russian project for a monumental city, they elaborated plans for new cities, the most famous being the design of Manchuria's capital city, Shinkyô (now Changchun), in large part constructed.[43] The urban plan featured boulevards and monumental circular spaces, including new sanitary techniques as well as telephones and electricity, all of them symbols of China's 'modernization', as intended by the Japanese.[44] (Fig. 6)

As previously mentioned, Japanese planners in the 1930s were very interested in issues of regional planning, greenbelt and neighborhood design. In 1933 came the publication of a landmark study concerning hierarchical regional planning, German geographer Walter Christaller's *Die zentralen Orte in Süddeutschland* (Christaller later became a well-known figure in Japan). In the same year, a group of Japanese architect-planners proposed a settlement pattern for villages of about 150 houses each for Manchuria. (Fig. 7) The group

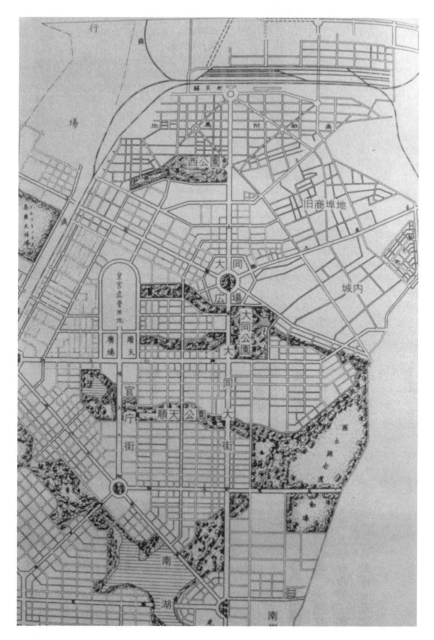

Figure 6. *Japanese plans for Shinkyô, 1937*
Source: *Manschukoku no shuto keikaku (Capital City Planning in Manchuria) (Tôkyô: Nihon keizai hyôronsha, 1991), p. 127*

included two well-known architects: Utida Yosikazu,[45] who was a professor at Tokyo University from 1921 to 1945 and its president from 1943 to 1945, and Kishida Hideto, also a teacher at Tokyo University (holding various positions between 1923 and 1955) and a major influence in the architectural field.

Their visionary plan suggested dividing the entire region in a grid, assigning fields to villages. Three of these villages were to collaborate. One of them was to become the seat of major institutions, thus establishing a hierarchy. Probably in response to the traditionally walled Chinese cities, Utida Yosikazu suggested a square city of 150 houses, each allocated a 10-hectare area outside the village to be reached by foot within 30 to 40 minutes. One of his major aims in elaborating this proposal was to show that urban planning concepts could be applied to agricultural planning. Similar topics were discussed simultaneously in Germany, where the Nazi's applied Christaller's ideas, among others, to the occupation of neighboring countries.

Throughout the 1930s, Japanese planners kept on top of Western developments in planning theory and practice. Projects for the colonies, considered by many planners a blank slate, demonstrated the Japanese knowledge and understanding of Western practice as well as the relative absence of doctrinaire convictions. The most elaborate urban proposal was that for Datong, prepared in 1939 by Utida Yosikazu, who had been invited to set up planning

Figure 7. Utida Yosikazu, regional plan for agricultural settlements in Manchuria, proposal, 1933
Source: *Uchida Yoshikazu Sensei beiju shukuga kinen sakuhinshû kankôkai, Uchida Yoshikazu Sensei sakuhinshû, Kashima kenkyûjo shuppankai, (1969), p. 166*

and building rules, and a group of young planners. One member of the group was Takayama Eika, who would later, in 1962, become the founder of Japan's first urban planning section at Tokyo University.[46] Prior to the trip he had compiled a study of housing schemes that was published in 1936 and had also been a great influence on planners in Japan.[47] On his trip to Datong, Takayama Eika is also known to have taken numerous books with him, the content of which is reflected in this study. The Datong project is thus a major example of the simultaneous import and export of planning ideas.

The proposal for Datong is remarkable in several regards. First, it is a project on a regional scale. In fact, in order to limit the growth of the city, the planners called for its connection with other existing cities, and for the creation of satellites around it. Taking ideas for the creation of new cities developed since the 1920s by planners like Paul Wolf or Raymond Unwin, which had found a large interest in Japan, the group proposed two decentralized industrial cities for 30,000 inhabitants. The first was an industrial center, the southern part being used for industry and separated by a green zone and a major roadway from the housing areas in the north. The second was a mining town, connected with the first by a major road, and organized in a half circle around the station – a feature that could be found in many of the Russian planned cities occupied by the Japanese. (Fig. 8)

Figure 8. Utida Yosikazu, a village for Japanese settlers in Manchuria, proposal, 1933
Source: Uchida Yoshikazu Sensei beiju shukuga kinen sakuhinshû kankôkai, Uchida Yoshikazu Sensei sakuhinshû, Kashima kenkyûjo shuppankai, (1969), p. 167

As to the overall city plan, which was intended for 180,000 people, the planners appear to have conceived the design as a finished one, the actual form being limited by a green area along the railway on the northern side and the river on the southern side. A green belt running through the city became the site of railways and roads, separating them from the neighborhood. This idea had already been used in the urban plan of Radburn from 1928, which is mentioned by the authors of the Datong plan. At the same time, green belts and parks were also being discussed by planners in Japan itself. Their realization, however, was more related to military concepts than to social ideas. The rivers bordering the area did not connect with the urban plan, and mainly formed the backdrop for industry and airports as well as a cemetery and a racetrack. The housing areas, consisting of regular rectangular shapes, set in the form of a half-moon, surrounded the administrative and commercial city center. A new, Beaux-Arts-style monumental area for the major administrative buildings was to be constructed adjacent to the old walled city. (Fig. 9)

The decision to maintain the existing center seems to particularly reflect the work of Sekino Musaru, the architectural historian of the Utida group, who researched old Chinese buildings. Apparently the group considered the maintenance of the old areas as a cultural mission and confronted it with the new development, reflecting the French attitude of opposing indigenous areas with urban districts realized by the colonizers. The only element in the plan that reflected the identity of the Japanese colonizer was the shrine on the northeastern side, a place of worship for Japan's native Shinto religion. While Japan has a long history of architecture, it did not seek to export its building traditions as their subdued character did not lend itself to colonial imposition in a way that monumental Western architecture did. This concentration on shrines as elements of urban representation is thus coherent with the development for the mother country, as shown by the plan for the Ise shrine.[48]

Utmost attention was given to the design of the neighborhood unit. Groups of 859 families, or about 5000 persons, were to be housed in one urban unit, corresponding to a rectangle 800 meters large and 1000 meters long that was further divided into five entities. In order not to disturb life in the neighborhood, all through traffic was banned and most units were accessible only through dead-end streets connected through greenways ending in a central park. (Fig. 10) This plan appears as a masterpiece on a par with other neighborhood plans elaborated during the period. However, a closer look at Takayama Eika's collection of housing districts shows that this was a nearly identical copy of an American Garden City neighborhood plan from Detroit in 1931. (Fig. 11) The planners of Datong made only minor adaptations to the original design, for example changing the orientation of a number of buildings, replacing apartment houses with courtyard buildings, and especially eliminating the churches, which were originally placed on the ends of the diagonal streets.[49] The Utida report insisted on the necessity of building large houses

Figure 9. Utida Yosikazu, Takayama Eika, Utida Yosifumi, and others.
The regional plan for Datong, 1938
Source: *Uchida Yoshikazu Sensei beiju shukuga kinen sakuhinshû
kankôkai, Uchida Yoshikazu Sensei sakuhinshû, Kashima kenkyûjo
shuppankai, (1969), p. 168*

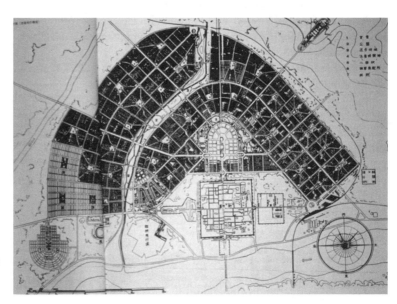

Figure 10. *Utida
Yosikazu,
Takayama Eika,
Utida Yosifumi,
a.o., The urban
plan for Datong,
1938*
Source: *Uchida
Yoshikazu Sensei
beiju shukuga
kinen sakuhinshû
kankôkai, Uchida
Yoshikazu Sensei
sakuhinshû,
Kashima kenkyûjo
shuppankai,
(1969), pp. 170–1*

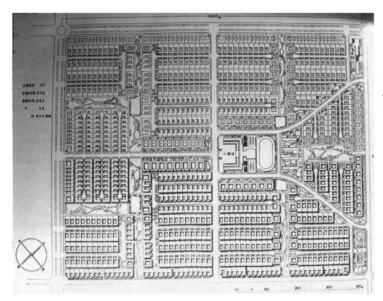

Figure 11. *Utida Yosikazu, Takayama Eika, Utida Yosifumi, a.o., The neighborhood unit proposed for Datong, 1938 Source: Uchida Yoshikazu Sensei beiju shukuga kinen sakuhinshû kankôkai, Uchida Yoshikazu Sensei sakuhinshû, Kashima kenkyûjo shuppankai, (1969), p. 172*

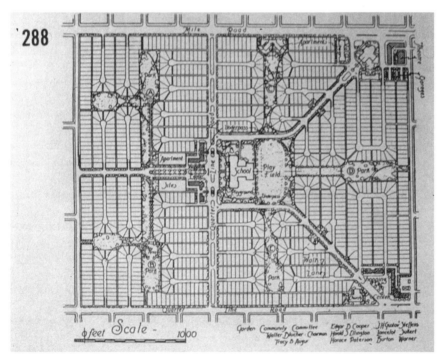

Figure 12. *Garden city neighborhood in Detroit, 1931*
Source: Takayama, Eika, Gaikoku ni okeru jūtaku shikichi: wari ruireishū (Dôjunkai, 1936)

for Japanese immigrants, referring to the housing policy of Western countries in their colonies. In regard to the housing design itself, the planners referred to the typical Chinese courtyard buildings of this area as the most appropriate for the climate. (Fig. 12)

The Datong project is an exercise in applying Western ideas, and includes elements from earlier projects by Utida Yosikazu, such as his plans for a garden city or the regional settlement plan. It is, however, important as a visionary Japanese-designed conception that reflects the understanding and the status of imported planning ideas from Europe and the US in Japan. Of particular importance to urban planning in Japan was Takayama Eika's financial concept that accompanied the project. Takayama was convinced that there should not be private profits from land amelioration and he therefore tried to fight speculation. His financial plan suggested a three-stage development, enabling the financing of the development of the outside areas through the sale of land in the inner part of the city.

Planners who returned to Japan from the colonies brought with them new ideas based on their experiences. Nevertheless, in many cases it took decades until the innovations that had been incorporated within the planning laws of the colonies found their way into the planning laws and strategies of Japan. The attitude towards urban design displayed by the planners in Datong is very similar to projects prepared by architects in the early rebuilding period after the Second World War, and indeed the war destruction in Japan seemed to offer a field of experimentation, just as Japanese colonialism had. However, the desire for rapid reconstruction and the constraints of land ownership, planning and building laws promoted a reconstruction based on pragmatic land readjustment plans instead of large-scale visions, the Hiroshima competition offering perhaps the best example of a rare realization.

Although attempts at planning on the scale of the Datong project exist for the reconstruction of Tokyo after the Second World War, only a few elements of these were realized. Ishikawa Hideaki, who had been influential in planning Shanghai, authored a large-scale reconstruction plan for Tokyo and inspired several competitions for major urban areas as well as for central campuses in Tokyo. Among the participants in these competitions were numerous planners who had been active in the colonies. Takayama Eika worked with such a group to develop a reconstruction plan for a larger area around the campus of Tokyo University in 1946. The resulting proposal reflected major developments in the West. In fact, buildings by Le Corbusier were used as sources for prominent constructions in this plan. Another example inspired by the architectural forms of Le Corbusier was the proposal for the Shinjuku area in Tokyo, prepared by Utida Yosifumi, the son of Utida Yosikazu and another prominent member of the Datong planning group. None of these plans were implemented, even though most of them concentrated on the capital, the heart of political and economic representation.

In the colonies and during the early reconstruction period, Japanese planners practiced a role as architect-planner more typical in a Western setting.
Their attempt to impose comprehensive plans and integrate three-dimensional
architectural design and two-dimensional urban layout failed in the reconstruction period, just as Gotō Shinpei had been unable to realize projects on
the scope of his colonial plans on his return to mainland Japan. The particularities of urban Japan did not allow for large-scale comprehensive urban
implementations,[50] strong planning interventions and the integration of the
fields of architecture and planning – confirming trends that were established
since the Meiji period.

CONCLUSION: IDEOLOGY IN PLANNING IMPORT AND EXPORT

Japanese urban planning developed over a period of time when the country
was undertaking rapid modernization and Westernization. Never colonized,
Japan did not experience an imposition of planning concepts. Instead,
Japanese leaders carefully selected models, importing and adapting them, and
innovating on the basis of these. Interventions by foreigners, such as Waters
or Böckmann and Ende, appear as model case studies that were tried out once
and quickly abandoned if they did not work. This direct foreign influence was
mostly a dead-end street, as there was no urban tradition of architectural and
urban integration and no place in politics for planning professionals to impose
comprehensive design ideas on the cities.

Modern Japanese planning developed as a field for specialists inside the
central administration, and has focused on tools and projects rather than on
large-scale plans, urban design or an integration of urban and architectural
design. These experts were interested in planning techniques and eagerly
took up ideas presented by technocrats such as Hoehn or Feder. Japanese
planners had an organizational rather than a political role, developing
planning techniques rather than creating urban monuments as political mani-
festoes as did many of their Western counterparts. As we have seen, powerful
individuals influenced the emerging modern Japanese planning discipline, but
they were more influential in the creation of planning tools than the application of plans. Neither the planner-politician nor the planner-architect could
counter the planner-technocrats in central government. Even administrators
like Gotō Shinpei or Seki Hajime, who obtained political roles, could not
impose their ideas on comprehensive planning. It was not so much citizen
opposition that caused them to fail – Japan's centralized system did not have
any citizen participation or even a strong civil society, as André Sorensen
has argued.[51] But neither was there widespread public support for the
proposed beautification; had there been any, this may have helped to overcome the resistance from landowners.

The situation was similar for administrators who ventured into the field of urban and architectural design, or architect-planners who were invited to plan in the colonies or called upon in the early reconstruction period. Their ideas remained mostly on paper, such as the colonial projects by Takayama Eika or the reconstruction competitions and projects conceived by Ishikawa Hideaki for Tokyo. After the Second World War, many of the authors of these plans went into education (for example Takayama Eika), or returned to architectural practice – most famously Tange Kenzō, whose Hiroshima Peace Center remains a unique case in postwar reconstruction after 1945.[52] The postwar influence of other planners and the continuity in their work needs further research. Hideshima Kan (1917–73), for example, is very interesting in this regard. Hideshima was one of the planners of Shinkyō and participated in the 1942 revision of the Manchurian Town and Country Planning Act (Manshū koku toyū keikaku hō). A visionary planner of the colonial era, he was also active as a planning consultant after the Second World War, and became one of the major visionaries of postwar Japanese planning.[53]

Bureaucrats were most instrumental in shaping urban form, as they selected knowledge in the West and therewith shaped urban planning. The structure of Japanese planning vested individual planners inside the ministries with great powers.[54] Their influence was mediated as they confronted each other; their names are less known and their work remains less studied. The impact of selected individuals in the import of planning tools and the creation of a Japanese planning system has been discussed in the present text.[55] Planning thus developed as a field of bureaucrat experts using a tool to shape the city. The continuity of urban planning in Japan lies in the continuity of this instrument, and is not limited to the presence of selected individuals.[56]

Japanese urban planning techniques, which have evolved through integrating, transforming and adopting Western ideas, are very attractive for other Asian countries. As we have seen, planning techniques, when they relate to local practice or needs, are more easily integrated than visible symbols of a specific culture into a different national context. This finding seems to support Takayama Eika's explanation of the failure of visionary projects in the colonies and in post-Second World War Japan. Takayama argued that export is only a problem if it is connected to ideology and the transmission of culture, for example, as he points out, in the case of the Algiers project from Le Corbusier.[57] Instead he sees the export of planning techniques simply as the work of merchants without ideological background. Pragmatic planning in contrast to urban design hence becomes a technical means to be exported without hesitation. Japan can therefore be seen as a transformer of Western planning ideas, importing and transforming techniques and concepts and adapting them for use in Japan and elsewhere in Asia.

NOTES

1. On the impact of the American occupation on Japanese urban reconstruction, see Carola Hein, Jeffry M. Diefendorf and Ishida Yorifusa (eds) (2003) *Rebuilding Urban Japan After 1945*, London: Palgrave/Macmillan. On the American attempts to implant their convictions in the political, economic and social fields, see also Olivier Zunz (1998) *Why the American Century?*, Chicago, London: University of Chicago Press. Beyond attempts at land reform and industrial restructuring, issues of city planning are not discussed in the latter.

2. The author plans to research further the theme of the Japanese position in the international exchange of planning ideas. A recent study by Nishiyama Yasuo on the particularities of Japanese urban planning discusses selected issues in this context. See Nishiyama Yasuo (2002) *Nihon gata toshi keikaku to ha nanika?*, Kyoto: Gakugei Shuppan.

3. See also André Sorensen's argument that the post-Second World War reconstruction is the best application of the 1919 Town Planning Act, which focused on the creation of streets and parks; André Sorensen (2002) *The Making of Urban Japan: Cities and Planning from Edo to the Twenty-First Century*, London: Routledge, p. 159.

4. Stephen Ward (2000) 'Re-examining the international diffusion of planning', in Robert Freestone (ed.) *Urban Planning in a Changing World, The Twentieth Century Experience*, London: Spon, pp. 40–60.

5. David Stewart, Dallas Finn and Jeffrey Cody discuss various aspects of the impact of foreigners and their works on Japan. Jeffrey W. Cody (1996) 'Erecting monuments to the God of business and trade: The Fuller construction company of the Orient, 1919–1926', *Construction History*, Vol. 12; Dallas Finn (1995) *Meiji Revisited: The Sites of Victorian Japan*, New York, Tokyo: Weatherhill; David Stewart (1989) *The Making of A Modern Japanese Architecture*, New York: Kodansha International.

6. This process of adoption and reflection is discussed in regard to German planning ideas in Carola Hein and Ishida Yorifusa (1998) 'Japanische Stadtplanung und ihre deutschen Wurzeln', *Die alte Stadt*, March.

7. Ward, op. cit.

8. See also David Tucker (2003) 'Learning from Dairen, learning from Shinkyô: Japanese colonial city planning and postwar reconstruction', in Hein, Diefendorf and Ishida, op. cit.

9. Torsten Warner (1998) 'Der Aufbau der Kolonialstadt Tsingtau: Landordnung, Stadtplanung und Entwicklung', in Hans-Martin Hinz and Christoph Lind (eds) *Tsingtau. Ein Kapitel deutscher Kolonialgeschichte in China 1897–1914*, Berlin: Deutsches Historisches Museum.

10. Carola Hein (2000) 'Land development for the modern metropolis'. Paper given at a symposium on Architecture and Modern Japan, Columbia University.

11. See also Ishizuka Hiromichi and Ishida Yorifusa (eds) (1988) *Tokyo: Urban Growth and Planning 1868–1988*, Tokyo: Center for Urban Studies, Tokyo Metropolitan University.

12. See also Okamoto Satoshi (2000) 'Destruction and reconstruction of Ginza town', in Fukui Norihiko and Jinnai Hidenobu (eds) *Destruction and Rebirth of Urban Environment*, Tokyo: Sagami Shobo, pp. 51–84.

13. See also Fujimori Terunobu (1982) *Meiji no Tôkyô keikaku*, Tokyo: Iwanami Shoten; and Ishida Yorifusa (ed.) (1992) *Mikan no Tôkyô keikaku*, Tokyo: Chikumashobō.

14. Ishizuka and Ishida, op. cit., p. 12.

15. See also Ian Nish (ed.) (1998) *The Iwakura Mission in America and Europe: A New Assessment,* Richmond: Curzon, The Japan Library.

16. Ishida Yorifusa (1988) 'Mori Ogai no "okusei shingi" to Tôkyô shi kenchiku jôrei' [Mori Ougai's 'New Discussions on Building Law' and the Tokyo Building Law], in Ishizuka Hiromichi and Ishida Yorifusa (eds) *Tôkyô: seichô to keikaku 1868–1988.* Tokyo: Tôkyô toritsu daigaku toshikenkyū sentaa.

17. Jeffrey E. Hanes (2002) *The City as Subject: Seki Hajime and the Reinvention of Modern Osaka,* Berkeley, CA and London: University of California Press.

18. Used particularly in France, this technique was also part of German planning praxis and was mentioned in an early draft of the Adickes Law of 1893 (see note 21).

19. Hein and Ishida, op. cit.

20. Tatsuno Kingo was a student of Josiah Conder who taught at Tokyo University from 1877 to 1888. Tatsuno graduated in 1879. Kataoka, a disciple of Tatsuno, graduated from Tokyo University in 1897.

21. Hein and Ishida, op. cit.

22. Named after Franz Adickes, mayor of the city of Frankfurt, the law was used for a planned extension of the city and included techniques for redistribution and expropriation of the concerned land.

23. Ishida Yorifusa *et al.* (1987) 'Nihon ni okeru tochi kukaku seiri seido no seiritsu to Adikesu hō' [Influences of Lex Adickes upon legislation of Japanese land readjustment system], Papers of the annual conference of the City Planning Institute of Japan, no.22, pp.121–26; Ishida Yorifusa (1986) 'Nihon ni okeru tochi kukaku-seiri seido shi gaisetu, 1870–1980' [Short history of Japanese land readjustment 1870–1980], *Comprehensive Urban Studies,* 28, pp. 45–87.

24. Shoji Sumie (1993) 'The life of Hideaki Ishikawa', in *City Planning Review,* 182, pp. 25–30.

25. Carola Hein (2002) 'Visionary plans and planners', in Nicolas Fièvé and Paul Waley (eds) *Japanese Capitals in Historical Perspective: Place, Power and Memory in Kyoto, Edo and Tokyo,* Richmond: Curzon.

26. Watanabe Shun'ichi (1980) 'Garden city Japanese style: the case of Den-en Toshi Company Ltd, 1918–1928', in Gordon E. Cherry (ed.) *Shaping an Urban World,* London: Mansell.

27. Watanabe Shun'ichi (1988) 'Japanese vs Western urban images: Western influences on the Japanese architectural profession, 1910s-1920s', in *The History of International Exchange of Planning Ideas.* Tokyo: The Third International Planning History Conference [IPHS], pp. 568–99.

28. Plot reduction is done to create new public space for streets and green spaces and land reserved for sale to cover some costs of the redevelopment.

29. Gottfried Feder (1939) *Die neue Stadt: Versuch der Begründung einer neuen Stadtplanungskunst aus der sozialen Struktur der Bevölkerung,* Berlin: Verlag von Julius Springer.

30. Itō Goro (1942/43) 'Nachisu doitsu no toshi keikaku' [City planning in Nazi Germany], *Shinkenchiku,* Part 1: 11/1942, pp. 835–41, and Part 2: 1/1943, pp. 25–35.

31. Ishikawa Hideaki (1943) '100 nengo no toshi' [The city in 100 years], in *Toshi no Seitai,* Shunjūsha. Nishiyama Uzō (1942) Seikatsu no kōzō to seikatsu kichi, *Kenchikugaku kenkyū,* 110 and 111, later included in his 1968 book *Chiiki kūkan ron* [The structure of life units and the base of life], Tokyo, Keisō Shobo.

32. See for example Akiyama Masayuki (1980, 1985, 1993) *Toshi keikaku* [Urban Planning], Tokyo: Rikō Tosho; Higasa Tadashi (1977, 1985, 1986, 1992, 1993, 1996) *Toshi keikaku* [Urban Planning], 3rd vol., Tokyo: Kyôritsu Shuppan;

Katsura Hisai, Adachi Kazuo and Zaino Hiroshi and Takei Kōshirō (1975) *Toshi keikaku* [Urban Planning], Tokyo: Morikita Shuppan, reprint 1988; Takei Kōshirō (1958/60) *Toshi keikaku* [Urban Planning], Tokyo: Kyōritsu Shuppan; Toshikeikaku kyōiku kenkyū kai (1987, 1995, 1996) *Toshi keikaku kyōkasho* [Urban Planning Textbook], tome 2, Tokyo: Shōkoku Sha.

33. Carola Hein (2000) 'Nishiyama Uzô and the spread of Western concepts in Japan', in *10+1* (Ten Plus One), 20 (in Japanese), pp. 143–48.

34. Bruno Taut (1920) *Die Auflösung der Städte or Die Erde eine gute Wohnung or Der Weg zur Alpinen Architektur,* Essen: Folkwang Verlag. Taut's text was criticized by Ishikawa in the above mentioned '100 nengo no toshi'.

35. Closer to the Japanese understanding was the research of Martin Wagner, the director of city planning in Berlin (1926–33). His research, which focused particularly on economic issues, was translated into Japanese by 1935.

36. An earlier version of portions of the following part was included in conference proceedings as Carola Hein (1998) 'Japan and the transformation of planning ideas – some examples of colonial plans', in Freestone, op. cit., pp. 352–57.

37. Gwendolyn Wright (1991) *The Politics of Design in French Colonial Urbanism,* Chicago and London: The University of Chicago Press; Paul Rabinow (1989) *French Modern: Norms and Forms of the Social Environment,* Chicago and London: University of Chicago Press.

38. Mark Peattie points this out in his chapter on Japanese attitudes towards colonialism; Ramon H. Myers and Mark R. Peattie (1984) *The Japanese Colonial Empire 1895–1945,* Princeton, NJ: Princeton University Press, pp. 80–127.

39. Ishida Yorifusa (1998) 'War, military affairs and urban planning', in Freestone, op. cit., pp. 393–98.

40. Fujimori Terunobu and Wan Tan (eds) (1996) *Zenchōsa higashi Asia kindai no toshi to kenchiku, A Comprehensive Study of East Asian Architecture and Urban Planning: 1840–1945,* Tokyo: Chikuma Shobō.

41. Natacha Aveline (1994) 'The Japanese land readjustment system: a model for Asian countries? The cases of Seoul and Taipei', Paper given at the EAJS conference in Copenhagen.

42. The Government-General building in Taiwan is still preserved.

43. See Koshizawa Akira (1991) *Manshū koku no shuto keikaku,* Nihon Keizai Hyōron Sha; and Tucker, op. cit.

44. Fujimori and Wan Tan, op. cit.

45. At the request of his family, I am using here the transcription of the name as used by Uchida himself in the 1920s. The romanized spelling of the name would be Uchida Yoshikazu. The most complete collection of works by Uchida is: Uchida Yoshikazu Sensei biju shukaka kinen sakuhin shū kankōkai (1969) *Uchida Yoshikazu Sensei sakuhinshū* [Collection of the Works of Professior Uchida Yoshikazu], Tokyo: Kajima Kenkyūjo huppankai.

46. In 1934, in his diploma thesis, Takayama designed a fishing village that stretched along the Japanese coast. In this project, he covered planning topics as much as architectural ones, and his work reflected that of major French planners like Tony Garnier, whom he admired. Takayama also showed a desire for comprehensive planning, which was rare in Japan. See Ishida Yorifusa (2000) 'Eika Takayama, the Greatest Figure in Japanese Urban and Regional Planning in the 20th Century', Paper given at the IPHS conference in Helsinki.

47. Takayama Eika (1936) *Gaikoku ni okeru jūtaku shikiji wari ruireishō* (Dōjunkai)

48. Koshizawa Akira (1997) *Shinto keikaku: Jingū kankei shisetsu seibi jigyō no tokushoku to igi* [Planning of the Shrine City in Ise: Its Characteristics and Significance], Papers on City Planning, City Planning Special Review Issue.

49. Takayama, op. cit., p. 188.
50. This topic and the later careers of planners who had held important positions in the colonies need further analysis. Norioki Ishimaru started to address this topic in his paper at the European Association of Japan Studies conference in Lahti, Finland, in 2000: Ishimaru Norioki, 'On the Actual Conditions of Employment and Transference of City Planners in Japanese Local Government'.
51. Sorensen and Watanabe both argue that there is no tradition of civic society, of decentralized planning and citizen participation; Sorensen, op. cit.; and Watanabe Shun'ichi in Freestone, op. cit., pp. 947–52.
52. Architect such as Kishida Hideto regretted the lack of architectural interest and three-dimensional development in reconstruction planning, as Tucker points out (Tucker, op. cit.), but despite their colonial projects they were not really leaders in postwar urban planning.
53. Kimura Saburō(1988) 'Toshikeikaku who was who (8): Hideshima Kan', *Toshikeikaku* [City Planning Review], no.155, p. 69. Hideshima designed the Waseda Bunkyō-chiku Plan in 1946, which later became the basic concept of the present campus of the Faculty of Engineering, Waseda University. In 1955 he designed the Tokiwadaira housing estate in Matsudo city, Chiba prefecture, and was awarded the planning prize of the City Planning Institute of Japan in 1962. He later participated in many major development projects, including Kobe's Port Island.
54. This assessment seems to be confirmed by Watanabe Shun'ichi, who states: 'In terms of the decision-making process, many orders and circulars issued by the ministry regulate in detail who can authorize and implement which matters and how. Such rules are prescribed in terms of detailed technical standards. Thus, these rules ostensibly regulate so as room for policies and political decisions would be extremely small; in contrast, technical bureaucrats virtually have large authority to make decisions'. Watanabe Shun'ichi (1998) 'Changing paradigm of the Japanese urban planning system', in Freestone, op. cit., p. 950.
55. Whereas research exists for the early period, it is much more difficult to assess later years, due to the Japanese practice of shifting individuals from one position to another. See: Ishimaru, op. cit.
56. Carola Hein (2003) 'Change and continuity in postwar urban Japan', ch. 11 in Hein, Diefendorf and Ishida, op. cit.
57. In an interview with Izosaki Arata, in Tokushū kindai Nihon toshi keikaku shi, hito to shisō, jōkyō, *Toshi Jūtaku* 7604 (4/1976).

CHAPTER 4

LEARNING FROM THE US: THE AMERICANISATION OF WESTERN URBAN PLANNING

Stephen V. Ward

Oxford Brookes University

> Having saved the world, it would not thereafter be easy to imagine that there was still much to learn from it.[1]

With this telling observation on the dominant tone of American political thought in 1945, the historian Daniel Rodgers ends *Atlantic Crossings,* his justifiably acclaimed account of European influences on the social politics of the US. In his view, the era of deference to European ideas on social reform closed with the Second World War. Amongst much else, this former openness to Europe had allowed the entry of much of the thinking that underpinned the formation of an American city planning movement. Ending his book at this point, Rodgers knows, perhaps, that he can safely leave his readers to infer what followed – an insular and self-regarding America, mistrustful of foreign thinking and exuberantly confident in the superiority of its own way of life. It is an image that matches the familiar postwar story of the US.

Yet there is another side to the story, probably familiar to relatively few of Rodgers' readers – the impact of these important changes outside the US. So how far did the self-absorbed Western superpower of the postwar years (consciously or unconsciously) shape the thought and practice of the world around it? In the words used to frame this whole collection, how far did the balance of trade in ideas shift so that pre-1945 imports were replaced by post-1945 exports?

This is a large and complicated question, worthy itself of a book at least on the scale of *Atlantic Crossings.* However, within the rather modest confines of this chapter, it is possible to sketch only a few aspects of the story. Rather than the broader front of progressive thought that Rodgers took as his subject, we concentrate here specifically on urban planning. The geographical emphasis is also limited, to the Western, advanced capitalist states, the countries that have most closely matched American prosperity and strategic alignment. The story of American influence on the developing postcolonial world or the more ideologically filtered American influence on the communist world form other and, in many ways, quite different stories.

TYPOLOGY OF DIFFUSION

This concentration on relatively affluent countries is important for several reasons, not least because of the nature of the national contexts into which American ideas were received. Elsewhere I have proposed a simple, somewhat idealised typology of the international diffusion of planning ideas, which asserts the primacy of the 'power relationship' between the importing and exporting countries.[2] The term 'power relationship' is, in this context, a very shorthand term for the economic, geopolitical, cultural and technical balance between the national parties to the international flow of ideas. At one extreme, the model asserts that a country that is economically and geopolitically dependent on another is also very likely to be dependent on it for planning ideas and practices. Moreover, these obligatory imports are likely to be imposed with very little expectation of critical evaluation or adaptation in the receiving country. Classically this situation is found only in the immediate aftermath of military conquest or colonial appropriation of the territory into which the exotic ideas are being received. In other words, the process is conceived as being entirely under the control of the exporter, which effectively imposes its will on the other party.

At the other extreme are highly developed countries, where the power relationship between them is more equal. Here, ideas and practices are likely to be imported in an altogether more promiscuous fashion. In turn, the imports themselves are likely to be critically evaluated, deconstructed and substantially adapted in their application in the receiving country. The essential control of the process therefore lies in the importing country. It is analogous to a process of borrowing, whereby the borrower can decide how much to borrow and from whom.

In practice, of course, most transactions in this international trade in planning ideas and practices, whether acts of borrowing or imposition, lie somewhere between these two extremes. Even in the most authoritarian of contexts, external control is rarely total, and some form of local resistance or negotiation, if not of the planning proposals then of the implemented outcomes, is common. There are also many examples of countries that, because they are small or have historic or cultural ties to larger or more powerful countries, tend to follow predictable and recurrent patterns in their borrowing. If they have planning movements that are undeveloped in their reformist and professional capacity, then the borrowing may well be rather uncritical, leading to a cloning of planned intentions in the emulated country. (Outcomes will, of course, always be more subject to forces that are indigenous to the receiving countries.)

Moreover, we should note that even amongst adaptive, synthetic borrowers with highly developed planning traditions, the reductive fit with the 'power relationship' is rarely, if ever, perfect. Finally, the 'power relationship' is itself something that may undergo dramatic change. These general observations are of great importance in considering the changing role of American influence on the course of planning history in the wider West.

BEFORE 1945: A RISE IN INTEREST

Despite Rodgers' interest in the processes by which ideas crossed the Atlantic from East to West, even before the Second World War, there had in fact also been a growing movement in the opposite direction. Since the late nineteenth century, Europeans had become increasingly fascinated by the apparently unconstrained dynamism of American cities. Cohen, for example, documented a growing continental European fascination with the American city between the two world wars.[3]

Of most obvious interest were the gigantic skyscraper buildings, which by the early twentieth century were sprouting in growing numbers, especially in New York and Chicago. The great structures of American industry, particularly the huge grain silos, were beginning to inspire the first generation of European modernists with their unadorned functional design. There was also a continuing wonderment at the extraordinary range of technological innovations Americans applied to their cities and urban buildings, most apparent in all aspects of urban transportation, along with building design and construction. All of this was complemented by a somewhat condescending interest in the way Americans seemed to be civilizing their workaday cities by emulating the traditions of European urbanism on a grand scale. Great avenues and major public and cultural buildings were being built to house collections of largely European art donated by growing numbers of American multimillionaires. And Europeans envied the way that wealth was allowing a widening section of American society to live in generously proportioned residential suburbs.

Europeans were learning about all these things via various means. European architects, planners and others working in or visiting the US came back with reports of the American way of doing things, and the Great Columbian Exposition held in Chicago in 1893 gave many Europeans their first sense of the potential of the US to be a major influence on the cities of the world.[4] In the new century, the numbers of European visitors interested in American city planning increased.[5] For example, the French Garden City reformer Georges Benoît-Levy visited the US in 1904, publishing his results in a book the following year. The German architect Werner Hegemann was another early visitor,[6] and from 1909 he became an active participant in the development of the American city planning movement. However, the immediate impact of this experience within the rather authoritarian atmosphere of the Kaiser's Germany was rather limited, and Hegemann did not return to Europe until after the First World War.

This conflict had significant effects on the opening of Europe to American influences, particularly so in France where, even before the US became a combatant nation, the American Red Cross sponsored the involvement of a group of American architects in their reconstruction efforts. Most important amongst this group was George B. Ford who in 1920 produced the plan to rebuild Reims, the largest French city to suffer extensive destruction.[7] Ford's influential plan, the first to be approved under the new planning law of 1919, introduced to France many of the principles and techniques of American city planning. However, though this was significant, encounters such as this were still relatively rare. Closer to a more typical perspective was that of the French urbaniste Jacques Gréber, who in 1917 produced the implemented design for the Fairmount Parkway in Philadelphia.[8] In 1920 Gréber gave his own account for French readers of American architecture and city planning;[9] the thinking that underpinned was apparent in the title, which can be translated as 'The architecture of the United States: evidence for the dynamic expansion of the French genius'.[10] Like many European visitors, Gréber was most impressed by those features of the American scene that seemed to reproduce or confirm what was familiar to him.

Though British visitors were by no means immune to such viewpoints, the impact of the US on the Anglophone world was somewhat different from that of the other European countries due to the sharing of a common language. This allowed early American planning efforts, especially Daniel Burnham and Edward Bennett's great 1909 plan for Chicago (itself very strongly influenced by European, especially French, urbanity), to become well known in Britain earlier than was possible in continental Europe. But there were more active agents in the spreading of lessons. The British planner Thomas Adams, for example, moved to Canada in 1914 and was a regular visitor to the US before taking charge in 1923 of the otherwise American team that prepared the New York Regional Plan.[11] Although his appointment was indicative of the extent of continuing American deference to European planning, it also exposed Adams (and through him other parts of the British world) to emergent American thinking.

During the 1920s, the trend towards an Americanisation of planning started to become noticeable in countries such as Canada and Australia. Here, the quite limited local reformist and technical capacity in these matters led to a more ready uptake of external ideas. The imperial power had initially provided this, but increasingly the US seemed to offer a model of what a 'new world' settler nation could become. Not surprisingly, this process was more complete in Canada, where American 'city efficient' ideas became the dominant strand of planning thought and action in the 1920s.[12] Though for the time being this trend remained more muted in Australia, as early as 1912–13, the new Australian federal capital, Canberra, had in fact been planned by an American, Walter Burley Griffin, in the city beautiful idiom.[13] And American-style city planning commissions also appeared in Melbourne (1922) and Perth (1928).[14]

In Europe, the much more highly developed national traditions of urban planning meant American ideas and influences, especially those that were distinctively different from their own national approaches, were sifted more critically. Despite this, however, British interest in American planning had increased substantially by the end of the 1930s. Thus the official Barlow Report of 1940, which presented the results of an extremely important Royal Commission on planning, actually gave more attention to American examples than to those of any other foreign country.[15] The New York Regional Plan, by now widely known throughout the world, remained a major source of interest. Alongside this, there were also large numbers of impressive plans prepared for other big American cities, and many of these outshone British or other European examples in their technique and presentation. There was also an emerging theoretical dimension within the burgeoning American literature on planning and the city. In particular, the eloquent writings of Lewis Mumford were beginning to be read by British urban reformers and planners.[16] In part this reflected his links with earlier British theorists such as Ebenezer Howard and Patrick Geddes, but he was now updating their message for bigger and more technologically advanced cities.[17]

In many ways, though, it was the bold practical achievements of American planning that excited the greatest British interest during these years. This was a time when the totalitarian states of Europe seemed to many to be setting the pace for decisive public action. In this context, as Europe was drifting towards conflict, the planning efforts associated with President Roosevelt's New Deal, intended to lift the US economy out of depression, became a symbol of hope to progressive opinion in Britain. Here, it seemed, was the middle way between totalitarian planning and democratic 'muddling through' that seemed so elusive in the major countries of Europe during the 1930s.

The (initially) comprehensive approach to regional development planning practised by the Tennessee Valley Authority (TVA) was studied most closely (even though some of its most ambitious planning aspirations were quickly diluted). So too were the Garden City-inspired greenbelt towns and various other exercises in resettlement. The first peacetime American forays into public housing provision were also of interest. Yet the appeal was certainly not confined to the progressive social agenda. The massive public works programme initiated by Robert Moses in New York was another counterblast to the achievements of Hitler, Stalin or Mussolini. Extensive parks and recreational facilities were developed close to the city, along with new networks of limited access high-speed urban roads, huge futuristic intersections and vast bridges. Here, in the world's biggest city, was proof that a democratic society could implement projects at least as impressive as Hitler's *Reichautobahnen* or Mussolini's *autostrade*.

Although British planners showed much the fullest understanding of recent American planning innovations during the 1930s, these certainly did not go unnoticed elsewhere in Europe. But the perspectives from which these were viewed were markedly different than in Britain. For example, it was extremely awkward for planners in totalitarian states to be too open in their admiration, and American influences therefore had to be ideologically filtered or disguised. This was especially so in Nazi Germany, where anti-Jewish sentiments also made it very difficult to openly discuss the work of several leading American figures, except in scathing tones. However, various prominent planners in Nazi Germany, such as Konstanty Gutschow of Hamburg, certainly visited New York and studied aspects of its planning.[18] And there was also German interest in the traffic-segregated residential layouts developed at Radburn in New Jersey from 1928 to 1931 by Henry Wright and Clarence Stein.[19]

In France, the planning of highways in Gréber's 1933 proposal for Marseilles or Henri Prost's 1934 proposal for Paris clearly demonstrates an American influence.[20] Even more obvious was Môrice Leroux's contemporary emulation of the stepped-back high-rise architecture produced by New York's zoning ordinance at Les Gratte-Ciel (literally, the skyscrapers) in Villeurbanne, adjoining Lyons.[21] Although the political climate in France was quite different from that in Germany, there were some common features. American influence was received more as a series of rather decontextualised urbanistic images, with less of the underpinning of political sympathy that was evident in Britain. Quite apart from the linguistic barriers that naturally delayed deeper understandings, the dominance of the Left in 1930s France was important. The generally more polarised state of French political opinion at the time, with the Left being countered by a strongly nationalistic Right, also meant that progressive middle opinion was much weaker compared to that in Britain. The preference was for bolder and more socialistic models than the temporary expedients of Roosevelt's America could ever provide. For example, aspects of this can be detected in Le Corbusier's 1930s writings in French about the US.[22] Although he saw much to admire, Le Corbusier also found a timid American city planning movement that was, in his view, unwilling to tackle or refine the crude dynamics of capitalist urban change. The Right, meanwhile, was less interested in and much less impressed by American examples.

THE SECOND WORLD WAR AS PIVOT: MARSHALL AID AND THE REBUILDING OF EUROPE

The Second World War dramatically changed the international engagement with all things American. If most Western countries before 1939 had viewed the US with varying measures of regard and scepticism, the relationship six years later was much closer to an uncritical dependence. This situation came about because the fighting, and especially the productive, capacity of the US quickly gave it the dominant role in the successful prosecution of the war. Nor was it just American food, tanks, aircraft, trucks and ships that crossed the Atlantic. So too did many other aspects of American culture and know-how. By varying means, Europeans found themselves beguiled by the American way of life, including, to some extent, the American way of building and living in cities. However, the way this took place was not as straight-forward as might at first sight seem.

By 1945, the US was the supreme military power in the Atlantic and Pacific regions. Its former, or would-be, rivals as the main Western power were either defeated or so impoverished by war as to pose no further challenge. The global hegemony of the US was challenged only by the Soviet Union, which, apart from its own vast and enlarged territory, was or soon would be dominant in Eastern Europe and over large parts of the Asian continent. Within the US there was, understandably, a growing sense in 1945 that the country had more than done its duty for the wider world. Yet it soon became clear that with-drawal into a more insular stance carried serious risks. The speed of the postwar communist advance in Eastern Europe and China showed the fragility of capitalism and parliamentary democracy, a reminder to the US that it needed to continue to intervene decisively in world affairs if it was to main-tain its influence in Europe. (In the slightly longer term, it also underlined a need to find ways of countering communist influence in those territories from which European colonisers were now beginning to withdraw.)

Therein lay many of the motivations for the more active role assumed by the American government from 1946 in aiding the economic and political recovery of Western Europe and later the wider world. (Another was the desire to appropriate European, especially German, industrial and military technology and know-how, however this does not seem to have been a factor in relation to urban planning.) By 1948, what had originated as an incre-mental series of American loans had become the European Economic Recovery Program, known commonly as the Marshall Plan.[23] For their part, the devastated and near-bankrupt countries of Western Europe were pathet-ically eager to receive whatever material and other aid the US cared to give them. The image of half a continent seduced by candy bars and nylon stock-ings is a caricature but is certainly symbolic of a larger truth.

The US was thus extremely well placed to impose its own solutions. This was especially the case in Germany, but also substantially so in other parts of Western Europe. Even Britain and France, the other Western occupation powers in Germany, were far from being equal partners; both had been obliged to seek massive American loans, making them very dependent on the US. Yet the US used this dominance principally to shape the larger para-meters of the postwar Western European economy and governance. The essential concern was with establishing the preconditions for capitalism to flourish and democratic government to prevail. In other words, it wished to create a Western Europe that was likely to be broadly sympathetic to the United States. In some countries (for example Italy), the propaganda that surrounded the Marshall Plan quite explicitly promoted the message that 'you too can be like us'.[24] Beyond this, however, there was relatively little interest in specifying the finer grain of public policy, such as city planning. So far as physical reconstruction (other than industrial plants) was concerned, the main focus was on major infrastructure projects.

The closest the Americans came to making a real exception to this general practice was in Germany, which we will examine in further detail. Even here, though, it acted with reluctance and its efforts were of a rather 'broad-brush' nature.[25] (This was in sharp contrast to the close and at times heavy-handed interest in the physical planning of reconstruction shown by the British, French and Soviet occupation authorities in their respective zones.[26]) In part, the American approach reflected informed decisions by its occupation administration. In 1947, for example, the Americans commissioned advice from Walter Gropius, one of the leading German modernist architects during the Weimar Republic, who had emigrated to the US via Britain during the Nazi years. He made a variety of suggestions, essentially advising that responsibility for planning be given to the most technically competent Germans, albeit with opportunities for contacts with American expertise. His visit became mired in controversy over the planning of Berlin and the possible future role of Frankfurt as the capital of West Germany, which was being strongly urged in some American quarters. Overall, though, his recommendations probably reinforced the general pattern of very limited American involvement in planning matters.

More detailed recommendations followed in 1949 when Samuel Zisman, then head of the Philadelphia citizens' planning organisation, was commissioned to advise on urban planning in the American occupation zone.[27] Zisman, who spoke little German, asked another planner then working in the city and with more relevant (but controversial) experience to join him. This was Hans Blumenfeld, a German Jew who had fled the Nazis to work first in the Soviet Union before moving to the US in 1938. Blumenfeld had been a member of the German communist party and remained very sympathetic to Communism, even though he disliked Stalinism. In the growing anti-communist mood of postwar America, it was uncertain whether Blumenfeld would even be given an American passport to allow him to undertake the German commission. However, he benefited from a more liberal interlude in such matters and largely authored the joint report that followed.[28]

The report urged against the pressing of an American planning approach, which the authors saw as being rather weaker than the (pre-Nazi) German tradition. Again, they urged the easing of contacts between German and

American (and other Western) planners. This included granting financial support to bring German officials to the US for study tours and young Germans to American universities for city planning education.

But perhaps the most important aspect of the Zisman/Blumenfeld report was to encourage the importance of supporting the construction of social housing, as Gropius had done. Yet the American occupation authorities remained unenthusiastic because their remit explicitly excluded doing anything to raise the German standard of living. They were also rather exasperated by German reluctance to accept temporary emergency housing programmes built in non-traditional ways. However, Zisman and Blumenfeld's advice, coming just after the fracturing of Germany into a capitalist and a communist state, was more timely than that of Gropius. The American authorities could now see that the relative housing successes of the two German states would be critical in a wider ideological sense, beyond the housing field alone.

In the wake of this, American influence had important effects on German architectural and planning discourse. Competitions and demonstration projects were promoted that did much to raise interest in housing matters. The general outcome was to encourage the re-establishment of the modernist, standardised and industrialised approaches to housing design (and, indirectly, city planning), a tradition that had largely been eradicated during the Nazi period. In effect, therefore, the Americans were reintroducing to Germany approaches that the US had itself learnt from Europe in the late 1930s and 1940s. The ironies of this were not lost on those refugee modernists from Nazi Germany who now served on adjudication panels for the US-funded model housing projects. However, the quantitative effects of all this should not be exaggerated; American aid, even at its peak in 1950, contributed no more than 5 per cent of the total housing budget of the new German Federal Republic.

Everywhere in Western Europe, it was the relative modesty of Marshall Aid contributions to urban reconstruction planning that was most striking. Certainly in some countries there were, as in Germany, important contributions on the housing front. In France, for example, roughly an eighth of American aid went into housing.[29] Italy had the most ambitious American-aided housing programme, most notably through the INA-CASA Plan.[30] Significantly, though, the reasons for this were only partly housing-led, and it was actually wider economic considerations to combat unemployment through stimulating the building industry that took precedence. This served to underline the point that the general presumptions of Marshall Aid were that economic and governmental reconstruction were critical. If these larger projects could be implemented, then more detailed aspects of reconstruction would follow automatically.

It is interesting to speculate what would have happened after 1945 were the US to have had a strong tradition of formal Empire in the manner of Britain or France. In such circumstances, it is difficult to believe that urban planning would not have been more central to the postwar scene. Certainly the other power in Europe at that time, the Soviet Union, adopted a very different style in asserting its own hegemony in Eastern Europe. Under direct Soviet instruction, urban planning was here used in a more direct way to form the identity for the new communist states.

AMERICAN INFLUENCES ON EARLY POSTWAR EUROPEAN PLANNING

Although the US did not in any very real sense *impose* its own city planning conceptions on Western Europe, there was nonetheless a very marked Americanisation of urban planning discourse and practice across Europe during the 1940s. As in Germany, the Americans to some extent encouraged this by promoting a flow of information. But in general it was a fairly voluntaristic process, taking the form of borrowings by the governments and professionals of Western Europe. The wider context of European dependence on the US at this time of course shaped the basic parameters of this borrowing, yet it did not determine it in any meaningful sense. To a greater extent than ever before there was now widespread European admiration for the successes of the US as a society and, of course, real gratitude for its wartime and postwar role in Europe. This quickly transposed itself into a desire to learn about, and to apply, the American way of doing things.

It is instructive, for example, to consider how the attitudes to the US of French architects and planners had shifted compared to the 1930s. As Cohen has put it, a rather stylistic interest in *Americanism* gave way to a more deeply rooted *Americanisation*.[31] French reconstruction planners and their political masters were thus active in seeking American examples after the liberation. The Ministry of Reconstruction and Planning set up an office in Washington DC in 1945, and with governmental encouragement, delegations of prominent architects and planners were soon visiting the US.[32] Such visitors included Marcel Lods, Le Corbusier, Michel Écochard and a future postwar reconstruction minister, Eugène Claudius-Petit. In addition, several significant figures in French architecture and planning had spent at least part of the war in the US and were now well placed to act as intermediaries. Perhaps the most important of these from the planning point of view was Maurice Rotival, a former associate of Henri Prost, who had worked in Venezuela and taught at Yale University from 1939.[33]

The visiting French planners at this time were especially impressed by both the New Deal projects and the wartime new settlements and housing schemes. Their perceptions were by no means uncritical but the overwhelming impression was positive. Here, it seemed to many of them, was much of what communism promised, though delivered by the world's greatest

capitalist country, mobilised in a great cause. (It is worth noting that some
Soviet planners had openly shared these perceptions in their own country
in 1943–4 when American-Soviet relations were at their warmest.[34]) The
developments of the TVA won many plaudits amongst French visitors, as did
the industrialisation of housing provision. Both, it seemed, were models for
reconstruction and modernisation that could readily be transferred to the
French world. The signs that this was happening came soon after in June
and July 1946 in the form of a major exhibition, at the Grand Palais in Paris,
devoted to American wartime techniques in housing and planning.[35]

The late 1940s saw the start of a major push towards the acceleration of
housing production. For example, there were serious (though largely fruitless)
attempts to engage major French industrial manufacturers in prefabrication,
emulating the American wartime experience with firms such as Ford and
Kaiser.[36] Ultimately, though, the main effect of these efforts was to stimulate
change in the construction industry. During the 1950s, regional development
planning also began to assume greater significance, inspired partly by the
experience of the TVA.

Unsurprisingly, given the dominant British thinking of the late 1930s,
American experience was regarded most favourably in France's offshore
neighbour. The New Deal initiatives, especially the TVA and the greenbelt
towns, continued to be reported and studied closely, particularly in their
most radical phases.[37] There were also very favourable reports of American
experience with the prefabrication of housing both in the Tennessee Valley
and, even more, in the wartime schemes.[38] For example, Britain's own emergency wartime housing programme, which eventually resulted in the building
of over 150,000 bungalow 'prefabs', was influenced by these efforts.[39]

Another strand of American influence that was most strongly apparent in
early postwar British planning concerned community projects. Knowledge of
Clarence Perry's interwar writings on neighbourhood planning had begun to
be applied in Britain in the 1930s, but it was not until the following decade
that the concept became widely adopted.[40] By this time, Lewis Mumford's
growing volume of writings on this theme was exerting a growing influence
in Britain. The official Dudley Committee[41] recommended the neighbourhood
unit as the norm for the planning of public sector housing (which constituted much the largest proportion of early postwar housing supply), and two
years later the Reith Committee[42] gave it a similar endorsement in the planning of the new towns. The advice of both reports was closely followed.

As might be expected, though, the neighbourhood unit idea adopted in
Britain showed important differences from the American exemplar. It was
larger, with an ideal of 9000 people rather than Perry's original 5000 (itself
developed partly from Ebenezer Howard's concept of the 'ward'),[43] and was also
more inward looking, with community facilities at its centre, rather than at the
edge. Finally, the British ideal also became linked with the very ambitious

objective of achieving social mix. This intention reflected the prevailing egalitarian social ethos of wartime Britain – that different classes of the community would henceforth live in close proximity.

Partly through these important British variations, as exemplified in the important wartime plans for London and the early new town plans, the neighbourhood unit idea soon became widely known in Western Europe. Its influence can be traced in plans for some of the earliest of the large postwar French housing projects, for example at Parilly on the outskirts of Lyons, where the first dwellings were completed in 1952. It also had a major influence on postwar reconstruction in West Germany, in part because it bore a striking resemblance to the concept of the *Ortsgruppe als Siedlungzelle* (literally, local party chapter as residential cell) favoured by planners during the Nazi period.[44] The Anglo-American notion of the neighbourhood unit effectively became an acceptable ideological relabelling of this concept, allowing it to continue in postwar plans, especially in Hamburg.

The neighbourhood unit was also widely adopted in Sweden and its neighbours during the 1940s and early 1950s. This particular diffusion casts important light on the way in which the influence of American planning spread across early postwar Europe, because Sweden had remained neutral and therefore experienced neither the large-scale American presence on its soil, nor large-scale American aid for reconstruction. The first signs of a reorientation of Swedish planning from its earlier deference to German precedents towards American (and British) urbanism had in fact emerged prior to 1939. Weimar modernism had remained the strongest external influence on Swedish architects and planners between the wars, yet Stockholm could also boast what were probably Europe's first skyscrapers, the twin Kungstornen erected in 1924 and 1925. Within a few years, it also added Europe's first cloverleaf intersection at Slussen (1931–4), conceived barely a year after the first example in the US, on the Lincoln Highway in New Jersey.[45]

The war years brought a more marked reaction against German thinking and a closer engagement with American ideas, most notably with regard to community planning. Thus, in 1942 Sweden's extremely influential co-operative movement published a Swedish translation of Lewis Mumford's *Culture of Cities*.[46] This influenced planners throughout the region, especially those in Denmark and Norway who were already more Anglo-American in their orientation than their Nordic neighbours. However, it was in Sweden that real developments informed by this thinking appeared most rapidly, notably in the pioneer Stockholm neighbourhood unit at Årsta, planned from 1943. Others soon followed, and the doyen of American community planners, Clarence Stein, was captivated by what he saw in Stockholm during visits in 1949 and 1952.[47]

Stein's enthusiasm was motivated partly by pride at seeing his own ideas implemented on a large scale. During these early postwar years, Sweden, and especially Stockholm, became the earliest (and in relative terms remained the most enthusiastic) adopter of the road-safety residential site plan that Stein and his former partner, Henry Wright, had developed at Radburn in the late 1920s,[48] and which was applied later in a few other places such as at Greenbelt, Maryland, the first of the New Deal new settlements. Its widespread adoption in Sweden stood in sharp contrast to the growing indifference to the concept that prevailed in Stein's own country. In part, it reflected the stronger planning culture of Sweden but also its greater prosperity and higher levels of motorisation than was evident in other early postwar European countries. As wartime austerity receded, British planners, mainly in the new towns, also began to adopt the same layout as predictions of motor-vehicle use began to increase during the 1950s (this was also the case in other countries, albeit on a smaller scale).

The fate of the Radburn idea in the US was a symptom of a much larger shift. During the late 1940s and 1950s, Americans retreated from the belief in interventionist government that had been dominant in the Depression and Second World War years. There had been some signs of this in the later 1930s, though these had gone largely unnoticed by European admirers. Moreover, the collectivizing experiences of war seemed to have comprehensively reversed the anti-interventionist trend. In the event, though, the victory for the more socialistically minded planners in the 1940s was also more apparent than real. The US quickly shifted back to what had been its more usual pattern, granting a far more important role to market forces rather than planners in the shaping of cities. New Deal and wartime initiatives were abandoned or very substantially diluted.

Paradoxically, therefore, the examples that so inspired planners in other Western countries during these years remained atypical oddities in their country of origin. Some European planners also experienced at first hand an America that was more difficult to admire. During the anti-communist hysteria orchestrated by Senator Joseph McCarthy, Hans Blumenfeld who had readily found a role in Roosevelt's America now found his career path blocked. The prominent British planner Gordon Stephenson, meanwhile, was penalised for imagined communist sympathies when he was refused entry to take up a professorial chair at the Massachusetts Institute of Technology. In 1955, both moved instead to the more welcoming atmosphere of Canada.[49]

Yet if the US was rejecting the kind of planning that left-minded Europeans could readily admire, and the whole ideological mindset that had fostered it, a further paradox was in the making. Despite being born out of a move away from planning, the market forces that were released from the late 1940s onwards themselves triggered significant new planning innovations. In some cases these were directly responsible for the creation of new forms of planned environments; in others, planners were obliged to develop ways of comprehending and responding to the totality of countless individual decisions. But in both cases the innovations that resulted began to offer important new lessons to other Western countries.

MATURING INFLUENCES: PLANNING FOR A MASS CONSUMER SOCIETY

The results of these efforts put the US at the forefront of two important, and related, aspects of Western urban planning during the 1950s and 1960s – the planning of shopping centres and planning for the motor car. The first of these had a more immediate influence on planning practice in Western Europe. By 1949 a retailing revolution was underway in the US, as large planned shopping malls rapidly began to appear in suburban locations, oriented towards the car-based shopper.[50] The first of these showed relatively little design sophistication. Soon, however, there were moves to create a purely pedestrianised circulation area between all the stores. Gradually, more protection from the weather was given to these pedestrian malls, culminating in 1956 with the world's first fully air-conditioned mall at Edina in suburban Minneapolis.

The continuing effects of rationing and shortages throughout postwar Europe meant that mass consumerism was much slower to develop there. However, wartime destruction and the strong commitment to planned reconstruction gave planners an opportunity to rethink retail provision. Accordingly, developments in the US were watched closely. The Lijnbaan in Rotterdam, generally considered to be the world's first purpose-built pedestrianised central area shopping mall, was designed after its planners had inspected the latest American developments.[51] And an even more direct American contribution came in Britain in 1950 when, through his friend Gordon Stephenson, Clarence Stein played an important role in the early planning of the fully predestrianised town centre at Stevenage New Town.[52]

The new American retail developments of the 1950s were watched with some interest but, for the moment, with little emulation in Europe. Sweden and Britain showed the closest appreciation, mainly in the centres of their new towns. German cities, led by Essen, meanwhile followed a different path by pedestrianizing existing central area streets.[53] But in some ways, the most fertile territories for the American retailing model were those with the space and affluence to develop more American-style suburbs, thus the first out-of-town shopping mall in Canada appeared in 1950, very soon after the first American examples, at Park Royal in Vancouver.[54] In 1955 Gordon Stephenson was recommending the concept for adoption in Australia, in a major metropolitan planning report for Perth,[55] and actual examples were already beginning to appear in Melbourne.[56]

By the 1960s, Western Europe had moved on from postwar austerity and physical reconstruction, and circumstances were altogether more favourable for more dramatic changes in retailing forms. Once again, Britain proved itself to be the principal entry point for American thinking into Europe. In 1964 the Bull Ring Centre in Birmingham became the first European example of the fully enclosed shopping mall.[57] This scheme (recently demolished) was designed after extensive study of American practice. Another early British example was at the Elephant and Castle in London, itself now (in 2002) about to be demolished and redeveloped. Yet, for all the evident deference to American ideas, this British approach was in one important respect quite different from the pattern that had evolved in the US. These British examples (and those that followed in much larger numbers in the later 1960s and 1970s) were not out-of-town greenfield developments. Instead, they were the result of the planned redevelopment and modernisation of well-established existing shopping areas, which were still oriented at least as much towards public transport as the car.

Coincidentally, 1964 also saw the first serious British move to establish a large-scale, car-oriented out-of-town retailing mall at Haydock Park in Lancashire,[58] however the scheme was rejected following a public inquiry. This set back British policy on out-of-town retailing for many years, and it was not until 1976 that the first large and substantially car-oriented out-of-town shopping mall appeared, at Brent Cross in suburban London.[59] Even this was subjected to the long agonizing of London's strategic planners, and went ahead only when they were certain it would not damage existing centres. In fact, Britain had to wait until 1986 to get something that was more completely American in style – the MetroCentre in Gateshead on Tyneside. By this stage, though, the governments of Margaret Thatcher had significantly deregulated the planning system, and one of the principal effects of this was to permit very substantial commercial developments in locations other than established traditional town and city centres.

Despite these lags, Britain was the European country that most closely followed the 'American' path in its approach to retail planning, acting partly as a staging post for this and other American planning ideas. In this case, though, the active agents of the adoption of these retail planning ideas across Britain were largely commercial property developers rather than planners or architects. And over successive decades, it was they who took British interpretations of the evolving American shopping mall concept to cities in other countries and continents. Again, though, a paradox was evident, at least in the 1960s and 1970s. The principal British variation on the mall, making it a central area rather than an out-of-town phenomenon, was close to what the leading American retail planner, Victor Gruen, actually wanted for the US.[60] Instead, though, he had a greater immediate impact in the decentralisation of retailing, and it was not until the later 1970s and 1980s that sizeable downtown malls began to appear in the big American cities.[61]

MATURING INFLUENCES: PLANNING FOR MASS CAR-OWNERSHIP

During the 1950s and 1960s, the US also became the world leader in large-scale metropolitan highways and transportation planning.[62] To some extent this reflected the large pre-existing body of American expertise on highway engineering matters. The US was, of course, the world's most motorised society, and from the 1950s it was busily rebuilding its cities to allow unrestricted car use. Triggered partly by this and by the huge interstate highways programme, highways planners began to make growing use of electronic computers for large-scale data processing. This allowed predictive and dynamic modelling of transportation and land-use relationships within urban regions, and in turn meant, for example, that the impact of new highways on activity patterns could be predicted and decisions regarding routes and networks made accordingly. A landmark in this aspect of planning was the 1955 Detroit Metropolitan Area Traffic study, which with the equivalent Chicago study of the following year firmly established American supremacy in this field.

Within a few years, this deepening and widening pool of American highways planning know-how was stirring international interest. One of the most notable examples was the 1963 Oslo transportation study, an early European (and widely studied) application of the Detroit methodology,[63] though in many cases the techniques were applied directly by American experts. By the early 1960s, specialist American highways planning consultants were finding their expertise eagerly sought by cities in other countries. Apart from a growing export trade in this methodology to less developed parts of the world, especially Latin America, the most immediate impact was in the Anglophone world. Thus the De Leuw Cather highways consultants of Chicago were commissioned to advise the Australian city of Sydney about planning expressways in 1961,[64] and subsequently produced similar reports for Perth in 1964 and 1967. There was also comparable activity in Canadian cities, for example, when the San Francisco-based consultants Parsons, Brinkerhoff, Quade and Douglas were commissioned to prepare a citywide highway plan for Vancouver in 1966.[65]

The same process was also evident in Britain where, despite lower levels of motorisation, cities were facing acute problems arising from the increased use of motor vehicles. From about 1960, American consultants such as Wilbur Smith and Alan Voorhees were being retained to advise on aspects of planning with regard to the motor vehicle.[66] Of more profound significance, however, was the admiration of American achievements in transportation planning evident in the extremely important official report *Traffic in Towns*, prepared by a team headed by Colin Buchanan and published in 1963 to very widespread acclaim.[67] International interest in the report was so great that it was translated into German in 1964,[68] and some of its key parts also appeared in French the following year.

Though it also looked at the experiences of West German cities, Stockholm and Venice, the bulk of the above report's international lesson-drawing came from the US. There was particular admiration of the way urban renewal in American cities such as Philadelphia was being planned with car access in mind, especially through what Buchanan termed 'traffic architecture'. There was also high regard for the convenience of car-based shopping at out-of-town malls. Above all, though, the report demonstrated a pervasive admiration of American traffic-planning methodology (to the extent that the majority of the literature it cited was of American origin).

Buchanan disapproved of several ways in which motor traffic had changed American cities. In particular he disliked their ill-considered sprawling suburbanisation and the destructive and blighting effects of major freeway construction in parts of some US cities. Yet the report also indicated the sense that the US of the Kennedy era was on the point of changing its ways. The 1961 Washington plan, which proposed a growth corridor model with major investments in rail transit and high-density development in planned new communities, was cited with approval. This plan showed many European references, borrowing especially the planning concept pioneered in the 1947 'finger' plan for Copenhagen and the 1952 plan for Stockholm. It also encouraged a growing interest among Anglophone planners in metropolitan corridor planning models, especially so in Australia.[69] As far as Buchanan was concerned, however, it helped bolster his belief that an integration of the advanced American transportation planning techniques with Europe's stronger urban planning traditions would forge a winning combination. Certainly British planners (and, to a lesser extent, those in other European countries) tried hard to follow this guidance.

The 1960s were marked by a growing emphasis on rational 'scientific' planning approaches. Though this originated in transportation planning, it was soon being extended to other aspects of planning. In many ways, this trend reached its peak with the 'systems' approach popular, especially amongst Anglophone planners, in the 1970s. Again, the original source of this approach was American, developed essentially in connection with the space programme but elaborated most completely in the field of planning by British planning academics.[70]

GROWING DOUBTS

In retrospect, it is clear that there was little long-term basis for Buchanan's optimism about an increasing salience of planning in the US during the 1960s. His criticism, in the report, of American experiences might also be seen as beginning the trend of more negative external perceptions, even in the European country usually most disposed to draw positive lessons from across

———

the Atlantic. More significant events from the mid-1960s further encouraged this adoption of such critical perspectives, particularly the unrest associated with the Civil Rights movement, urban rioting and growing unease regarding the Vietnam War. To many critics, American cities were no longer places to emulate. By extension, therefore, American planners, for all their impressive techniques and methodologies, could be said to have failed. Ultimately their powers were seen as too few to allow real achievements. Thus the team despatched in the wake of the 1965 Schéma directeur for the Paris region to study and draw lessons from new town planning throughout the world could find little they wished to learn from the US.[71] This was quite different from the thinking of twenty years earlier.

Despite this, and in yet another paradox, it was also largely an American critical discourse that articulated the growing Western unease with planning by the later 1960s. Jane Jacobs' trenchant critique of city planning, *The Death and Life of Great American Cities,* first published in 1961, had within a few years reached a wide international readership,[72] and the more measured writings of Herbert Gans were also of seminal importance in highlighting the social blindness of much planning activity.[73] Admittedly, the more theoretical critiques of planning were of European origin, yet these too were partly Americanised as some of the leading European urban theorists, such as David Harvey and Manuel Castells, succumbed to the lure of American academic life.[74]

Alongside these important contributions to planning thought, the US also became a world leader in the formation of citizens' movements to challenge the actions of the planners. The anti-freeway movements that began in San Francisco in the late 1950s spread to most American cities during the following decade.[75] In part, perhaps, this reflected an almost instinctively less deferential attitude of Americans to governments than was typical in Europe, at least until the later 1960s. The international environmental movement similarly had its origins in the US during the 1960s, informed by several seminal books, of which the first was Rachel Carson's *Silent Spring*, published in 1962.[76] More practically, the Friends of the Earth organisation was formed in California in 1969, and Greenpeace two years later in Vancouver, albeit by Americans avoiding the draft to fight in Vietnam.

CONCLUSION

The story of American influences on wider Western planning obviously did not close with the 1960s. Nor did it shift from offering positive models to coining the conceptual vocabulary of a critical discourse. In the 1980s, for example, the Baltimore model for regenerating waterfront areas exerted tremendous influence throughout the world, especially, though by no means exclusively, in Anglophone countries. Yet we have reviewed enough of the twentieth century to be able to draw some valid conclusions.

We can identify a broad evolution in the way the wider Western world understood and was influenced by American city planning. Initially, between the two world wars, the dominant engagement was with the image of the American city and its unique visual features. At this stage, though, there was relatively little real understanding of the work of American city planners and the impact of their efforts in actually shaping cities. Deeper understanding began to develop from the late 1930s, when the growing social and economic content of American planning meant that it had wider relevance. In general, though, there was no strong imperative that impelled other Western countries to adopt American approaches. However, attitudes changed fundamentally during the Second World War, out of which came an unprecedented interest in learning and applying the American way of doing things.

Yet as the role of planning in shaping urban development was downgraded and the forces of market capitalism reasserted themselves in the US from the late 1940s, the wider salience of the American model changed. American cities were increasingly seen as providing an early warning of the pressures for change that were soon likely to affect the wider West. Certain aspects of American planning could still be admired and adopted, albeit often in a consciously modified form. Yet the US also became an increasing source of negative lessons, the adoption of which was all the easier due to the existence of a more assertive American culture of critical research and comment. Nowhere, though, did planners safely feel that they could ignore the American experience.

Considering this evolution in terms of the broad typology of diffusion outlined earlier, we can identify some ready parallels. Before the late 1930s, the American experience was not particularly well understood and, in so far as it was borrowed, this usually occurred in a rather critical and adaptive, synthetic fashion. The most uncritical borrowing was in those countries (such as Canada or, to a lesser extent, Australia) that were becoming increasingly dependent on the US and/or for other reasons showed some degree of cultural or technical deference to the American experience. The nature of the wider power relationship was also important in the most typical Western responses. The US was clearly a major but not yet the hegemonic Western power. Thus the larger European countries would feel no particular sense of dependence or deference that would cause them to feel they had to adopt (or even properly to understand) its experience.

Self-evidently, this position changed radically during the 1940s, when the US emerged as the dominant Western power. This was to remain the case until the late 1980s, when American global hegemony became total. Yet the real sense of wider Western dependence on and deference to the US was greatest in the 1940s when all the former actual or would-be hegemonic

Western powers were humbled or exhausted by war. This situation obviously also challenged traditional patterns of deference amongst the smaller and less powerful countries, in Europe and beyond. Those that had traditionally looked to one or more of the major European planning traditions now looked more to the US. Those that were already looking in that direction now did so to a greater extent.

Without the wartime and early postwar support of the US, most of these countries, in Europe at least, would have collapsed, or at least fallen harder than they actually did. As we have seen, though, the US did not use its dominance to impose its own solutions on the secondary detail of governmental policies in the many countries that now looked to it for support. Its concerns were broad brush, to create a West that was capitalist and democratic. However the realities of their countries' dependence on the US strongly encouraged the planners of other Western states, particularly the former sceptics in Europe, to view American planning experiences in a rather uncritically positive light. In particular, Europeans failed at this time to see how shallow and temporary the US commitment to interventionist planning really was.

As the US retreated from this position during the 1950s, Western Europe also recovered and its real sense of dependence on the US declined. In turn, these larger realities encouraged the return of more sceptical attitudes to American planning. Yet the scepticism never went so far as being able to ignore American experiences. The West remained a spatial and ideological construct that existed only under an American guarantee. As the decline of the remaining European empires showed, there was to be no return to the prewar position. Just as the US could not be ignored in the larger arenas of geopolitics and economics, neither could it be disregarded in the more limited arena of planning.

There are, though, limits to the extent of these rather structuralist and deterministic perspectives. In a story that is littered with paradoxes, the most important of these is that the US has never developed an urban planning tradition commensurate in influence with its broader global significance. In the long term, therefore, it has supplied fewer positive models to the wider Western discourse of planning than have the major European traditions. Yet perhaps it is false ever to expect such neat parallels. In reality, the urban planning movements of different countries should be seen as more autonomous and reflective of specific historical experiences. Thus the pre-industrial and formal imperial experiences of European countries undoubtedly contributed to the formation of more ambitious ideologies and practices of modern planning than those of the US. This has been paralleled by a generally stronger European belief in the State as a positive agent of change. Only when America seemed to come closest to sharing these beliefs was it actually possible for Europe to borrow extensively and uncritically from the US.

NOTES

1. Daniel T. Rodgers (1998) *Atlantic Crossings: Social Politics in a Progressive Age*, Cambridge, Mass.: Harvard University Press, p. 508.
2. Stephen V. Ward (2000) 'Re-examining the international diffusion of planning', in Robert Freestone (ed.) *Urban Planning in a Changing World: the Twentieth Century Experience*, London: Spon, pp. 40–60; Stephen V. Ward (2002) *Planning the Twentieth-Century City: the Advanced Capitalist World*, Chichester: Wiley.
3. Jean-Louis Cohen (1995) *Scenes of the World to Come: European Architecture and the American Challenge 1893–1960*, Paris: Flammarion/Canadian Centre for Architecture.
4. Mel Scott (1969) *American City Planning Since 1890*, Berkeley, CA: University of California Press, pp. 31–37; William H. Wilson (1989) *The City Beautiful Movement*, Baltimore, MD: Johns Hopkins University Press.
5. Anthony Sutcliffe (1981) *Towards the Planned City: Germany, Britain, the United States and France 1780–1914*, Oxford: Basil Blackwell, pp. 149–50.
6. Christiane C. Collins (1996) 'Werner Hegemann (1881–1936): formative years in America', *Planning Perspectives*, 11, no. 1, pp. 1–22.
7. Marc Bédarida (1991) '1918: une modernisation urbaine frileuse', in Archives Nationales (ed.) *Reconstructions et modernisation: La France après les ruines 1918 . . . 1945 . . .*, Paris: Archives Nationales, pp. 262–66; Gwendolyn Wright (1991) *The Politics of Design in French Colonial Urbanism*, Chicago: Chicago University Press, pp. 49–51.
8. Scott, op. cit., pp. 57–60.
9. Isabelle Gournay (2000) 'Revisiting Jacques Gréber's *L'architecture aux États-Unis*: from city beautiful to cité-jardin', *Urban History Review*, Vol. XXIX, no. 2, pp. 6–19; Cohen, op. cit., pp 49–56.
10. Jacques Gréber (1920) *L'architecture aux États-Unis: preuve de la force d'expansion du génie français*, Paris: Payot.
11. Michael Simpson (1985) *Thomas Adams and the Modern Planning Movement: Britain, Canada and the United States*, London: Mansell, pp. 122–67; David A. Johnson (1996) *Planning the Great Metropolis: the 1929 Regional Plan of New York and Its Environs*, London: Spon.
12. Walter Van Nus (1979) 'Toward the city efficient: the theory and practice of zoning, 1919–1939', in Alan Artibise and Gilbert Stelter (eds) *The Usable Urban Past*, Toronto: Carleton Library, pp. 226–46.
13. John W. Reps (1997) *Canberra 1912: Plans and Planners of the Australian Capital Competition*, Melbourne: Melbourne University Press.
14. Robert Freestone (2000), 'Master plans and planning commissions in the 1920s: the Australian experience', *Planning Perspectives*, Vol. 15, no. 3, pp. 301–22.
15. Barlow Commission (Royal Commission on the Distribution of the Industrial Population) (1940) *Report* (Cmd 6153), London: HMSO, pp. 288–316; Stephen V. Ward (2000) 'American and other international examples in British planning policy formation: a comparison of the Barlow, Buchanan and Rogers reports, 1940–1999', Paper presented at the International Planning History Society Seminar on Americanization and the British City in the 20th Century, University of Luton, 6 May.
16. Lewis Mumford (1938) *The Culture of Cities*, London: Secker & Warburg.
17. Peter Hall (1988) *Cities of Tomorrow: An Intellectual History of Urban Planning and Design in the Twentieth Century*, Oxford: Basil Blackwell, pp. 137–73.

104

18. Jeffry M. Diefendorf (1993) *In the Wake of War: The Reconstruction of German Cities after World War II*, New York: Oxford University Press, p. 163.

19. Carmen Hass-Klau (1990) *The Pedestrian and City Traffic*, London: Belhaven, pp. 77–82.

20. Marinke Steenhuis (1997) 'Paris 1934 Plan d'aménagement de la région parisienne', in Koos Bosma and Helma Hellinga (eds) *Mastering the City: North-European City Planning 1900–2000*, Rotterdam: NAI Publishers/EFL Publications, II, pp. 226–33; Norma Evenson (1979) *Paris: A Century of Change 1878–1978*, New Haven, CT: Yale University Press, pp. 332–36.

21. Alain Vollerin (2000) *Histoire de l'architecture et de l'urbanisme à Lyon au XXe siècle*, Lyon: Editions Mémoire des Arts, p. 54.

22. Le Corbusier (orig. 1937) *When the Cathedrals Were White*, New York: McGraw-Hill.

23. Michael J. Hogan (1987) *The Marshall Plan: America, Britain, and the Reconstruction of Western Europe*, Cambridge: Cambridge University Press.

24. Donald W. Ellswood (1993) 'The Marshall Plan', *Rassegna*, 54, pp. 84–88.

25. Jeffry M. Diefendorf (1993) 'America and the rebuilding of urban Germany', in Jeffry. M. Diefendorf, Axel Frohn and Hermann-Josef Repieper (eds) *American Policy and the Reconstruction of West Germany, 1945–1955*, New York: Cambridge University Press, pp. 331–51; Diefendorf, (1993) *In the Wake of War: The Reconstruction of German Cities after World War II*, New York: Oxford University Press, pp. 246–51.

26. On the French in Germany, see: Jean-Louis Cohen and Hartmut Frank (eds) (n.d.) *Les relations franco-allemandes 1940–1950 et leurs effets sur l'architecture et la forme urbaine*, Paris: Ecole d'Architecture Paris-Villemin, Département de la Recherche, and Hamburg: Hochschule für bildende Künste Hamburg, Fachbereich Architektur. The Soviet case is illustrated clearly in the article by Strobel, in this volume.

27. Hans Blumenfeld (1987) *Life Begins at 65: The Not Entirely Candid Autobiography of a Drifter*, Montreal: Harvest House, pp. 208–20; Diefendorf (1993) 'America and the rebuilding of urban Germany', op. cit., pp. 331–51.

28. City Planning in Germany, NA/RG 59/State Department Central Decimal Files/Box 6778/no. 862.502/12–849. Reference cited from Diefendorf, (1993) *In the Wake of War*, op. cit., p. 324.

29. Gérard Bossuat (1991) 'L'aide américaine 1945–1955', in Archives Nationales, op. cit., pp. 291–300.

30. Sergio Pace (1993) 'Solidarity on easy terms: the INA-Casa Plan 1948–1949', *Rassegna*, 54, pp. 20–27.

31. Cohen, op. cit., p. 163.

32. Ibid., pp. 162–77.

33. Carola Hein (2002) 'Maurice Rotival – French planning on a world scale' (in two parts), *Planning Perspectives*, 17, nos 3 and 4, pp. 247–66 and 325–44.

34. Alessandro de Magistris (1993) 'USSR, the other reconstruction', *Rassegna*, 54, pp. 76–83.

35. Cohen, op. cit., p. 173.

36. Dominique Barjot (1991) 'Les entreprises du bâtiment et des travaux publics et la Reconstruction (1918–1945)', in Archives Nationales, op. cit., pp. 231–44; Dominique Barjot (2002) 'Un âge d'or de la construction', *Urbanisme*, 322, pp. 42–74.

37. Julian Huxley (1943) *TVA: Adventure in Planning*, Cheam: The Architectural Press; David Lilienthal (1944) *TVA: Democracy on the March*, Harmondsworth: Penguin.

38. Hugh Casson (1946) *Homes by the Million: An Account of the Housing Methods of the USA 1940–1945*, Harmondworth: Penguin.

39. Brenda Vale (1995) *Prefabs: A History of the UK Temporary Housing Programme*, London: Spon, pp. 52–74.

40. Dirk Schubert (2000) 'The neighbourhood paradigm: from garden cities to gated communities', in Freestone (ed.), op. cit., pp. 118–38.

41. Dudley Report (1944) *The Design of Dwellings: Report of the Sub-Committee of the Central Housing Advisory Committee.* London: HMSO.

42. Reith Committee (1946) *Final Report of the New Towns Committee* (Cmd 6876), London: HMSO.

43. Stephen V. Ward (2000) 'Re-examining the international diffusion of planning', op. cit., pp. 46–47.

44. Schubert, op. cit., pp. 127–32.

45. Olof Hultin (ed.) (1998) *The Complete Guide to Architecture in Stockholm*, Stockholm: Arkitektur Förlag; Blake McKelvey (1968) *The Emergence of Metropolitan America 1915–1966*, New Brunswick, NJ: Rutgers University Press, p. 106.

46. Thomas Hall (1991) 'Urban Planning in Sweden', in Thomas Hall (ed.) *Planning and Urban Growth in the Nordic Countries*, London: Spon, pp. 167–246.

47. Kermit C. Parsons (1992) 'American influence on Stockholm's post World War II suburban expansion', *Planning History.* 14, 1, pp. 3–14.

48. Clarence S. Stein (1958) *Toward New Towns for America*, 2nd edn, Liverpool: Liverpool University Press, pp. 37–69.

49. Gordon Stephenson (1992) *On a Human Scale: A Life in City Design*, ed. Christina de Marco, Fremantle Arts Centre/Liverpool University Press, pp. 154–56; Blumenfeld, op. cit., pp. 221–2.

50. Victor Gruen and Larry Smith (1960) *Shopping Towns USA: The Planning of Shopping Centers*, New York: Van Nostrand Reinhold; Scott, op. cit., pp. 458–62.

51. R. M. Taverne (1990) 'The Lijnbaan (Rotterdam): a prototype of a postwar urban shopping centre', in Jeffry M. Diefendorf (ed.) *Rebuilding Europe's Blitzed Cities*, Basingstoke: Macmillan, pp. 145–54.

52. Stephenson, op. cit., pp. 97–106.

53. Hass-Klau, op. cit., pp. 194–6.

54. Robert N. North and Walter G. Hardwick (1992) 'Vancouver since the Second World War: An economic geography', in Graeme Wynn and Timothy Oke (eds) *Vancouver and Its Region*, Vancouver: UBC Press, pp. 206–7.

55. Gordon Stephenson and J. Alastair Hepburn (1955) *Plan for the Metropolitan Region Perth and Fremantle*, Perth: Western Australian Government Printing Office.

56. Ian Alexander (2000) 'The post-war city', in Stephen Hamnett and Robert Freestone (eds) *The Australian Metropolis: A Planning History*, London: Spon, p. 107.

57. Oliver Marriott (1969) *The Property Boom*, London: Pan, pp. 247–68.

58. Stephen V. Ward (1994) *Planning and Urban Change*, London: Paul Chapman, p. 186.

59. Ibid., pp. 238–39.

60. Victor Gruen (1964) *The Heart of Our Cities*, New York: Simon & Schuster.

61. Bernard J. Frieden and Lynne B. Sagalyn (1989) *Downtown, Inc.: How America Rebuilds Cities*, Cambridge, Mass.: MIT Press.

62. Peter Hall, op. cit., pp. 326–31.

63. Rolf H. Jensen (1997) 'Norwegian city planning – Oslo: from provincial to cosmopolitan capital', in Bosma and Hellinga (eds) op. cit., p. 35.

64. Paul Ashton (1993) *The Accidental City: Planning Sydney Since 1788*, Sydney: Hale and Iremonger, pp. 84–87; Peter Newman (1992) 'The re-birth of Perth's suburban railways', in David Hedgcock and Oren Yiftachel (eds) *Urban and Regional Planning in Western Australia*, Perth: Paradigm Press, p. 175.

65. D. Gutstein (1975) *Vancouver Ltd*, Toronto: James Lorimer, p. 154.

66. Ward (2000) 'American and other international examples', op. cit.

67. MT [Ministry of Transport, Great Britain] (1963) *Traffic in Towns: A Study of the Long Term Problems of Traffic in Urban Areas: Reports of the Steering Group and Working Group appointed by the Minister of Transport*, London: HMSO.

68. Ward (2002), op. cit, p. 241.

69. Ian Morison (2000) 'The corridor city: planning for growth in the 1960s', in Hamnett and Freestone (eds), op. cit, pp. 113–30.

70. J. Brian McLoughlin (1969) *Urban and Regional Planning: A Systems Approach*, London: Faber; George Chadwick (1971) *A Systems View of Planning*, Oxford: Pergamon.

71. Pierre Merlin (1971) *New Towns: Regional Planning and Development*, London: Methuen, pp. 176–92.

72. Jane Jacobs (1964) *The Death and Life of Great American Cities: The Failure of Town Planning*, Harmondsworth: Penguin.

73. Herbert J. Gans (1962) *The Urban Villagers: Group and Class in the Life of Italian-Americans*, New York: Free Press; Herbert J. Gans (1967) *The Levittowners: Ways of Life and Politics in a New Suburban Community,* London: Allen Lane.

74. David Harvey (1973) *Social Justice and the City*, London: Edward Arnold; Manuel Castells (1977) *The Urban Question: A Marxist Approach*, London: Edward Arnold.

75. Sally B. Woodbridge (1990) 'Visions of renewal and growth: 1945 to the present', in Paolo Polledri (ed.) *Visionary San Francisco*, Munich: Prestel, p. 122.

76. Rachel Carson (1962) *Silent Spring*, New York: Houghton Mifflin.

Part II

CITY-BUILDING, STATE-BUILDING AND NATION-BUILDING

CHAPTER 5

Urbanism as Social Engineering in the Balkans: Reform Prospects and Implementation Problems in Thessaloniki

Alexandra Yerolympos
Aristotle University of Thessaloniki

The Balkan Context

Little is known about the important changes that took place in the Balkan cities in the hundred years between 1820 and 1920. On the periphery of Europe, bearing a name that has come to signify a geographically localized chaos and having won their independence at the expense of their reputation, the Balkan countries seem to have been among the most eager importers of Western planning concepts in the nineteenth century. In an attempt to evaluate the Balkan experience within European planning history, the particular course of urban restructuring the Balkan countries embarked upon in the nineteenth century needs to be briefly discussed. Indeed, the violent changes and resulting transformation of the Balkan cities fuelled the arduous processes of nation building.

While every import presupposes an export, and importing does not always imply free will and an open range of choices, it appears that in the case of the Balkans the import aspect is more pertinent. Having lived for five centuries under Ottoman rule, the will to modernize, at the time interpreted as a desire to catch up with the more developed European countries (mainly France and England), was strong within the Balkan peoples. It involved all levels of government, administration, education, cultural expression (literature, music, etc.), way of life, clothing and everyday behaviour. 'Westernization' was much more than a political goal – it was a deeply rooted, widespread wish, regarded as an index of the vitality of the new nations, of their capacity to bridge gaps of many centuries and retrieve an identity that had been forcibly taken from them. In their interpretation of history, the Ottoman conquest was the main reason why they had been separated from their natural family, the European nations, and left behind on the road to progress.

Created between the 1820s and the 1920s, paralleling the dismantling of the multiethnic Ottoman Empire, the new Balkan states had to cope with extensive damage to existing towns and countryside, deserted areas and millions of refugees in search of new homes. New networks of settlements had to be established within the newly traced national boundaries, and the planning of new cities and the reconstruction of existing ones were placed at the heart of the modernizing programmes of the nations concerned.[1]

The reasons behind this effort were practical and functional, as well as ideological. The new state should motivate production and economic activity, redistribute old and new inhabitants within the national territory, colonize abandoned regions, and at the same time emphasize its proper identity by creating its own urban culture. Urbanism was thus viewed as a vehicle of universally accepted principles, political freedom, economic progress and social well-being, to be promoted through the form of the city. Meanwhile, traces of Ottoman rule, identified by social and political underdevelopment, had to be effaced from the urban fabric and landscape. In the struggle for political emancipation and social, economic and cultural progress, 'Westernization' and 'de-Ottomanization'[2] appeared as two strongly inter-woven objectives that spurred major planning initiatives. Thus, appropriate planning legislation, along with specific operations, was included among the very first decisions of the new independent governments. Throughout the Balkans, more or less elaborate planning schemes and urban legislation, reflecting the contemporary state of the art, were prepared during the nine-teenth century.

The traditional Balkan city, as it was inherited from Ottoman times, seemed quite different from the Western European city: it had no political autonomy or legal identity, nor any authority or institution directly respon-sible for the city. From a social point of view, the city was the home of a bourgeoisie related to the state and the central administration.

With respect to the physical structure and form of Balkan cities, although a general description could not easily be applied to all of them they still shared some common characteristics: anarchic development along with rural areas inserted within city limits; no specific role assigned to ancient fortifi-cations, if they existed; a multiethnic population living in separate residential areas, each with an introverted, strictly controlled communal life of its own; specially reserved areas for market places and workshops; the absence of a civic centre; low building densities, allowing each house to stand in its own garden; an extremely intricate system of narrow, ill-maintained streets; few public buildings made of stone, while individual houses were made with poor, non-solid materials; and a total lack of infrastructure.[3] Urban life was frag-mented and capital was not invested in immovable property, as long as the property and other rights of non-Muslims were not safeguarded by the State.

What can be seen as a lack of visual and structural order, and what had been a fundamental aspect of the traditional city, had in the past supported intricate patterns of social and economic relations. It had not hindered the functioning of the city, yet under the new sovereignty, neither was it instrumental in preparing for change. The physical setting was an all too eloquent testimony to a part that was seen as a medieval, retarded and ultimately repulsive, and appeared incapable of responding to and supporting the radical changes in economic and social organization, and in cultural and political behaviour, introduced by the new national regimes.

Throughout the nineteenth century, the young Balkan countries made great efforts to recompose and reconquer their cities. People of all origins, natives and foreigners – military engineers, geographers, technicians, even teachers – offered their general ideas or specific expertise to help recreate the city. This 'ideal city' may be described as the exact opposite of the traditional city. It was *grosso modo* the model of the 'colonial city', as it incorporated the rich planning experience of the eighteenth century in terms of the provision of public space and buildings, technical infrastructure, practical considerations and ideals of embellishment. It was a well-organized city, shapely, orderly, functional, equipped with roads and networks, extroverted, properly oriented, well maintained and sanitary; but above all it was clearly defined and 'egalitarian', a city defying the past, an exact reflection of a new society for free people.

Geometric order, equal advantages for private plots, uniform regulations, capacity for growth, clearly defined public spaces and freedom to live wherever one wished in the city were the main imports of European urbanism in the nineteenth century as interpreted in the Balkans. Beginning in the 1830s, hundreds of cities were designed or redesigned according to this model, while planning developed as a rather centralized procedure under government control, often in collaboration with foreign experts. Local authorities, if they existed, were seldom asked for their opinions.[4] In any case, many people took a favourable view of the new plans, which fulfilled their deepest wishes for a new kind of living environment.

THE NEW PLAN FOR THESSALONIKI

The replanning of Thessaloniki in 1917 may be considered a triumphant epilogue to the endeavours of the new Balkan countries to affirm their 'Western' orientation and profile through urban replanning. It was actually an avant-garde operation that went far beyond the experience accumulated on the spot, and in fact conformed to the evolution of planning in the early twentieth century. Indeed, the case of Thessaloniki shows that modern town planning, as a convergence of reformist thought and theories about control of urban space, was adopted in Greece almost simultaneously with its first inclusion in operational planning in the West, in the early twentieth century.[5]

Thanks to a series of coincidences, it did not simply supply informed politicians or enlightened technocrats with rhetoric, but was in fact implemented. In addition to the political and ideological considerations prevailing in the nineteenth century, Thessaloniki confirmed the firm belief of contemporary statesmen and reformers in 'social engineering', that traditional society could be transformed through the implementation of new 'physical' patterns of space. It is also the last radical redesign operation to be recorded in the Balkans before the 1960s.

Thessaloniki is perhaps the only coastal city in contemporary Greece to have maintained its commercial importance since its foundation in the fourth century BC. It was laid out on a regular chessboard plan, and adorned with important civic buildings and spaces in the Hellenistic, Roman and Byzantine periods. Taken by the Ottomans in 1430, and abandoned by its population, the city soon recovered and was colonized by Jewish fugitives from Spain. By the middle of the seventeenth century it was again a densely populated city and a major commercial crossroads of the Balkans. It accommodated a multilingual, multireligious society, living in separate neighbourhoods and quarters, with close-knit ethno-religious Christian, Jewish and Muslim communities, Jews being the most populous group. When the city was integrated into Greece at the end of the first Balkan War in 1912, it presented a hybrid aspect, partly 'oriental' and partly 'European'. New forms of social stratification were tending to gravitate outside its walls, while the city's ancient centre retained its inherited social structure formed centuries before. The Greek government immediately formed a committee to prepare plans for the embellishment of the city, but the First World War put an end to all such projects.

In 1917, during the war, a devastating fire destroyed the greater part of the historic centre,[6] clearing away all the obstacles to change that an ossified, centuries-old urban structure could present, and thus speeding up the city's adaptation to its future role as a regional metropolis of the modern Greek state. The Liberal Party, in office at the time under the great Greek statesman Eleftherios Venizelos, immediately decided to redesign the city by adopting entirely new spatial patterns in its urban fabric. This meant the complete overthrow of the old land-ownership system and of existing patterns for the occupation and use of space.

Through the new city plan and specific legislation to implement it that ignored all former practice, the government aimed to implement the following stipulations:

1. The old pattern of ethno-religious spatial segregation would be rearranged according to modern residential requirements.
2. A political and economic centre (*point fort*) would be created with the function of directly organizing socioeconomic life and expressing the unitary authority of the State.

3. Investments would be attracted to Thessaloniki from Greeks living else-
    where in Greece and in the diaspora, and the local economy would be
    restructured with a view to concentrating capital.
4. Efforts would be made to document certain parts of the city's historical
    past, mainly Roman and Byzantine, by giving prominence to selected
    historic buildings.
5. The scheme would also allow the official implementation of up-to-date
    theories concerning such matters as the social character of town plan-
    ning, the appropriation by the community of the surplus value of land
    created by the planning scheme itself, and the role of the state in the
    organization of space.
6. It would also permit central control of the area and its economy for years
    to come, and a substantial degree of public administration in the city,
    while engaging international interest thanks to the ambitiousness of the
    redesign operation.[7]

Within two weeks of the fire, all the main questions that were to dominate
the next six to ten years had already arisen and been dealt with in principle.

The scheme was entrusted to an international commission of architects
and engineers, proposed by Greece's French and British allies and the Greek
government itself. The chief planners were Ernest Hébrard and Thomas
Hayton Mawson, and the commission was placed under the chairmanship of
the Mayor of Thessaloniki.

Foreign experts immediately regarded the replanning of Thessaloniki as
'one of the most unique opportunities for the replanning of a great city which
have ever engaged the genius of the City Planning expert', and observed that
'the new Salonika will emphasize in a remarkable degree the advance which
the art and science of City Planning has made in recent years'.[8] Hébrard
grasped the opportunity to apply to a real city the principles and ideas he
had formulated in his utopian project of the World Centre, which had made
him famous before the war.

It was mainly Hébrard and the powerful cabinet minister Alexandros
Papanastassiou who put their stamp on the whole scheme. Hébrard passion-
ately believed that the new discipline could greatly help to accelerate social
processes and promote modern modes of living in the world's underdeveloped countries, alongside the scope for experimentation it also offered there.[9]
He was supported at a political level by Papanastassiou, a learned sociologist
and a fervent social-democrat who detected socialist features in the new
ideas. Papanastassiou saw these features as supporting the concept of community as opposed to private interest, developing the State's interventionist role,
and offering opportunities to pass measures of an essentially reformist nature.
In this way, he attempted to use the legislation involved in the replanning
of Thessaloniki as a vehicle for genuine social reform. The joint enthusiasm
of the town planner and the politician, and at the same time their lack of

clear-sightedness as to the possible side-effects of the plan's implementation, are crucial points in the understanding of the Thessaloniki project.

The plan drawn up for Thessaloniki was classical in form, but based on much updated concepts of town design and legal organs to implement it. The city was organized around a single major centre, with a greenbelt limit confining it to a surface area of 2400 hectares (eight times greater than the old historic city) for a population forecast of 350,000 (as compared to the existing 170,000). Prescribed land uses, such as industry, wholesale trade, warehouses, essential transport facilities (a goods and passenger railway station, and extension of the port, workers' housing, retail commerce, shops and offices, middle- and high-income housing and neighbourhood centres were organized in a sequence that drew on the industrial organization of production (Taylorism).

Workers' residential districts were planned according to Garden City principles, and proposed as social housing schemes. In the central, devastated zone particularly, space was allotted for administrative and financial buildings (including courts, public offices, a Stock Exchange and Chamber of Commerce) complying with specific architectural restrictions (ordinances), while the east end, a fashionable bourgeois resort of the 1890s, was intended only for residential and recreational use. It stretched for eight kilometres along the coast and consisted of high-income housing on the sea front, a shopping zone along the main artery, middle-income neighbourhoods inland divided by parks with watercourses running seawards, small neighbourhood centres with schools and kindergartens, and space for sports and cultural facilities.

A green belt surrounding the city ended in an ambitious seaside amusement centre on the southeast headland at the entrance to the bay. The eastern and central sections were separated by a wide park, where a large university campus was to be located, along with entertainment areas including theatres, concert halls and smart restaurants and cafés.

In the historical centre, the city's ancient grid system was enriched with parallel thoroughfares and a system of diagonal thoroughfares, either linking Byzantine and other monuments or opening up vistas centred on them. A major innovation proposed by the commission was the Civic Boulevard, which linked two large squares: the first was conceived as an imposing civic centre with the City Hall, law court and government departments; the second opened into a piazza on the sea front. This unified composition was reinforced by programmatic architecture on the buildings fronting the squares. For the facades, Hébrard and the commission introduced the neo-Byzantine style in an effort to establish a historical allusion to the city's illustrious past. (Figs 1 and 2)

Further eastward, and at right angles to the sea front, was another boulevard, this time linking the Roman Rotunda with the Arch of Galerius and the probable site of his palace, before descending to the sea. The archaeological discovery of the imposing palace complex on that same site in 1945–50 vindicated Hébrard's efforts, integrating the promenade into an archaeological space.

Figure 1. Thessaloniki intra-muros before the fire of 1917.

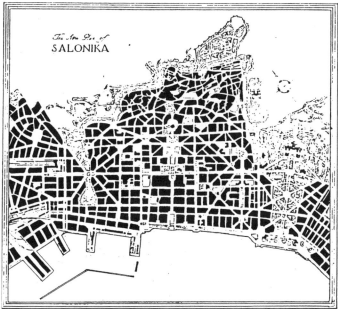

Figure 2. The new plan for the entire intra-muros city after the fire (the non-burnt area is at the top of the plan). Source: These plans, drawn by the author, are simplified illustrations of official documents. They circulated in many different versions in order to publicise the work of the International Commission of the Plan.

In an effort to preserve a part of the city's traditional character, as he perceived it perfectly in line with French planning ideas of the 1920s, Hébrard also proposed the integral conservation of the picturesque Upper City (which had survived the fire), as well as the rebuilding of the old covered markets (the bazaars), again in a neo-Byzantine style. But the conservation of the Upper City was indeed an exception; in no other case was any proposal made that favoured the preservation of old street or neighbourhood patterns or of architectural styles reminiscent of the city's oriental past; 500 years of history had to be erased and agreement on this point was unanimous.

But the new plan could not have been implemented without the support of legislation specially devised to meet the case. Old property boundaries within the devastated zone could not possibly be respected, nor could the existing plots be individually adapted to fit the new alignments, as had previously happened, and still happens nowadays, in Greece. (Figs 3 and 4)

Papanastassiou's solution was to set up a Property Owners' Association, incorporating all owners of land within the burnt-out zone. The entire area was then expropriated in the association's favour (Law 1394/1918). By this means, immediate compensation was not necessary, since former proprietors no longer owned any particular piece of land, but became shareholders in the total building land available. Former building sites were to be valued, and a price would be reached on the basis of the land register and of values for the three years before the fire. Owners were to receive a share certificate in the form of a special title deed. This certificate was non-transferable, but could be used as security for bank loans. (This was an attempt to prevent speculation and monopolization of the title deeds. In short, land prices were not to be freed, nor was property to be amassed in the hands of a few.)

After the new sites had been plotted, land for private rebuilding, which now belonged to the Property Owners' Association, would be subdivided into new plots in conformity with the approved city plan. The new building sites would be valued, by determining a minimum price according to the advantages of their situation, and sold off by open tender. Price increases were controlled and in the event of equal bids the original owner would have priority. Resale within three years was forbidden. Once all the property had been sold off, the profits would be shared equally between the Property Owners' Association and the Municipality of Thessaloniki (which would spend the money on laying out public spaces and on infrastructure).

PROBLEMS OF IMPLEMENTATION

Predictably enough, these proposals led to protests by political opposition groups, and also by local agents, namely the former property owners, the local authorities and the powerful Jewish community, the members of which composed the majority of the landowners and saw the proposals as an attempt to reduce their presence in the city.

With the exception of the Jewish community, whose arguments will be discussed later, the concerns of the opposing parties, which in any case did not question the overall logic of the redesign operation, focused on the following issues.

In Parliament, local representatives together with leaders of the opposition (the powerful Populist Party and some representatives of the Left) argued that the plan was over-ambitious in its formal aspects ('Thessaloniki is not Paris')[10] and too generous in terms of public space (the plan proposed 50 per cent, against 23 per cent before the fire). The Athens plan, providing narrower streets and fewer and less spacious squares, was used to make comparisons and support demands to modify the Thessaloniki plan to the advantage of private land. Local authorities backed the demands, thinking of the financial burden of building and maintaining public space and infrastructure.

Land owners and local businessmen objected to the size of the new plots, arguing that the local economy would not tolerate large properties (and the concomitant large sums of money that would have to be invested in the purchase of land). Refusing to cooperate with the government in the venture to encourage the infusion of capital and create larger (and more viable) units, they systematically boycotted the auctions, at the same time opposing competition with outside investors.[11]

The local authorities (the City Council) also supported the further division of the properties, fearing the emergence of 'collectivist practices' in land occupation habits.[12] On the other hand, they were enthusiastic about the modernization of the city, and also expected a significant increase in local taxes because of the new high-rise buildings to be erected. They argued that the municipal authority should play a leading role in the rebuilding process by constructing not only modern market halls to replace the unacceptable oriental covered bazaars, but also housing for the poor.

Though the latter idea was seriously considered,[13] it had to be abandoned when the French Allied authorities demanded that the City Council purchase the hospital facilities of the Armée d'Orient (which was leaving now that the war was over) in the eastern suburb. The demand was put forward as a precondition for a loan of four million drachmas from French banks for the municipal authority to repair the damage caused by the fire. The City Council was obliged to give way and pay up on receipt of the loan.[14] The hospital buildings were used to accommodate Jewish victims of the fire, and the City Council never again concerned itself with projects of housing for the poor.

It is worth looking in greater detail at the intervention of the large group of Thessalonian Jews in the rebuilding process. The fact that most of the ruined properties belonged to Jews, and that objections to the government's plans were put forward by the opposition in association with prominent members of the Jewish community (leagued together in the Landowners' Union),[15] put a distinctive complexion on the confrontation. Furthermore, the community's links with the Paris-based Alliance Israélite Universelle (AIU) and the Anglo-Jewish Organization meant that these two international bodies actively intervened on behalf of their fellow Jews in Thessaloniki, strengthening the impression that something out of the ordinary was going on.

Two questions have been asked at various times. Were Venizelos and the government turning against the Jews of Thessaloniki through the process of redesigning the city? And conversely, was the (not very significant) change made to the original plan due to Jewish objections, and were they therefore responsible for the famous 'missed opportunity to get a modern city' (a cliché often used in cases of replanning)?

These questions lurked in the background for many years, though they were never asked openly or in public since they touched sensitive spots in recent history with eventful and frequently tragic outcomes (for example the near-annihilation of Thessaloniki's Jews in concentration camps during the

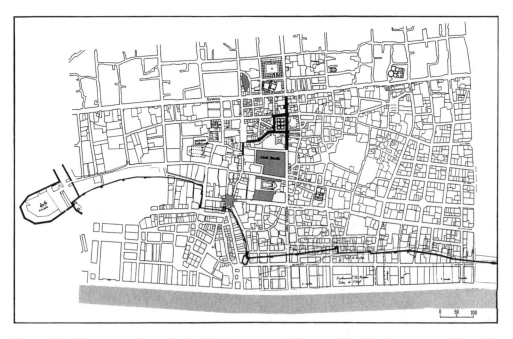

Figure 3. *Old property boundaries in the commercial part of the burnt-out zone. Plans of important buildings -churches, mosques, baths- and also of demolished sea walls have been included; covered commercial streets have been shaded. Source: plan prepared by author on the basis of cadastral documents (by block, originally at 1:500 scale), plans of buildings and old photographs*

Second World War). It is significant that the protagonists of the redesign project themselves devoted no more than a few lines to the subject in their political speeches. It is unclear whether the reason might have been that they did not want even to mention it or perhaps that they regarded it as part of other, more general issues that the replanning of the city and the revival of its economy raised?

Whatever the case, Papanastassiou skirted the issue in Parliament: 'This government has been unfairly accused of seeking, through the measures it wished to implement, to oust the population of Thessaloniki and replace it with another'. Prime Minister Eleftherios Venizelos briefly explained: 'You can be certain that it is our desire that the old property owners should own again, and all our efforts are directed toward this end, so that the old property owners of a certain religious faith should be re-established. Do not protest because I have had to discuss these matters several times in London. This accusation has been levelled against the government . . . We have therefore made every effort to ensure that not the slightest suspicion will persist that this is our intention'.[16]

The archives of the AIU (Alliance Israélite Universelle) in Paris contain data and documents that are quite enlightening about the demands and fears of the

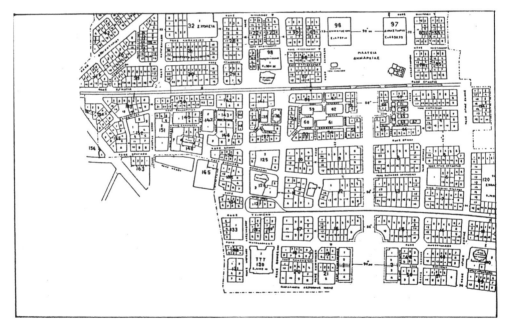

Figure 4. Subdivision of new plots in the (same as above) burnt-out area. Source: the plan was prepared by the Property Owners' Association and it was distributed to all potential buyers.

Thessalonian Jews, as well as their negotiations with the government.[17] The subject matter covers three broad areas: one group of documents describes the fire, the damage, and all the steps taken to look after the victims; another concerns the deliberations and the interventions 'against' the replanning of the city, covering the period from 1918 to early 1921; and a third includes newspaper articles about the rebuilding process with reference to current problems of implementing the plan.[18]

From the start, Joseph Nehama, who conveyed the views of the Thessaloniki community to the headquarters of the AIU in Paris and the powerful Jewish community in France, was against the Liberal government's Law 1394 and the International Commission's design proposals, and welcomed the changes effected by the Populist leader Gounaris' administration.[19] Nehama felt that the proposals were inspired by megalomania, and his main concern was financial. This was understandable, yet his lack of vision is striking here. It is interesting to see how, as the years went by and the rebuilding still had not begun, Thessaloniki's economic elite began to perceive how rational the plan was and to realize what a favourable effect it would have on the value of land. This is the main explanation for the fact that the new party in power did not significantly modify the plan, despite its leader's explicit election promises that he would annul it.[20]

The correspondence of the president of the community, J. Misrahi, contains letters including information about the ongoing negotiations with the government, excerpts from the special legislation for the rebuilding, preliminary reports on legislation, and an extract from the constitution concerning expropriation, all translated into French.[21] Seeking legal assistance from the Alliance on the crucial matter of expropriation,[22] Misrahi also submitted a number of documents relating to the steps taken by the property owners, their demands and how these were being asserted. The file is particularly revealing about how the various issues were raised.

The demands may be summed up as follows:[23]

* The property owners wish, first of all, to retain their plots, reduced proportionately by the amounts imposed by the new plan. Despite all that has been said on this subject, the owners feel that a system that combines reduced plots with partial and total expropriation, always with compensation, can resolve the problems in the most acceptable way.
* Nonetheless, if a serious and assiduous investigation shows this proposal to be unfeasible, the owners request that the government expropriate their land in accordance with the constitution.

Realizing that the government could not buy up the entire city centre, the property owners agreed not to demand that all the compensation be paid at once, but gradually. Finally, if neither of these solutions proved acceptable, the property owners proposed setting up a state-controlled cooperative and distributing the plots themselves, on condition that they could decide on the new plan and the building regulations in the centre.

Alongside these demands, they sought permission for the title deeds to be bought and sold freely.

Misrahi includes his own opinions in his letters, and notes that the only feasible proposal is expropriation: 'The government says that general expropriation is necessary. The property owners are almost ready to accept it. But they argue that there can be *no expropriation without immediate compensation*'. Commenting on the aspects of the law that provided for the sharing out of the (future) profits, he writes: 'There is so little faith in these profits that the victims of the fire would gladly give them to the government, if only it would agree to compensate them for the land at 1917 prices'.

It is interesting, and quite surprising, that the demands of the Thessalonian Jews (expropriation and monetary compensation, plus an unrestricted exchange of title deeds) would have led to the ownership of land in the centre of Thessaloniki completely changing hands; and this is precisely the objection the government raised with its interlocutors (who included the local MPs H. Cohen and N. Yermanos – an ardent opponent of the plan – among others). The government's rejection of the demands was based on the following arguments:

* Who would ensure that anyone who received compensation for expropriation would not leave the city?[24]
* If title deeds were bought and sold freely, how would it be possible to prevent the richer owners from forcing the poorer ones to sell to them (owing to difficult economic conditions, delays and so forth)? How, ultimately, would it be possible to prevent price rises?
* In either case, departure or rising prices, how would the rebuilding of the city be funded, how would it be financially provided for?

Studying this material it becomes apparent that the whole issue was polarized along two main lines. On the one hand, the opposing Thessalonian camps simply did not believe that the project to redesign the city could succeed amid the prevailing turmoil, and this lack of faith eventually expressed itself in opposition to the government. And on the other hand, there was a demand for economic freedom in reaction to the paternalistic reformism of the plan; freedom that would ultimately benefit the economically stronger (as indeed it manifestly did in the end).

The Liberal government rejected all the above arguments, except for the further subdivision of the properties. In Thessaloniki, the procedures for land registration and tendering were systematically boycotted, and thus rebuilding was blocked. Opposition to the plan soon became politicized and was used against the Liberal government by the Populist Party, which won the 1920 elections. The new prime minister, royalist Dimitrios Gounaris, hastened to assure the people of Thessaloniki that both the plan and the law of 1918 would be annulled.

In fact the retreat did not go so far. The urgent need for a modernized city and the opportunities offered to speculative capital by new plots and planning regulations had been clearly understood by potential investors, who eventually focused their objections on partial clauses in the 1918 law that sought to control speculation and protect the original small property owners. The plan remained, with the public spaces somewhat reduced (from 50 per cent to 42 per cent) and the building land subdivided into smaller individual plots (the number of which rose from 1300 to 2600).

With regard to the implementation law, major amendments modified basic clauses covering the purchase of new plots (new Law 2633/1921). The pretext was that the former owners should be protected against outside investors, and also that the freedom of individuals to dispose of their property as they wished should be guaranteed. Law 2633/1921 stated that

* The auctions were open only to bidders with title deeds in their possession. At the same time free sale of title deeds was permitted and numerous former property owners were driven to sell, as they considered themselves unable to buy the new plots five years after the fire.
* No maximum prices were fixed in the auctions, which were no longer secret, thus permitting unrestricted competition among bidders that resulted in high rises in land values.
* The profits were to be used to finance the reconstruction of the most expensive plots, located in the commercial sector, as the high land prices were expected to absorb all the capital available for the construction of buildings.

The changes that Law 2633/1921 effected upon Papanastassiou's Law 1394/1918 essentially encouraged speculation. Certainly the new law did not allow bidding by people who did not possess title deeds (which was loudly hailed as a 'victory for the Thessalonians'); but it permitted the unrestricted sale of title deeds, made the auctions open and the bidding public (which sent prices soaring), and abolished price ceilings.

As soon as the modifications came into effect, the boycott on auctions and rebuilding ceased. The Thessalonians accepted the changes without complaint, and the fiercely competitive auctions were over within two-and-a-half years (by mid-1924). However, although public opinion (duly manipulated) had originally given the modifications a favourable reception, it soon became clear that the fragile equilibrium between the interests of the community and the strictly controlled activity of private initiative (an equilibrium theoretically ensured by the original proposals of Law 1394/1918) had been destroyed. In fact the accounts from 2400 auctions (which showed a huge profit) reveal the accelerating pace of speculation.

The last letter on the subject in the Alliance archives was written in 1921 by Nehama, who took a very positive view of the Gounaris administration's changes to the Papanastassiou law. In fact, the sales records in the Thessaloniki Town Planning Office show that large numbers of the city's Jews took part in the auctions, clearly abandoning the boycott they had launched earlier. In the book of land purchases, which contains all the names of buyers up to April 1923, out of 3350 entries, 1931 (57.6 per cent) are manifestly Jewish, 980 (29 per cent) Christian, 405 (12 per cent) Muslim, five Armenian and 29 are company names.[25]

Many writers refer frequently to Nehama to support the argument that the Jewish community was badly hurt when Thessaloniki was rebuilt. In the last volume of his history of the Jews of Thessaloniki,[26] Nehama asserts that the redesign struck the community a severe blow; however he goes on to explain that this was because, by changing the spatial organization that had been in place for centuries, the new disposition of space triggered or hastened a restructuring of the community that had been brewing for some time anyway, but had been held back by the inertia of the physical aspects of the space. In the same book, which was written a considerable time after the fire and not published until 1978, Nehama takes a favourable approach to the redesign project. This volte-face from fierce opposition to the plan to a sober, perceptive interpretation of the sociological repercussions of the radical spatial changes should not be viewed as odd. A similar change may be noted as early as 1923 in the city's newspapers, which had supported Gounaris' changes.

The redesigning of the city, as proposed by the political party of the emerging bourgeoisie (the Liberals) intent on modernizing the space, originally came up against the landowners, whose political mouthpiece was the Populist Party, and left unmoved the working classes who were hoping, simply, that the rebuilding would bring them relief and work. However, the increased land values and the rationalized urban space introduced by the new plan did not ultimately go unnoticed by the economic elite, who by and large accepted it. The fundamental objections to the legislation covering the implementation of the plan had focused on the regulations that protected small landowners, and it was precisely these that were revoked by Law 2633/1921. In the whole affair of the redesigning of the city, the winners were the higher-income group, which was made up of all religious groups, with the Jews in the majority; and the losers were the small landowners, again with Jews in the majority. Also on the losing side were those who had been living in rented accommodation in the city centre who were forced to move to camps on the outskirts of the city (some 25,000 of them were Jews).

As early as 1918, Misrahi wrote: 'I do not believe that the plan intends to drive the Jews out, but it will de facto lead to their destruction'. By 1923 he had been proven wrong as the auctions took their course. Both the numerous purchases of sites by Thessalonian Jews and their major investments in buildings (which they commissioned and/or designed themselves) show that at the beginning of the 1920s Thessaloniki's Jews had no reason to fear that their presence in the city was in jeopardy.[27]

CONCLUSIONS

A careful review of the replanning operation presents the following conclusions.

As was to be expected, the acquisition of new plots and rebuilding in the historic centre were accompanied by the first signs of spacial stratification according to income group.[28] A modern society began to emerge in line with the new patterns of spatial distribution. Although the physical form of the modern city was a product of the new plan, all the reformist features of the new appropriation of urban space were severely modified to the profit of purely speculative attitudes.

Despite this major failure, other initial objectives were more successful. For example, the structure and form of the city were modernized with a low investment cost for the state, through the mobilization of local and nation-wide private capital. New, regular building plots, properly equipped, offered the opportunity to construct high-rise buildings of up to five storeys in the place of the traditional two-storey houses with gardens and the covered markets. The use of concrete was mandatory; and the Planning Commission offered ready-made plan types to new owners, proposing the optimum arrangement of internal space according to prescribed use and for maximum exploitation.

A great deal of private capital flowed into Thessaloniki from other parts of Greece and the diaspora, and this was invested in building, made attractive by modern planning advantages and high exploitation ratios.[29] The historically constituted spatial structure of the city was radically transformed: the traditional ethno-religious clusters disintegrated. People settled according to their economic capacity and social-professional preference and not according to their religious affiliation. Traditional activities were redistributed according to their revenue capacity and were either relocated in the new central district or forced to leave it.

Extensive reconstruction works revitalized the local economy, also offering jobs to increasing numbers of unemployed refugees, though this did not lead to a restructuring of the building sector. The production of urban space remained in the hands of small capital, engaged in the rebuilding of small plots of land endowed with the possibility of intensive development, using traditional techniques and production methods and an abundant non-specialized labour force. The profits were shared by landowners and entrepreneurs, turning the building sector and land speculation into the cornerstones of the growth of the city's economy. This has been the profile of Greek town planning ever since, and shows the limited potential of imports when they encounter local economic conditions.

The fate of imported planning concepts and tools for the replanning of Thessaloniki in 1917 is an eloquent illustration of the gap between the local society's intellectual and material readiness to receive them. Still, the powerful ideas that were imported, although only partially implemented, radically transformed the urban scenery and erased all features of the traditional city to the benefit of its highly valued 'Westernization'.

NOTES

1. For the first two parts, the paper draws mainly from Alexandra Yerolympos (1996) *Urban Transformations in the Balkans, 1820–1920,* Thessaloniki: University Studio Press.
2. It should be remembered here that similar transformations were also in progress in the Ottoman Empire, which had been undergoing reform since the 1850s. In fact, town remodelling was immediately regarded by Ottoman officials as an efficient and tangible means to express the State's will to modernize, and cities appeared as a terrain *par excellence* for the implementation of new policies with regard to urban space, activities and institutions.
3. Traian Stoianovic (1970) 'Model and mirror of the premodern Balkan city', *Studia Balkanica,* 3, Sofia, pp. 83–110; Nicolai Todorov (1977) *La ville balkanique sous les Ottomans,* London: Variorum Reprints; Bernard Lory (1985) *Le sort de l'héritage ottoman en Bulgarie: L'exemple des villes bulgares 1878–1900,* Istanbul: Isis Editions; Alexandra Yerolympos (1997) *Between East and West: Cities in Northern Greece During the Ottoman Reforms Era,* Athens: Trohalia (in Greek).
4. In their internal development, new regimes followed a similar general pattern, which opted for centralized bureaucratic monarchies and shifted political control from traditional local communities to the central authority of the capital city. See Barbara Jelavich (1983) *History of the Balkans, 18th and 19th Century,* Cambridge: Cambridge University Press, p. 298. We must also consider the urgent nature of the planning operations, as well as their powerful ideological connotations, especially in the making of the new capitals: Athens, Sofia and Belgrade had been insignificant cities with fewer than 10,000 inhabitants at the beginning of the nineteenth century, while in this period the great Balkan centres of the Empire had been Constantinople/Istanbul, Thessaloniki and Adrianople/Edirne.
5. It is no exaggeration to say that the replanning of Thessaloniki was the greatest planning operation ever undertaken in Greece and, as Pierre Lavedan asserts 'the first great work of twentieth-century European city-planning'; Pierre Lavedan (1933) 'L'oeuvre d'Ernest Hébrard en Grèce', *Urbanisme,* May, p. 159.
6. All central areas, including the busy commercial sector, were totally destroyed: modern shops and traditional bazaars, hotels, banks and warehouses, the post and telegraph offices, the city hall, the water and gas boards, European consulates, three important Byzantine churches, ten mosques, sixteen synagogues, the Chief Rabbi's residence, denominational, foreign and other private schools, newspaper offices and the homes of 70,000 people. A zone of 128 hectares had ceased to exist.
7. For the replanning of Thessaloniki, see Yerolympos (1996), op. cit., and Alexandra Yerolympos (1988) 'Thessaloniki before and after 1917: 20th-century planning vs 20 centuries of urban evolution', *Planning Perspectives,* vol. 3, no. 2, pp. 141–66.

8. Thomas H. Mawson (1927) *The Life and Work of an English Landscape Architect*, London: Richards; and Thomas H. Mawson (1918) 'The New Salonika', *Balkan News*, 29, 30, 31 January.

9. G. Wright and P. Rabinow (1982) 'Savoir et pouvoir dans l'urbanisme moderne colonial d'Ernest Hébrard', *Cahiers de la recherche architecturale,* 9, January.

10. *Journal of Parliamentary Debates* 1919, Athens: edited by the Greek Parliament, pp. 149–61.

11. See articles in the newspapers *(Efimeris ton Valkanion [Balkan Journal]* from 1918 to 1920) with interviews of prominent Thessalonians and statements by the Landowners' Union steering committee.

12. The Soviet revolution was all too recent; see the *Minutes of the Municipal Council of Thessaloniki*, 1919 and 1921, Thessaloniki City Hall.

13. Archive of the Municipality of Thessaloniki (hereafter AMT), Thessaloniki, *Minutes of the Meetings of the Municipal Council*, 24 April 1919 and 20 May 1919. A committee of councillors made up of architects and engineers drew up the relevant plans.

14. AMT, Thessaloniki, *Minutes of the Meetings of the Municipal Council*, 5 June 1919.

15. A private body set up in 1914. In 1918, the Landowners' Union was chiefly made up of Jews: Alliance Israélite Universelle (hereafter AIU), Paris, Archive AIU Grèce VII B 27 (Communauté de Salonique 1914–1935, see letter from Misrahi, 29 August 1918). In 1921, the Union was administered by a five-member committee made up of two Jews, two Christians and one Muslim: *Efimeris ton Valkanion (Balkan Journal)*, 3 January 1921.

16. *Journal of Parliamentary Debates*, op. cit., p. 159 (in Greek) and detailed reports by diplomats and political officials in the Historical Archive of the Greek Foreign Ministry, Athens, file 1918, A 5 (9) Jewish community.

17. The material relating to the fire of 1917 and the redesigning of the city is mainly to be found in the files containing the correspondence of Joseph Nehama, director of the Alliance school, and in the files containing the documents of the Jewish community of Thessaloniki, many of which – mainly accounts of the fire – are also written by Nehama.

18. Paris, Archive AIU, Grèce XVII E 202 b, c, d (Nehama 1914–15, 1915–21, 1916–17); Grèce VII B 27 (Communauté de Salonique 1914–35); Grèce II C 53–54 (Journaux de Salonique 1924–5).

19. See Paris, Archive AIU Grèce VII B 27, letter 23 January 1919 and letter 16 January 1921: 'Le nouveau gouvernement a, d'un tour de main, jeté à bas les élucubrations juridiques de M. Venizelos ainsi que les plans fastueux et mirifiques élaborés par des ingénieurs en chambre, qui, rêvant de faire de Salonique une ville merveilleuse, ne s'étaient pas souciés de tenir en compte les ressources de la population et ses possibilités'. (The new government has, at a stroke, knocked down the legal constructions of Mr Venizelos as well as the grandiose and fantastical plans elaborated by desk-bound engineers, who dreaming of turning Thessaloniki into a marvellous city did not concern themselves with the resources and the potential of the population.)

20. See Nehama's previous letter and the local newspapers during December 1920.

21. Paris, Archive AIU Grèce VII B 27, documents 21 and 29 August 1918.

22. By 'expropriation' is meant the transfer of an entire plot of land into the possession of the Property Owners' Association. The Greek constitution permits expropriation by the state for duly justified reasons of public benefit, on condition that the property changes hands only after full compensation has been made to the private individual.

23. Paris, Archive AIU Grèce VII B 27, doc. no. 2, Solutions proposées par les proprié-taires; doc. 29 August 1918.

24. See Misrahi's correspondence and *Journal of Parliamentary Debates,* op. cit., pp. 152–59.

25. See the Archive of the Thessaloniki Town Planning Office (section of the 'burnt zone', book of new buyers, minutes of the auctions). Investigation has shown that the book lists the buyers of land in four of the six sectors in the devastated zone. For one more sector (the city's main commercial quarter) investigation focused on the records of the auctions themselves. It is certain that the speculative frenzy that broke out over the plots in the commercial centre (around Venizelou Street) and in the Bazaar (Vlali, Vatikioti, Bezesten) was provoked equally by all the buyers, irre-spective of religious affiliation, and they all played a prominent part both in the auc-tions and in the constant transfers that followed the initial purchase of the plots. A random sample of contracts in the commercial quarter reveals that the same plot was transferred up to four times in two weeks! By 1928, more than 1500 buildings had been erected, i.e. two-thirds of the city centre. Meanwhile, there was an impres-sive flow of capital (for example investment in housing, public works and increased employment). *Annual Report of the National Bank of Greece, 1930.*

26. Joseph Nehama (1978) *Histoire des Israélites de Salonique,* vols VI and VII, Thessaloniki: Publications of the Jewish Community of Thessaloniki.

27. Vassilis Kolonas (1995) 'The rebuilding of Thessaloniki after 1917: architectural implementation', in *The Jews in Greek Territory: Historical Questions in the Longue Durée,* Athens: Gavriilidis Publications (in Greek).

28. The Records of the Property Owners' Association show that only 56 per cent of the total value of title deeds was used for the purchase of new plots. (It is impor-tant to note here that it is not known whether the title deeds were used by former owners or by new investors.) Of the remaining 44 per cent, 18.5 per cent were not used and were sold out after the end of auctions, and 25.5 per cent remained inactive in the hands of owners, who consequently lost all rights to former prop-erty or compensation.

29. Statistical evidence is included in the *Annual Reports of the National Bank of Greece,* 1928–1936.

CHAPTER 6

FROM 'COSMOPOLITAN FANTASIES' TO 'NATIONAL TRADITIONS': SOCIALIST REALISM IN EAST BERLIN

Roland W. Strobel
Independent scholar

At the close of the Second World War, Germany lay in ruins. Not only had its cities been destroyed during the course of the war, but as the result of postwar reorganization, most of its social, political and economic institutions were also demolished. The four sectors into which Germany and its capital city, Berlin, had been divided, were at a *Stunde Null* ('zero hour'); the two countries that emerged, East and West Germany, had to be rebuilt. It was during this period that Stalinism left on East Germany an indelible mark through what became known as 'socialist realism'. This imposed 'realignment' into socialist thinking not only encompassed a new architectural and urban design aesthetic, but also reformulated more deeply seated cultural views and traditions, such as the content and purpose of the arts, institutional behavior, and even popular perceptions of socialist and capitalist societies.[1] The new political leadership also used socialist realism as a means to establish a firm control over the development and direction of the fledgling state. It was one of the instruments used to consolidate the grip of Stalinism on East German society.

In the transitional period immediately after the fall of the Nazi empire, modernist architecture and urban planning were starting to re-establish themselves after being suppressed during the 1930s and the first half of the 1940s. The architectural and urban design guidelines embodied in socialist realism were Stalin's attempt to squash the re-emerging Modernism, supplanting its legacies with a new aesthetic that extolled the virtues of a socialist society. The adoption and dissemination of socialist realism were primarily through a re-education campaign that was directed not only at architects and planners under the guise of professional 'discussions' and articles in scholarly and trade journals, but also at the general public through the popular print media.

Socialist realism was pervasive wherever Stalin's dominion reached, and the Eastern Bloc countries produced several residential and industrial complexes, in some cases even entirely new cities, that followed these design guidelines. Nevertheless, outside the Soviet Union (where it had been adopted since the 1930s), the movement was relatively short-lived: introduced in East Germany in 1949, it effectively ended with Stalin's death in 1953.

This article examines how East German leaders used socialist realism as a nation-building tool, as well as the methods by which the movement was disseminated among the rank-and-file of East Germany's architects and urban planners. After sketching the historical backdrop in the late 1940s to the unfolding Cold War situation in Berlin and the precarious political situation in East Germany, the article reviews the main architectural and urban design characteristics associated with socialist realism. It investigates the local imposition of socialist realism within East Berlin by way of the city's inaugural project, the *Wohnzelle Friedrichshain/Hochhaus an der Weberwiese* (see below), which was used to introduce a new cultural and design aesthetic. This represents an interesting case where new authorities from within and without the country pressed local architects who were immersed in the Modern Movement and its universalist tenets to reconnect to local traditions from which they had been striving to move away.

HISTORICAL BACKGROUND

Through the course of the war, large sections of Berlin had been destroyed. The extremely high population density of the city was due to private land speculation and development during its rapid industrial-revolution growth in the latter half of the nineteenth century. Berlin's General Building Plan of 1862 had created a skeletal network of municipally funded streets, but because private developers chose not to subdivide the large blocks by building additional streets – instead preferring to place tenement houses behind one another within the deep blocks – the tenement districts became very dense in terms of building masses (Fig. 1). Rampant overcrowding of the tenements only served to worsen the situation.

Because of this overcrowding and the lack of what came to be considered as basic amenities (such as running water and toilets in the buildings), almost as soon as the tenements had been constructed, urban reformers repeatedly clamored for their destruction and for a general rebuilding of the city. Therefore, with much of the city lying in ruins after the war, Berlin's new governmental leaders and urban planners identified this as a unique opportunity to fundamentally overhaul the city.[2] Because Berlin's networks of streets and rail lines were inadequate and considered outmoded, planners devised rebuilding schemes around new transport systems that used freeways and the private motor car as the primary means of mass mobility. As for housing, since the building stock was seen as dense and largely unhygienic, many planners advocated that the city be rebuilt much less densely, in a modernist style.

Figure 1. *Typical structure of tenement districts. The Frankfurter Allee crosses from the bottom right to the top left. At the center is the old weaver's meadow (Weberwiese).*
Source: Senatsverwaltung für Bau- und Wohnungswesen V (Vermessung)

The blockade and splitting of Berlin

In the first years following capitulation, an increasing antagonism between the US and the Soviet Union caused Berlin to bear the brunt of the unfolding Cold War politics. For example, when a pro-Western government replaced, under free elections, the initial Soviet-installed postwar municipal government, and the inclusion of Berlin in the monetary reform of Western Germany strengthened the ties of Berlin's western sectors to West Germany, the Soviet Union retaliated in 1948 with a blockade of these western sectors for a period of 11 months.[3] When the blockade ended in 1949, Berlin emerged as a city divided, and two separate municipal governments laid claim to sole legitimacy for the right to govern the city.[4]

As a result of the above, the earlier opportunities for redesigning Berlin seemed lost. Although the various governments and other entities produced a myriad of widely divergent rebuilding plans that ranged from very conservative repairs to whole-scale demolition and reconstruction of the city, the lack of consensus even on basic issues meant that none of the plans were likely to be implemented. In addition, private landowners were already starting to rebuild on top of old foundations, and the city was therefore beginning to be re-erected largely as it had been prior to the war.

Ironically, and despite their separate development, the reconstruction plans eventually adopted by East and West Berlin were very similar (even if irreconcilable). The division of Berlin forced both sides to react quickly to popular pressures that demanded official rebuilding plans. As a result, both sides adopted plans that incorporated elements of modernist architectural and urban design ideas, without requiring such extreme actions as the razing of large portions of the city.

Since both municipal governments felt that the division of the city was only temporary, competition fueled the desire for each of them to adopt and begin to realize its own rebuilding plan, even if implementation was restricted to each government's respective half of the city. If nothing else, the blockade firmed up the use of Berlin by both sides as a showcase for Cold War political grandstanding. With the creation of separate West and East German states in 1949, West and East Berlin became intimately tied (politically, economically and socially) to their respective states. To the chagrin of the Soviets, as a result of the blockade, West Berliners suddenly viewed the Allied (American, French and British) troops not as an occupying force but as a protective shield against Soviet aggression. Similarly, West Germans saw the US as an amicable partner in rebuilding the country's economy. Ties between the Soviet Union and the East Germans also deepened, but the blockade and later events, such as the military intervention in the uprising of 17 June 1953[5] and the erection of the Wall in 1961, indicated that this relationship was to be based mainly on subservience and obsequiousness on the part of the East Germans.

A Cold War showcase

The division of Berlin had several consequences for the reconstruction of the city. First, as mentioned above, East and West Berlin adopted different reconstruction plans.[6] West Berlin used 'Plan 1948', as created by Karl Bonatz, while East Berlin quickly distanced itself from this plan and drafted the 'General Reconstruction Plan of 1949'. Although the plans were implemented very partially only within the confines of their respective sides, inconsistencies and conflicts between the plans were especially noticeable along the intra-city border. Because the boundaries of Berlin's boroughs (established – often haphazardly – in the city's political reorganization of 1920) were used as the basis for division, the new 'frontier' cut neighborhoods in half and separated industrial districts from residential bases. Consequently, East and West Berlin, as separate entities, were unbalanced in terms of the distribution of industry, commerce, wealth and social services, and neither plan allowed for the correction of these imbalances.

Second, the desire to extol the merits of each side's new societal organization (and to expose the pitfalls of the other) placed Berlin's two municipal governments in direct competition with each other. Both sides saw the rebuilding process as an ideal propaganda tool in which a new urban design would reflect its new societal values. Therefore, East and West Berlin, as a showcase for socialism and capitalism, respectively, embarked on projects such as housing for the working classes, the architecture and urban design of which purportedly expressed these values. The communication of these values to the residents of the entire city was of paramount importance because, even though politically split, the city was still physically integrated, and residents, at least for the time being, could still travel (and relocate) across the border.

Finally, the East and West German national governments, and to varying degrees the Soviet Union and the US, also became involved in the reconstruction of the city. Most of the involvement of the parent states was in the form of infusions of capital and material. However, East Berlin was also the country's capital city, thus involvement of the national government and the Soviet Union here was significant.

SOCIALIST REALISM: PROPAGANDA TOOL AND DESIGN GUIDELINES

Socialist realism and modernism were not necessarily antithetical architectural styles or urban planning concepts; rather, they could be seen as alternative approaches that sought to meet the needs of modern society.

For both architecture and urban planning, modernism, as crystallized in the 1933 'Athens Charter' of the International Congress of Modern Architecture (CIAM), used a fundamentally new aesthetic to visually underscore its departure from historical precedents. By rejecting the inherited notion of the city (which through the Industrial Revolution came to signify squalor and poverty in dense tenements on dark and crowded streets), modernism devised a fundamentally new type of urban environment. A strict separation of land uses and complex technological structures – high-rise towers set apart from each other by green spaces, and high-speed urban freeways – became its hallmarks.

In contrast, socialist realism, as defined and explained by Stalin, embraced the pre-Industrial Revolution urban form – a dense agglomeration of buildings and people – and attempted to recast the city in a way that made use of its advantages while alleviating its worst excesses. For example, though tenement housing is not bad *per se*, the way in which it devolved in capitalist societies – especially Berlin, with its multiple rear 'courtyards' that often crowded people and livestock together or included noxious land uses such as steel foundries – could be explained through the exploitation by greedy capitalist land developers. Dense cities were not the problem; nonetheless density should not be at the cost of the standard of living of the inhabitants. Thus socialist realism tried to 'preserve the unique face of Berlin, to care for and critically develop the national [architectural and urban design] traditions [it contained], while at the same time integrating new [constructions] that express [the socialist] societal system, and thereby introducing new elements into the urban setting'.[7]

Socialist realism is defined by the maxim 'socialist in content and national in form'. Specifically, 'socialist content' means that the city must be monumental in its proportions, timeless in its architectural styles, democratic in its accessibility, and well-functioning for all of society. 'National in form' means that the city's architectural styles should be drawn from local or national historical traditions. This does not entail a blind copying of past architectural styles, but a recycling of, or reference to them, in ways appropriate for a modern, socialist society. In general, socialist realism borrowed heavily from classicism, permitting – unlike modernism – ornamental details on the facades of buildings. Other characteristics of the style included baroque traditions, such as symmetry in building facades, the primary street, the urban square or plaza and closed, block-perimeter construction.[8]

In theory, socialist realism also demands that its cities be more than a series of strictly functional elements. As a work of art, the city must also express the political ideology of socialism. One of the ways this can be achieved is through the diligent development of the city's silhouette. For example, a socialist realistic 'high-rise' (or, more appropriately, mid-rise), allegedly symbolizes the magnificence and upward mobility of socialist society. According to this viewpoint, skyscrapers in capitalist cities lack human scale, and their lack of harmony with nature or surrounding structures demonstrates their antisocial and egomaniacal disposition. Cities like New York therefore express the exploitation and excess of the capitalist society. Because the socialist realistic high-rise is built in harmony with the existing cityscape and, especially when rooted in an ensemble, does not try to eclipse the surrounding structures, it serves as the focal point for its setting.

Even if the evidence for national or local variation is scarce, the idea of drawing on historical precedent was not to remain solely an academic activity. Instead, widely publicized public debates and grassroots discussions were to be used as avenues to develop a new understanding of, and foundation for, socialist society.[9] Functioning as a vehicle for public education and instruction, the architecture and urban design of socialist realism, as a form of public art, in this way regained the pre-twentieth-century notion that art existed primarily to inform, educate and elevate society.

FROM *WOHNZELLE* TO *HOCHHAUS*:
THE LOCAL IMPOSITION OF SOCIALIST
REALISM IN EAST GERMANY

Modernist precursor: the Wohnzelle Friedrichshain

East Berlin's first official rebuilding project, the *Wohnzelle Friedrichshain* (Residential Cell Friedrichshain), was a veritable resurrection of the modernist ideas popularized during the 1920s. Reconstruction would depart radically from the tenement settlements: buildings destroyed during the war would not be rebuilt; those left standing would eventually be torn down; and the State, either through people's collectives or municipally owned contractors, would replace private builders to ensure the end of the squalid housing conditions that had characterized Berlin's tenements in the past.

In a setting of trees and greenery, the design of the *Wohnzelle* embodied modernist ideas in architecture and urban design. Several apartment buildings, ranging from three to six stories, were to be lined up in north-south and east-west directions, proportionately spaced to ensure maximal exposure to sunlight. Six blocks of 180 single-family 'L'-shaped residences with yards would provide low-density housing for families with children. Two squares, a market place, a school and a 'plaza of social life' would be the main elements of the cell. To underscore the bucolic setting, streets and parking structures would be restricted to the periphery of the cell, and access to the interior would be provided only by walkways and bicycle paths. The population would be limited to 5000 people, based on the assumption that 10 per cent of these would be of school age, as 500 children were deemed necessary to run a school efficiently.

Work on the *Wohnzelle* began at a feverish rate. On 4 October 1949, three days after Hans Scharoun (Berlin's former Building Commissioner who had been appointed to the Soviet-installed government) made the first sketches of the cell's layout, an associate, Ludmilla Herzenstein, completed plans for the first phase of the project (Fig. 2). Time was of the essence because the East Berlin government wanted to capitalize on the advantage in materials and supplies it had over West Berlin, the supplies of which had been perilously depleted through the blockade. But perhaps even more importantly, the laying of the cell's cornerstone, as well as the renaming of the street (from Frankfurter Allee to Stalinallee) upon which the cell bordered, were already scheduled to take place on 21 December 1949 – Stalin's seventieth birthday.

Construction was progressing nicely when Walter Ulbricht, Deputy President of the ruling German Socialist Unity Party (SED), suddenly put a stop to the *Wohnzelle* in July 1950.

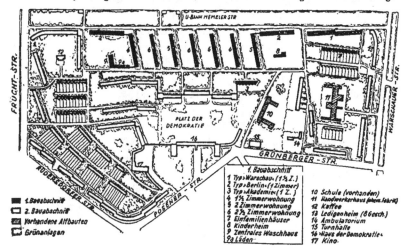

Das Gesicht der ersten Wohnzelle

In diesem Frühjahr beginnen die Arbeiten / 576 moderne Wohnungen für die Werktätigen

Figure 2. The Wohnzelle Friedrichshain as developed by
Scharoun/Herzenstein. It was officially presented on 8 January 1950 in
Berliner Zeitung.
Source: Berliner Zeitung 8 January 1950

Consolidation of Political Power and Change in Urbanism

Although several buildings of the *Wohnzelle* were already under construction, two unrelated developments caused the SED leadership to abandon the project. First, the heavy-handedness of the Soviet military during the blockade turned popular opinion against the Soviet Union as well as the political leadership of the SED within Berlin. Scores of East Berlin residents and refugees from the eastern provinces, including members of the SED, fled to the western sectors, and many eventually moved on to West Germany. Realizing that a new housing program based on Bauhaus ideas was not enough to recapture the high moral ground, the party leadership felt the need to find new ways to stop the mass exodus.

Second, as the émigrés who went to the Soviet Union during the Third Reich and the war returned to East Berlin, they expressed shock and dismay at the reconstruction plans. In particular, Lothar Bolz, a returning exile who had been appointed as East Germany's Minister of Reconstruction, was alarmed at the design of the *Wohnzelle*. Knowing that Stalin despised modernist architecture, Bolz tried to persuade East Berlin's architects and political leadership to substantially modify the project. When his attempts were rebuffed by the architects, he sought from Ulbricht an explanation. Bolz argued that the *Wohnzelle* was based on an outdated and reactionary 'Garden City' paradigm that stemmed from England and America. Soviet urban design, i.e. socialist realism, in contrast, was progressive because it satisfied the aesthetic needs of the people. Therefore, Bolz stated, it should form the basis for a new German architecture.[10]

Ulbricht, quick to grasp control of the SED and East Germany, used the celebration of Stalin's seventieth birthday to help rectify the situation. Traveling to Moscow as the official East German delegate, Ulbricht outlined the political and reconstruction problems facing East Berlin and solicited Stalin's advice.[11] Stalin responded on both counts: first by endorsing him as the sanctioned leader of the SED; and second by giving him a crash course on the architecture and urban design of socialist realism. Furthermore, Stalin suggested Ulbricht send a delegation of architects and planners to Moscow so that they could be instructed on the experiences and principles of proper Soviet architecture and planning.[12]

On his return, Ulbricht readily complied; he assembled a delegation that included some of East Germany's most prominent architects and planners, which he sent to Moscow for six weeks in April and May 1950. They presented to their Soviet colleagues their plans for the reconstruction of East Berlin as a series of residential cells. Dismayed by what they saw, the Soviet architects responded: 'Obviously we value Germany's urban planning traditions more highly than you do in Berlin . . . One should not want to strive for something new without having an internal need'.[13] This 'internal need' was to rediscover building traditions beyond those that flowered during the Weimar Republic, most notably the city's early nineteenth-century neo-classical architecture by Schinkel, Langhans and Gilley.

Explaining by way of examples from the Soviet Union's vast and largely unhappy experiences with modernist architecture and urban design, the Soviet colleagues outlined what was wrong with this style. Design-related problems that did not appear on the neighborhood scale became evident on a larger scale. Berlin's reconstruction under the current plans threatened to repeat the same mistakes: gross economic inefficiency by denying that land values in the center of the city were higher than at the periphery (i.e. the center of the city should be more dense); monotonous and unvarying building designs in residential complexes that caused depression, suicide and other psychological problems among the residents; and finally, utter disregard for the city's individual topographical, cultural or social identity. Instead, the Soviet architects recommended that Berlin's reconstruction plans pay particular attention to the city's historic housing type (the tenements) and existing land values, striving to rebuild within the old framework as compactly as hygienic standards would allow while eradicating existing shortcomings such as an incompatible mix of land uses.[14]

In other words, the East German architects were instructed to do an about-face: they were to distance themselves from the reform ideas of the 1920s and adopt the Soviet ideology for urban reform. Realizing that these marching orders were not open to debate, the delegation remained in the Soviet Union for over six weeks studying the architectural styles, construction methods and urban design principles of socialist realism, and together with their instructors they formulated the 'Sixteen Principles of Urban Planning', a manifesto that based East Germany's rebuilding program on the Soviet model.[15]

On returning home, the East German delegates disseminated the new building guidelines among their colleagues with similar tactics to those the Soviets had used on them – through the guise of a 'discussion'.[16] Although many East German architects were strongly critical of the 'Sixteen Principles', Minister of Reconstruction Bolz approved only the most minor of changes to their wording. Therefore, with new guidelines in place by mid-1950, Ulbricht stopped work on the *Wohnzelle* and announced the first new demonstration project: the *Hochhaus an der Weberwiese* (High-rise on the Weaver's Meadow). Located directly on the site of the *Wohnzelle*, the new architectural style would symbolically kill modernism's germinating cell and unmistakably signal the new architectural direction of East Germany.

Towing the party line

The year 1950 was consumed with discussion among East German architects and urban planners of the 'Sixteen Principles' and passage of the Reconstruction Law (*Gesetz über den Aufbau der Städte in der DDR und der Hauptstadt, Berlin*, or simply *Aufbaugesetz*) that established socialist realism as the basis for the reconstruction of East Berlin. At the third Party Conference of the SED on 22 July 1950, the same day that construction workers were celebrating the completion of the first buildings of the *Wohnzelle*, Walter Ulbricht declared an end to the 'egg-crate', i.e. modernist, architectural style. In his speech, he made the following remarks:

> The most important accomplishment is that out of the ruins of the cities that were destroyed by the American imperialists, new ones are arising that are more beautiful than ever. This is particularly true for our capital, Berlin. The experts should begin with the concern for the people in their urban planning duties, as well as in their relation to work, dwelling, culture, and recreation. During the Weimar period building complexes were constructed in many of our cities whose architectural designs do not address the wishes of the public, and that do not correspond to the national characteristics. Instead, these buildings were the result of formalistic conceptions of a set of architects who transferred the primitive nature of factory buildings onto residential structures. This barracks style was further developed under Hitler's fascism.

Certain architects, especially those in the Division of Construction in Berlin's municipal government, wanted to play down the importance of the capital by building small houses, and rebuild portions of central city according to the guidelines used for peripheral regions. The basic mistake these architects made is that they do not tie into the structure and architecture of Berlin, but through their cosmopolitan fantasies, they believe that one should build houses in Berlin that could just as well be situated in the South African landscape.[17]

Party conferences, architectural meetings and literature, and even the popular media were all used to disseminate the ideas of socialist realism to the rank-and-file architects and urban planners. Scores of articles written by many well-known East German architects and political leaders appeared, particularly in *Deutsche Architektur*, East Germany's principal monthly architectural journal. Towing the party line of socialist realism, not only in the form of designs and drawings but also in terms of the new hierarchical arrangement of society as a result of the conversion to socialism, made dissension and non-compliance increasingly risky.

It seems that no architectural detail was too small to escape the attention of the purveyors of socialist realism. For example, Kurt Liebknecht, president of East Berlin's newly created *Bauakademie*, addressed the question on the correct form of windows, i.e. horizontally or vertically oriented, in an article in *Neues Deutschland*, the official newspaper of the SED.[18] And an apparently private rebuttal from a Dr Graefrath prompted Liebknecht to fire off another article, this time in *Deutsche Architektur* and intended for the architectural community. Liebknecht wrote:

It is important to make note that the large participation of wide circles of the people on significant sub-problems of architecture is especially welcome, because it demonstrates the openness of our workers and their feelings of responsibility with respect to our cultural development. These contributions have given us, particularly the architects, impetus for new and livelier discussions, and thereby helped us speed up the clarification of important questions in architecture. German architecture, upon which our best architects are working, has a totally new quality, when compared to all former architectural epochs, and especially the building epoch of imperialism . . . Our architecture stands in the strongest contrast to the 'architecture' of imperialism, which tries to misuse its arch reactionary goals for the interests of a small band of unscrupulous hyenas of finance and industry . . .

The socialist architecture of the Soviet Union gives us wonderful examples for the recasting of cities, especially its capital city, Moscow. A characteristic trait of socialist architecture is that the single element, the single building, integrates itself in an organic fashion into the overall picture, and that each building, through the heightening of its artistic architecture, contributes to the beauty of the city. In Soviet architecture, individual buildings and their larger urban design form an inseparable artistic union . . .

We are no longer hindered by the property boundaries of private capitalism, by closed-minded views, or by philistine interests in the solutions of [architectural and urban design] questions. The main boulevards of capitalistic cities, especially the streets of its proletarian sections, are usually comprised of indistinguishable and systematically lined up rows of narrow tenements, whose firewalls embody the ugliness of this world . . .

If one begins with the total composition of the street, it is possible to find the correct solutions to all questions of architecture, among which is the form of the windows. The window is the most often repeated architectural element of a building, and is, thus, in the apartment complexes of large cities, of exceptional importance. . . .

In my prior article I remarked that I do not consider the question of window forms to be an elemental question. But I also expressed at the same time that I consider the tall window to be that window form upon which we should direct our attention because it is a satisfying form, not only in a technical perspective, but also in an artistic one. Pointing this out was necessary because the wide window played a paramount role in formalistic architecture, which I do not, at all, consider to be a coincidence. This fact has doubtlessly led to an abandonment and an undeserved discrediting of the tall window even among the general public. Dr Graefrath recommends we employ the low, wide window. But he, in no way, offers a convincing reason. The multi-storied apartment buildings from the Weimar Period, which favored the use of the wide window, cannot convince us of the 'beauty' of this window form. To the contrary: they are an example of something obviously frightfully ugly. No one will deny that these apartments are cold and loveless boxes of a pessimistic time, and that this expression is largely determined by the unsightly wide window. Yes, comrade Dr Graefrath, due to this, we are in favor of the tall, rectangular window, because it allows more light into our rooms that have taller ceiling heights, because it complies with our good and venerated tradition, because this window restores to us the character of the apartment house, and because it is a main element of our upwardly-striving architecture . . .[19]

This article is characteristic of the many 'instructional' articles, often following a basic formula. The effect of such articles and public criticisms was multi-fold: first, they inculcated and explained the values embedded in socialist realism; second, they demonstrated that the Soviet Union could always be relied upon for the correct solution; third, they exposed the fallacy of following Western or modernist examples; fourth, they provided both technical and artistic explanations and solutions for the problem at hand; and finally, they often embarrassed specific, and often well-known nonconforming individuals for their unabashed outspokenness. Of course, looking to the Soviet Union for the correct solutions gave the further insinuation that by questioning the direction East Germany's leaders were taking, one was indirectly questioning the wisdom and authority of Stalin himself.

Nevertheless, by the end of 1950, the break with modernist architecture was still far from complete. As tenants moved into the first (and only) buildings of the *Wohnzelle* in early 1951, a photo was printed on the cover of the East German monthly technical journal *Planen und Bauen*, heralding the houses as the grand beginning of the new 'Five-Year Plan'. Shocked by this endorsement, Liebknecht published a series of articles in *Neues Deutschland* in which he unequivocally derided the 'cosmopolitan' architecture of the modernist style.[20] In his lead article on 13 February 1951, he reprinted the photo of the *Wohnzelle* that had been used in *Planen und Bauen*, and placed a photo of a Soviet apartment building in the socialist realist style (Figs 3 and 4) directly beside it. The photo captions stated the Party's official position in no uncertain terms.

Having seemingly rooted out (or rather forcibly converted) the last remaining proponents of modernist, functionalist and 'cosmopolitan' architecture, Ulbricht commissioned the *Bauakademie* architects Hermann Henselmann, Richard Paulick and Hans Hopp to draw up new plans for the *Wohnzelle* area. They were to develop new urban and architectural designs

Figure 3. *The building of the newly erected Wohnzelle as depicted in Neues Deutschland on 13 February 1951. The original caption read: "The houses along the Stalinallee built by the Baubetreuung Berlin are a typical example of the erector-set style [Baukastenstil] that can no longer be condoned for our workers."*
Source: Neues Deutschland 13 February 1951

in keeping with socialist realism. However, when the Central Committee and several leading architects reviewed the initial drafts of the *Hochhaus* on 25 July 1951, the assembly was flabbergasted: instead of conquering 'formalism' and 'cosmopolitanism', their designs seemed to champion these unsanctioned ideas. Henselmann and Paulick were strongly reprimanded for their work and ordered to devise new designs in keeping with socialist realism immediately.

This reprimanding was not, however, in the form of a simple and private chastisement, but again made known throughout East Germany via an article in *Neues Deutschland* by Central Committee member Rudolf Herrenstadt. An excerpt of this article is reproduced here since Herrenstadt's manner exemplified the character of these public criticisms:

Figure 4. *A building in the Stalin-approved socialist realist style as depicted in the same issue of Neues Deutschland on 13 February 1951. The original caption read: "One of the many apartment buildings that was erected in the last fifteen years along Moscow's main boulevards that does not only fulfill its function, but also addresses the sense of beauty of the people."*
Source: Neues Deutschland 13 February 1951

These and similar charges [of formalism and cosmopolitanism] were presented to our architects. How did they respond? Let us not do a disservice to our architects and reveal the ending right away. The discussion on 25 July ended as follows:

The representatives of the Central Committee: 'We need satisfactory designs as soon as possible. When can we have them?'

'In two months.'

'Two months is too long.'

'How much time will you give?'

'Eight days.'

'Eight days! That's impossible. What is the outermost limit?'

'Eight days.'

Silence. They look at each other and then:

'Okay, in eight days the drawings will be ready.' (On Wednesday, 1 August, the eight days will be up. *Neues Deutschland* will report on the outcome.)

The next day the same people paid a visit to the studios of the *Bauakademie*. It turned out that Professor Paulick did not need eight days but only 24 hours to develop a new sketch that still needs improvements, but unmistakably tows the new, healthy line. It also turned out that a whole row of architects is already working on new designs in the new spirit with considerable success. And a characteristic conversation – again in the studio of Professor Paulick – took place.

The members of the Central Committee: 'How do you reconcile these progressive designs on which you are working with those of the egg-crate model you showed us yesterday?'

Answer: 'Not at all . . .'

'If we had agreed to your egg-crates yesterday, would you have built it? Or would you have protested against your own models?'

'If the Party had decided it should be built, I would have built it.'

'Do you understand that your behavior is inconsistent?'

'Of course I understand that. But do you also understand that one only develops slowly, that in the course of the last year I have learned a great deal, that one does not cast off all egg crates at once?'

'You are right.'[21]

This had a chilling effect not only on the rest of the architectural cadre in East Germany, but also on all organs of the State and society, and gave a strong warning to all individuals who were not in step with official policy. Furthermore, by educating the masses on architecture and other tangible products of socialist realism, each East German resident could observe (and, ostensibly, report to Party representatives) anyone who was not following official policy.

As for the *Hochhaus*, the new drawings were ready for presentation to the Central Committee five days later, and Henselmann's design was approved for construction (Fig. 5). On 1 September 1951, ground breaking took place even before the drawings were finished, and the topping-off celebration was held a mere 141 days later on 19 January 1952.

The progress of the construction of the *Hochhaus* became an event of national importance, and *Neues Deutschland* dedicated a special series of articles on the building, continually extolling socialist realism as the new foundation for architecture and urban design. Amid great fanfare, political speeches and general celebration, Friedrich Ebert, mayor of East Berlin, ceremoniously handed over the keys to the new 65-square-meter apartments on 1 May 1952 to thirty working-class families, an architect, a policeman and a teacher.

In accordance with socialist realism's tenet of recycling past architectural styles, the *Hochhaus* made direct links to Schinkel's *Feilnerhaus* not by copying, but, as Henselmann described it, by 'critically developing' details of the house's facade such as the use of ceramic tile around the windows (compare Figures 6 and 7). Furthermore, through the adaptation of past building styles, Berlin's gray and 'Prussian' tone was to become more colorful, bright and uplifting. However, all new constructions were to remain true to the city, 'captured in the breeding grounds of its traditions, with the inheritance of its slowly growing and reasoned culture, here and there reminiscent of Schinkel, not slavishly copied, but instead recalling the aura of "Berlin" that we know so well'.[22]

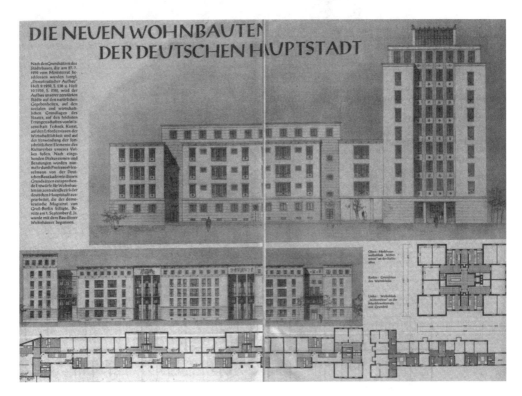

Figure 5. *Henselmann's plan and design for the Hochhaus an der Weberwiese in the socialist realist style.*
Source: Demokratischer Aufbau, March 1952, p. 76

Figure 6. *Schinkel's Feilnerhaus.*
*Source: Carl von Lorck, Karl Friedrich Schinkel (Berlin: n.p., 1939), p. 73,
reproduced in Johann Friedrich Geist and Klaus Kürvers, Das Berliner
Mietshaus: 1945–1989 (Munich: Prestel, 1989), p. 335*

Figure 7. Facade detail of the Hochhaus an der Weberwiese.
Source: Photo by the author

FROM *HOCHHAUS* TO STALINALLEE: THE BRIEF GLORY OF SOCIALIST REALISM

Model project: the Hochhaus an der Weberwiese

The *Hochhaus* ensemble comprises a nine-story mid-rise tower and two flanking buildings five and seven stories tall (Fig. 8). Constructed in 1951/52, the 'L'-shaped ensemble blends into its setting among the tenements and the *Wohnzelle Friedrichshain*.[23] Despite its mid-rise tower being somewhat taller than the surrounding tenements, the overall scale of the buildings is comparable as the flanking buildings copy the area's predominant five-storey height. Similarly, the setbacks from, and their orientations to, the street (and the adjacent park) generally replicate typical tenement patterns.

Exemplary of socialist realism, the *Hochhaus* employs a style that draws on Berlin's classicist era of the early 1800s. For example, the facade of the tower uses both stucco and fine ceramic tile. This decorative tile covers the recessed middle segments of the building, giving the tower a feeling of upward movement, a movement strengthened by the 'standing' orientation of the windows. This verticality is further accentuated by the filigreed tile edging of the building's crown, which gives the tower a flair that is not uncommon

Figure 8. *The setting of the Hochhaus an der Weberwiese project after completion.*
Source: Landesarchiv Berlin-Breitestraße

to the tenements, though here expressed in new ways. The attractiveness of the flanking buildings is deferential to the tower, even though they boast columns rising over four floors to support reliefs of happy children and burly workers.

The general demeanor of the site is attractive and inviting. The buildings frame the park, which includes a small pond, trees, walkways and benches for the pedestrians. The landscaping makes the site much greener than typical tenements and provides opportunities for children to play while remaining under the watchful eyes of adult users of the park. The ensemble only slightly modified the original street pattern, and its land uses are primarily residential and recreational (there are two stores on the tower's ground-floor), which is in contrast to the mix of land uses often found in Berlin's tenements during the Industrial Revolution.

The architectural style and urban design of the *Hochhaus* break with those of the *Wohnzelle*. For example, while the modernist strip buildings of the *Wohnzelle* try to establish a new order and visual appearance in the city, the *Hochhaus* emulates its tenement neighbors. Its buildings show their ornate facades to the street, and the harmonious arrangement with the existing structures ties the ensemble into the neighborhood, the tower even creating a visual reference point in its skyline.

The park, from which the project derives its name, is also significant; as a place to read, relax, play or stroll, with its benches and walkways it is decidedly public, and the encounters are of an urban nature. The open spaces of the adjacent *Wohnzelle*, in contrast, seem disconnected and uninviting since there is no outdoor furniture and the ability and desirability for the general public to enter is ambiguous.

Propaganda icons: Hochhaus and Stalinallee

Because the *Hochhaus* was a pilot project for the *Stalinallee*, a much larger and costlier housing project, the East German leadership announced a 'National Construction Program' (*Nationales Aufbauprogramm*) to raise money as well as awareness for the construction projects. Citizens were encouraged to donate either their spare time to work shifts on the *Hochhaus*, or a percentage of their earnings from their normal job. To encourage voluntary contribution, many of the *Hochhaus'* apartments were to be allocated on a lottery system, where chances to win were based on the number of shifts worked or amount of money donated to the program. The lottery was publicly announced in *Neues Deutschland*, and the newspaper kept East Berlin and the rest of the country informed on the current stage of the *Hochhaus'* construction. Human-interest stories on the 'hero of the workplace' (*Held der Arbeit*) increased public curiosity, and placed in the national spotlight individuals who had, typically, worked an inordinate number of shifts or endured extreme hardships to be able to contribute to the program.

The *Hochhaus* tower became a national icon for the socialistic reconstruction of the nation. Speeches by public officials derided the 'cosmopolitan' *Wohnzelle* and praised the new socialist architecture that was rising in its place. Soon, likenesses of the *Hochhaus* tower could be seen everywhere with slogans encouraging all residents of the nation – even those in West Berlin – to pool their resources and help create the socialist basis of the country (Fig. 9). Even school children could contribute to the national effort by depositing their lunch money into special piggy banks in the form of the *Hochhaus* tower, which were set up in each classroom.

The tower gained further recognition as a national icon through its lavish construction and dedication celebrations. Despite construction cost over-runs, the city government threw a party at the topping-off ceremony of the tower that included members of East Berlin's two opera companies as entertainers.[24]

The propaganda value of the *Hochhaus* was not just aimed at residents in East Berlin, but at West Berliners too. Claiming that the media (radio, print) in the western sectors were disseminating malicious misinformation about life in the Soviet sector, the East Berlin municipal leadership went as far as to organize exhibitions and bus tours for residents of West Berlin to see for themselves how the socialistic state was rebuilding the city.[25]

However, though it served as the icon for the 'upswing of socialism' (*Aufbau des Sozialismus*), the *Hochhaus* was soon eclipsed, both figuratively

Figure 9. The Hochhaus an der Weberwiese as an icon for the National Construction Program of Berlin 1952. Text on the poster: It is not hard, purrs the bear, so keep apace and build with us. Our successes in April: 4,376,130 bricks salvaged, 702 tons of rubble reclaimed, 65,557 cubic meters of waste disposed of.
Source: Gerhard Puhlman, Die Stalinallee: Nationales Aufbauprogramm 1952 (Berlin [DDR]: n.p., 1953)

and literally, by the Stalinallee, East Berlin's largest example of socialist realism. Just when the *Hochhaus* was enjoying the zenith of its public awareness, public attention shifted to the building projects along the Stalinallee. Even though the *Hochhaus* lay only 100 meters to the south, the almost two-kilometer length of the Stalinallee dwarfed the *Hochhaus* which, as a result, soon slipped out of the public eye (Fig. 10).

The buildings of the Stalinallee were not only taller and more elaborately decorated than those of the *Hochhaus*, but, keeping in line with the tenets of socialist realism, they were endowed with a much greater symbolic value. The Stalinallee (formerly, and once again today, called Frankfurter Allee) was Berlin's main thoroughfare to the east and, reputedly, the avenue over which the Russian army marched into Berlin during the Second World War. To commemorate this historical significance, the Stalinallee was widened to 90 meters, and the architecture and urban design of the housing (with commercial uses on the ground floor) were correspondingly monumental in scale.

Figure 10. *The Hochhaus an der Weberwiese eclipsed, figuratively and literally, by the Stalinallee. This photo shows the three building phases: on the right is the original Wohnzelle Friedrichshain, in the center the Hochhaus an der Weberwiese, and on the left, a portion of Stalinallee under construction.*
Source: Landesbildstelle Berlin (West) II/3843, reproduced in Geist and Kürvers (1989), p. 348

CONCLUDING REMARKS

The architectural and urban planning style of socialist realism remains unmistakable even today in the urban fabric of Berlin (and East Germany). Most buildings erected in this style are even protected by being listed on historic registers. Their worth is reflected in their value as real estate and their desirability as residences.

It is interesting to note that one can speak of socialist realism as a distinct 'style' across all former Eastern Bloc countries, even though the intent was to incorporate local architectural traditions to develop a country-specific or even region-specific architectural and urban design form that blended with historical antecedents. Perhaps this can be partly attributed to its short life: socialist realism, although never officially revoked in East Germany, was quickly abandoned after Khrushchev assumed power in the Soviet Union in 1953 and ordered the discontinuation of these large and costly building projects. Instead, Khrushchev embraced the advantages that could be gained through modernistic buildings and modern building technologies. With slogans such as 'bigger, better, cheaper', he favored mass production of entire neighborhoods and urban districts (precisely those objects and styles that engendered the negative social consequences that led Stalin to abandon modernism) over the principally handcrafted, and therefore slow and expensive to build ensembles of socialist realism.[26]

But despite its short lifespan, socialist realism did leave a physical presence in East Germany through the major projects scattered across several of the larger cities, and had unmistakable political and social effects. Ulbricht used socialist realism as one means to consolidate political power, thereby being enabled to reorient and recast East Germany into a socialist nation. The ability to detect who was unquestioningly towing the party line was made much easier because the officially approved products and manners of behavior, i.e. subservience to official policy, were widely known and easily discernible. Also, the ubiquitous use of 'criticism and self-criticism' in socialist countries, as well as the educating of the general populace to recognize and employ socialist realism in their daily life, made the adoption and dissemination of this style all the more pervasive.

Finally, the methods by which socialist realism was disseminated are particularly noteworthy. This architectural style imposed a new aesthetic that, although it claimed to revere national traditions (which, in many ways, it did), also chose to be very selective about which national traditions it would honor. In addition, even though Stalin made no secret of his derision of modernism, the speed and thoroughness with which socialist realism was successfully disseminated among the rank-and-file architects and urban designers in East Germany is surprising. This may be explained (at least in part) by the pervasiveness of the indoctrination and fear of public exposure for individuals not compliant with official policy. Alas, for many it may have also been more comfortable to simply follow the new guidelines after the ravages of war and East Germany's tumultuous postwar political and social circumstances. Whatever the cause, socialist realism, as a cultural movement as well as an architectural style, played a vital and indelible role in the early years of East Berlin's reconstruction – a role that can be intriguingly understood as an 'imposition of localism'.

NOTES

1. For a full coverage of the reach of socialist realism, see Thomas Lahusen and Evgeni Dobrenko (1997) *Socialist Realism without Shores*, Durham, NC: University of North Carolina Press.
2. Note, however, that while extensive, the destruction was far from total in most of the city's districts. This fact did not prevent many planners from acting as if it were total.
3. The Soviet Army did not blockade Berlin's western sectors solely because of the outcome of the municipal election, but as the result of many factors, the main – or at least final – one being the monetary union of the western sectors which deliberately excluded the Soviet (eastern) sector of Berlin and Germany.
4. The Soviet Union's tight control over the city had begun to erode after democratically held municipal elections installed a pro-Western Parliament. Although the Soviet Military Administration was able to block Ernst Reuter (of the Social Democratic Party, or SPD) from being elected mayor, it was unable to retain other top governmental positions to which the Soviet administration had appointed members of the newly created Socialist Unity Party (SED). When the Western Allies (France, Great Britain and the US) announced a monetary reform and economic union of the zones they occupied in Germany to the exclusion of the Soviet zone in March 1948, the Soviets feared that Western Berlin would be integrated into Western Germany, as well as cause a devaluation of its own Eastern German currency. Thus, in a move designed to drive out the Western Allies from Berlin and regain its control over the city, the Soviet Military Administration closed the land and water avenues. American and British forces responded by supplying the city with food and other provisions from the air, thereby ensuring the survival – if nothing more – of the Western sectors. Realizing that the blockade had failed, the Soviet Union restored land and sea passage on 12 May 1949, nearly eleven months later.
5. 17 June 1953 was an important date in the history of East Berlin. The working classes were becoming increasingly disgruntled over working and living conditions, and over their inability to effect changes in their government. As the movement grew in intensity, a general strike was called for 17 June. The Soviet Army crushed the strike by deploying tanks on the streets of East Berlin to restore order.
6. Planners felt the root of Berlin's problems of spatial congestion lay in the inadequate system of radial and concentric streets as laid out in the General Building Plan of 1862; thus, any solution would have to restructure, or at least retrofit, that network. The network was never fully implemented according to James Hobrecht's original designs. Between 1945 and 1949, planners designed several restructuring plans, four of which received serious consideration: 1) the 'Kollektivplan' of 1946

by Hans Scharoun's Building Commissariat; 2) the 'Zehlendorf Plan'; 3) West Berlin's 'Plan 1948'; and 4) East Berlin's 'General Reconstruction Plan 1949'. For a detailed account of these and other plans, see Johann Friedrich Geist and Klaus Kürvers (1989) *Das Berliner Mietshaus: 1945–1989*, Munich: Prestel, pp. 222–71.

7. Edmund Collein (1952) 'Das Nationale Aufbauprogramm – Sache aller Deutschen!', *Deutsche Architektur*, 1, pp. 13–19. The idea of recasting the capitalist city in a form fitting for a socialist society is a central element of the socialist realism movement in East Germany. The literature, as in the example cited here, often speaks of a socialist revamping of the city's 'capitalistic inheritance'. In this way, socialist realism also differs from modernism: modernism tried to remold society through new architectural forms; socialist realism remolded traditional architectural and urban design to be fitting for a socialist society.

8. Obviously, Stalin's vision of urban design was very different from the conceptions of modernist architects, but his dismissal of modernism was primarily due to the Soviet Union's unhappy experiences with modernist architecture. Between 1926 and 1939, plans for hundreds of new cities and urban extensions were implemented largely by German architects of the modernist school, such as Ernst May, Hannes Meyer and Bruno Taut. However, problems in urban design that did not appear on small-scale projects, such as the monotonous design and gross economic inefficiencies, became painfully evident in the Soviet Union's full-scale projects. Unhappy with these results, Stalin was additionally displeased with modernist architecture because he felt it did not sufficiently express the political ideas of socialism. As a result, he quashed the Russian architectural avant-garde and forced the profession to reform in keeping with his ideological and aesthetic lines. For more information on the development of socialist realism under Stalin, see Anders Åman (1992) *Architecture and Ideology in Eastern Europe during the Stalin Era: An Aspect of Cold War History*, Cambridge, Mass.: MIT Press.

9. Historical translation for countries like Poland, which did not exist as a nation state for generations at a time, was rather problematic since they did not necessarily have a clearly identifiable historical epoch to refer to. Thus Poland had to go back to the Middle Ages and Renaissance to find and lay claim to a 'Polish' architecture.

10. Lothar Bolz (1951) *Von Deutschem Bauen: Reden und Aufsätze*, Berlin: n.p, pp. 32 and 56.

11. To make sure that the Party leadership understood the message, Ulbricht asked Friedrich Ebert, the mayor of East Berlin, and Otto Grotewohl, president and chairman of the SED, to accompany him on his trip to Moscow. Grotewohl feigned illness and stayed at home, thereby effectively removing himself as a contender for power within the SED. For further description, see Simone Hain (1993) 'Reise nach Moskau: Erste Betrachtungen zur politischen Struktur des städtebaulichen Leitbildwandels des Jahres 1950 in der DDR', *Wissenschaftliche Zeitschrift der Hochschule für Architektur und Bauwesen Weimar*, 39, 1/2, pp. 5–14.

12. For a detailed account of this trip and its consequences, see Simone Hain (1992) 'Reise nach Moskau: Wie Deutsche 'sozialistisch' bauen lernten', *Bauwelt*, 83, 45, pp. 2546–58.

13. Ibid.

14. Simone Hain (1992) 'Berlin, "schöner denn je": Stadtideen im Ostberliner Wiederaufbau', in *DAM Architektur Jahrbuch,* Munich: Prestel, pp. 9–22.

15. An English translation can be found in Doug Clelland (1982) 'From ideology to disenchantment', *Architectural Design*, 52, 11/12, pp. 41–45. The 'Sixteen

Principles of Town Planning' are both prescriptive and proscriptive in nature. They establish the function and purpose of the city as well as the role of architecture and urban planning in creating urban form. Loosely grouped and summarized here under four different themes, the 'Principles' address the city's history and purpose, its urban design and growth, the urban ambiance and the theoretical basis for architecture and urban planning (the numbers in parentheses refer to the Principle involved).

First, the historical purpose of the city has been to provide an economically efficient settlement for community life, whose structure expresses the political life and national consciousness of the people (1). Even though contemporary cities are built largely by and for industry (3), urban planning draws on science, technology, and art to reshape the historical structure in a way that ameliorates its shortcomings and satisfies the human needs for work, living, culture, and recreation (2, 5).

Second, the city is organically structured with decreasing density from the center to the periphery. The center is the focal point of the city not only because it contains the most important and monumental buildings, and is, therefore, the focus of political and social life, but also because it dominates the city's architectural composition, as well as its silhouette (6). 'Residential complexes' or neighborhoods are grouped together to form residential districts, whose secondary-tiered cores provide all the goods and services needed for daily life (10). City size is determined by the size of its industries, administration, and cultural institutions, but the city's growth is subject to the ability for further expansion without compromising economic efficiency or utility (4). Traffic must serve the city, but not become a hindrance to its inhabitants. Through traffic should be diverted around the center and away from residential areas, and rail and water shipping must be kept out of the core (8).

Third, the ambiance of the city is, by definition, urban, and a city cannot be turned into a garden, i.e., no garden cities (12). Multi-storey buildings are more in keeping with the character of a city (13), although population density, geographic orientation, and traffic must ensure a healthy and peaceful living environment (11).

Finally, there is no abstract scheme for urban planning or architectural design (15). A city must be carefully planned and designed (16). Urban planning and architecture must ensure that each city has a unique and artistic urban design that is determined by its squares, main streets, and dominant buildings (9), and in cities that lie on a river, the river and its streets form one of the main architectural axes (7). The architecture must be democratic in content and national in form, thereby incorporating progressive traditions from the past (14).

16. Hain (1992), Bauwelt op. cit., pp. 2546–58.
17. Walter Ulbricht (1950) 'Die Großbauten im Fünfjahrplan (Rede auf dem III. Parteitag der SED)', *Neues Deutschland*, 23 July.
18. Kurt Liebknecht (1952) 'Hohes oder breites Fenster', *Neues Deutschland*, 20 March.
19. Kurt Liebknecht (1952) 'Zur Frage der Fensterformen', *Deutsche Architektur*, 2, pp. 87–89.
20. Liebknecht's series of articles in *Neues Deutschland* was entitled 'In the fight for a new German architecture'; see Kurt Liebknecht (1951) 'Im Kampf um eine neue deutsche Architektur', *Neues Deutschland*, 13 February.
21. Rudolf Herrenstadt (1952) *Die Entwicklung Berlins im Lichte der großen Perspektive: Aufbau des Sozialismus*, Berlin: Druckerei Tägliche Rundschau.

22. Rolf Göpfert (1951) 'Die Neubauten an der Weberwiese', *Planen und Bauen*, 5, 21, pp. 485–87. Göpfert, an architect in Henselmann's studio who worked on the design, elaborated further on the symbolic content:

> These buildings had a special duty from the outset: the architectural-artistic expression should be an expression of the changes and the new construction of our society, of the will and the dominance of a new general contractor, namely the working public, and with this building indicate the future prosperity and the broad development possibilities of the democratic and freedom-facing order . . . [These buildings] should be a document for the new contents of the structural changes in the political, economic, social and cultural [arenas] . . . That precisely the apartment house should get the task of being a document of the times is a telling sign of the new social and humanistic contents . . . The Weberwiese was designed from these signals, as a contribution to the discussion on a new architecture, as a first step in a new direction that begins to demonstrate the drawing together of the mental and social situation in an ever-tighter dynamic relationship.

23. Credits for the *Hochhaus* go to the architectural collective headed by Hermann Henselmann, with Rolf Göpfert as the executing architect.

24. However, not all the news surrounding the *Weberwiese* celebrations were positive. When it became clear to the construction workers that the city was not going to celebrate the completion of the flanking buildings with similar pomp despite newspaper accounts to the contrary, the workers signaled their protest by hanging a broom – instead of the traditional construction crown – from the building. The broom was taken down when the city held a smaller celebration. Desperate to find a way to make the dedication ceremony of the ensemble more impressive than the opera singers at the tower's construction celebration, the deadline for completion of the project was moved forward to 1 May, 'Labor Day', when the mayor of Berlin would personally hand over the keys to the residents of the first flats; see Landesarchiv-Breitestraße, Rep. 110, Nr. 808.

25. Stiftung Archiv der Parteien und Massenorganisationen der DDR im Bundesarchiv IV/2/606/30.

26. For a review of the successive shifts in urbanistic and architectural paradigms in East Berlin, as well as parallel developments in West Berlin, see Roland Strobel (1994) 'Before the Wall came tumbling down: urban planning paradigm shifts in a divided Berlin', *Journal of Architectural Education*, 48, 1, pp. 25–37; and Greg Castillo (2001) 'Building culture in divided Berlin: globalization and the Cold War', in Nezar AlSayyad (ed.) *Hybrid Urbanism: On the Identity Discourse and the Built Environment*, Westport, CT and London: Praeger, pp. 181–205.

CHAPTER 7

THE PRESERVATION OF EGYPTIAN CULTURAL HERITAGE THROUGH EGYPTIAN EYES: THE CASE OF THE COMITÉ DE CONSERVATION DES MONUMENTS DE L'ART ARABE

Alaa El-Habashi

American Research Center in Egypt

> The foreign competitors won and the four Egyptian counterparts failed. This strange result was surprising to us [Egyptians] because Egypt, the land of various historical remains, provides its architects with all the fundamentals to win such a competition . . . In my point of view, the failure of the Egyptian architects is a fiction.
>
> – a wondering architect*

The Comité de Conservation des Monuments de l'Art Arabe (hereafter the Comité)[1] had an enormous impact on the status of Arab monuments in Egypt during the late nineteenth and first half of the twentieth centuries.[2] There is no single object remaining in Egypt that belonged to what the Comité's founders agreed to call 'Arab Art' that was not studied and/or conserved and restored by the Comité, which intervened through various preservation philosophies and technologies for it was, and still is, regarded as being the savior of that heritage. During the course of its work, which extended from 1881 to 1961, alongside the continuous appointment of Egyptians the Comité included, among other nationalities, French, British, Italian, German and Austro-Hungarian members. Throughout the early years, and despite the constant, relatively higher percentage of Egyptian members, the Comité was largely dominated ideologically by its European members who were consistent in attending its meetings and in following up on technical and administrative matters. Such domination continued until the 1920s when, due to the internal climax of nationalism, it was resisted, and gradually started to dissolve.

This article investigates the complexities of this very time when resistance to 'foreign' control over Egyptian affairs began to mount. It focuses on the case of the Comité where the matter was more intellectual. Egyptian members of the Comité felt they had the right to preserve a living and an intimate portion of their heritage, while foreign members claimed to possess the know-ledge and the expertise to do so. The tension was subtle as it was concealed under the governmental status of the Comité, which was then functioning under the auspices of the Egyptian Ministry of *Awqaf* (pl. of *waqf* – religious endowments), formed to administer the various charitable endowments and to maintain religious cult.[3] The tension, however, can be inferred from a close reading of the Comité minutes, and through pursuing some of the heated debates between its members that reached the press. The question of Egyptian versus foreign members, or 'us' versus 'them' as it was described by the 'wondering architect', a key figure in this paper and the author of its prologue, arose, interestingly, in a 1926 international competition for the reconstruction of the Mosque of 'Amr ibn al-'As in Cairo. Although the compe-tition had not been launched by the Comité, the majority of its protagonists were, or later became, members. Away from the institution's formalities, the Comité affiliates involved in the competition – Egyptians or foreigners, jury members or competitors – were able to express themselves freely. For the purpose of this research, the participation of Mahmud Ahmad in this compe-tition offers an ideal case. Being the only Egyptian participant who was a Comité affiliate, the competition provided the perfect opportunity for Mahmud Ahmad to refute earlier claims that Egyptian members could only be functionaries, and to challenge their image of being passive implementers of the Comité's foreign philosophy and technology on his own heritage. Along with his Egyptian competition partner Muhammad Abdil-Halim, Mahmud Ahmad failed shamefully in the competition, a result that surprised and infu-riated the wondering architect. His later promotion to chief architect of the Comité, however, was a reward for his continuous efforts and consistent will-ingness. Was he able to assert a new vision where Egyptians could actually take care of their own heritage?

THE COMPETITION

In 1926, the Ministry of *Awqaf* launched the international competition for the 'reconstruction of the mosque of 'Amr ibn al-'As'.[4] Being the oldest in Egypt and in fact in Africa, the mosque had continuously received special attention since its foundation in the seventh century.[5] Its *waqf* had main-tained the building until the end of the nineteenth century[6] when, following its task to select from the *waqf* registers those buildings of 'Arab Art' worthy of conservation, the Comité had recognized the historical importance of the mosque and taken over its *waqf* responsibilities, registering it in the Comité's 1886 first list of monuments.[7] The conservation approach of the Comité towards the Mosque of 'Amr, as well as towards most of its monuments, focused on the physical aspects of the building. Such an ideology did not conform to the *Awqaf* principles that mainly targeted sustaining the perpetual utility of the *waqf* buildings.[8] Being the then official proprietor, the Ministry of *Awqaf* was primarily responsible for the upkeep of the cult in the Mosque of 'Amr, and its attitude towards the building was therefore based on that very understanding. Mainly concerned with performing their religious practices, the users of the mosque sided with the *Awqaf* approach, thus the Comité's emphasis on conservation was alien to the local context, and despite several philosophical and administrative shifts in its approach,[9] its preservation activities remained, to a certain extent, detached from the ideologies of the *waqf* and the users of these religious buildings.[10]

This ideological conflict sometimes resulted in clashes, one of which was related to the Mosque of 'Amr. In 1914, Prince Muhammad 'Ali of the royal family signified the position of al-*Awqaf* and the public in his proposal to sponsor a major intervention to 'reinstate the religious value of the Mosque'. The Comité could not incorporate the proposed funding within the scope of its work as the project was not by any means directed towards the conservation of the building. Facing a sensitive situation, it approved – though only internally – the withdrawal of the mosque from its list of monuments. However, the decision was blocked immediately by the Council of Ministers due to the harsh criticism it received from the Society of Antiquaries of London and other international associations. Lord Kitchener, then British Consul-General in Egypt, communicated with the Comité to ensure that the ancient mosque would not be touched and that it was reinstated on the Comité's list of monuments.[11] The incident proved that the Comité had powerful international support that could back it against any opponent – even the very government under which it was functioning.

Though for the time being it appeared that Prince Muhammad 'Ali's proposal had been rejected, it was not forgotten. Twelve years later, in 1926, a similar but rather more official move came from the Ministry of al-*Awqaf* when it launched the aforementioned competition. This time the ministry was supported by King Fu'ad (r. 1917–36) who sought through such intervention to claim a religious leadership of the muslim world. Fu'ad was trying to take advantage of Mustafa Kamal's recent abolition of the Caliphate in Turkey, in order to transfer this famed religious institution to Egypt.[12] Unlike Prince Muhammad Ali's earlier proposal, the competition was well funded – and well supported. A number of the Comité's members were selected to participate in writing its program as well as to sit on the jury. The hope, arguably, was to side the Comité with the move by involving its members in the competition procedures, thus preventing any external veto.

The stated goal of the competition emphasized this very maneuver. It aimed to 'reconstitute the mosque's most splendid epoch', pointing to neither physical nor utilitarian aspects of the mosque. Such vagueness was undoubtedly intentional; the statement assumed wide interpretation and therefore any criticism or attempts to block the competition would lack concrete foundations. The Ministry of al-*Awqaf* appears to have favoured appointing an external – preferably foreign – architect to realize its proposals for the mosque, and it therefore publicized the competition so widely that it received 525 inquiries in response, only 72 of which came from Egypt.[13] However, due to the apparent – and perhaps deliberate – ambiguity of the program, only seven projects were eventually submitted.[14]

The authors of four of the seven presented projects were Egyptians: Ibrahim Fawzi sent in his entry from Paris,[15] Mahmud Fu'ad from Upper Egypt, Hassan Sabri from Cairo, and Mahmud Ahmad and Muhammad Abdil-Halim from London.[16] The authors of the remaining entries were Noel Dawson and K. A. C. Creswell, a British team residing in Alexandria; Wulffleff, Verrey and Gavasi, a multinational team residing in Cairo; and Maurice Mantout, a French architect living in Paris.[17]

At a meeting of 3 May 1927, the competition jury decided to dismiss the four Egyptian entries and selected the project of Wulffleff, Verrey and Gavasi for first prize, that of Noel Dawson and K. A. C. Creswell for second prize, and Maurice Mantout's entry in third place.[18] The result might not have been so surprising had the goal of the Ministry of *al-Awqaf* to select an 'outsider' been considered. However, due to the surge in the local nationalists' movement of the time, the local press lashed out against the jury's selections. The prologue to this article, which refers to the competition result, is quoted from *al-Handasa*, the journal that reproduced a series of seven short essays published in *al-Balagh al-Yawmi* (The Daily Balagh), a contemporary newspaper that aimed to inspire a sense of local nationalism to oppose foreign domination over internal affairs.[19] The author preferred to remain anonymous and signed as 'a wondering architect'.

'US' AND 'THEM'?

In his series of essays the wondering architect set a clear polarity between those he referred to as 'us' and those he described as 'them'. For him, 'us' were the local inhabitants of Egypt including the four 'Egyptian' architects who participated in the competition. 'Them' were the foreign participants and all the jury members who supported them. He had either disregarded the fact that five among the eleven members of the jury were Egyptians,[20] or had considered Egyptians who sided with foreigners as being 'foreigners'. For the wondering architect, the very decision to dismiss the Egyptian designs was 'foreign', or rather 'strange',[21] and consequently anyone who participated in selecting the foreigners and dismissing the Egyptians belonged to the foreigners' camp. The author's absolute distinction of identities raises the question of who were the Egyptians and who were the foreigners in Egypt at that time.

At the legal level, the years of the competition – 1926–27 – fell right in the midst of several international and local attempts to define nationalities. The 1920 Sèvres Treaty, 1923 Lausanne Treaty[22] and several other local laws, namely those of 1926 and 1929, were all attempts to regulate the then international and local affairs with the question of local nationalities.[23] Capitulations had been largely reshaped, and resolutions to identify Ottoman residences were being contemplated. According to the 1926 and 1929 local laws, Egyptian nationality was basically granted if the 'father is Egyptian, or if a foreign father who is born in Egypt, is related by race to a majority of population of a country that adopted the Arabic language, or Islam'.[24] Race, Arabic language and Islam were, then, the legal parameters upon which Egyptian nationality was evaluated. Egyptians, however, certainly did not require this legal definition in order to feel 'Egyptian'. Indeed it was not any treaty or law that induced the wondering architect to react against the result of the competition. What motivated him was his sense of belonging to the people, to the religion and to the locale, feelings reported to have been rooted in the inhabitants of Egypt since ancient times.[25]

At the time of the competition there were a number of attempts to capitalize on the strength of this feeling, each with its own champions and motivated by a specific agenda. After the abolition of the Caliphate in Turkey, and with the support of local religious groups, the king heavily encouraged this desire for the establishment of an Islamic identity that would gather not only the people of Egypt but also all Muslims under his sway.[26] The restoration of an important Islamic monument like the Mosque of 'Amr provided the ideal propaganda tool to convey this message. Taking a more local approach, the opposition parties called for the emergence of an Egyptian identity based on the specificities of the locale. One principal chord that those parties' protagonists had played was the note of the rich history of Egypt manifested in the extensive historical remains found in its lands. 'The inheritors of the Greatest Civilizations' was how they referred to Egyptians.[27]

While treatises and laws formed the basis for local nationality from the legal standpoint, Egyptian identity was in fact emotionally rooted, but incited and directed differently to suit some leaders' prospects. It was this identity, regardless of its incentives, that was the foundation of the wondering architect's notion of 'us'. 'Them' (foreigners), on the other hand, were those people living in Egypt who did not emotionally belong and who preferred to live in Egypt under the protection of foreign consulates, profiting from Capitulations and detaching themselves from local circumstances.[28]

At the time of the competition, Capitulations were so privileged that they attracted the largest number of foreigners living in Egypt.[29] This must have irritated the anonymous author, but what really provoked him to write his harsh criticism was the fact that foreign domination was now touching on one of the key representations of his identity – the ancient Mosque of 'Amr

Ibn al-'As. The wondering architect was aware of the Comité, and also recognized Mahmud Ahmad's long experience in implementing its projects.[30] It was for this reason that the anonymous architect argued that all the technical aspects of the project of Mahmud Ahmad and his partner 'were correct' and that 'none of the other competitors were able to discuss these points'.[31] Being 'Egyptians' gave them an advantage in the competition since, unlike the actual winners, they were able to express local self-identity in their design for the reconstruction of the Mosque of 'Amr. An Egyptian as well as an affiliate to the Comité, Mahmud Ahmad was the ideal candidate to produce a design that could address the social values in addition to the technical aspects. The author thus concluded that Ahmad's project should have been awarded the first prize.[32]

RISING TENSION

The ideological clash of Prince 'Ali's case did not leave an apparent transfiguration in the internal affairs of the Comité. Being an outsider, the prince might not have grasped the essence of the Comité's work, and thus his proposal was neither blamed nor did it receive much attention. Clashes between Comité members – even if they were minor – would certainly be more eloquent. Despite sharing the same goals and objectives, the members did not always necessarily agree on all issues, and several internal debates and disputes arose throughout the lifetime of the institution. Of most relevance to the discussion here were those conflicts that were founded on ideologies of preservation, the antagonists of which were the Egyptians versus the foreigners. Examining a number of such instances below will highlight the position of the Egyptians with regard to the approaches of the institution.

Soon after the formation of the Comité, the famous 'Ali Mubarak, appointed a member of the Comité in 1882,[33] objected to the conservation of the *sabil* of Farag Ibn Barquq, a small, fifteenth-century water fountain that blocked the widening of Taht al-Rab' Street. Mubarak advised that the fountain be demolished in order to proceed with the plans of the Ministry of *al-Ashghal al-'amma* (Public Works), of which he was minister,[34] to open up avenues and wide streets in the dense fabric of the historic city.[35] He argued that there was no 'need for so many monuments', and that it would be enough to conserve only a sample of each type.[36] Mubarak generally opposed the conservation of such water fountains, since most had ceased to be used and water could anyway be supplied to individual residences through newly installed pipelines. His position would certainly be different had the future of a working mosque been the subject of debate. In the same line of thought, he argued through the voice of his controversial figure *'Alam al-din*, that 'forms from earlier times which are unacceptable now, should be eradi-

cated'.[37] For Mubarak, insistence on the preservation of every historical frag-
ment would restrict the State's modernization of the city of Cairo,[38] thus he
stressed that only those buildings still in use should be preserved. To clarify
his position, he used the analogy of the French demolition of the Bastille,
symbolizing that such a building type had no use in the new climate of
freedom. The historical importance of the building had not prevented the
French from eradicating this prison, thus it should not deter the Egyptians
from demolishing the water fountain. So for Mubarak, the utility of the
building was the main parameter that mandated its preservation.

It is interesting to note the position of the Frenchman Pierre Grand with
regard to Mubarak's argument. At the time, Mubarak and Grand were working
together in the Ministry of Public Works – Mubarak as minister with Grand
directing the Department of the Streets of Cairo.[39] Both had been appointed
Comité members in the decree of November 1882. In his 1874 map of the city,
Grand presented Cairo not simply as it was but as it might be, for it included
wide avenues through the fabric of the old city, and consequently the decision
to demolish the *sabil* Farag Ibn Barquq was in part his. However, the majority
of Comité members, of course with the exception of Pierre Grand,[40] rejected
Mubarak's proposal, and instead decided to conserve the monument. As a
result, Ali Mubarak resigned after attending only three of the Comité's meetings.[41] In his letter of resignation, Mubarak claimed that he was so busy with
his ministerial duties that he would no longer be able to participate in Comité
activities. Though at the time the Ministry of Public Works was very busy working on the modernization of Cairo, this reasoning is not very convincing as
Mubarak had previously been able to manage three ministries at the same time.
It thus appears that the ideological clash between Mubarak and the Comité in
general was the hidden reason behind his withdrawal from the organization.
Despite being often accused of being on the side of Western ideology,[42]
Mubarak, a French-educated engineer, rejected clashed with – an approach
developed in Europe to save historic objects – when it clashed with the socially
rooted doctrines of utility that he and his ministry adopted.

Like Ali Mubarak, several other Egyptian members raised their voices
against the dominant doctrines of the Comité. For example, Sabir Sabri, chief
engineer in the technical bureau of the *Waqf* administration of the time, insti-
gated a series of other clashes during his period of membership.[43] In 1897
Sabri dismissed a scheme proposed by Max Herz, the Comité's chief architect, for the repainting of the interior frieze of the Mosque of Barquq.[44] The
latter sought the approval of the Comité on a suggested color scheme that
included the use of pale-colored paint so as not to change the historical aspect
of the frieze. Sabir Sabri did not like Herz's approach, commenting that:
'. . . the colors are too pale and invisible for the spectators'. Sabri's preference was instead 'to re-touch the frieze with sufficient colors so that it would
provide the goal and the effect for which they were originally conceived'.[45]

So while Sabri was for complete restoration that would bring the monument to a specific point in time, Herz was more concerned with showing the historicity of the architectural elements of the mosque, highlighting the effect of time on the building. But except for a few surviving fragments, Sabri did not have any definite reference for the original color scheme, and his proposal would actually bring the monument to a state that had in fact never existed. His approach can be compared with that of Viollet-le-Duc (1814–79), the busiest restorer in France during the nineteenth century. He had adopted what had been described by Viollet-le-Duc as restoration 'not just to preserve it, to repair it, and to remodel it', but to 're-instate it in a complete state such as it may never have been in at any given moment'.[46]

Seeking to show the effect of time on the colors of the frieze, Herz, on the other hand, appeared to be more reinstating and conforming to the 'conservation' task of the Comité that was declared in its very title. However, Herz was flexible in his interpretation; rather than reinstating the original color fragments in their entirely original form, he proposed painting these, and the rest of the frieze, with an old-looking modern paint layer that mimicked historic colors. Neglecting the different, uneven and sometimes random effects of time on a building, he instead offered a 'complete' and ideal representation of the deteriorated monument that was not in fact real. So in effect, in neither Herz's nor Sabri's scheme would the original colored fragments of the monument survive. While Herz, concerned with the historicity of the building, suggested a formulized state of degradation for the wooden frieze, Sabri wanted to recreate the initial impact of the freeze on the worshippers when it was first introduced into the mosque. However, dismissing the opinions of Sabri the Comité agreed to 'paint the wooden frieze . . . according to Mr. Herz bey's sample reproducing the [hue] of the ancient paint whose traces are visible on several locations in the frieze'.[47] The Comité certainly seems to have adhered to its conservation task, but in reality not only had it fantasized the effect of time on the historic object, it had also obliterated all of the original color scheme of the frieze.

Though the ideological approaches of the two Egyptians were very different, they did, however, agree on the basic understanding that any act of preservation must be useful, and opposed approaches that were primarily based on romanticism. Both also recognized that the objectives of the Comité did not match the locally rooted utilitarian perspective. While Mubarak was impatient to clarify his position and quickly resigned, Sabri, whose accomplishments within the *al-Awqaf* administration had already proved exceptional,[48] was persistent in highlighting his viewpoints during his 23 years of membership – one of the longest in the lifetime of the Comité. For example, referring to the *sabil-kuttab* (water fountain and Koranic school) of Mussalli Khurbagi, the architecture of which was praised by Max Herz, he pointed out that its listing and restoration would not be of any utility, arguing that it had 'no artistic or historic interest and all the expenses that the Comité will allo-cate for its consolidation and its restoration will be useless'. However, a number of European members supported Herz, declaring that 'the building in question has to be conserved because even if it does not bear special char-acter, it still represents the architecture of its époque'.[49] In a sense, the statements of Herz and his fellow Europeans acknowledged the lesser archi-tectural significance of the *sabil*, but if their rationale had been adopted throughout, all of the buildings of historic Cairo, and elsewhere, would have been included in the Comité's list of monuments. Their opinion must thus have been quite strange to Sabri, who by this time was supported by his fellow countryman and colleague Abdil-Hamid Fawzi, then deputy chief engineer of *al-Awqaf*. The Comité never declared its position on the *sabil-kuttab* of Mussalli Khurbagi, since no decisive opinion prevailed among its members.[50]

Although Sabri's propositions were sometimes accepted, he never ceased voicing his disagreements whenever he found the opportunity, a persistence which, on occasion, resulted in his opinions being taken into consideration. For example, when he pointed out that the French translation of a number of verses of the Koranic inscription were not always 'exact', and that publishing these translations in the Comité bulletin would lead to miscon-ceptions, the Comité agreed to verify these before publishing the reports.[51] Though this incident may have little direct connection with the preservation of historic buildings, it undoubtedly illustrates the growing internal concerns at the time among the Egyptian members of the organization.

Objections from Egyptian members, if they were raised, were not usually considered, while in contrast the opinions of the foreign 'experts', even if they were not well grounded, were rarely questioned. This was more or less the general trend that prevailed within the Comité right up until the First World War. Thus this period was characterized by dominant foreign control over the objectives, philosophical approaches and technological aspects of Comité activities. After the war, the percentage of foreign members continued to increase until, as mentioned earlier, it reached its peak in 1927. Yet the new postwar climate and the rise of local nationalists' movements in the struggle for independence[52] allowed the Egyptian members of the Comité, like Mubarak and Sabri before them, to gain a stronger voice and greater prominence within the organization. For example, Ali Bahgat, who joined the Comité in 1900,[53] succeeded Max Herz in heading the Museum of Arab Art in 1914[54] at the same time that he was involved with a secret nationalist group.[55] Then in 1923, Ahmad al-Sayyid, chief architect of the Ministry of *Waqf*,[56] replaced the Italian Achille Patricolo,[57] chief architect of the Comité. Thus an apparent power, at least over the technical aspects of preservation, had been handed to the Egyptian members. While Bahgat enjoyed a remark-able and consistently distinguished career working on several excavations and in the organization of the Museum of Arab Art,[58] al-Sayyid rarely spoke during the meetings he attended.[59] Even when responsibility for the Museum of Arab Art was handed over to him after the death of Bahgat in 1924, Ahmad al-Sayyid failed to prove himself worthy of such a position. Thus it was probably because of al-Sayyid's negative contribution and weak leadership of the Comité's technical section, and later the museum, that the decision was taken to appoint the Frenchmen Gaston Wiet as head of the museum in 1926,[60] and in 1929 to appoint alongside him a Frenchman, Edmond Pauty,[61] who was more experienced in preservation, as an 'expert architect'.[62]

MAHMUD AHMAD AND THE RECONSTRUCTION OF THE MOSQUE OF 'AMR

Another Egyptian who actively influenced the Comité's path in the 1920s and 1930s was Mahmud Ahmad (1880–1942) (see earlier) who initially joined the Comité's technical bureau as a draftsman.[63] Ahmad was newly graduated from the Egyptian School of Arts and Crafts (*madrasat al-finun wa al-sina'at*) where he had shown an enthusiasm for 'Arab monuments' during the school's weekly scheduled visits to different mosques.[64] In 1922 he was transferred to work for the newly formed 'Bureau of Monuments' of *al-Awqaf* as a *muhandis* (engineer/architect).[65] At the time of the competition for the reconstruction of the Mosque of 'Amr, Mahmud Ahmad was directing this bureau, responsible for implementing conservation and restoration projects on the orders of the Comité. The projects were subsequently presented to the Comité, which in turn accepted, commented on, enhanced or dismissed them. After the granting of final approval, Mahmud Ahmad and his team in the Bureau of Monuments supervised and reported on the execution of the required work. It was his enthusiasm for the work of the bureau that in 1924 had led its director, Ahmad al-Sayyid, to allow Ahmad to attend meetings of the Comité's technical section on his behalf when he was unable to attend himself.[66]

By 1926, when Ahmad and his partner, Muhammad Abdil-Halim, conceived their design for the reconstruction of the Mosque of 'Amr, Ahmad had still not been granted a Comité membership, and this was probably why he was able to participate in the competition.[67] However, by 1934 the Comité's 'expert architect', the Frenchman Edmond Pauty, had recognized Mahmud Ahmad's hard work and supported membership for the latter in order to increase the number of architects in the Comité's technical bureau,[68] advocating that Ahmad be appointed to the position of 'supplementary architect' for Cairo monuments.[69] In May the same year, several Egyptian Comité members nominated Ahmad as an ex officio member. They argued that 'his presence in the meetings is necessary to enlighten the members about the on-going works' and 'his assistance to the meetings of the Comité Technical Section will better reflect the Comité viewpoints regarding the various decisions taken during the execution phases'.[70] Despite resistance from a number of the foreign members, Mahmud Ahmad finally became a member in December, even being granted the title 'Architect of the Comité'.[71]

In 1920, whilst he was still a draftsman working for the Comité's technical bureau, Mahmud Ahmad and several other Egyptians founded *al-Handasa* (Engineering), the first local Arabic engineering review.[72] Until its demise in 1937, Ahmad was not only the main editor of the review but also an active contributor of its articles, and he was also behind the decision to publish the 'wondering architect's' criticism that appeared as a series of articles in *al-Balagh al-Yawmi* (The Daily Balagh), and as a brief note in *al-Balagh al-Usbu'i* (The Weekly Balagh).[73] In *al-Handasa*, Mahmud Ahmad divided this series into three sections, reserving the first for the criticism of the winning entries, the second to introduce the Egyptian entries, except that of Ahmad and Abdil-Halim, which was praised in the third where it was also suggested – almost emphasized – that this project should have been the winning entry. The wondering architect was so informed of all the details of the competition, and some of the Comité's internal administrative matters, that he must have been one of the affiliates of the institution who participated, as a competitor or a jury member, in the competition. In addition, his nationalist aspirations indicate that he was an Egyptian. One might well speculate that he was indeed Mahmud Ahmad himself.[74]

It is of a little interest to prove Ahmad's relationship with the wondering architect. What is important, however, is to analyze the claims that were presented in the anonymous argument. The wondering architect confirmed that Ahmad's long involvement with the conservation and restoration in Cairo, and his responsibility for implementing the Comité's decisions, meant he was well versed in the technical issues of preservation; furthermore, as a Muslim Egyptian he had a better understanding of how the mosque should respond to local needs. But was this actually the case? Was the author's assessment of Ahmad's credentials accurate?

The reconstruction that Ahmad and Abdil-Halim proposed for the Mosque of 'Amr was based on 'the description of the edifice during the famous historical period, namely the Fatimy [Fatimid]'. Their approach conformed with Viollet-le-Duc's definition of 'restoration', and to a certain degree with the one Sabri adopted in proposing his color scheme for the Mosque of Barquq. According to Ahmad and Abdil-Halim, their design adhered to 'the architectural characteristics, composition and details, also the utilization of building materials obtainable in the country, with due consideration to climatic conditions and religious [requirements and providing for] modern methods of construction for economical purposes and sound structure . . .'[75] In the report that accompanied their drawings, Ahmad and his colleague covered all the technical aspects that might be involved in the reconstruction process, from recommending shallow piles for the foundations to specifying Torah lime-stone, to the use of *homra* (brick dust) in the mortar mix and so on. These technical specifications confirm that the pair were indeed aware of the context in which they conceived their design, an awareness that was based on experience in the field rather than literature reviews since published studies describing local, traditional techniques were scarce at the time.[76]

In terms of technical expertise, Mahmud Ahmad's knowledge of local building materials and building techniques, which he gained through his involvement with the Comité, set his design apart from any other entry. However, this was not also the case in terms of its design concept. In their report, Ahmad and Abdil-Halim described their proposed 'lay-out' as follows:

> The accompanying suggestion for a lay-out is to show suitable surroundings which explain the scheme and manifest the dignity of a religious edifice, with efficient circulation and cheerful outlook . . . Beyond this treatment, are informal surroundings limited by a secondary circulation road which links up the main roads running south and north, being the important flow of traffic to and from Old Cairo and places beyond . . . On that secondary circulation road and on the other side of which, are the neighboring buildings which, whether private or public are well away from the mosque, and overlook the gardens, as shown on the drawing, and this will, no doubt, increase their value considerably . . . However, such treatment helps to maintain a quiet atmosphere round the mosque, being also public gardens of a peaceful and cheerful nature.[77]

The 'suitable surroundings' they proposed in fact took the form of a rigidly symmetrical and proportioned French garden, with a master plan that echoed a basilica. The scale of this garden actually overshadowed the sizable Mosque of 'Amr (Fig. 1). The mosque may have been the focal point of the design but here it was subsumed by gardens and a gateway in Baroque forms that had certainly never previously been part of the composition of the mosque. The 'dignity of a religious edifice' was emphasized in a proposed gateway that con-stituted, as the architects suggested, 'the main approach from an important feature leading to the north-western front of the mosque . . . There are palm-walks, enclosing waters in the form of ponds or low basins'. (Fig. 2) The mosque, as shown in the submitted perspective view (fig. 3), became alienated – more like an object displayed in a museum with an extrinsic entourage. The park was so imposing that it did not relate to the surrounding urban fabric, as was evident in the architects' drawings that did not include any of the existing context. The efforts of Ahmad and his partner to adopt foreign preservation philosophies were so self-conscious that their scheme for the reconstruction of the Mosque of 'Amr was more European than the European entries. Ahmad was influenced by the expropriation work he had undertaken around most of the 'Arab monuments' of Cairo upon orders from the Comité, and followed a similar approach in his mosque reconstruction scheme.

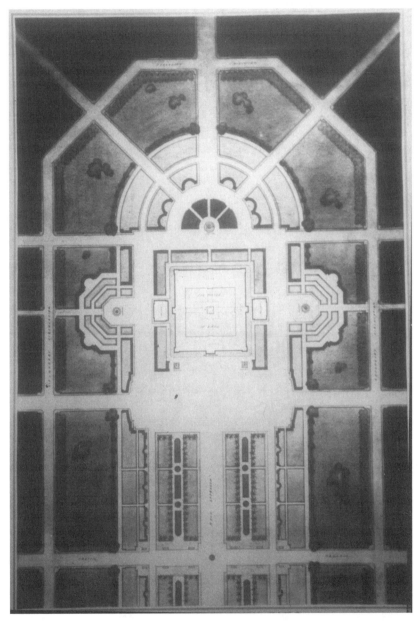

Figure 1. *Mahmud Ahmad and Muhammad Abdel-Halim: Site plan, project for the reconstruction of the Mosque of ʿAmr, 1926 (Project entry, plate n° 3, Archives of the Supreme Council of Antiquities, Cairo)*

Figure 2. *Mahmud Ahmad and Muhammad Abdel-Halim : The entrance gateway, project for the reconstruction of the Mosque of 'Amr, 1926 (Project entry, plate n° 10, Archives of the Supreme Council of Antiquities, Cairo)*

Figure 3. *Mahmud Ahmad and Muhammad Abdel-Halim: Perspective view, project for the reconstruction of the Mosque of 'Amr, 1926 (Project entry, plate n° 6, Archives of the Supreme Council of Antiquities, Cairo)*

However, theirs was not the only Egyptian composition influenced by foreign philosophies. Ibrahim Fawzi, a student at the Beaux-Arts in Paris at the time, took a similar approach. Fawzi proposed clearing out a park around the mosque. Like Ahmad and Abdil-Halim, he wanted to 'respect the dignity of the mosque', however Fawzi's park was not as rigid as that of his countrymen, instead being more organic and interwoven with the surrounding urban fabric (Fig. 4). This is particularly interesting if one considers that in another of his compositions – that for the competition for the courthouse of Cairo two years earlier – Fawzi appeared much more willing to embrace European approaches in his proposal for an imposing classical building which, as his perspective drawing depicted, was intended to be used mostly by those in non-traditional dress (Fig. 5).[78] But for the Mosque of 'Amr, an exemplar of heritage and religious legacy, Fawzi portrayed men praying in the mosque, wearing traditional dress, and in this regard was more sensitive to the environment and more respectful of the existing urban fabric than Ahmad and Abdil-Halim (Fig. 6).

The reconstruction plan of Ahmad and Abdil-Halim placed so much emphasis on the historicity of the mosque that it deprived the mosque of the chance to interact with its existing surroundings. Fawzi, on the other hand, though demonstrating more respect for the existing fabric, appeared unaware of the history of the mosque and his scheme was technically weak.

This was expected of Fawzi, who was detached from his homeland and very much influenced by the Beaux-Arts tradition in which architects were trained to be excellent designers but not builders. He proposed a mix of architectural styles, a Fatimid arcade that surrounded the interior courtyard, and a central place of ablution that mimicked the existing one in the fifteenth-century mosque of the Mamluk Sultan Hasan. In his report, under a section entitled '*La description technique de la mosquée*', Fawzi failed to include any of the technical aspects of the reconstruction of the mosque and described only the architectural elements, which anyway were not historically convincing.[79]

Regardless of their weak points, however, both designs were praised by the 'wondering architect'. Although the anonymous author acknowledged that all the competition entries had been coded,[80] he took his nationalism to an extreme level in demonstrating his total distrust of the jury members and suggesting that the marks he noticed on the drawing panels of the three winning projects were 'clear indications to the designers' identities'.[81] Fawzi failed, the wondering architect argued, 'just because he is "Fawzi" and Mahmud failed because he is "Mahmud"'.[82]

The remaining competition entries also merit brief mention here.[83] For example, Mahmud Fu'ad, an Egyptian architect working for the Ministry of

Figure 4. Ibrahim Fawzi: Site plan, project for the reconstruction of the Mosque of 'Amr, 1926 (Project report, Archives of the Supreme Council of Antiquities, Cairo)

Figure 5. *Ibrahim Fawzi, Perspective view, design project for Cairo Mixed Courts, 1924 (Al-Handasa, vol. 4, issue n° 3, 1924, p. 178)*

Figure 6. *Ibrahim Fawzi, Perspective view, project for the reconstruction of the Mosque of 'Amr, 1926 (Project report, Archives of the Supreme Council of Antiquities, Cairo)*

Awqaf in Qina (a city on the Nile in southern Egypt), presented a scheme the elements of which were a mix of Fatimid (the openings) and Romanesque (the towers) architecture (Fig. 7). Despite the discrepancy in the architectural conception that was depicted in his drawings, Fu'ad, in his report, maintained one line of religious concern through which he regarded the reconstruction of the Mosque of 'Amr as a means to reinforce Islam. Through the reconstruction, Fu'ad hoped not only to revitalize the 'splendeur' of the mosque but also of Fustat, Cairo and Egypt in general.[84] It is even possible that he had recognized the incentives of the King of Egypt to bring the Caliphate to Egypt (see earlier).

While Fu'ad addressed the issue from an emotional stance, Noel Dawson and his partner K. A. C. Creswell – yet to be appointed a Comité member[85] – focused on concrete and historical evidence. For example they paid great attention to determining inter-column spacing to be followed in the reconstruction process. These were measured and an average dimension calculated, upon which Dawson and Cresswell based their reconstruction. They confirmed that the suggested spacing matched the description of historians, travellers and artists' plans.[86] Unlike any of the other participants, they devoted great care to surveying the different ornaments of the architrave and suggested conserving these during reconstruction.

Each of the entries focused on different aspects of the reconstruction process. While an apparent emotional inspiration was manifest in the proposals of the Egyptian entries, the designs of Noel and Creswell, Wulffleff, Verrey and Gavasi, and Maurice Mantout concentrated more on historical and substantive evidence. Mahmud Ahmad and his partner were caught between the two camps. Besides their explicit historical and technical studies, they depicted a strong sympathy for the symbolic message that would be conveyed by the reconstruction of the mosque. Thus Mahmud Ahmad and

Figure 7. *Mahmud Fu'ad: Western façade, project for the reconstruction of the Mosque of 'Amr, 1926 (Project entry, plate n° 5, Archives of the Supreme Council of Antiquities, Cairo)*

Abdil-Halim's competition entry represents an appropriate case for investigating the viewpoints of Egyptians towards the preservation of their heritage for a number of reasons: Ahmad was the only local participant who was both an architect and a conservationist; he was the only Egyptian who was involved in Comité activities; and furthermore he was an expert historian who had written extensively on local heritage.[87] As the 'wondering architect' asserted, Ahmad's broad-based expertise made him a favourite to win.

AN 'AWAKENING'?

No other international competition held in Egypt at the time attracted such high levels of publicity as the competition for the reconstruction of the Mosque of 'Amr ibn al-'As, which was unique and crucial to the local sense of identity. The insistence of the 'wondering architect' that only Egyptians be selected to win the competition had not been emulated in other cases where Europeans had won contemporary international competitions in Egypt. For example, the success of European architects in the 1921 competition for the design of the Kasr al-'Ayni hospital, and the 1924 competition for the design of the Mixed Courts Building, both in Cairo, had received little local attention. It was only when the subject touched on the very essence of heritage and religious legacy that Egyptians such as Ahmad were accredited, or rather it was felt that they should be.

In the event, immediately after declaring the winners the jury decided that 'none of the competitors had achieved a project that deserved, even after modification, to be executed'. The jury realized that during the reconstruction process, a great deal of archaeological heritage would be lost, and concluded that the main benefit of the competition was to 'bring to the Ministry of Waqfs from an artistic and archaeological viewpoint, the new elements which could be of serious utility for a definitive project'.[88] Mostly composed of Comité members,[89] the jury decided against the execution of any of the competition projects to avoid the destruction of the archaeological remains of the mosque – an approach that matched the Comité's objectives of conserving 'Arab' remains. Contradicting the intentions inferred from the program of the *Awqaf* competition, the Comité, represented here in the jury, had proved that it possessed a stronger voice than that of the Ministry of *Awqaf* in determining how its selected monuments should be preserved.

Since its reorganization in 1879, the local government had constantly employed an average of 10 per cent foreigners in its workforce.[90] The number of foreigners appointed to the Comité, however, was always much greater. The Comité had started out in December 1881 with a total of 11 members: eight 'Egyptians' and three (i.e. 27.3 per cent) foreigners.[91] By January the following year Husayn Fahmy, chief architect of *al-Awqaf*, and Jules Bourgoin, a French artist who was interested in Arab art,[92] had also become members. The appointment of Ali Mubarak, Ya'coub Artin and Pierre Grand in November the same year meant that the Comité by this time included 11 Egyptians and five (or 31.2 per cent) foreigners. However, this decline in the percentage of Egyptian members of the Comité did not appear to be an issue. On the contrary, some even argued for a further increase in the number of European members. Indeed, a report published in English in *The Architect* suggested that a 'Ministry of Fine Arts' be created that would have 'control over all the monuments of Egypt', the staff of which would mainly be 'properly trained Europeans'.[93]

In 1927, responding to the peak in the number of foreigners in Egypt's population, the State tended to replace foreigners with Egyptians whenever possible, and consequently a large number of foreigners left their governmental posts.[94] Only those foreigners whose expertise was not available locally were kept in their positions – and 'conservation' represented one such area. It was for this reason that despite local concern about the growing number of foreign employees, the percentage of foreigners in the Comité during the same year reached one of its highest levels (33.3 per cent).[95] In 1930 this percentage reached its climax at 47 per cent.[96] A local law issued in 1936 decreed that the State was not to employ any foreigner unless an Egyptian equivalent was not available;[97] a substantial decline was then noted in the number of foreigners working for the government.[98] This law was also reflected in the internal structure of the Comité and within its different ministries. For example, the law highlighted the fact that foreigners did not have a justifiable role in the Ministry of *al-Awqaf* since its internal procedures were based on *Shari'a* (Islamic law).[99] However the knowledge and expertise of the Comité's foreign members were indispensable, and this is perhaps why control was transferred to its Ministry of Public Instruction (*wizarat al-ma'arif al-'umumiyya*) which still permitted the highest number of foreigners.[100]

Even after the ministerial transfer, the Comité continued to lose its foreign members due to the unfavorable working conditions dictated by the 1936 law. Not only did the law impose restrictions on the contracts of foreigners if they were to be hired at all, it also reserved the right to dismiss any of them without notice if their specified duties were not fulfilled.[101] In 1936, only four foreign members attended the Comité meetings alongside 12 Egyptians.[102] The matter was exacerbated after the Montreux Convention of 1937 that abolished foreigners' privileges given under the Capitulations.[103] The independent status of the country was strengthened. In the following Comité meeting in March 1938, only 2 foreigners attended along with 7 Egyptians (22 per cent foreigners).[104] The number of foreign Comité members kept declining steadily,[105] until 1952, the year of the revolution, when no foreigners attended.[106]

THE PRESERVATION OF EGYPTIAN CULTURE HERITAGE THROUGH EGYPTIAN EYES

A year after the revolution, in 1953, the Comité was combined along with *maslahat al-athar al-masriyya* (Antiquities Service), *al-mathaf al-masri* (Egyptian Museum), *al-mathaf al-qibti* (Coptic Museum), and *mathaf al-fann al-islami* (Islamic Museum), in the '*maslahat al-athar*' (the Egyptian Antiquities Organization or EAO).[107] The EAO's Permanent Committee for the Islamic and Coptic Monuments was then formed to pursue the Comité's goals.[108] The EAO entirely excluded foreigners, and handed all responsibility to Egyptians. These Egyptians were a local elite who had consciously or unconsciously adopted a European image of Egypt. In an effort to assert themselves as European,[109] they often identified with many aspects of the European culture.[110] Mahmud Ahmad did this to the extreme by imposing a European architectural sensibility over his own heritage – his self-identity. Even after political independence, Egyptians continued adopting the same preservation doctrines which were the Comité's legacy. The power is currently in their hands, but oddly enough, Egyptians still praise these doctrines, and blindly feel obliged to implement them. Surely, the EAO's decision to exclude foreigners would have pleased the 'wondering architect' who wanted to get rid of 'them' and leave Egypt's heritage to 'us'. Did this 'wondering architect' ever consider that 'them' are already internalized in 'us'.

NOTES

*. Source of the quotation: 'Musabaqat tajdid jami' 'Amr' [The competition for the reconstruction of the Mosque of Amr], al-Handasa [Engineering], vol. 7, no. 10, 1927, p.421.
1. The Comité was founded in December 1881 by a decree of Khedive Tawfiq. The Khedival Decree is published in *al-Waqa'i al-masriyya* [Egyptian Gazette], December 1881, and in the first bulletin of the Comité published in 1882, pp. 8–10.
2. This committee is also referred to in Arabic as *Lijnit hifz al-athar al-'Arabiyya*. Throughout this article this committee will be referred to as the 'Comité'. The Comité bulletins are referred to as B.C., the *Procès-Verbaux* (minutes of meetings) as P.V., and the *Rapports* (reports) as R.
3. For a brief history on the Ministry of *al-Awqaf* in Egypt, see Al-Sanhuri (1949) *Fi qanun al-waqf* in *Majmu'at al-qawanin al-masriyya al-mukhtara min al-fiqh al-islami*, Cairo: Matba'at Misr, vol. 1, pp. 4–45. For the history of the Ministry up until 1996, see Ghanim (1998) *Al-awqaf wa al-siyasa fi misr*. Cairo: Dar al-Shuruq, pp. 386–499.
4. See Ahmad Rabi' al-Masry (1926), *Jami' 'Amr Ibn al-'As bi-misr al-qadima*, in *al-Ahram* (newspaper), 11 April, p. 1.
5. For the history of the mosque see Mahmud Ahmad (1939) *The Mosque of Amr Ibn Al-As, at Fustat*, Cairo: Government Press, Bulak.
6. *Waqf*, singular of *Awqaf*, literally means to stop, to retain, to prevent, to immobilize, etc . . . There are, however, many definitions offered for the term which are all referring to a banned charity which cannot be sold, bought, given or inherited and its revenues go to charity. For the different definitions of *waqf*, see Abdel-Wahab Khalaf (1953) *Ahkam al-waqf*, Cairo: Matba'a al-Nasr, pp. 6–7. For

the role of the *waqf* institution in preserving *waqf* buildings, see Muhammad Afifi (1988) 'Asalib al-intifa 'al-iqtisadi bi-al-awqaf fi misr fi al-'asr al-'uthmani', in *Annales Islamologiques*, vol. 24, pp. 108–27. For a comparison between the approach of the *waqf* system and the Comité to building preservation, see Alaa El-Habashi (2001) *From athar to Monuments: the intervention of the Comité in Cairo*, Ph.D. dissertation, University of Pennsylvania.

7. The Mosque of Amr ibn al-'As was registered under number 516 in the first Comité's unpublished list of monuments (known as the 1886 Rogers' list). On Rogers' list and other lists of monuments produced by the Comité, see Alaa El-Habashi, and Nicholas Warner, (1998) 'Recording the Monuments of Cairo', *Annales Islamologiques*, vol. 32, pp. 83–84.

8. For a comparative study of the *waqf* preservation principles and the Comité's preservation philosophies, see El-Habashi (2001) *op. cit.* For the Comité's and locals' different preservation objectives, see Alaa El-Habashi, and Ihab Elzyadi, (1998) 'Consuming Built Patrimony, Social Perspectives and Preservation Strategies in Modern Cairo: A Chronological Cross-Disciplinary Analysis', in *IASTE working paper series*, vol. 1.

9. For the shifts in the Comité early phases, see Achille Patricolo, (1914) *Histoire du Comité, La Conservation des monuments arabes en Égypte,* Cairo. For the continuous changes in the Comité's administration structure, see Donald Reid, (1992) 'Cultural Imperialism and Nationalism: the Struggle to Define and Control the Heritage of Arab Art in Egypt', *International Journal of Middle East Studies* 24, pp. 57–76. See also Philipp Speiser, (2001), *Die Erhaltung der arabischen Bauten in Agypten, Reihe ADAIK*, Heidelberg.

10. On the contradiction of approaches between the Comité, and the *Awqaf* and the users of Mosques, see El-Habashi and Elzyadi, *op. cit.*

11. See B.C. 31 (1914): P.V. 210, pp. 79–80; P.V. 211, pp. 88–89; P.V. 214, p. 125.

12. On the question of the Caliphate, see Elie Kedourie, (1963) 'Egypt and the Caliphate', *Journal of the Royal Asiatic Society*, pp. 208–48.

13. The inquiries were sent from the following countries: 2 South Africa, 2 Algeria, 86 Germany, 33 United States, 44 England, 3 Australia, 42 Austria, 17 Belgium, 2 Bulgaria, 1 Belgian Congo, 1 Denmark, 72 Egypt, 8 Spain, 62 France, 3 Greece, 5 Hungary, 2 India, 3 Yugoslavia, 61 Italy, 1 Kenya, 7 Palestine, 1 Poland, 3 Riga, 8 Romania, 2 Russia, 5 Singapore, 26 Switzerland, 14 Czechoslovakia, 3 Tripoli, 6 Turkey. See the Competition Jury (1927), 'Procès-verbaux du jury pour le concours de la Mosquée de Amr', unpublished report.

14. See Ahmad Zaki's opinion on the concept of reconstruction in *Tajdid Jami' 'Amr: hal yaguz tanfiz al-risum?, al-Ahram*, 25 June 1927, p. 1. Other critics explained the shortage of submissions as due to the complexity and lack of clarity of the competition's program. See, for example, Angelo Sammarco (the court official historian), *Tajdid jami' 'amru wa musabaqat wad' al-rusum lahu, al-Ahram*, 1 July 1927, p. 1.

15. Ibrahim Fawzi was studying architecture at that time in the Beaux-Arts of Paris. In Paris, Ibrahim Fawzi was a neighbor of Maurice Mantout, another participant of the competition.

16. The following were the returning addresses for the Egyptian teams: Architect Ibrahim Fawzy, 12 rue Victor-Considérant, Paris XIV; Mahmoud Fouad, engineer in *ma'mouriyyat al-awqaf* in Qena (Upper Egypt); Hassan Sabri in No. 8, Atfet el-Chorbagui, El-Hayatim, Cairo; Mahmoud Ahmad and Mohammed Abdel Halim, Architectural Association, 34, Bedford Square, London. See the Competition Jury, *op. cit.*

17. Competitors' names and residences listed here are copied from the Jury report as they appeared. Residences reflect the returning addresses of each submission not the actual residence of each of the architects. Noel Dawson (fellow of the Royal Institute of British Architects) and K. A. C. Creswell (Honorary fellow of the Royal Institute of British Architects) had 'Rue de l'Ancienne Bourse, No 1, Alexandrie' as their returning addresses; Wulffleff, Verrey and Gavasi had '96, Rue de Grenelle, Paris, et 23, Rue Soliman Pacha, Le Caire' as their returning addresses; and Maurice Mantout had '10, Rue St. Florentin, Paris 10e' as his returning address.

18. See the Competition Jury, *op. cit.* The jury's decision was declared on 19 May in *al-Waqai' al-masriyya* and published in *al-Ahram* on 1 July 1927.

19. See *al-Handasa*, Vol. 7, No. 10, October 1927, pp. 418–36; and No. 11, November 1927, pp. 474–88. I could not locate the issues of *al-Balagh al-Yawmi* to check on the publication of these series in it.

20. The members of the jury were: Muhammad Shafiq, president of the jury and ex-Minister of Public Works; Sayyid Mitwalli, the chief architect of the Ministry of *Waqf*; Ahmad al-Sayyid, the director of the Monuments Services at the Ministry of *Waqf*; Aly Hassan Ahmad, the under secretary general of the State buildings department at the Ministry of Public Works; Mustafa Fahmy, the general director of State buildings and later the general director of *Tanzim*; Ernesto Verrucci, the chief architect of the Egyptian Royal Palaces; P. Conin-Pastour, the general director of the State Buildings department at the Ministry of Public Works; Gaston Wiet, the director of the Arab Museum; Pierre Lacau, the general director of the Egyptian Antiquities Service; P. Albert; E. G. Newnum.

21. To describe the competition's result, the wondering architect used the Arabic term '*gharib*', which has a dual meaning: either 'foreign' or 'strange.'

22. For an interpretation of those international treaties at the time of their release, see A. Assabghy, and E. Colombani, (1926) *Les questions de nationalité en Égypte*, Cairo: Imprimerie Misr.

23. See Mahmud Muhammad Suliman, (1996) *Al-ajanib fi misr dirasa fi tarikh misr al-ijtima'i*, Giza: Ein for Human and Social Studies, pp. 17–18. For a brief and a concise reference on the evolution of laws concerning Egyptian nationality, see Suliman pp. 11–51. See also Frédéric Abecassis, and Anne Le Gall-Kazazian, (1992) 'L'identité au miroir du droit: le statut des personnes en Égypte (fin XIXe-milieu XXe siècle)', in *Egypte/Monde Arabe*, 11, p. 11–38.

24. Article 10 in both 1926 and 1929's laws. For the laws and their interpretation, see Abecassis and Le Gall-Kazazian, *op. cit.*, p. 19.

25. Laila Shukry El-Hamamsy traces the basis of this identity in Egypt back to antiquity. See Laila Shukry El-Hamamsy, (1975) 'The Assertion of Egyptian identity', *Cairo Social Research Center Reprint Series*, Series No. 24, Cairo: The American University in Cairo Press.

26. Such a call was initiated, though with the aim of religious reform, by Jamal al-Din al-Afghani (1838–1897), and later by Muhammad 'Abdu (1849–1905). On the assertion of Islamic versus Arab identity, see Muhammad 'Imara (1967) *Al 'urubah fi al-'asr al-hadith*, Cairo, p. 276. See also by the same author, *Tajdid al-fikr al-islami: Muhammad 'abdu wa madrasatuh*, Kitab al-hilal: 360, December 1980. See also Tariq al-Bishri, (1998) *Bayn al-islam wa al-'uruba*, Cairo: Dar al-Shuruq, specially pp. 19–33.

27. Hussein Mu'nis stated that that was how Sa'd Zaghlul (1857–1927), the leader of the 1919 revolution, referred to the people: see Hussein Mu'nis (1936) 'Misr wa madiha', *Turath misr al-qadima*, *Muqtataf*, September, pp. 1–8.

28. For a concise discussion on the development of local identity in Egypt at the beginning of the twentieth century, see Sawsan al-Messiry, (1978) *Ibn al-Balad: a Concept of Egyptian identity*, Leiden, pp. 30–35.

29. The number of foreigners in Egypt was chronologically as follows: in 1843 there were 6,150; in 1871 the number was 79,696; in 1882 there were 90,886; in 1897, 11,300; in 1907, 151,414; in 1917, 183,015; and in 1927, 225,600. See Suliman, *op. cit*, pp. 56–68.

30. Muhandis ha'ir (a wondering architect), *Musabaqat tagdid jami' 'Amr, al-handasa*, Vol. 7, No. 11, 1927, pp. 477–87.

31. Ibid., p. 486.

32. Ibid., p. 478.

33. Mubarak was appointed upon the Khedive decree of November 1882.

34. With the reorganization of the local government in 1878, beside his appointment as the Minister of Public Works, Ali Mubarak was also appointed as the first Minister of *al-Awqaf*, and *al-Ma'arif* (education). See F. Karam (1994) *Al-nizarat wa al-wizarat al-misriah (Egyptian Ministries)*, second edn., Cairo: al-Hay'a al-misria al-'ama li-il kitab, pp. 641, 645 and 655.

35. For Mubarak's opposition to the conservation of *Zawiya* and *Sabil* Farag Ibn Barquq see B.C. 1 (1882–83), P.V. 2, 14. See also B. F. Musallam, (1976) 'The modern vision of 'Ali Mubarak', in *The Islamic City* (edited by R. B. Serjant), Faculty of Oriental Studies, Cambridge, from 19 to 23 July 1976.

36. 'A-t'on besoin de tant de monuments? Quand on conserve un échantillon, cela ne suffit-il pas?' Quoted from Marcel Clerget, (1934) *Le Caire*, vol. I, Cairo, p. 337.

37. Ali Mubarak, *'Alam al-din*, first published in 1882, vol. III, p. 863.

38. See Ali Mubarak, *al-Khitat al-Tawfiqiyya*, vol. I, p. 83; vol. III, pp. 63, 67–68, 82–83, 118–120; vol. IX, p. 53.

39. For Fraud's career, see Mercedes Volait's contribution, in this volume, p. 23. For Gran's activities in the Comité, review the minutes and technical reports published in the Comité's bulletins 1 to 14.

40. Arthur Rhoné, (1883) 'Le Comité de conservation et le conseil du Tanzim', *Chronique des Arts*, pp. 43–44.

41. Mubarak's three meetings with the Comité were: meeting No. 2 (16 December 1882), No. 3 (20 January 1883) and No. 4 (3 March 1883) of the Comité sequence of meetings. B.C. 1, 1882–83, P.V. 2, 3, and 4.

42. See, for example, F. Robert Hunter, (1984) *Egypt under the Khedives 1805–1879: From Household Government to Modern Bureaucracy*, Pittsburg: University of Pittsburgh Press, pp. 123–38.

43. Sabir Sabri was appointed as a Comité member in 1893, and attended his last meeting on 24 June 1915. He had been a member for 23 years. See B.C. 32, P.V. 222, p. 383.

44. Max Herz was an Austro-Hungarian architect who joined the Comité in 1887. He was responsible for the execution of important restoration work at the complexes of Qalawun, Sultan Hasan, Barquq and for the completion of the building of al-Rifa'i. He also served as the Director of the Museum of Arab Art. He was expelled from Egypt as an enemy alien after the outbreak of the First World War in 1914. On Max Herz, see István Ormos, (2001) 'Max Herz (1856–1919): his Life and Activities in Egypt', in Mercedes Volait, (ed.) *Le Caire-Alexandrie: Architectures européennes, 1850–1950*, Cairo: IFAO/Cedej, pp. 161–77; and 'Preservation and Restoration: the Methods of Max Herz Pasha, Chief Architect of the Comité de Conservation des Monuments de l'Art arabe, 1890–1914', in Jill Edwards, (2002) *Historians in Cairo: Essays in Honour of George Scanlon*, Cairo: The American University in Cairo Press, pp. 123–53.

45. B.C. 14, 1897, R. 217, pp. 81–82. Saber Sabri's own words were: '*les couleurs
    . . . sont trop pâles et invisibles pour le spectateur, il serait bon de les retoucher
    suffisamment pour qu'elles puissent donner l'effet et le but pour lesquels elles
    sont conçus; c'est de détacher visiblement l'octogone de la calotte sphéroïde.*'
46. Viollet-le-Duc, *Dictionnaire raisonné de l'architecture française du XIe au XVIe
    siècle*, 1868–74, VII, p. 14.
47. B.C. 14, 1897, R. 217, p. 82. The Comité's decision was to '*peindre la frise en
    bois qui couronne les lambris de la coupole, conformément à l'échantillon que
    M. Herz bey a fait faire en reproduisant l'ancienne peinture dont les traces sont
    visibles à plusieurs endroits de la frise*'.
48. Sabri, for example, was involved in designing and constructing several mosques
    for the *Awqaf* department. See Sabir Sabri (1906) *Sura al-muzakirra allati rufi'at
    li-al-janib al-'ali al-khidiwi*, Cairo: al-Awqaf.
49. Antoine Batigelli, an Italian architect, and Dr. Moritz, the director of the Khedivial
    library, supported Herz's opinion. Both figures, as I was told by István Ormos who
    is writing a biography on Herz, were reported to be friends of Herz. See B.C. 15,
    1898, R. 237, p. 65.
50. Ibid., P.V. 83.
51. Ibid., p. 56.
52. P.J. Vatikiotis, (1992) *The History of Modern Egypt from Muhammad Ali to
    Mubarak*, 4th edition, Baltimore: The Johns Hopkins University Press, pp. 249–72.
53. See Khedival decree No. 6 of 14 January 1900. See also B.C. 17, 1900, P.V. 96,
    p. 2, and B.C. 17, 1900, P.V. 98, p. 19.
54. Ali Bahgat was appointed director of the Museum of Arab Art after the resigna-
    tion of Max Herz who had to leave the country after the outbreak of the First
    World War as an enemy alien. See B.C. 31, 1914, P.V. 215, pp. 134–36. For a
    short account of Herz, see note 44 above.
55. See Ahmad Lutfi al-Sayyid (1998), *Qissa Hayati* (The story of my life), Cairo: al-
    hay'a al-'ama li-al-kitab, (new edition), pp. 28–29.
56. Ahmad al-Sayyid was eventually appointed a member of the Comité by Royal
    decree of 25 May 1922. For the Royal decree see B.C. 33, 1920–1924, P.V. 263,
    pp. 225–27. In 1927, Ahmad al-Sayyid was appointed the director of the Service
    of Arab Monuments, leaving his position, chief architect of the Ministry of Awqaf,
    to his colleague Sayyid Mitwalli.
57. See B.C. 33, 1920–1924, P.V. 264, pp. 249–52.
58. Ali Bahgat (1858–1924) made remarkable contributions to the excavation work
    in Fustat, and was able to publish several studies on the discoveries. Bahgat also
    had noteworthy publications and translations that described the contents of the
    Museum of Arab Art. See, for example, Ali Bahgat, and Albert Gabriel, (1921)
    Fouilles d'al Foustat, Paris: E. de Boccard; and Ali Bahgat, and Felix Massoul,
    (1930) *La céramique musulmane de l'Egypte*, Cairo: l'Institut Français
    d'archéologie Orientale.
59. For the negativity of Ahmad al-Sayyid see, for example, his position towards the
    reconstruction of the Mimbar of the Mosque of Baybars. B.C. 33, 1920–1924, P.V.
    263, pp. 223–224.
60. See B.C. 34, 1925–1926, P.V. 265, pp. 58–62.
61. Pauty was a graduate of the Ecole des Beaux-Arts in Paris, and an ex-director of
    the Service des Monuments Historiques du Maroc. He was hired in the Comité
    as '*Architect Expert*' beside Ahmed al-Sayyid. See B.C. 35, 1927–1929, P.V. 271,
    p. 123.

62. Gaston Wiet had contributed to this structural change. He, on the one hand, highlighted the inefficiencies of Ahmad al-Sayyid's work and, on the other, had introduced his countryman Pauty to the Comité. See B.C. 35, 1927–1929, P.V. 270, p. 86.

63. For the formation of the Comité's Technical Bureau, see B.C. 7, 1890, P.V. 40, pp. 3–4. Max Herz was the architect in chief of the Bureau. Mahmud Ahmad was first mentioned in 1920 when the president of the Comité, Hussein Darwish, requested a rise for him during the institution's meeting of February 1920. See B.C. 32, 1915–1919, P.V. 252, p. 755.

64. The School of Arts and Crafts was first established in 1839 under the name of *madrasa al-'amaliyyat* (School of Operations). It was forcibly closed in 1854, and re-opened under the same name in 1868. In 1877, it was named *madrasa al-'amaliyyat wa al-sina'at* (School of Operations and Crafts). It is only after 1885 that the school was named *madrasat al-finun wa al-sina'at* (School of Arts and Crafts). See Yacoub Artin, (1890) *L'instruction publique en Égypte*, Paris: Ernest Leroux, p. 196. For the program of the school and the courses taught it, see Amin Sami, (1917) *Al-ta'lim fi misr*, Cairo: al-Ma'arif, pp. 17–19. See also J. Heyworth-Dunne, (1939) *Introduction to the History of Education in Modern Egypt*, London: Luzac & Co., pp. 357–58.

65. For the relationship between the *awqaf*'s 'Bureau des Monuments', the Comité and the *awqaf*'s Technical Service, see *Waqf* decree of 30 January, 1922, published in B.C. 33, 1920–1924, pp. 189–198.

66. Ibid., R. 596, p. 327.

67. It seems that the members of the Comité were not allowed to participate in the competition, but only in its jury committee. Mahmud Ahmad and K.A.C. Creswell were not members at the time when the competition was held. After their appointments, however, each definitely played an important role in shaping the institution's agenda.

68. See B.C. 37, 1933–1935, P.V. 280, pp. 33–34.

69. Ibid., p. 34.

70. The Comité's own words were: '. . . *sa présence aux réunions étant nécessaire, pour qu'il puisse éclairer les Membres sur les travaux en cours*' and also ' . . . *en assistant aux réunions de la Section Technique, sera à même de mieux pénétrer les vues du* Comité, *en vue des décisions à exécuter.*' See B.C. 37, 1933–1935, R. 686, p. 142.

71. Ibid, R. 692, pp. 198–99. For more information on Mahmud Ahmad see the biography that Hassan Abdel-Wahab provided in the obituary published in *al-Ahram*, 30 November 1942, p. 3. Also see Khayr al-din al-Zirikli, *al-A'lam: qamus tarajim li-ashhar al-rigal wa al-nisa' min al-'arab wa al-musta'ribin wa al-mustashriqin*, second edition (first edition in three volumes published in 1927), Cairo: Costatsomas Press, 1955, p. 40.

72. *Al-Handasa* is a monthly review that was published from 1920 up until 1938. For the foundation constitution and the list of the founders of *al-Handasa*, see *al-Handasa*, vol. 1, No.1, December 1920, pp. 29–36.

73. See Muhandis Ha'ir (the wondering architect), 'Musabaqat tajdid Jami' 'Amr', *al-Balagh al-Usbu'i*, No. 35, 22 July 1927, pp. 18–19, republished in *al-Handasa*, Vol. 7, Nos. 8 and 9, August and September 1927, pp. 389–91.

74. It should be noted that Mahmud Ahmad had a long publishing relationship with *al-Balagh al-Usbu'i* and *al-Yawmi* (weekly and daily). He had published in them several articles during the years 1927–1928. If the hypothesis was proved true,

Ahmad's familiarity with the publishing procedures in *al-Balagh* had definitely facilitated publication of his criticism of the Jury's decision under an anonymous name.

75. Mohamed Abdel-Halim, and Mahmoud Ahmad, (1926) 'Concours pour la reconstruction de la mosquée d'Amrou au temps de sa plus grande splendeur,' unpublished report submitted to the Ministry of Awqaf. Note the linguistic mistakes made by Ahmad and Abdel-Halim.

76. Among the very few studies that described local building materials, one can point to Édouard Mariette, (1886) *Traité pratique et raisonné de la construction en Égypte*, second edition, Paris: Librairies Générale de l'Architecture et des Travaux Publics; and the explicit discussion of Muhammad 'Arif devoted to the subject in his 1897's book, *Khulasat al-afkar fi fann al-mi'mar* (Cairo: Bulaq). A. Lucas and W. F. Hume had contributed some detailed studies on building stones in Egypt during the first two decades of the twentieth century. Apart from the short and few essays related to the subject published in *al-Handasa* in the 1920s, it is only after the 1930s that some Egyptian engineers devoted special attentions to list and analyze local construction materials. See, for example, Husayn Mohamed Salih, (1930) *Handasa al-mabani wa il-insha'at: muad al-bina'*, Cairo: Dar al-kutub al-misriyya.

77. Abdel-Halim and Ahmad, *op. cit.*

78. Ibrahim Fawzi came fifth in this competition. For Ibrahim's design, see 'Ibrahim Fawzi: A congratulation for the winning of the fifth position', *al-Handasa*, vol. 4, No. 4, 1924, p. 178.

79. See Ibrahim Fawzi, (1926) 'Concours pour la reconstruction de la mosquée d'Amrou au temps de sa plus grande splendeur', unpublished report submitted to the Ministry of *Awqaf*.

80. See the Competition Jury, *op. cit.*

81. 'A wondering architect', *Musabaqat tajdid jami' 'amr*, *al-Handasa*, Vol. 7, No. 10, October 1927, pp. 418–436.

82. Ibid., No. 11, November 1927, p. 478.

83. For a complete analysis of the competition, its entries, the competitors and the jury members, see Alaa El-Habashi's forthcoming 'The Competition of the Reconstruction of the Mosque of 'Amr'.

84. In his report, Fu'ad wrote: '*Nous invoquons Dieu pour qu'il inspire aux Egyptiens de se préoccuper de la ville de Fostat et de lui rendre la magnificence islamique qu'elle possédait à l'époque des Fatimides quand elle était contiguë au Caire et était le centre de l'industrie et du commerce. Ce n'est pas impossible à Dieu.*' See Mahmud Fu'ad, (1926) 'Concours pour la reconstruction de la mosquée d'Amrou au temps de sa plus grande splendeur', unpublished report presented with a set of architectural drawings as entry I for the competition of the reconstruction of the Mosque of 'Amr, Ministry of Waqfs.

85. K.A.C. Creswell was appointed a Comité member in 1939.

86. Noel Dawson, and K.A.C. Creswell, (1926) 'Projet de reconstruction de la moquée d'Amrou au Caire au temps de sa plus grande splendeur', unpublished report, Ministry of Waqfs, pp. 27–30.

87. See, for example, Mahmud Ahmad, (1938) *Jami' 'amru ibn al-'As bi al-Fustat min al-nahiyatin al-tarikhiyya wa al-athariyya*, Cairo: Bulaq, which was translated a year later into English; and 'al Fustat', a series of articles he published in *al-Balagh al-Usbu'i*, vols. 54, 56, 58 in 1927, and vols. 61, 63, 65, 69 in 1928.

88. See the Competition Jury, 'Procés-verbaux du jury pour le concours de la mosquée de Amr', unpublished report, 1927.

89. All of the jury members, except P. Albert and E. G. Newnum, were members of the Comité.

90. Suliman states that in 1879 not less than 208 foreigners were working for the State. This number had reached 250 in 1880. The year 1882 had reinstated the status of the foreigners working for the State as their number reached 1355. This number started to decline, to 690 in 1896 (7.5 per cent of total State employees). In 1906 the number of foreign employees had grown once more, to reach 1252 (9.4 per cent of total State employees). Suliman, *op. cit.*, p. 116.

91. The Egyptians were: Muhammad Zaki, Mustafa Fahmy, Mahmud Sami, Mahmud al-Falaky, Ismail al-Falaky, Izzat effendi, Ya'coub Sabry, Aly Fahmi; and the foreigners were: Julius Franz, Edward Rogers, Ambroise Baudry. On the founding members of the Comité, see Mercedes Volait, (2002) 'Amateurs français et dynamique patrimoniale: aux origines du Comité de conservation des monuments de l'art arabe', in Daniel Panzac, and André Raymond, (eds) *La France et l'Egypte à l'époque des vice-rois (1805–1882)*, Cairo: Institut français d'archéologie orientale, pp. 311–26. The Khedival decree is published in *al-Waqa'i al-masriyya*, December 1881, and in the first bulletin of the Comité published in 1882, pp. 8–10.

92. See Jules Bourgoin, (1879) *Les éléments de l'art arabe: le trait des entrelacs*, Paris: Librairie de Firmin-Didot et Cie.

93. Anon., 'The protection of the monuments of Cairo', *The Architect*, 4 August 1883, p. 66.

94. Suliman, *op. cit.*, p. 129.

95. In April 1927 a total of 18 members constituted the body of the Comité: 12 Egyptians and 6 foreigners. For the names of the Comité members, see B.C. 34, 1925–26.

96. In December 1930 a total of 17 members constituted the body of the Comité: 9 Egyptians and 8 foreigners.

97. Law No. 44 of May 1936. For the law, see *al-Waqa'I' al-masriyya*.

98. In 1936 foreigners numbered 1623 in State positions. The Ministry of Public Instruction had the largest share of this number. Suliman points out that the majority of these foreign employees were British. See Suliman, *op. cit.*, p. 129.

99. See Khedive Abbas Helmi II's decree of 13 July 1895 and published in *al-Magmu'a al-dayma li-il-qawanin wa ql-qararat al-misriyya*, vol. 6.

100. See the report of the Ministry of Public Instruction on the work of the Administration of the Conservation of Arab Monuments (1949) *Idarat hifz al-athar al-'arabiyya risalatuhafi ru'yyat al-athar al-islamiyya fi al-qahira*, Cairo: dar al-ma'arif, p.4. See, also, Mahmud Ahmad, the then Director of Arab Monuments, Avant-Propos, in B.C. 36, 1930–32.

101. See Suliman, *op. cit.*, p. 132.

102. See P.V. 284, 285 and 286, B.C. 38.

103. The number of foreigners working for the State declines in 1937 to 186,515, and fell to 145,912 in 1947.

104. B.C. 38, 1936–1940, P.V. 287, p. 135.

105. Three foreigners attended the meeting of 1951 along with 12 Egyptians (20% foreigners). See P.V. 302, B.C. 40, 1946–1953, p. 304.

106. Ibid., P.V. 303, pp. 363–64.

107. Decree 22/1953. See *Al-mawsu'a al-tashri'iyya al-haditha*, Hassan al-Fakahani (lawyer), 26 volumes, Cairo: al-dar al-'arabiyya li-al-mawsu'at.

108. See the explanatory law no. 529 issued in 1953. A further revision of this law was issued in 1970 (Law no. 27 of 1970), published in *al-Waqa'i al-masriyya*, issue 21, September 21, 1970.
109. See Muhammad Khalifa Hasan, (1997) *Athar al-fikr al-istishraqi fi al-mujtama'at al-islamiyya*, Cairo: Ein for Human and Social Studies, pp. 88–89.
110. See, for example, El-Hamamsy, *op. cit.*

PART III

POWERFUL SUBJECTS

CHAPTER 8

FROM EUROPE TO TRIPOLI IN BARBARY, VIA ISTANBUL: MUNICIPAL REFORMS IN AN OUTPOST OF THE OTTOMAN EMPIRE AROUND 1870

Nora Lafi

Independent scholar

The nineteenth century in North Africa witnessed the advance of European imperialism and diminishing Ottoman influence. Only Tripoli in Barbary, or Trâblus al-Gharb (Libya's current capital) was to remain under the authority of the Sublime Porte until the latter part of the century.

Located on the southern shore of the Mediterranean, Tripoli was, in the early decades of the nineteenth century, a modest city surrounded by a 'green belt' – the Manchia. Its *intra muros* population at the time can be estimated at about 12,000 inhabitants. The city experienced continuous growth, becoming an urban center of approximately 30,000 inhabitants by the 1870s.[1]

Between sea and sand, the town nevertheless appeared as an important strategic location between East and West, as well as between Europe and Africa. Trade and the other activities of the city had created a unique urban society. A pirate stronghold, it functioned as a virtually autonomous city-state during the Qaramânlî Dynasty (1711–1835).[2]

Tripoli later became a city of the Ottoman Empire directly administered from Istanbul, and was to remain as such until the Italian colonization (1911). Several *hûma* (quarters principally inhabited by Muslims), two *hâra* (Jewish quarters) and a mixed neighborhood composed the *intra muros* space of the walled city. A commercial and military harbor, houses, forts (12), mosques, synagogues, a church, baths (*hammâm*), souks, caravanserais, coffee shops, mills, schools and a castle (*al-hisâr*) made up the physical structure of the town.

The last bastion and peripheral province of the Ottoman Empire from 1835 onward, Tripoli is a unique case in the context of expanding imperialism in the Mediterranean. At the time, prey to various problems and in reaction to developments in Europe, the Ottoman Empire launched major modernization initiatives based on European models. The military reorganization was a success, and these *Tanzîmât* reforms were to be applied in other fields. Local administration was one such area, and cities, vital settings for modern life, were the object of particular attention. While borrowing from the West, the achievements and organization of which were envied, a considerable effort was necessary to adapt such achievements to the Ottoman context – in short they had to be 'Ottomanized'.

A study of the impact of such reforms – at the forefront of which was municipal reform – in the province of Tripoli, implies taking into account the development of the Western European model and how this was transformed in its application. This article, after an overview of administrative reforms in the Ottoman Empire, will focus on the case of Tripoli in the mid-nineteenth century. We are dealing here with the development of an imported, borrowed model that was subsequently re-exported to a region far from the heart of the Empire. The article attempts to show how the model as known in the West, that is an administrative body composed of a group of people, mayor and elected representatives managing an area in urban, social, economic and even political terms according to a set of institutionalized rules, was accepted, modified and finally applied in such a peripheral province.

What is of particular interest in the case of Tripoli is to examine how, in a town that remained isolated from direct influence of the European colonial powers for much longer than its neighbors,[3] a 'European-inspired' reform of the local administration could be implemented. In such a reform, the impact of two distinct dynamics can in fact be detected: on one hand, the indirect influence of the European municipal model channeled through the Ottoman efforts of administrative modernization, and on the other a local process of transformation of the traditional exercise of power by the elites on urban society and space. The case study of Tripoli thus offers an excellent opportunity to discuss the role of the periphery and its elite in the modernization movement of the Ottoman Empire. It also allows analysis of the extent to which administrative modernization was, for the central power, a crucial stake in maintaining its influence on the provinces.

NINETEENTH-CENTURY ADMINISTRATIVE REFORM PROJECTS IN THE OTTOMAN EMPIRE: THE CASE OF THE EUROPEAN-STYLE MUNICIPALITY

There has been much research into the *Tanzîmāt*, the legal reforms conducted by the Ottoman State in the nineteenth century, both at the local and central levels.[4] In the case of urban reforms there are a number of high-quality pieces of research.[5] However, the smallest entity in the administrative system, intermediary between population, experts and authorities – namely the *baladiyya*, or municipality – has attracted much less attention, and studies on the transfer or importation of European-style municipalities to the Ottoman provinces are still quite rare.[6]

Social, political and economic factors led the Ottoman rulers to seek to modernize. Little by little the paradigm of modernity through modernization took root, in multiple forms, appearing as essential to the elite on whom the future of the Empire depended. The desire for change and development implied by 'modernity' came from Europe, and at a time when a journey to the East was essential for anyone who claimed intellectual allegiance to the Enlightenment, when writers, scientists and merchants were developing a passion for the Orient, it was to the West that the Ottomans turned with growing curiosity. The economic successes of old Europe, its military expansion and scientific achievements were undoubtedly of huge interest to the Ottoman leadership, and Europe and modernity were intimately linked in its collective mind. The new technologies in diverse domains would have to be adopted one way or another.

However, regarding the city, this importation of European models was not to take place simply or on the basis of a continuous process of borrowing. Taking the example of the Western municipality, the transfer process was a slow one, beginning in the first quarter of the nineteenth century.

A number of stages are clearly identifiable before the establishment of two model municipalities effectively copied from the West, namely in the Beyoghlu and Galata neighborhoods of Istanbul. The first stage began with the study of European institutions and urbanism by Ottoman ambassadors, students, military experts and emissaries of all kinds who traveled widely in Europe, observing and gathering information. Projects were then designed back home, and the two experimental municipalities founded. It was only later that the municipal experiment was widened to include other cities in the Empire – among the first of which was Tripoli in Barbary.

The observation of European institutions and the design of reform projects

Reforms were first launched under Mahmud II (1807–39), although initially they concerned only military matters. Civil reforms were to follow somewhat later. Officials and others were sent westwards on short special missions or for longer periods of study, while foreign technical experts were recruited in Istanbul, notably for the navy and the army. The Ottoman Empire opened up to the West, and in particular to France, and there was a huge growth in contacts between Ottomans and Westerners. A mixture of fascination and curiosity led the Ottoman leadership to draw inspiration from advances in Western techniques and institutions.

The task of determining what were the exact sources of inspiration, the places, the actors and the circumstances still remains to be applied to the municipal institution. Although it is relatively easy to discover precise details regarding the transfer of a piece of military technology or organization, this task is much more difficult with regard to administrative reforms.[7]

Reforms, of course, cannot be reduced to the results of simple fascination with the Other and the Ottoman desire for change. The factors were much more complex, and there were major shifts – economic, social and political – taking place in the nineteenth century that underpinned the institutional developments of the day. Whatever the case may be, Istanbul, for example, underwent major organizational changes, and these have been well researched by Lewis, Dumont, Yerasimos and Çelik. The point to be stressed is that, from the early nineteenth century, there was a heightened – or quite simply new – awareness of the city as an entity in itself. The Western city was observed by the Ottomans, as was the organization of Istanbul, and the result was the drawing up of a design for a European-style municipality.

One of the first notable innovations in the capital of the Sublime Porte was a reform that made 'the urban services that were at one time undertaken by the janissaries – for instance the police and the fire brigade – into the responsibility of specialized urban bodies: the *muhtasib*, formerly officially responsible for markets, received the title of *ihtisab aghasi* (1828), and became one of the leading elements of the city, with neighborhood officials (*mukhtar, kahya*) under his authority; he was assisted by a Council of Elders, representing the different components of the city (religious, ethnic and economic communities)'.[8]

A new phase began in 1854 (1271 H.), when the *Majlis Ali lil-Tanzîmāt,* the High Council on Reform, decided 'to create a municipal commission (*intizam-i shehir komisyonu*)'. 'The leading light in this commission was one Antoine Allion, member of a wealthy French banking family that had settled in Turkey during the French Revolution. The other members were mainly drawn from the local Greek, Armenian and Jewish communities, with a few Muslim Turks, including the *hekimbashi* Mehmed Salih Efendi, one of the first graduates of the school of medicine founded by Sultan Mahmud. The commission was charged with presenting a report on European municipal organization, its rules and procedures, along with recommendations on this question to the Sublime Porte.'[9]

The commission worked away for four years. The archives of the High Council on Reform, with its lengthy deliberations, show that it was felt that there was a very real need for the creation of a European-type urban administration. The main recommendations of the commission, regarding improvements in city conditions, 'concerned the building of pavements, sewers, water conduits, the daily collection of refuse, public lighting, street widening – where possible, the organization of municipal financial autonomy, the establishment of a city rate, and a request to be made responsible for the application of municipal regulations'.[10] Following this period of discussion, the recommendations were submitted to the authorities, and it was decided to test the reforms at a small scale before implementing them in all the towns and cities of the Empire.

Testing the reforms: two pilot municipalities

It was not until 1857 that the High Council decided to experiment with the new form of municipal management in two neighborhoods of Istanbul. The aim was to see what risks and problems could arise alongside the hoped-for advantages. The two areas chosen, Beyoghlu and Galata, had large populations of foreign residents. The experiment should be seen as a clear attempt to adapt the new model to local realities. The objective was clear: 'When the merits of these institutions have been shown by this example, and understood and accepted by all, then it will be time to apply them to all neighborhoods'.[11] The apparent slowness with which the reform was applied should perhaps be seen as an attempt to 'Ottomanize' the model.

This Ottomanization began with the selection of a suitable translation for the term municipality within the Empire. According to Bernard Lewis, the neologism *belediyye* in Turkish and other Near Eastern languages (in Tripoli, the Arabic adaptation is *baladiyya*) was chosen specially to designate the modern European-style municipal institutions in contrast to older Muslim forms of urban government. However, the term, derived from the Arabic *balad*, often used to designate the town, should be seen as an expression of the will of the reformers to modernize in accordance with local conditions without alienating the population. In fact, one quarter in Tripoli has been named *baladiyya* since at least the end of the eighteenth century; an important figure of the management of the city was located there – the *shaykh al-bilâd*, chief of the council of notables (primarily merchants and heads of guilds).[12]

The merits of the new institution were clear by 1868 (1285 H.). After numerous difficulties (as described by Lewis), including some cautiousness, or at least tardiness (14 years) in implementing the new reforms, most probably due to the weight of bureaucracy, the wariness of the decision-makers and the inertia of the established powers,[13] it was decided that the 'Ottoman' municipality, or *belediyye,* of Istanbul would be created as follows: 'Each neighborhood would have a committee of eight to twelve members, who would choose a president from among themselves. A general assembly (*jemiyyet-i umumiyye*) for Istanbul with 56 members would be set up, with three delegates for each neighborhood, named and remunerated by the imperial government. These two bodies would function under the control of the Prefect (*shehremini*), who would remain a State civil servant'.[14] The whole city was thus governed by some sort of municipal administration and conditions changed considerably, enabling it to compete with European capitals.

The Ottoman model surely had the secret ambition to imitate the administrative efficiency and opulence of Paris. Just like the French capital, Istanbul was divided into several *arrondissements* (*daire*). However, 'for the moment, only the sixth [*arrondissement*], covering the Galata and Pera neighborhoods, was created. The city officials [for this area] were given the task of making it into a model neighborhood with paved streets, pavements, public gas lighting, tap water, and regularly aligned buildings . . .'[15]

By 1868, the 'modern' instruments of urban management had finally won a place in the reforming Ottoman system. Thanks to the success of the pilot municipalities, the Ottomanized European model was to be subsequently transferred to other provincial Ottoman cities, among them Tripoli in Barbary, discussed here in the light of new archival research.

THE LOCAL ADVOCATES AND SPONSORS OF REFORM

An examination of the adaptation, or Ottomanization, of the European model in Istanbul gives us an idea of what was to be exported in terms of urban planning and administrative organization to one of the seven 'test cities' in the eastern Mediterranean.[16]

Before moving into details about this re-exportation of the European model, two points need to be emphasized. First, the context must be taken into consideration. Tripoli was the westernmost bastion of the Ottoman Empire, and thus represents a special case in North Africa, a paradox in more than one way. It was thanks to a detour via Istanbul that the Western model was imposed in Tripoli, in contrast to the other countries of the region where the establishment of the European model resulted from direct influence from Europe. However, it is also true that the authorities in Tripolitania were from outside. Although these authorities might appear less radically different from the power structures imposed by the French on other North African populations – the Ottomans were Muslim, the dynasty overthrown in 1835 had never pushed its autonomy as far as total independence, and the historic and commercial links had never been broken – they were nevertheless imposed from above, from the center of the Empire, without much finesse. There is no doubt that the inhabitants of Tripolitania had little enthusiasm for the powers that be, and there was certainly strong resistance: the reoccupation of the whole territory by the Turkish army was to take some 20 years.

The second point that needs to be stressed is that it seemed more useful to seek out the local figures responsible for the implementation of the municipal reforms, or the 'anonymous reformers' in Mantran's words. (Mantran has long stressed the importance of considering actors other than the major figures of the Sublime Porte in the implementation of the reforms.) These individuals are the best illustration of the human aspect of the issue, for as in many other human matters a taste for power and money accompanied a good dose of enthusiasm and hard work. The personalities and behavior of key individuals were essential to the success (or failure) of a project, often independent of other factors, be these economic, political, social or cultural. Another aspect of the reforms is that they were to lead to huge changes in the everyday habits of the population.

Among the reformers who played a leading role in Tripoli and who had remained 'anonymous' until very recently were the governor, representative of the Porte and the local *shaykh al-bilâd*, both of whom were crucial to the success of the enterprise at the local level. However, the population as a whole was involved – accustomed as it was to work against decisions taken at the central level.

An outstanding governor of Tripoli, ʿAlî Ridha al-Jazayrî

ʿAlî Ridha al-Jazayrî, governor-general, or *walî*, of Tripoli, was a fervent partisan of reforms and of the modernization movement. In this he stands out from his predecessors – and even from his successors – for the other governor-generals appointed to Tripoli considered their posting there as a form of purgatory where the only possible activity was quick self-enrichment while ignoring the country and its people. It is also true, however, that their short periods of office were unlikely to lead them to undertake major projects or become heavily involved in local matters. ʿAlî Ridha al-Jazayrî is thus an outstanding and unusual figure, and it is thanks to this individual that Tripoli set out on the path to modernization. He is undoubtedly the leading figure in the implementation of municipal reform.

As his family name – al-Jazayrî – indicates, this governor-general was a native of Algeria, and he held the post on two occasions, from 1867–70 and from 1872–73. He was born some time in the first quarter of the nineteenth century, in all likelihood in Algiers since 'his father had been *qadhi* of Algiers and his mother was still living in that city'.[17] However, he was to leave Algiers at an early age due to the French conquest of 1830.

Father and son took up residence in Constantinople, perhaps because of a parental desire to see his offspring equipped with an Ottoman education. The choice of Istanbul may have been a reaction to the French colonization of their homeland. The sources give us no information on this point, however it is ironic to note that ʿAlî Ridha Pacha 'was sent to France with other young men to receive a French education. He spent five years at the military school and three years at the Ecole d'application in Metz'[18]. His native language was Arabic, although he spoke perfect French having spent eight years in France. As he had lived and been educated at Istanbul as well, he probably spoke Turkish too, although Féraud (one of the best sources on him) states that this was not the case.

Although as governor 'he was surrounded by Arabs and Algerians', according again to Féraud he seems to have maintained excellent relations with the French consulate in Tripoli or, at the very least, with the consul-general, one M. Botta. In fact, even though he was not the son of a diplomat, he was a member of that generation of Ottomans who studied in the best French or English schools and who, once they had returned to Turkey, were among those to push hardest for reform.

The archival documents examined so far show that he also had close links with the sultan of the day, 'Abdul-'Azîz (1861–76), and with the Ottoman State apparatus. He would seem to have had full liberty to implement reforms in Tripoli. No doubt this was due in great part to the desire of Sultan 'Abdul-'Azîz to see the governors push forward the *tanzimât* in the provinces. In fact, 'at the suggestion of Ali Ridha Pacha, the Ottoman governor decreed in 1869 important measures to develop the resources of the vilayet of Tripoli and breathe new life into a province which had fallen into decadence'.[19] The construction of colossal new infrastructure at Tobrouk, and of a new city, shows the extent to which major Ottoman support, both financial and technical, was made available.

The confidence placed in 'Alî Ridha al-Jazayrî is also demonstrated by the fact that the Sultan adopted his major project without passing through the Council of State. The project consisted of developing the uninhabited land along the coast at Bomba for settlement (along with similar proposals for Tobrouk and Benghazi). Given the fact that it was an excellent natural harbor, Bomba had for many years been of interest to a number of maritime powers who had attempted to get the Ottoman Empire to cede the land to them. In all likelihood this was one of the reasons contributing to 'Alî Ridha Pacha's decision to undertake a major land development there. The following is an extract from Féraud's account of the project:

> . . . the travels of several foreign explorers had drawn ['Alî Ridha Pacha's] attention to this coast. He understood the advantages that the creation of the Suez Canal could bring to this naval port, situated in the middle of an inhospitable coast between Crete and Libya. He thus presented the project which was adopted by an imperial decree emanating directly from the Sultan, without the approval of the Council of State. . . . [E]quipment was made available to facilitate the execution of his plans. . . . A large quarantine facility was constructed, along with barracks and storage depots. Families settling there were to benefit from ten years of tax exemption and received free food for a year, the animals necessary to work the land and sea and building materials. A small town thus grew up, protected from the nomads, within the perfectly conserved walls of a Roman castellum, whose ruins provided ready made construction material. The surrounding land seemed suitable for cereal growing, and wells were sunk and the ancient dams for river waters rebuilt. Ali Riza Pacha intended to visit the site as soon as possible and establish a small garrison chosen from among the married soldiers, who would receive plots of land and the means to farm them. A land concession was offered to the Missionary Fathers so that they might build a hospice and a chapel, with a view to attracting Maltese immigrants. Free trips were organized for anyone wishing to study the area with a view to creating an

establishment of some kind. Already, the Prefect of the Catholic Mission, a number of merchants and a certain number of workers and craftsmen had announced their intention to accompany the Pacha. In June 1869, Ali Riza set sail on the Ottoman vessel for Bomba and Tobrouk to attempt to implement the colonization plans he had conceived. There were around four hundred people on this first expedition. Although it began under the best auspices, the enterprise was totally unsuccessful. Certain powers had designs on the natural ports of Bomba and Tobrouk, and manoeuvred to portray the project at Constantinople as though Ali Riza Pacha had drawn inspiration from the procedures used by the colonising French in Algeria, which would lead to the natives being ill-disposed towards the Turkish government. Without any detailed explanation, Ali Riza Pacha received the order to abstain henceforth from any innovation and in the following May, this intelligent Pacha was recalled.[20]

This edifying example brings together the procedures for the use of new techniques, along with 'concepts' in vogue at the time, such as colonization by creating settlements and the construction of new cities, inspired no doubt by the colonization projects undertaken by France in Algeria.

Nevertheless, 'Alî Ridha's projects were not just simply derived from Western 'procedures'; he was working to establish genuine technical co-operation with the French. He had modern machinery, along with French engineers, brought over from his native Algeria.

> Aware of the magnificent results achieved by the drilling of artesian wells in the Oued Rir region of Algeria, Ali Ridha got the Porte to accept similar projects in the Regency. He addressed himself to the French Consulate, and via them he obtained from the Government General of Algeria a project manager from one of our drilling units in the South, managed by the engineer Jus.[21]

'Alî Ridha Pacha's projects were numerous and varied, and all were strongly marked by a desire to modernize – following a French template: 'He was interested in improving the postal service, and had inaugurated the first telegraph line from Tripoli to Homs. He built the Aziziya market, named for the Sultan 'Abdul-'Azîz, the name of which was later given to a street in the modern town. He gave Tripoli a public park and a clocktower, and he restored the Citadel Mosque'.

He also played an influential role in establishing a Western form of urban management in Tripoli. It was mainly thanks to 'Alî Ridha Pacha (and the *shaykh al-bilâd* as we shall see below), that the project was undertaken as an extension of the decision by the Council of State to introduce new forms of urban management in the capitals of the Ottoman provinces.[22] The correspondence of the Pacha and the decrees he issued clearly demonstrate that he was the driving force behind this project.

The walî and the shaykh al-bilâd

As regards re-exportation of the institution of the municipality, or *baladiyya* in Arabic, it would seem that the Sublime Porte, prior to 1867, had requested 'Alî Ridha Pacha – then posted in Tripoli – to give his informed opinion on the matter of creating a municipality there. On 1 August 1867, the Pacha replied favorably to the idea of creating a European type of municipal management in Tripoli, and included with his reply a report on the situation of Tripoli in terms of urban administration. He thus aimed to get the Porte to understand that modernization would be linked to this new type of city management and that at the same time certain elements of local administration should be retained given that they would benefit the reforms.

The arguments presented in order to have Tripoli benefit from the new style of municipal management are based on a presentation of the merits of the *shaykh al-bilâd*'s function, and of the person holding the position at the time, 'Alî al-Qarqanî. We thus have a good idea of the nature of this local position of authority that had taken root under the Qaramânlî Dynasty and had survived its fall from power.[23]

The different attributes of the *shaykh al-bilâd* are enumerated in 'Alî Ridha's report, including his responsibilities with respect to trade: 'he is responsible for circulation patents and contracts'. The *shaykh*'s social position is also established: he 'is one of the local notables[24] and he is even the example and model, the representative of the leading merchants of the corporations and the sheikh of the city streets and of the notables who represent the whole population resident in this locality (*al-bilâd al-mazkura*)'. It was most probably because his old functions and the new ones needed for the job were comparable in many ways that 'Alî Ridha Pacha considered the *shaykh* the person best suited to hold the office of *ra'îs* (chief), as provided for in the reform project. This is all the more true since 'he is known to all and because of this the *shaykh* in question will keep the official function of sheikh of the commune (*bilada*) in question, continuing to be what he has always been, loyal to the Sublime Porte and undertaking everything of which he is capable in his brilliant work'.

Loyalty to the central authorities was certainly one of the most important arguments, for the primary objective of the Porte, in addition to its reforming designs, was to keep the province in question in its possession. However, beyond these considerations it should be remembered that any reform project would be implemented with great caution so as not to alienate the local people, and above all the notables. Although he was a great enthusiast of 'European recipes', our governor drew up his projects on the basis of the pre-existing local traditions. In short, his vision of modernity was of one springing from the old system.

Just as on the Bomba project, where an old Roman site was to be used for the creation of a new, modern city, the use of already existing municipal management methods while adopting the modern European form, although certainly indicative of a reforming spirit, shows a high degree of skill and prudence. In the final analysis it is quite possible that the hidden drive behind all this reforming activity may quite simply have been personal ambition.

The formula put forward by this reformer was to maintain the *shaykh al-bilâd* in his office while expanding his prerogatives by making him president of the new municipality, with the title of *ra'îs al-bilâd*, even though this municipality did not yet in fact exist. Thus before getting the go-ahead from the central authorities, 'Alî Ridha al-Jazayrî had a decree promulgated and approved by the local *diwan* (the Council of the province), abolishing the office of *shaykh al-bilâd* and instituting a new post for the leading official of the town. Of course, for this decision to come into force it would have to be approved by the authorities in Istanbul. However, the decisions taken in Tripoli may be considered as a way of forcing the hand of the powers that be, of pushing forward change.

The policy based upon *fait accompli*, on undertaking projects independently, planning and obtaining the necessary human and financial means, whatever the obstacles, is clearly that of a reformer, fitting the general trend at the time towards reform. But any reformer must make use of other people to achieve his designs. At Tripoli, our Pacha was to find great support from the *shaykh al-bilâd*.

The role of the shaykh al-bilâd and the population of Tripoli

It was thus that 'Alî al-Qarqanî, ex-*shaykh al-bilâd*, became president of the new municipality, even before this institution had been formally established and before the central authorities had had time to accept the export of an Ottomanized municipality based on the experimental Istanbul model. It is true – and this is clear from a number of sources – that there were close relations between the *shaykh al-bilâd* and Governor-General 'Alî Ridha al-Jazayrî. For example, the explorer Nachtigal tells us that 'among the close entourage of the *vali* was the burgmeister of Tripoli (*cheikh-el-bled*), Ali el-Kerkeni'.[25] While it is not surprising that these two figures, at the top of the local hierarchy, should maintain close relations due to their official positions, it is also true that the preceding governors and the *shaykh al-bilâd* had never been as close.

Was it thus a matter of shared personal interests? Did they share the same desire to see urban and social modernization implemented? This is difficult to judge – after all, the *shaykh al-bilâd* was hardly going to reject a reform leading to a considerable extension of his powers.

The role of the *shaykh al-bilad* made ʿAlî al-Qarqanî the most important locally born individual in the town. The office made of him an intermediary between the population and the central authorities. His role was to deal with the urban and social development of the city, as well as with certain commercial issues. At the urban level he was responsible for maintaining regulations on the buildings, construction and development of the town. From a social point of view he was responsible for guaranteeing morals and public order. He could settle certain differences, essentially of a commercial nature, arising between the inhabitants of Tripoli. However, on occasion his prerogatives might assume greater importance, as was the case when the Porte requested him to have all the forged currency in circulation destroyed.

The *sheikh al-bilâd* thus had a leading economic role, as monitor of the weights and measures in use in the markets, and also as president of the Chamber of Commerce. This was of course a highly strategic office, both for the trading activities he undertook for himself and on the governor's behalf. This position brought him into contact with foreigners and locals. If there was litigation to be settled at the Commercial Tribunal, the *sheikh al-bilâd* was responsible for informing the different parties concerned; he had to provide the Tribunal with lists of the goods and properties of debtor parties so that they could be seized if necessary. From an administrative point of view, he was the guarantor of commercial transactions between two individuals or two companies. He was also responsible for drafting letters of exchange for major transactions, and this activity, a purely financial one, was a further source of income.

This role of commercial mediator was a major source of power and influence, and doubtless a source of considerable wealth, both in terms of fees for official services and of various unofficial pay-offs. The *shaykh al-bilâd* also attributed certain contracts, notably with foreign companies. In addition, he was in an extremely good position to take the best contracts, since he could award himself those contracts that seemed most financially interesting.[26]

For ʿAlî Ridha Pacha, ʿAlî al-Qarqanî was clearly the man of the hour. Thus in his recommendations to the Sublime Porte he stressed the need 'to adopt an authentic project in which the Porte will find a governor of confidence.[27] You, assembly of official figures whom I address, I beg of you to ensure that the shaykh in question remain shaykh of the city and leave him all his attributes'.[28]

The participation of the *shaykh al-bilâd* may therefore be deduced from his activities when it became necessary to set up a municipal team to second him in his tasks. There is, however, a paradox here: hardly had he assumed his new functions than a section of the population accused him of abusing his authority.

As a result, it is legitimate to hypothesize that ʿAlî al-Qarqanî had worked for the establishment of the new municipality out of personal ambition. But whatever the case may be, a number of developments in Tripoli were implemented thanks to him. He was to be *shaykh al-bilâd* for 18 years, and during his period of office extensive new neighborhoods were laid out. He worked for the creation of the Tripoli Chamber of Commerce that he was to preside over. Local poet Ahmad al-Faqih Hasan, in an elegy composed a few years later, was to describe 'Alî al-Qarqanî's achievements to the benefit of people and city.[29] However, it would also seem that 'Alî al-Qarqanî was certainly not a man to neglect his own interests – in contrast to Al-Jazayrî who had a reputation for being fair and uncorrupt.

Al-Qarqanî and 'Alî Ridha al-Jazayrî were not, however, the only people to be concerned with the creation of a European-type municipality. In fact, there were local residents who displayed radical opposition to any extension of the *shaykh's* prerogatives – and were certainly against the abuses of power of which he had been guilty for quite some time. We cannot go into details here of the different demonstrations against the *shaykh al-bilâd*; the fact that there were such reactions shows just how attentive the notables of Tripoli were to changes in their local government. In fact, in the end, following a major scandal,[30] the population managed to get 'Alî al-Qarqanî arrested in late September 1871; he was subsequently stripped of his assets and exiled. 'Alî Ridha Pacha was recalled to Istanbul at the same time, which could lead one to suppose that he was the object of the population's wrath as well. This petition, however, never questioned his authority – quite the opposite in fact.

The Birth of a Hybrid Institution: The Municipality of Tripoli in Barbary between Traditional Institutions and Tanzîmāt

Despite numerous vicissitudes, the Municipality of Tripoli was established, at the same time as similar bodies were being created in other towns across the Ottoman Empire. Local actors played an important role, and private matters did not ultimately form an obstacle to this administrative project. A series of official measures, emanating both from the Sublime Porte and the governor-general of Tripoli, was to lead to the creation of the municipality. Archival research has produced a chronology of the main decisions, decrees and reports leading to this – as seen in the Appendix below. We thus have an idea of the models used to endow the city as a modern municipal institution.

It was on 7 December 1870 that the Municipality of Tripoli actually came into being with the signature of a decree, concerning the payment of salaries, by the president of the *baladiyya* and its members. The new municipality was henceforth to be called *baladiyya*, as in Istanbul, and was to deal with the city's problems, participating as well in the economic revival of the city – and even that of the country, for according to 'Alî Ridha Pacha this new institution 'counts among the greatest tools for the construction of the city.

It has limitless merits. There is no doubt that the objectives of the Porte are linked to this intermediary which can guarantee the city's tranquility and the well-being of its population'.[31]

The idea was that an urban rates system would finance the needs of the city in terms of urban development and major public works. A municipal council was evidently vital to this. Giving a town its own development finance system represented a minor revolution and a convincing argument to the central authorities. Putting forward a team, already at work and with a reputation for competence and honesty, would no doubt be a convincing argument as well. 'Alî Ridha writes how a team was constituted as 'municipal council, the head of which was a town notable, 'Alî al-Qarqanî (the ex-*shaykh al-bilâd*), with his assistant the merchant Omar Efendi, whose salary was to be 1500 *qûrûsh* . . . We also took the decision to nominate a doctor, M. Dickson, as treasurer, with a salary of 400 *qûrûsh* . . ., a secretary (*kâtib*) . . ., a factotum (*mubashir*) . . ., and according to the project, we will use the persons already employed in the *wizara* with a salary from the Municipality . . .'. 'Alî Ridha also mentions the name of an engineer, Al-Kul Aghasi Efendi, a graduate of the Ecole militaire impériale d'Istanbul, and already an Ottoman civil servant who 'in this function will receive a salary from the *baladiyya*'. He adds a list of the members unanimously elected (missing in the document),[32] and mentions the presence of a Jewish member of the Council.[33] The list of members in this team, in the form of a decree issued by the governor-general and drawn up by this official, no doubt with the participation of the city notables and their representative 'Alî al-Qarqanî, was sent to the Sublime Porte for approval.

The council members were in all likelihood convinced that there were more advantages to be drawn from an officially constituted municipal organization than from a loose network composed of leading figures without any set regulations and no guiding principles regarding responsibilities or attributes. The constitution of the Municipal Council, with the election of members and the distribution of official posts, is incontestably European in form. Nevertheless, this system resembles the one already in existence in as much as it was the same sector of Tripoli's population, the notables, who remained in charge and the former *shaykh al-bilâd* who became the new *ra'is*.

This reform was to help establish a body where recruitment and responsibilities were established on a formal legal basis for the first time in Tripoli. Replacing traditional local institutions, such an administrative instrument was to make the city more autonomous; it was more efficiently run, thanks to a qualified, salaried personnel working at specific tasks as in the French and British models.

But there is a relative silence in the sources concerning how the new *baladiyya* was received by the people of Tripoli. This silence is difficult to interpret: was it that the reform brought about few real changes in the daily life of Tripoli's inhabitants in the years immediately following its application?

The silence is perhaps not really surprising. There was no huge change in the governing group – apart from the introduction of a doctor and an engineer. Even the site of the old administration was retained by the new municipal institution, the café belonging to the *shaykh al-bilâd* in the Baladiyya district[34] in the medina, or old town.

The local notables and the chief of their assembly were very quick to adopt the idea of reforms. The municipal institution, re-exported from Istanbul, was to take root and develop in Tripoli from the 1870s right up to the arrival of the Italians in 1911. What was originally an experiment had in fact proved so successful that the model was extended to Benghazi, Homs and Misrata. The social actors responsible for the *baladiyya* ensured that it was a logical continuation of the old model of urban and social management, once upon a time made concrete in the office of the *shaykh al-bilâd*. The Municipality was to become a means via which the people of Tripoli could develop their city and reduce its isolation.

Other innovations in the Ottoman Empire were not as positive as the introduction of new municipal administrations. The reasons for the success of the latter are no doubt due to the fact that an essentially European institution was Ottomanized at Istanbul and was easily grafted onto existing systems. To the local populations, the changes thus seemed minimal and purely formal in nature.

CONCLUSION

It is an irony of history that the arrival and development of the Western-style municipality seems such a positive and successful re-exportation in the case of Tripoli. It was functioning so well that when the Italians arrived they left its structure and responsibilities untouched, changing only its name from *baladiyya* to *municipio*. This *municipio*, however, was not Italian, although it delivered what the new occupiers expected of a municipal body. Throughout the nineteenth century and right up to the Italian conquest of 1911, municipal management had been a feature of Tripoli life, and it survived ('resisted', if we take the point of view of the local people) successive changes of ruler – the Qaramânlî Dynasty, the Sublime Porte and Italian colonial administration. The example of Tripoli is thus highly revealing in terms of the importance of local actors in the success or failure of an imported piece of administrative machinery, and the quality of the project or reform is therefore really only of secondary importance.

This conclusion, then, leads into wider debates about local authorities and their relationships with foreign powers, be these colonial or otherwise. The case study of Tripoli in the implementation of Ottoman municipal structures within the framework of the reforms suggests that the idea of the importation of a model in one direction only should be relativized, and also that the reform had more chances of successful implementation where the new institutions could lean on pre-existing structures. In Tripoli, the continuity between the function of the *shaykh al-bilâd* and that of the mayor is striking.

One further wonders if the very inspiration of the municipal reform was so external to the Arab world: in a way Tripoli offers the example of a city where a Western-style reform succeeded because it was superimposed on a network of notables and a type of functioning of local power configurations that were themselves in a process of significant redefinition. Imperialism and colonialism have had such a tremendous impact on the functioning of the local elites in the Arab world that it is almost impossible to assess whether these societies could, during the nineteenth century, have experienced a genuine process of institutional reform. The case of Tripoli, although it does not bring a definite answer, nor represent an experimental example totally closed to any external influence, helps assess the role of premodern structures of urban management in the movement of administrative modernization, as well as the dynamics of reform in the Ottoman framework.

APPENDIX

Chronology of the early development of the Municipality of Tripoli, 1867–77

Date	Event/Decree
30 rabi' I 1284/ 1 August 1867	The Porte agrees to the creation of the Municipality of Tripoli. Decree issued by Governor-General 'Alî Ridha Pacha re. *shaykh al-bilâd*. Nomination of 'Alî al-Qarqanî as *ra'îs al-baladiyya* and report of governor on the establishment of a municipality, based on institutions existing already in Tripoli. Report sent to Istanbul to Ministry of Interior to have decree approved.
9 Safar 1285/ 1 June 1868	Letter from the Porte (Ministry of the Interior) to 'Alî Ridha to inform him of the Porte's desire to implement new reforms concerning municipalities and rates (constitutional law laying down details of the implementation of the *arrondissements* (*dawa'ir*) supported by 'Alî Ridha Pacha).
Rabi' I 1285/ July 1868	Report sent by 'Alî Ridha Pacha to the Porte in which he supported the setting up of a municipal administration (*idarat al-baladiyya*).

Date	Event/Decree
5 Dhu al-Hijja 1286/ 8 March 1870	Letter from ʿAlî Ridha Pacha to Mutassaraf *markaz al-wilaya* informing him of the Porte's agreement with the decision to abolish the office of *sheikh al-bilâd* and create a municipality headed by a *raʾîs al-baladiyya*.
10 Rabiʾ II 1287/ 16 July 1870	Census of the male population of Tripoli undertaken by the *baladiyya*.
4 Jumada al-Akhar 1287/1 September 1870	Decree promulgated by the *Majlis daira al-baladiyya* (the Municipal Administrative Council), re. first works undertaken by the Municipality, including street lighting and cleaning.
7 Jumada al-Akhar 1287/4 September 1870	Decree from the *raʾîs al-daʾira al-baladiyya* Mahmud Faʾiz re. the boring of a fresh water well.
17 Ramadhan 1287/ 7 December 1870	Decree issued by the Municipal Council re. payment of salaries signed by the president of *baladiyya* and its members.
1294/1877	Law voted on by the recently created Parliament in Istanbul, extending the Istanbul municipal system to all the cities of the Empire.

NOTES

1. These figures, based on various sources, do not include the inhabitants of the Manchia. This zone had, however, strong links since the very beginning with the built area, and at the end of the nineteenth century it became ever more integrated with it. But it is difficult to evaluate its population. See Nora Lafi (2002) *Une ville du Maghreb entre Ancien Régime et réformes ottomanes: Genèse des institutions municipales à Tripoli de Barbarie, 1795–1911,* Paris: L'Harmattan, 305 pp.

2. Tripoli was the chief town of the Regency of the same name, Trâblus al-Gharb, which comprised, depending on the times considered, three regions: the Fezzan, the Cyrenaïc and the Tripolitania. In the sixteenth century, when the Ottomans stepped in, the region of Tripoli became a *Pashalîq* (in Turkish a territory submitted to the authority of a pacha). At the time of the Qaramânlîs, the region was known as Ayâla al-Trâblus al-Gharb, which can be translated as the Regency of Tripoli. See Dâr Mahfuzât Trâblus [Tripoli archives], religious court, file no. 60, 1253h./1837.

3. The Ottoman Empire lost its other North African provinces much earlier: Algeria in 1830 due to French domination, and Tunisia from mid-century, as a Regency, that was to be placed under a French Protectorate from 1881. At the time, Egypt had almost achieved de facto political independence from the Porte.

4. For our case study, see Lisa Anderson (1984) 'Nineteenth-century reform in Ottoman Libya', *International Journal of Middle East Studies* 16, pp. 325–48.

5. See in particular Stephane Yerasimos (1992) 'A propos des réformes urbaines des Tanzimat', in Paul Dumont and François Georgeon (eds) *Villes ottomanes à la fin de l'Empire*, Paris: L'Harmattan, pp. 17–32, where such reforms are mainly viewed as a means to regain control over the provinces. See also Zeynep Çelik (1993) *The Remaking of Istanbul: Portrait of an Ottoman City in the Nineteenth Century*, Los Angeles: University of California Press.

6. An early reference is Bernard Lewis (1960) 'Baladiyya', *Encyclopaedia of Islam*, pp. 1002–5 on the *Belediyye* institution in Turkey from its beginnings to the 1930s; see also William Cleveland (1978) 'The Municipal Council of Tunis, 1858–1870: A study in urban institutional change', *International Journal of Middle East Studies* 9, pp. 33–61, and Michael Reimer (1995) 'Urban regulation and planning agencies in mid-nineteenth-century Alexandria and Istanbul' (with Documentary Appendix), *Turkish Studies Association Bulletin* 19, no. 1, spring, pp. 1–26.

7. The subject has been dealt with in part in *Medjell-i ummur-i belediyye*, a voluminous study by Osman Nuri Ergin. Unfortunately, this is still only available in Turkish.

8. Robert Mantran (1989) (ed.) *Histoire de l'Empire ottoman*, Lille: Fayard, p. 154.

9. Lewis, op. cit., p. 1003.

10. Ibid.

11. Ibid.

12. On the origin and role of the *shaykh al-bilâd*, see Lafi, op. cit., pp. 131–66.

13. 'The movement favoring the introduction and expansion of Western-style municipal services continued however. In 1285/1868, a code of municipal regulations (*belediyye nizâmmâmesi*) was published, with the idea of extending the system of a municipal council to the 14 other districts of Istanbul.' Lewis, op. cit. p. 1005.

14. Ibid., p. 1004.

15. Paul Dumont (1989) 'La période des Tanzimât', in Mantran, op. cit., pp. 459–522 (quotation from p. 492).

16. Among these cities were Jerusalem, Alexandria, Beirut and Tripoli.

17. Charles Féraud (1927) *Les annales tripolitaines*, Augustin Bernard, Paris: Tournier-Vuibert, p. 421.

18. Ibid.

19. Ibid.

20. Ibid., p. 422.

21. Ibid., p. 421.

22. Baladiyya Trâblus (1973) *Baladiyya Trâblus fî mi'â 'âm: 1286–1391 H. (1870–1970)* (The municipality of Tripoli through a hundred years), Tripoli: Sharîka Dâr al-Tibâ 'al-Hadîth. Archives 1–2–3–4.

23. See the rich insights in the chronicle of Hasan al-Faqih Hasan, merchant in Tripoli, an important source for the study of the town during the first part of the nineteenth century: Hasan al-Faqih Hasan (1984) *Al-yawmiyyât al-lîbiyya, 958–1248 H./1551–1832*, with a commentary by al-'Ustâ Mohammad and Juhaydar 'Ammar, University al-Fâtah and Libyan Studies Center, p. 977.

24. The Arabic expressions used at the time in Tripoli were *al-'a'yân* or *ahl al-bilâd*. For the nuances, see Lafi, op. cit., pp. 110–12.

25. Gustav Nachtigal (1881) *Sahara et Soudan*, translated from German by Jules Gourdault, Paris: Hachette, p. 29.

26. See Lafi, op. cit., pp. 166–83 and idem. (2000) 'L'affaire 'Alî al-Qarqanî', in 'Abd al-Hamîd Henia, (ed.) *Villes et territoires au Maghreb, Itinéraires de recherche*, vol. 1, Dynamiques des configurations notabiliaires au Maghreb, Tunis (forthcoming).

27. When he mentioned 'a governor of confidence' he of course meant himself.
28. Baladiyya Trâblus op. cit., Archives 1.
29. This author was close to ʿAlî al-Qarqanî. He was the already mentioned son of the leading chronicler of Tripoli life in the nineteenth century, Hasan al-Faqih Hasan. See Ahmad al-Faqih Hasan (1988) *Al-Jadd: 1843–1866*, in texts and archives, 7, Tripoli: Markaz al-Jihad, p. 160.
30. ʿAlî al-Qarqanî was accused of various illegal activities, speculation, abuse of power and fraud by an important group of notables in a petition sent to the Porte. See Istanbul, Basbakanlik Arçiv, dosya 2004, D. 61, Arabic Mss. See also Lafi, op. cit.
31. Baladiyya Trâblus, op. cit., Archives 1.
32. The sources used do not indicate clearly the form of elections of these members. However, the organization of the census of Tripoli's male population in 1870 suggests the existence of an electoral reform.
33. Baladiyya Trâblus, op. cit., Archives 2.
34. As it was named for many decades, as stated above.

CHAPTER 9

BEIRUT AND THE ÉTOILE AREA: AN EXCLUSIVELY FRENCH PROJECT?

May Davie

URBAMA, University of Tours,
University of Balamand, Lebanon

In early October 1918, during the last days of the First World War, French troops occupied the city of Beirut, took over its administration and initiated the setting up of a completely new State organization. Beirut, the main port city of Ottoman Syria and the capital of a *wilaya* (province) that stretched from Jaffa to Lattakia, became the capital of Greater Lebanon, a mainly mountainous country to which it was annexed against the wishes of the population. The demographic composition of the city also changed: while the city exported, through emigration, a considerable portion of its own population, refugees flowed in from the hinterland, fleeing the consequences of the war. Armenian refugees were also brought in by the French and given Lebanese nationality, further modifying the religious balance that previously prevailed.

Almost immediately after their entry to Beirut, the French took a series of measures to rebuild three sectors of the city's centre: the port quarter, the old city centre and the land of the *musalla* (prayer and cemetery area) just to the north of the Petit Sérail. The previous urban fabric, which had already been restructured by the two openings cut through the old city by decisions taken by Jamal Pasha during the war but untouched since, was totally razed. In its place, a modern city centre was planned, reflecting the 'civilizing mission' that the League of Nations had entrusted to France among the Arabs of the Levant.

Of the three projects, the reconstruction of the city centre, today's Étoile area, was the most significant as that sector was the richest historically, symbolically and religiously and also offered a high heritage value. Named 'Beyrouth en cinq ans' (Beirut in Five Years), the Étoile project was thought up by French army engineers in 1927 and completed during the 1930s, giving birth to an urban composition that was in contrast with the preceding local land-use.

Quite French and colonial in its approach with its historical policy of *tabula rasa*, the star-shaped plan, wide gallery-lined avenues and its military undertones, the project aimed at making Beirut a showcase of French action in the Levant. This graft was, however, doubly original: contrary to North Africa, it was not applied on a pre-existing 'Arab' fabric but on a far more complex one that had been deeply influenced by the urbanistic ideas of the West, which were carefully adapted to the needs of the Ottoman late 1800s. The French were also not dealing with a relatively homogeneous and 'archaic' society but with a cosmopolitan group, the vector of merchant capitalism in the Orient, capped by a rich, powerful and Europeanized élite composed of landlords and bankers and seconded by a business and political bourgeoisie, some members of which collaborated directly with the French project.

Resistance to the Étoile project was not of a cultural order, as it was not really a conflict between two types of civilizations. It must be noted that the population readily accepted the imported models and local engineers participated in its planning. Opposition was rather of a political and economic nature, the project being instrumentalized in a power game between the French authorities and the local residents, or among the Beirutis themselves, which forced the project to stop before achieving its planned aims.

Despite the conditions within which the project was conceived, it remained the vector of technical and expertise transfers, while at the same time introducing new administrative practices, some of which are still operating in Lebanon today.

A CENTURY OF URBAN RENOVATION

When the French occupied Beirut in 1918, the townscape had very little in common with that of a century before. The city had been transformed from the inside, while its environs had been urbanized and its suburban orchards replaced by gardens and houses of a new style. The beginning of these transformations can be dated at around 1850, and they were the result of a series of circumstances that included the new conditions imposed by international commerce in the eastern Mediterranean and Ottoman reforms (the *Tanzîmāt*).

The first period

Two operations heralded the start of a new urban and architectural era in Beirut: the building, in 1853, of the imposing barracks and military hospital[1] on the Qubbat al-Qantari and the change in the alignment of the Damascus road, in 1858.

By their size, shape and colour, the barracks and the hospital, both covered with red tiles and offering neat and regular large windows, introduced new aesthetic norms in the public architecture of the city. They were both very distinct from the city's Old Seraglio, which had the aspect of a medieval citadel.[2] The new buildings were geometrically well laid out, and were surrounded by gardens; they overlooked the city and the sea, and were quite different from the 'traditional' town made up of low 'Arab' houses and their tangle of roofs.

As for access to the port from the Damascus road, which ended at the Tower Square (Sahat al-Burj), it no longer followed a road along the east of the city but now skirted instead the walls close to the as-Sur Square, then bypassed the city to the west[3] until it reached the landing point. This new road reorganized the urban fabric by forcing the previously marginal spaces inside and outside the walls towards a central position.

The urban expansion processes had in fact started at the Tower and as-Sur Squares as well as at the Chamiyyeh cape, with associated changes impacting the local way of life until the end of the nineteenth century and into the beginning of the twentieth century. Between 1860 and 1892, several public and social buildings were put up here, such as khan (trade hotels), cafés, shops and residential buildings that could not exist inside the walls for lack of space. During this same period, several suq (market streets) were built inside the town, thanks to the initiative of the city's notables. These market streets adopted a regular gridiron plan[4] and presented a 'modern' look: to the east, the suq al-Nuzhat, al-Hamidiyyeh[5] and Mar Jirjis, and to the northwest, on the Shamiyyeh cape, the Antun Bey and Fakhri Bey khan as well as the al-Tawileh, al-Sayyid, Ayyas, al-Kabbushiyeh, al-Jamil, Bustros and Sayyur suq (Figs 1 and 2).[6]

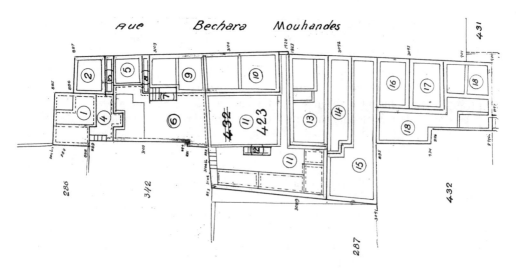

Figure 1. *The suq al-Muhandis's haphazard morphology.*
Source: Service du cadastre, Beirut

Urban policies of the Municipal Council

In order to organize this rapidly developing urban spread, the Municipal Council,[7] which was in the hands of local notables and an Ottoman administrator, launched a series of urban policies in 1878 that would be progressively implemented between 1879 and 1916. These would mainly be applied in three fields: the extension of public spaces, the improvement of communication networks and the setting up of public services.

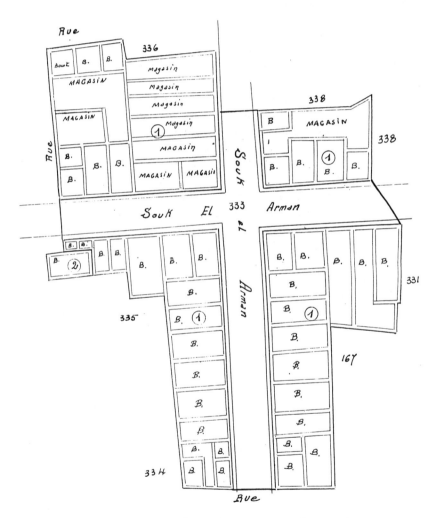

Figure 2. The gridiron plan of a 19th-century suq, the suq al-Arman.
Source: Service du cadastre, Beirut

A new administrative centre was planned for Sahat al-Burj, followed by the building of a new port and finally two straight roads through the old city, which would meet at its centre and thus connect the port to the outskirts. It was also decided to open up and embellish the old city, and to introduce public places and squares, public gardens and walks;[8] the same was decided for the suburbs. The size of the project, the importance of the investments and the originality of the building techniques meant that these urban plans would in effect be the starting point for the introduction of a new type of public works that would replace traditional development based on local *waqf* (family religious endowment) logics. Combined, these actions would radically change the aspect of both the seafront of the old city and its land approaches.[9]

Apart from the port, the planning and building of which were left to a foreign company, the restructuring of Beirut was entrusted to Bishara Afandi,[10] the engineer of the Wilayat. Bishara drew up the plans following what had already been tried out in Istanbul, Damascus or Cairo, imitating the Western bourgeois public places and following the use of a predetermined plan integrating the notions of axiality, symmetry and hierarchy while at the same time adhering to the new Ottoman regulations on buildings and land planning.[11]

At Sahat al-Burj, a public garden planted with Persian lilacs, together with a fountain, pools and paths, occupied the centre of the square. This clear-cut and regular space contrasted starkly with those of the 'Arab' *intra muros* city,[12] which were small, irregular and haphazard. All around the new square, land plots larger in size than those found inside the old city were aligned, and the roads along their sides were designed so as to be large enough for horse-drawn transport.

New buildings bordering this square were laid out following a regular plan while respecting the new urban regulations that took into account geometrical aesthetics and the question of perspective. At Sahat al-Burj, these buildings would be the seat of public administration and large companies: the seat of the governor and of the Municipality, the Qishlat al-Sawari (the gendarmerie), the headquarters of the port, railway, gas and tobacco companies, and finally the main offices of the Ottoman bank, the municipal medical dispensary and the post office.

These new 'urban gates' on the edge of the old town were then slowly filled by horse-drawn coaches and the tramway, and especially by hotels together with all the related activities: cafés, restaurants, casinos, theatres, music halls and reading clubs.

Architecture

The buildings were erected according to an original architectural style, adapting foreign models to local conditions; the archetype was the 'Central-

Hall House', with two floors, a red-tiled roof and a frontage consisting of three arches. Western in size, its colours and in certain exterior decorations, it was oriental in its interior organization and in its Arab-style arches. Also called the 'Three-Arched House', it was introduced by the local bourgeoisie and progressively adopted by all social categories.[13]

Certain buildings, such as the Kawkab al-Sharq hotel or the police headquarters, were built in this elegant local style so typical of the end of the nineteenth century. Others adopted more classical or baroque European styles, first adapted in Istanbul or in Egypt then re-exported to the provinces, and included the Ottoman Bank, the Hôtel de Marseille, the Orosdi-Back department stores and especially the Petit Sérail. The latter was typical of Ottoman civil public buildings, but also offered several details taken from medieval fortresses. However, religious architecture was the real domain of eclecticism, as was clear with the Roman-Byzantine and Italian styles of churches, such as those of the Capuchin, Maronite and Evangelical.

With their specific outward appearance, the new buildings contrasted with the 'Arab' structures of the old city, with their flat roofs, open patios and the blind lower-levels of their outer facades. As a result of this development, the character of the city centre was slowly modified, while offering a setting for trans-Mediterranean-inspired urban aesthetics that brought Beirut closer, in its physical aspect at least, to the cities to the north of the Mediterranean. As a result, Beirut distanced itself from its archetype, the oriental city, which characterized the interior of geographical Syria, most notably Damascus. From the compact unit that sheltered the specific elements of Arab communities of the Ottoman Empire, such as the *hammam* (public baths), the mosques, the *madrasa* (schools) and bazaars, the city evolved into a more open urban space, open both towards the sea and surrounding countryside and at the same time extending along the coast.

The centre was renovated according to a voluntary urban project that contrasted with the spontaneous urbanism of the *intra muros* old city. The project adopted geometrical norms, zoning principles, regular land-plots, alignment rules and considerations of visual perspective. Respect for these new norms[14] did not, however, imply an architectural or geographic break with the previous setting, as had been the case in certain cities of the colonized parts of the Arab world,[15] nor did it scorn the local forms. In Beirut, the population continued to build according to the old well-proven models and according to specific needs, producing a rather complex townscape. If Western-style buildings were introduced, this did not mean that *khan* and 'Arab' *suq* ceased to be built then (as would be the case in the near future). The new *suq*, with their larger shop-windows and wider streets, continued to function as before, in a traditional environment characterized by vaulted streets, fountains, compact buildings and street intimacy.[16]

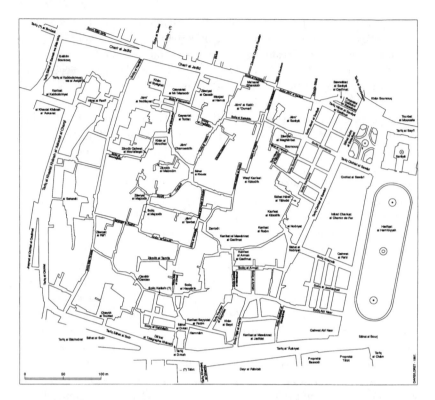

Figure 3. *The contrast between the organized layout and the irregular one. Source: Davie (1997) 'The History and Evolutions of Public Spaces in Beirut's Central District', unpublished report, Solidere*

The old city

The recent urban compositions on the outskirts of the old city (Fig. 3) signalled significant changes both in the political and the social fields. But while they naturally distanced themselves from the configurations that had survived from the past, they did not automatically eliminate them. The old city had itself evolved slowly, according to its own needs, introducing elements of modernity yet maintaining its position as the symbolic, economic, religious and historical heart of Beirut.

This old city could be construed as a barrier to the necessities of movement. But as economic changes and the need for road infrastructure had not brought its existence into question, it was easily bypassed without the need for a *tabula rasa* policy. Only the *shari'* (road) al-Jadid, which joined Bab Idriss to Bab al-Saraya, had been opened by the end of the century. Two other openings, perpendicular to the previous one, would have linked the port, Bab al-Dirkah and the New Seraglio;[17] work would begin on them only in 1916, during the war, just two years before the end of the Ottoman Empire.[18]

Thus a century of urban renovation gave the city centre of Beirut a morphological diversity and a remarkable architectural variety, a true palimpsest of additions, superpositions, corrections and renovations on an ancient urban context. It was on this complex urban heritage that the French mandatory authorities operated at the end of the First World War.

FRENCH URBANISM

As early as 1919, without waiting for the formal start of the mandate and before the official proclamation of the State of Grand Liban with Beirut as its capital, the French occupation forces took measures to rebuild and embellish the city centre. The old city thus became an urban laboratory and would subsequently sustantially disappear, to be replaced by a 'modern' centre built to satisfy the economic designs of France and its self-proclaimed cultural mission in the Levant.

The Moroccan connection

It was 1923 before the League of Nations voted in favour of the mandate; France thus governed the Levant according to experience gained in another protectorate, Morocco, applying the well-tested methods tried out by Marshal L.H. Lyautey.[19] As the idea of gaining new colonies was no longer fashionable, the newly created association formula was deemed more adequate as it proposed the sharing of responsibilities between Europeans and the local inhabitants while at the same time pursuing a colonial policy to the benefit of local interests. In other words, the French were forced to govern the local inhabitants using local governmental institutions and according to local laws and customs, a solution quite different from that used in other colonies, notably in Algeria, where a policy of total submission and assimilation had been applied.

The French military administration, in contrast, were faced with an ideologically sophisticated society, politically much better organized than that of Morocco and largely opposed to the idea of a mandate; a high commissioner (a Frenchman) was appointed to hold all the effective power.

If the local political organs were formally maintained, at least during the first years, the local bourgeoisie, which largely opposed the mandate and the idea of a Grand Liban, was excluded from all the public positions of importance and replaced by a bureaucratic élite. This élite had profited from the circumstances at the time to supplant the old aristocracy and impose its presence[20] by being sympathetic to the occupiers and working with the French counsellors who were mainly veterans from Morocco.[21] The latter represented the real power, as they were represented at all levels of the administration and in all the internal workings of the political life of the country.

In certain key sectors, such as education or public works, French officers were appointed to the highest posts. Work on the port quarter and on the two cuttings, named Allenby and Foch Streets, was started in 1919 under the authority of Commander Doizelet, the military governor of the city, and Commander Fumey, the administrative counsellor of the Wilayat, aided by the president of Municipality 'Umar Da'uq, and a committee of municipal engineers[22] and French technicians brought over from Egypt and Africa.[23]

In the interval, as all the members of the Municipal Council had been dismissed, municipal power had been placed in the hands of the *mutasarrif* (administrator). Najib Abu Suwwan, a pro-French émigré who had returned from Egypt, was the first to occupy this post; Abu Suwwan was seconded by Hasan Bek Makhzumi, the head of the *Nafi'at* (the public works department),[24] together with French counsellors and a provisional committee headed by Petro Trad that was put in place whilst awaiting the nomination also by the French of 'Umar Beyhum as head of the new Municipal Council[25]

In this context of institutional turmoil, Allenby and Foch Streets replaced several *suq*: al-Tujjar (the merchants' *suq*), al-Khamamir (the coffee-shop and wine merchants' *suq*) and al-Haddadin (the smiths' *suq*). The expropriated plots were levelled and consolidated, and two facades designed by Destrée[26] and Deschamps were chosen by Governor Doizelet as models for all future buildings in the area. At the same time, local Beiruti street names were slowly being replaced by a variety of new names, including those of French generals; for example Beqaa, Saint-Michel, Picot and Liban Streets respectively replaced Bustros, Saint-Nicolas, Prussia Street and Zarub al-Haramiyeh (or thieves') alleys.[27]

Later, and even though Lebanon was given a constitution and a new state organizational system in 1926, French direct control of the country's internal affairs was maintained. Urban works continued, under the supervision of Poupon, the counsellor to the *muhafiz* (regional state delegate), and Oudinot, the technical counsellor to the Municipality, both of whom were supported by Camille Duraffourd, the director of the land registry. Their efforts gave birth to an urban plan, the cost of which was estimated at 1.2 million gold pounds (Fig. 4). This sum was to be covered by a credit obtained through French banks in Beirut and paid back through the sale of plots of land or parts of buildings, built by the Municipality, to individuals. The Étoile project was approved in 1927 by the Council of Ministers and named 'Beyrouth en cinq ans' (Beirut in Five Years).[28]

The city centre remodelled by French engineers

The new project certainly had military aims. Planned in principle to open up the port area, the openings meant that it would be possible to police the city centre; the wide streets also linked up with those of the peripheral quarters where a series of barracks was built, effectively surrounding the city (Fig. 5).

Apart from the military aspects of the plan, i.e. controlling the *suq* through increased mobility for the troops, the project led the city into a new process of Westernization through the adoption of French urbanistic ideas. In this respect, a new land code and a land-register system were introduced, and laws controlling the *waqf* possessions promulgated. With all land-property obstacles having been removed,[29] a radically new model could be proposed – a radiocentred plan in sharp contrast to the previous Ottoman model, essentially of a gridiron type or the Arab model, which was largely a response to climatic factors such as heat and wind.[30]

Ridding the city of the old urban order, the project transformed Beirut from the inside and simultaneously produced a new centrality.[31] A colourful and eclectic new centre was built on the totally razed old Arab *suq* using the latest building techniques. The entire southern part of the *intra muros* city disappeared, along with its latticework of narrow streets, markets and workshops. To improve the movement of traffic, especially cars, a star-shaped

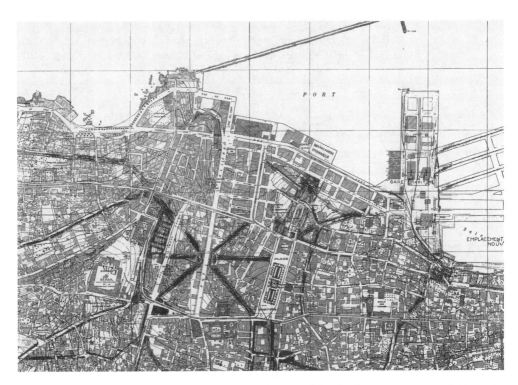

Figure 4. *Camille Duraffourd's original manuscript of the Étoile project, circa 1926*
Source: A. Farès, private collection

system of avenues,[32] named after generals, replaced the previous streets; wide gallery-lined avenues, with blocks built on both sides, converged on the Place de l'Étoile.[33] To compensate the previous land-owners, the Municipality used funds provided by French bankers and built two blocks on rue Foch, the rent from which was to be used for this purpose. However, these indemnities were not paid out until more than twenty years later.[34]

As if to disguise the operation behind an apparent respect for local traditions while highlighting the protective role of France, the authorities adopted oriental-style facades for the public buildings,[35] a style that paradoxically had previously hardly been known in Beirut but which was now used to mark the new centrality of the area. Youssef Aftimos Afandi, the chief engineer of the Municipality,[36] was instrumental in disseminating the *naw' sharqi*, a neo-oriental or Arab-inspired architectural language,[37] a product of an imagined Orient highlighted by exhibitions of colonial buildings.[38] This was to be used for the frontage of the public buildings, the internal layout being clearly Western-inspired. It would also be an *in situ* ersatz 'Arab' *suq* (the original was demolished). The Municipality building, designed by Aftimos himself, as well as the Parliament designed by Mardiros Altounian, are representative of this style.

With its 'oriental' frontage and decorated from top to bottom (Fig. 6), the Municipality building stood at the corner of Allenby and Weygand Streets, the

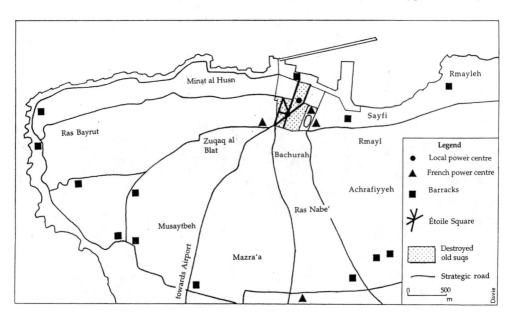

Figure 5. *The French military organization in Beirut*
Source: *Davie (1996), Beyrouth et les faubourgs (1840–1940).*

site of the *suq* al-Fachkha; however it had a modern internal plan that clearly differentiated it from the *khan* and *wikalat* (commerce house) (Fig. 7).[39]

The Parliament building was located on the western side of the Étoile and destined to introduce a 'national' style (Fig. 8). Wishing to adapt the Orient to the West, Altounian sought his inspiration in the palaces of the emirs of the mountain, which were themselves based on the palaces of the walis of Damascus. He thus conceived a building in the monumental 'Modern style' of the 1920s using simple geometric lines but incorporating a Mameluk-style gate and a facade with two stylized towers inspired from oriental architecture. This would symbolize the new sovereignty of the young Lebanese nation. With its narrow and elongated windows, the building resembled a closed temple built in an 'Arab' style.

Thus the two symbols of the new local authorities, the Parliament and the Municipality, now cut off from their previous bases of power, were reintroduced in a carefully cleansed new city; in the meantime, together with the *suq* the small traders of the city were also pushed out. Some, for example the jewellers, vegetable sellers, cheese sellers, butchers and others, emigrated towards the Mar Jirjis, Abi Nasr and al-Nuriyyah areas, the only *suq* to survive the remodelling of the city; other *suq* completely disappeared. In their place, large new Modern-style, Art-Deco and mainly oriental-style buildings[40] emerged, with shops on the ground floor and offices on the upper storeys (Figs 9 and 10). Finally, a new French-controlled financial district was developing at the foot of the Grand Sérail hill at the city centre's western edge.

Figure 6. *Beirut Municipality building's facade in 1998*
Source: Photo by the author

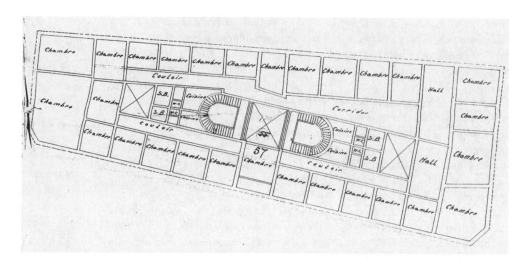

Figure 7. *Beirut Municipality building's layout*
Source: Service du Cadastre, Beirut

Figure 8. *The Place de l'Étoile and the Parliament in 1998*
Source: Photo by the author

COLLABORATION AND RESISTANCE

The Étoile project was the image of the near-total control of the city's admin-istration, together with its urbanism and its public works, by the French military authorities. The French inspiration and success of the project were underlined by its plan and the architectural language adopted, the modes of organization and the urbanistic regulations that were imposed, and the symbols projected. But an approach based exclusively on form and plan is clearly insufficient to understand the meaning of these urbanistic achieve-ments and their real motivations.

There was undoubtedly both importation and imposition of models. However, it must first be noted that the new local elite and the professional builders participated in the project, and that the forms and norms were adapted and assimilated; many locals were thus active collaborators. Second, it should be noted that there was also resistance to the project, and that certain modes of negotiation took place, the mandate authorities having to deal with local realities that had not necessarily been addressed in the thinking behind the original plans, resulting in a compromise between several positions and thus explaining why the project was never completed (two of the branches of the Étoile were never finished). Lastly, it must also be stressed that the contradictions were not only present in the attitudes of the French towards the locals, and that there were also conflicts within the local sectors themselves, between the mountain and urban elites, and among the urban inhabitants too.

The considerable resistance to the plan included those from the owners of the *suq* or the *waqf*, and from the urban communities, both Christian and Muslim, who waivered between several options, two of which are worth presenting here.

The first option was to agree to the project so long as there would be renewed activity in the city centre and business could resume after nearly ten years of decline and disorganization. This was the position of the nota-bles, albeit after some hesitation. Owners of the *suq* built during the nine-teenth century and occupying the eastern side of the Étoile area (the *suq* Sursok, Hani wa Ra'd, Abi Nasr, and so on), saw in the project an encroach-ment upon their interests. A considerable part of the merchant bourgeoisie and the urban aristocracy, such as the Sursok, Tabet, Kabbani, Tuéni, Hani and Khayyat families,[41] were little inclined to hand over their *suq*, which had been built less than half a century earlier and which were perfectly adapted to the workings of the world economy of that period. Nevertheless, this same bourgeoisie looked favourably on other parts of the project: the organizing of traffic, the opening up of the port area and especially the increase in usable land and creation of new business and investment opportunities.

Figure 9. *A rehabilitated 'neo-mauresque' building of the Étoile area in 1998*
Source: Photo by the author

Figure 10. The 'neo-mauresque' facade of the 'Grand Theatre' building in 1998
Source: Photo by the author

The second option was to resist the project: this was the attitude of the religious and civil heads of the urban communities and their followers who did not wish to see erased the central symbols of their presence in town, such as the mosques and cathedrals, the fountains and other urban *waqf* facilities, some of which were several centuries old. If they handed over the minor religious buildings to the planners, they were not ready to give up the cathedrals and mosques of the eastern site of the Étoile area, nor the *waqf's suq* of al-Arman, Mar Jirjis and Nuriyyeh. Deprived of a large part of their *waqf* revenue for more than ten years, they wavered between collaboration

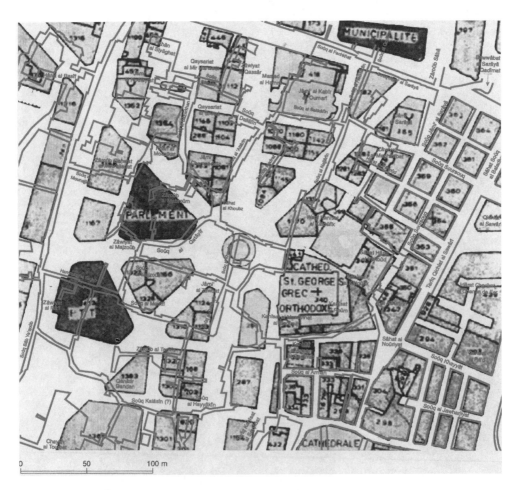

Figure 11. *The Étoile plan and the underlying old Beirut suq.*
Source: M. Davie (1997) 'The History and Evolution of Public Spaces in Beirut's Central District', Unpublished report, Beirut, Solidere.

and resistance before winning their case, thanks, it must be stressed, to the support of the notables. On one hand they agreed to rebuild quickly in order to ensure revenue for the *waqf*, but on the other they were not ready to give up their central places of worship, the Greek-Orthodox, Greek-Catholic and Maronite cathedrals, nor the Assaf mosque, which were the last survivors of a complex urban network of religious buildings. In this respect, the attitude of the Greek-Catholics is most relevant. Though a fervent ally of France, this community was the most watchful in defending its property and in questioning the compensation sums decided by the Municipality, and this attitude was central in blocking part of the project. The Saint-Élie cathedral, which the project planned to destroy, had been the symbol of the community's attachment to the West since the eighteenth century; by blocking the project and thus leaving the cathedral untouched, the French could claim the support of the community, which in turn would give the mandate a free rein.

Using their economic and social power, the notables were, among the opposition forces, the most efficient in opposing the project. The mandatory power could not take the risk of opposing them outright as it needed their support with regard to controlling the population in general and the religious communities in particular. In this context, the example of the Tabet family is anecdotal: the family was close to the high commissioner and owned the Grand Theatre, recently built to the south of the Étoile quarter, and was able to put an end to the plan to extend Allenby Street towards the southern suburbs of the city.

REVOLT AND REPRESSION

The most violent reactions were from those parts of the population that had been negatively affected by the new economic and political situation. Surprisingly they had very little effect on the plans of the reconstruction project. Those concerned had been pushed out of the *suq* with promises of compensation that were regularly postponed and eventually paid in a devalued currency. This disaffected section of the population was ready to join the political forces active at that particular moment in the restless suburbs, such as Basta and Musaitbeh, which had adhered to the Arabist tenets of the Sunni notables marginalized by the mandate authorities, or to those sympathetic to the Syrian cause, a development which gave birth to the Syrian National Party.[42] Through regular strikes and demonstrations organized by these parties in the city centre, they slowed down the project by a few years and increased its cost. The French, in order to neutralize these movements, encouraged the setting up of opposition groups that were confessionally linked to the Maronites or the Armenians, for example. This brought the city to the edge of a civil war, without however putting an end to the political activism and the economic difficulties it generated. These political events had also to be taken into account in the light of the Druze Revolt and the 1929 economic depression, and the consequent discrediting of the French government both in the Levant and in France.

In addition to the small traders and the political sympathizers, there were also here the journalists and the junior civil-servants as well as some prominent figures who did not hesitate to publicly criticize the project in the local press. In return, the mandatory authorities censored the press or simply suspended the incriminated newspaper; they also regularly imprisoned the more obstinate activists. The various municipal crises were also an expression of this opposition, and these too helped to slow down the project.

However, the French did not always use repressive methods; in the face of certain realities they were forced to negotiate. The weight of legal and administrative routine should be noted here: the French could not ignore the situation in the field nor local habits and usage, and nor could they shrug off technical considerations such as the estimates of compensations to be paid nor the question of lodging for the displaced or the expropriated. At the end of the 1920s, France was furthermore unable to impose the symmetry of the original plan by military means. The Druze Revolt, the recent difficult situation of French troops in Cilicia, the municipal deficit and the end of subsidies paid by the mother country all made it impossible for the high commissioner to further alienate the different positions of the Beirut bourgeoisie: the positions of those who had sided with the mandate from its inception, and of those, mainly Greek-Orthodox and Sunni, who had been compelled and had finally accepted the new political order as well as a new national homeland. Neither could the high commissioner always alienate the local population; the inhabitants of Mahallat at-Tawbah,[43] for example, were given two extra years before they had to leave. The incomplete project finally expressed the real power structure, the stakes at hand as well as the inertia of the local society in the face of imperious decisions taken by the mandate authorities.

However, France's financial disengagement, the reciprocal hesitations and the gradual paralysis of the Municipality also ended another important project that had been submitted by Najib Chakkur Pacha as a solution to the city-centre congestion problem and the negative reaction of the local bourgeoisie to some of its implications. The counter-project presented the building of a new city, Bayrut al-Jadidat, on the outskirts of Beirut itself, not far from Ouzai, taking Heliopolis as a model. Due to lack of funds, the plan was deferred.

CONCLUSION

Thus it appears that the Étoile area cannot be qualified as a purely Western creation. Rather it reflects a certain compromise between two unequal parties:

on one hand, the requirements of a domineering Western power and its vision for Beirut, and on the other the requirements of a merchant elite aided by the religious hierarchy, both very concerned about their respective interests and the profit-earning capacity of the central space of the city to which they were solidly attached. The urban forms finally produced by the project, i.e. a mutilated star and a hybrid architectural style difficult to define, express the importance of the forces present at a particularly unstable political and military juncture, and this perhaps highlights Beirut's specificity compared to other colonized cities at the time.

Aware of the notions of incremental value that the world economy could bring to land and business in the central part of the city, the bourgeoisie had already begun the modernization process during the Ottoman period. A solution of cutting through the old parts of the town and importing contemporary architectural styles for the new buildings had been adopted. The latter were adapted to replace the pre-existing Arab morphology that was judged to be unadaptable to the requirements of intensive business, to the various upheavals created by newly introduced machines, and to the uncontrolled migration from the countryside to the city. As such, the project can be seen as a continuation of the previous Ottoman urban programme.

However, the history of architecture cannot be content with simple technological observations, nor a comparative study of plans and facades. The finality of the French project can be grasped through several indicators. Quite apart from military considerations, there was the symbolic power of the quintessentially French star design, at both the semiological and figurative levels, a figure that projected the idea of progress and modernity. What could be more French than Paris' Place de l'Étoile? It is also important to stress the ideological message of the oriental décor of the public buildings, which suggested French respect for local traditions and heritage values, but also functioned to mask the very deep transformations forced onto the city by the mandate. On this point at least, Beirut's case is comparable to the colonial experience of cities of the Maghreb.

In retrospect, these projects do not seem to be particular to strictly colonial practice. Suffice it to examine the procedures and intentions of today's reconstruction project, which, just as during the mandate period, reinvented the 'Arab' *suq* after levelling nearly all the built environment of the city centre, while imposing an urban master plan the models of which were imported, and to which the local population could not relate. To hide the importance of the destruction, and especially the appropriation of the central spaces by a private company, the operation was cloaked in a heritage discourse produced by Lebanese and foreign archaeologists, specialists of the Hellenistic and Roman periods. The apparent expertise of local 'situationist' urbanists brought about the invention of a 'traditional' environment without reference to a historical analysis of the pre-existing forms, their functions or their future use.

A sign of the times or just fate, the Étoile and Foch-Allenby areas are the only parts of Beirut's centre to have been preserved, being designated as heritage objects *par excellence*. The colonial urban production has paradoxically become the old city, after having been the showcase of France in the Levant, the spearhead of progress.

NOTES

1. The *Qishlat Bayrut* and the *Khastah khanah*.
2. The origins of this edifice no doubt go back to the Mameluke period and perhaps even to the Crusader period. The Old Seraglio was sold and levelled and replaced by the *suq* al-Nuzhat and the contemporary *suq* Sursok, which belonged to the Sursok and Tuéni families.
3. Previously it was a dirt track cutting across the Tower Square to link up with the port through the Bab al-Dabbaghah gate.
4. Contrary to the irregular *suq* lined by narrow shops that characterized the *intra muros* town.
5. The *khan* Hani wa Ra'd, the future jewellers' *suq*, introduced a new type of building with a central covered gallery, spacious shops with wide windows, all neatly aligned, a copy of shopping arcades introduced across Western cities during the nineteenth century.
6. Contrary to the *suq* and *khan,* which were named according to the produce they offered, the contemporary *suq* were named after the notables who built them.
7. The organization of Beirut Municipality was subjected to the various reforms that came in the wake of the *Tanzîmat*, especially those of 1858 and 1863. In 1863 it was restructured by Qabbuli Pacha, *mutassarif* of Beirut. Its definitive organization was laid down by the Provincial Municipal Code of 1877. For more information on these reforms, see S.J. and E.K Shaw (1976–77) *History of the Ottoman Empire and Modern Turkey,* Cambridge: Cambridge University Press. On the communitarian organization of Municipal elections in Beirut, see M. Davie (1993) 'La millat grecque-orthodoxe et la ville de Beyrouth, 1800–1940: structuration interne et rapport à la cité', Dissertation, Université de Paris IV- La Sorbonne.
8. The as-Sur square, the gardens of the barracks, those of the Municipality and of the Arts et Métiers, as well as the walks around the lighthouse or in the pine forest.
9. On the history of Beirut port during the nineteenth century and the urban transformations it induced, see M. Davie (2000) 'Flux mondiaux, expressions locales, Beyrouth et son port au XIXe siècle ottoman', *Chronos* 3, pp. 139–72. On the exploitation of the new port, see Ch. Babikian (1996) 'La Compagnie du port de Beyrouth, histoire d'une concession, 1887–1990', Dissertation, Beyrouth, Université Saint-Joseph.
10. Bishara Afandi (1841–1925), whose real name was Manuk Avedissian, came from modern-day Turkey. The Arts et Métiers barracks and the Ottoman Bank buildings were his work. He also contributed to installing piped water in Beirut in 1875; S.H. Varjabedian (1951) *Armenians in Lebanon*, Beirut. At the end of the century the *muhandis* (engineers) Yusif Aftimos Afandi and Yusif Khayyat Afandi were appointed to work under him.

11. A. Abdelnour (1896) *Qanoun al-abniyat wa qarar al-istimlak*, Beirut: Matba'at al-Adabiyyat.
12. For a description of these small squares, see M. Davie (1997) 'The History and Evolution of Public Spaces in Beirut's Central District', Unpublished report, Beirut, Solidere.
13. For a description, see F. Ragette (1974) *Architecture in Lebanon: The Lebanese House During the 18th and 19th Centuries*, Beirut: American University of Beirut. The geographical extension of this architectural model seems to have been the territory of the future Wilaya of Beirut, as one can observe it between Jaffa and Lattakia. However, its favoured spaces were the Sandjaq of Beirut and Central Mount-Lebanon.
14. The texts of these regulations can be found in Abdelnour, op. cit.
15. For the Maghreb, see F. Béguin (1983) *Arabisances, décor architectural et tracé urbain en Afrique du Nord, 1830–1950*, Paris: Dunod.
16. The al-Arman, Jewellers', Mar Jirjis and al-Nuriyyeh *suq*.
17. The project also planned the building of a monumental stairway that would link the north side of the Small Seraglio to the port.
18. These cut-throughs were financed by donations to the Red Cross for the war poor by Syrians who had emigrated to the US; the money was used by Jamal Pacha to hire them for urban work; see *As-Salam* daily newspaper, 12 December 1916.
19. G. Wright (1991) *The Politics of Design in French Colonial Urbanism*, Chicago and London: The University of Chicago Press; Ph. Khoury (1987) *Syria and the French Mandate: The Politics of Arab Nationalism, 1920–1945*, London: I.B. Tauris.
20. The merchant bourgeoisie was shunted aside by the political elite of the mountain, to which, incidentally, the city was annexed. See M. Davie (1996) *Beyrouth et ses faubourgs (1840–1940), une intégration inachevée*, Beirut: CERMOC. It was also evicted by the action of some among its own ranks; Petro Trad, for example, was to be found high up in the state hierarchy, when previously his post had traditionally been held by a member of the Sursok family. On the political tensions of that period, see M. Zamir (1985) *The Formation of Modern Lebanon*, Ithaca and London: Cornell University Press.
21. Such as General Gouraud himself, who had worked under Lyautey in Morocco, or others such as Colonel Niéger and General Catroux, or civilians such as Robert de Caix, secretary-general to Gouraud.
22. Yusif Afandi, Aftimos Afandi and Raffler Afandi, an Austrian.
23. The civil engineer Hippolyte Michel and Commander Matthieu (*Lisan al-Hal* daily newspaper of 19 June 1920). Many immigrant Russians were also seconded to Municipality projects or to the land registry (Cadastre); A. Farès (n.d.) 'La participation active des ingénieurs et topographes russes au développement du cadastre, des municipalités, de l'urbanisme, de l'hydraulique et autres domaines techniques au Liban et au Moyen-Orient après la première grande guerre mondiale', Beyrouth.
24. He was replaced by Edmond Bishara.
25. Later, the Municipal Council would resign several times over questions of disputed authority or internal dissent.
26. The spelling of this name is uncertain, as the source is in Arabic. No mention of this name has been found in French sources. It is perhaps Dettray or D'Estrée.
27. Unhappy with the situation, several Beirutis replied that the city did not lack famous men and heroes, poets or saints and had no need of new ones brought in from the outside world (*Lisan al Hal* of 3 March and 22 May 1920). They were

also shocked that the *suq* al-'Umumi (the red-light area) had been named after Mutanabbi, a famous Arab poet renowned for his austerity.

28. This plan no doubt served as the basis for the Danger brothers' 1933 embellishment plan; they only brought minor modifications to the original project.

29. See Duraffourd's report in Haut Commissariat de la République française en Syrie et au Liban (1921) *Rapport général sur les études foncières effectuées en Syrie et au Liban*, Beyrouth: Services Fonciers.

30. The streets were narrow enough and irregular in alignment to block direct sunlight and to deflect gusts of wind.

31. For a brief overview of the first works, see Poupon (1928) 'La modernisation de Beyrouth', *Bulletin de l'Union Economique de Syrie*, vol. 1, pp. 23–29; Poupon (1929) 'La modernisation de Beyrouth', *Bulletin de l'Union Economique de Syrie*, vol. 5, pp. 18–21.; M. Berrard (1936) *Quinze ans de mandat, l'œuvre française en Syrie et au Liban*, Beirut: Imprimerie Catholique. For more details see M. Davie and M. Nammour (1995) 'Beyrouth 1920–1940, Municipalité et politiques urbaines durant le mandat français', unpublished research, Beirut, Université Saint-Joseph.

32. On the origin and the symbolism of the star-shaped plan in Europe, see Ch. Delfante (1997) *Grande histoire de la ville*, Paris: Armand Colin.

33. A clock tower was to be built at the centre of the square; the base was, however, disproportionately large in relation to the scale of the square and that of the overlooking buildings. It also blocked the planned view towards the sea.

34. On the conflicts between the Municipality and the previous owners, see the daily reports in the newspaper *Lisân al Hal* between 1918 and 1935.

35. In Syria this style is called 'neo-Ottoman'. In North Africa, this mix of ancient forms and decorations, reinterpreted by Western architects in the nineteenth century, is called 'mauresque' or 'neo-mauresque'. On the birth of this style and its evolution, see F. Béguin, op. cit.

36. Aftimos Afandi came from Deir el Kamar. He married Bishara Afandi's granddaughter. He designed, among other buildings, the Turkish and Persian pavilion at the Chicago Exhibition and the Egyptian pavilion at the Antwerp Exhibition. See L. Cheikho (1899) 'Manarat al-sa'at al-'arabiyyat fi Bayrout' (The Beirut Arabic tower clock), *Al-Mashriq* 17, pp. 769–74; Atelier de Recherche de l'ALBA (2000) *La malle de l'architecte: Youssef Aftimos (1866–1952)*, Beirut: ALBA.

37. Contrary to his predecessor, Bishara Afandi, who had introduced the Baroque and Classical styles in Beirut's official buildings. Émile Khachu was an associate of Aftimos Afandi in most of the buildings of that period. See M. Davie (2001) *Beyrouth 1825–1975, cent cinquante ans d'urbanisme*, Beirut: Ordre des Ingénieurs et Architectes de Beyrouth.

38. The Ottoman Empire took part in the world fairs. The *naw' sharqi* (oriental style) was used as an instrument to Ottomanize the provincial capitals. S. Diringil (1998) *The Well-Protected Domain, Ideology and the Legitimation of Power in the Ottoman Empire, 1876–1909*, London/New York: I.B. Taurus. However, in Beirut this style was not widespread: only the city's clock and the Hamidiyyeh fountain expressed it.

39. In most of these buildings, an airshaft, also used as a stairwell, would replace the open central courtyard of the Ottoman buildings.

40. Farid Trad, Rodolphe Elias, Behjat 'Abdelnur, Elias el-Murr, Salah 'Itani, were some of the famous engineers of the period; R. Ghosn (1970) 'Beirut architecture', *Beirut: Crossroads of Cultures*, Beirut: Librairie du Liban.

41. Other nineteenth-century *suq*, built by the Sunni bourgeoisie (the Beyhum, 'Itani, Hamadeh, Ayyas families), and by part of the Greek-Orthodox bourgeoisie (the Bustros and Sayyur families) were located to the northwest of the old centre and thus not affected by the project. However, plans to straighten the *suq* al-Tawileh were discussed, though nothing was decided for lack of funds and especially in the face of opposition from certain land owners and merchants.
42. Zamir, op. cit.
43. South of the Parliament building.

CHAPTER 10

LOCAL WISHES AND NATIONAL COMMANDS: PLANNING CONTINUITY IN FRENCH PROVINCIAL TOWNS IN THE 1940S

Joe Nasr

Independent scholar

The period during and immediately after the First World War is generally regarded as a watershed in France when urban planning became established as a basic function of the State.[1] French *urbanisme* has roots that can be traced back at least as far as the eighteenth century[2] and has been recognized as a legal concept since 1919,[3] but it is in the 1940s that a legal framework and political commitment enabled plans to be widely implemented for the first time. This development occurred within the context of a takeover of the urban planning process by the national government, in response to urgent rebuilding needs combined with pre-existing deficiencies in the building stock that had reached crisis level.[4] The French State devised detailed and uniform rules and administered all of them in a top-down manner from the capital,[5] pre-empting what little local powers existed.[6] This meant that the reconstruction process in France contrasted strongly with the decentralized processes in countries such as West Germany.[7]

This paper argues that despite the national government's appropriation of the urban planning process,[8] the plans that were produced in France absorbed many local concerns, priorities and aspirations by assimilating what the 'city fathers'[9] envisioned for their future, and built on concepts that were already 'in the air' locally. There were important continuities in some of the planners involved in certain cities and at the national level, and – more importantly – in planning ideas and frameworks from before, during and after the Second World War.[10] This paper does not deny that war destruction and the establishment of a national urban planning framework represented an important break, physically and otherwise, in the structure of the cities affected; it does, however, contradict the idea that devastation occasioned a complete breakdown in planning practices and in the plans generated through these practices.[11] Thus there is a danger of overemphasizing the fracture between before and after, even in countries such as France that directly experienced the effects of the war.

Besides what it brings to the understanding of the reconstruction period, the paper also has a historiographic contribution to make. Historians of the French reconstruction, including Danièle Voldman, the pre-eminent chronicler of the emergence of urban planning during that era, have tended to approach the rebuilding process by examining the relations between the national and the local, as seen through the prism of the national. Built into this approach is the inherent risk of overemphasizing the best-known planners and other actors.[12] Even those who have undertaken case studies of particular cities[13] have focused on the roles of those national actors who were assigned to replan and redesign these cities.[14] This paper hence represents a fundamental reversal of perspective by examining the reconstruction 'through local eyes' and by placing at its core the question of what happens to local wishes when they encounter national commands. When the local perspective is taken as a starting point, the dictate of the State is seen by many as an opportunity, but one also senses that it is regarded to a certain extent as an interference. In fact, it can be argued that the continuities in planning observed by other scholars can be understood only when seen as another facet of the 'local dimension' of planning, and when the interactions of that dimension with the external factors are analyzed.

In what ways did such interactions occur in the French reconstruction case? Both during and after the Second World War, a general doctrine prevailed, the principle of which was that the expression of all principal planning tendencies of the time would be allowed, but that planners would have to follow certain general rules and processes.[15] A hierarchical State mechanism was put in place to ensure that the rebuilding of the country would take place within this framework (in contrast to the rebuilding after the First World War when laws were put in place but were barely implemented at the local level).[16] Local actors, as well as those designated by the State to work specifically at the local level, generally co-operated, and the former often consented to the mold imposed by the national authorities. This article shows that the margin of action this mold provided was ample enough to accommodate prevailing local wishes.

The paper thus illustrates the formative role played by local priorities and local actors (especially professionals) in shaping planning schemes that were conceived within a resolutely centralizing process that was not particularly favorable to these local influences. Even in a situation where every step in the planning process is defined by the State (as was the case in 1940s France), locals may still find a voice or a means to channel their wishes to the planners assigned by that State. Links can thus be established here to more 'traditional' situations of dominance, and to the reactions of locals to such dominance – as dealt with elsewhere in this book. Hence there are even similarities between the treatment by the French State of provincial cities and that of colonial cities.[17]

The focus here is on Beauvais and Blois, two smaller historic cities that suffered important losses to their cores in June 1940, though the destruction in the former was far more extensive (170 acres/69 hectares) than in the latter (22 acres/9 hectares). The majority of structures in old Beauvais were lost, whereas the destruction in Blois was concentrated around the bridgeheads along the Loire river.[18] The two towns shared a certain number of traits. The size of their populations was almost identical at less than 25,000 residents each in 1940 (though they are more than twice that today). Their chief roles were as administrative centers (both were seats of *départements*) and regional market places, and industrialization in both was limited and specialized (Blois was known for chocolate production and Beauvais for textiles). Their surviving historic fabric was considerable, and both were tourist towns, each dominated by a single main attraction – the Renaissance château in Blois and the medieval cathedral in Beauvais.

The plans for rebuilding and extending the two cities, the *Plans de reconstruction et d'aménagement* (PRA),[19] were among the first to be adopted[20] in France in 1942.[21] While the Vichy regime under which they were developed was discredited after 1944, the plans were retained and implemented with only limited modifications after the war. Furthermore, important links could be found between these plans and those for the embellishment and renewal of these same historic towns before the war. This paper thus outlines some of the continuities among urban plans across dramatically different political contexts, and demonstrates that this can be explained largely by the persistence of the local through a process that, on the face of it, had become national.

BEAUVAIS

Planning Grand Beauvais in the 1940s

Beauvais, seat of the Oise *département* and capital of the southern Picardie region, is located less than 70 kilometers (45 miles) due north of Paris. While its rich history predates the Romans and was of particular importance in the Middle Ages, development of the city was fairly slow during the industrial era, and it was bypassed by the main northward railway and highway (autoroute). Until the Second World War, the small and stagnant city was too close to Paris to escape its economic pull, yet too far away to be integrated within its orbit, and a few factories had been scattered in the lowlands along the railway line east and west of the city. Largely contained within the ring road that had replaced its old walls, its historic urban fabric had not changed substantially, and its continuing role as a market for the region was complemented by the emergence of tourism.

Beauvais was one of the earliest cities to quickly and smoothly put in place the basis for rebuilding its ravaged quarters, so becoming one of the first cities in which the PRA was approved[22] and a precocious star of French reconstruction.

However, the circumstances in which the primary architects/city planners (*architecte/urbaniste en chef*) for Beauvais were selected were not typical. The process had been started very early and was linked explicitly to the *Plan d'aménagement, d'embellissement et d'extension* (PAEE) that had been initiated at the end of 1919. As early as July 1940 (a month after the devastation of Beauvais), the *Conseil Municipal* (CM) had contemplated the urgency of establishing a rebuilding plan. The architects of the future plan of the city were hired on 19 August, following a circular to the administrators of devastated cities from the general delegate of the French Government in the Occupied Territories, reasserting the applicability of the old laws of 1919 and 1924. Two days later, the two architects met with interim Mayor Brayet and architect and former city council member Bordez to discuss summarily the questions that would form the main points of the future plan, including the south-north route and the site of the market and theater. It was decided that the planning of the central part of the city would be undertaken first, to be followed by that of the newer districts.[23]

Thus when, on 12 October 1940, after deliberation by the Departmental Commission of Plans for Cities and Villages, the Prefect requested that Beauvais have a new PAEE drawn up, given the damage caused by the bombing,[24] the city had already begun this effort. Beauvais had been one of the first cities to take advantage of the law of 1919 to establish a master plan, and in a similar fashion it took the Prefect's decree in 1940 just as seriously.[25] At the end of October, the city was asking the architects to press on with their study; at the same time it addressed a letter to all architects residing in Beauvais and other 'local personalities . . . learned in artistic matters', beseeching them to be 'benevolent collaborators of the Municipality and the authors designated for the reconstitution', in order to 'give back to our dismantled [*démantelée*] old medieval City, some of its ancient appearance, while fitting our ideas to the demands of modern life'.[26]

The city's choice of the two architects responsible for the 'reconstitution' was a reasoned one. Albert Parenty, Officer of the Légion d'Honneur, had been the author of the PAEE of 1922, and though based in Paris had known Beauvais exceptionally well for over three decades. Georges Noël, a young architect from Beauvais (the son of local café proprietors) and a former student of Parenty, had recently won the 'Premier Grand Prix de Rome in Architecture'.[27] Although both architects resided in Paris, they clearly had strong ties with Beauvais and combined 'the experience of the seniors with the boldness of young competencies'.[28]

Consequently, when the reconstruction commissioner Jacques Muffang discovered that Beauvais had already begun (post August) the planning work for the city with a respected team,[29] and that this work was well under way,[30] it is not surprising that he chose to ratify the process and the actors by simply transferring the contract conditions (terms, payment methods) from the city to the State.[31] The city's activity had therefore preceded that of the *département*, which in turn preceded that of the State.

It should thus be noted that the architects in Beauvais, in contrast to nearly all the other cases of rebuilding in France, were not outsiders sent in from Paris. They had already received suggestions from local personalities and had been specifically charged by the municipality, to which they had special ties, to focus their attention not just on the destroyed central part of the city but on the totality of the communal territory, including 'locations of new residential centers', 'projected building needs', and the 'extension of the current water and sewer layout'.[32] Therefore, what became the PRA was only a continuation of the city planning that followed the First World War but with the additional brief of reconstruction.

The reparceling in the designated 'perimeters of reconstruction' was managed, financed and tightly supervised by the State. All the landowners within these perimeters were placed compulsorily in *Associations Syndicales de Remembrement* (ASRs), public entities with a professional staff (also State-appointed).[33] These were succeeded in April 1948 by *Associations Syndicales de Reconstruction* as the effort shifted from planning to building. In the case of Beauvais, those who lost their buildings had organized themselves independently in August 1940 into an *Association des Sinistrés Beauvaisiens*, with the Municipality, which lost the most buildings, at the top of its list of members. However, this association, the 'essential purpose [of which] would be the defense of the potential rights and interests of those who suffered losses, *vis-à-vis* the public authorities',[34] was permitted to function only after the Occupation. Since those affected had already organized themselves into this association, it was reconstituted into an ASR and granted the responsibility for executing the construction works; this nationally mandated grouping of locals therefore had an important influence on the details of what was rebuilt.

In the historic part of Beauvais, the existing streets underwent much widening and straightening and some extension, however significant shifts of their location were limited (Fig. 1). On the other hand, a much more important transformation in the patterns within the blocks took place. While the street network within the historic district changed little from the original proposal to that which was eventually implemented,[35] there was more of an evolution in what was built: from street-hugging individual buildings to an open layout of cooperative blocks with segregated uses.[36]

However, it is especially on the larger metropolitan area that the city fathers focused their attention (Fig. 2). The PRA thus emphasized major shifts in the routing of through traffic (taking it around rather than across the old city) (Fig. 3), the relocation of many public buildings, and the designation and reser-

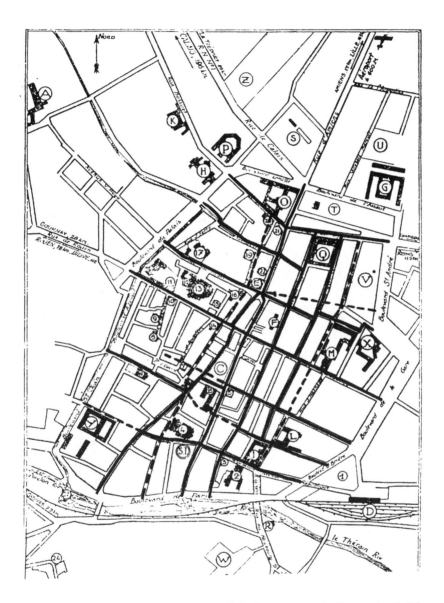

Figure 1. Full and partial crossings of the historic city in Beauvais. Solid lines: pre-Second World War crossings of the city. Broken lines: additional crossings created after the war.
Source: Drawing by the author, based on map from Charles Fauqueux, Beauvais: Son histoire de 1789 à l'après-guerre 1939–1945, 2nd edn. (Beauvais: Imprimerie centrale administrative, 1965), p. 201

vation of separate residential and industrial sectors. One particular administrative change that took place early in 1943 was separate from, though not independent of the rest of the urban planning efforts of the period – the annexation of four surrounding *communes* to the city of Beauvais, enlarging the area from 766 hectares (1893 acres) to around 3200 hectares (7907 acres).[37]

Context: Planning Grand Beauvais in the 1920s

The ease with which the enlargement of the municipality and the changes in its structure took place during the Second World War can be understood only by looking back at least two decades, to the planning efforts dating from the period after the First World War, which themselves had even older roots. Furthermore, these attempts at planning a 'Grand Beauvais' had an indirect influence on the 1940 plan for rebuilding the destroyed old city, and

Figure 2. 1942 zoning and circulation plan for greater Beauvais. The two industrial zones are to the east (hatched) and west (grey). The quartiers de compensation (light grey) radiate out to the north and south, following the main routes out of town (white). Source: Archives Nationales [A.N.], Centre des archives contemporaines (Fontainebleau) [CAC], 19810400 art. 86 (AFU 10191), folder 'Projet de reconstruction,' Aménagement du territoire et zonage, 16 May 1942

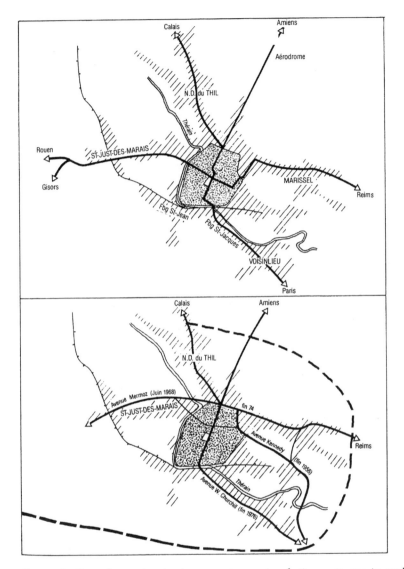

Figure 3. *Transformation in the cross-town circulation patterns in and around Beauvais: top, situation in 1939; bottom, in the late 1970s. The redesign of the arterial roads leading to and through Beauvais focused all of them on the Hôtel-Dieu area, the northern entrance of the old city. This resulted in congestion and high volumes of traffic from the time the planned roadwork was completed. Consequently, construction of a much larger bypass (in broken lines) started to be discussed in the early 1960s, circumventing the metropolitan area on three sides (north, east and south).*
Sources: Lines added by author on a drawing in Jean Ganiage, Histoire de Beauvais et du Beauvaisis (Toulouse: Privat, 1987), p. 269

enabled it to move faster than most other cities its in planning effort, if not in the rebuilding itself.

Indeed, the planners in 1940 had available to them a crucial document: a plan that had been prepared by Parenty in the 1920s.[38] Beauvais belonged to a small number of French cities that had jumped at the opportunity created by the law of 1919 that enabled cities to plan. Indeed, not only did Beauvais already have a plan approved by the CM in 1922, but this plan was in fact ambitious in goals, in time, and even in space, going well beyond the city limits at the time to include neighboring *communes*.[39] In effect it not only anticipated the expansion of 1943, but also laid the seeds for it.

The plan of 1922 virtually disregarded the city limits, and discussions with the other *communes* only began three-and-a-half years after the CM had accepted it. Differences were finally resolved in August 1927, at which time a 'syndicate' of six *communes*, including Beauvais, was formed, the goal of which was to implement the plan and deal with 'all matters pertaining to lighting, power, water supply, public transportation and, in general, all public services of inter-communal interest'.[40]

Within the historic district, what was of greatest significance in Parenty's original plan of March 1922 (Fig. 4) was a proposal to create two new north-south and east-west axes cutting through the fabric of the old city just east and south respectively of the existing main streets. At the southern entrance a new bridge over the river, tracks and ring road was envisioned, in almost the exact location of the bridge that would be realized mid-century (Fig. 5). Similarly, the eventual post-Second World War rebuilding included two new intersecting axes that would follow similar routes to those proposed in the 1920s.

The bridge and axes proposals in Parenty's original plan proved premature. They were the main subjects of critiques in CM meetings and were dropped from the plan when it was resubmitted two months later. While a bridge was still proposed, combined with improvements in the ring road, only minor street adjustments were retained in the plan for the old city.[41] The plan approved by the CM in May 1922 therefore included major developments outside the old city but very little change within it.

So the Parenty plan of the 1920s needs to be considered in all assessments of the conception and realization of the postwar city. As local historian Thibault remarks, the principal characteristics of the 1947 plan were already present in 1922:

* elimination of internal administrative barriers (through the annexation of neighboring *communes*);
* revision in the network of roadways in the urban area (limited improvements in the circulation inside town combined with more significant improvements in the circulation around town by relying on the existing

ring road as well as new access routes away from the city,[42] modifying in particular the most important and problematic route Paris-Calais);

* in combination with these improvements in circulation, extension of the built districts outside the old city;

* emphasis placed on industry (along the rail lines east and west of town following the Thérain river), on new residential districts for housing the workers of these production areas (on higher ground to the north and the south) and on reinforcement of the central functions within the inner city (administrative, commercial, cultural, etc.); and

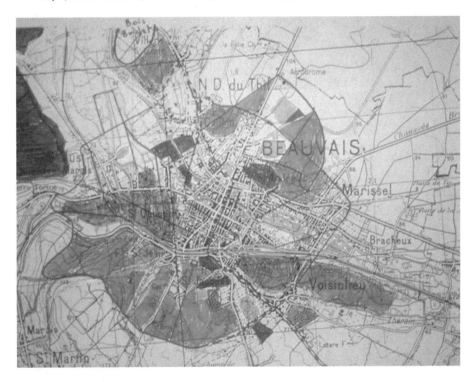

Figure 4. Main components of Parenty's plan of March 1922 overlaid on a 1932 map of Beauvais. The industrial areas (in dark grey) are essentially unchanged today. The main postwar residential zones match mostly the ones designated in the 1922 plan (in N.D. du Thil, St. André, St. Jacques and St. Jean areas). Woodlands and parks are in black. The routes that would be created are marked with a solid line, while the broken lines show existing roads to be improved. In the old town, in addition to two short east-west segments, there would have been two new cross-streets inserted in the existing fabric, shifting slightly the two traditional perpendicular axes of the city. When the plan was approved two months later, the only major alteration in the plan was the elimination of these two breakthrough streets.
Source: Drawing by André Thibault

Figure 5. *View from the south toward the old town of Beauvais: (top) before 1940; and (bottom) today. This view was the one Parenty wanted to offer to the visitor in the 1920s and was finally realized after the war with the construction of the bridge.*
Sources: Archives Municipales de Beauvais, photo collection; and photo by the author, 1994

* acceptance of the new (especially the growing role of the motor car and the spreading out and thinning out of housing) without drastically transforming the old,[43] as reflected in attention to the *extra muros* more than the *intra muros*.

Why plan for Grand Beauvais?

The same basic framework can be found in the Parenty plan of 1922, the Noël and Parenty plan of 1942, the Noël plan of 1948 and the present-day asphalt-and-concrete Beauvais. In other words, not only does the concept of *tabula rasa* not apply in the *rebuilding* of Beauvais (or most other cities for that matter), neither did it apply in the *planning* for that rebuilding. So Beauvais built on at least three decades of plans that had already been extensively debated, reviewed, revised and elaborated, and which had even undergone limited implementation. The ideas in the plans, as well as the idea of planning itself, had had time to ferment and gradually settle in the minds of both the civic leaders and the ordinary citizens.

So why do most of the essential elements of Beauvais today match so closely those in Parenty's plan of 1922? Perhaps Parenty was an astute and far-sighted thinker. Or maybe it was the case that his plan was just simply rational, and that any 'reasonable' planner would have reached more or less the same broad principles. Another answer to the question probably lies in the *existence* of the plan itself, which offered something to work from and a powerful image to refer to. Parenty's plan at least facilitated the acceptance of such planning for Greater Beauvais and provided the foundation for the relative ease of acceptance of Noël's plan a quarter of a century later. Whatever the case, it is quite certain that the successive plans, whether preceding the destruction of Beauvais or following it, and whether undertaken under local or national tutelage, all conformed to the key local actors' dominant vision for the future Beauvais.

The central trait of these plans was their focus on planning outside the ring road rather than inside. While Grand Beauvais underwent significant restructuring, this was largely avoided in the old city, except for the parcel structure, for two principal reasons.

First, no profound restructuring was needed. Despite the claims of the planners in the 1940s, the old city was not particularly congested (partly because of its very slow development since its medieval golden era). Its layout was roughly gridded with no shortage of long through-streets and no complex and narrow mazes. Therefore, the scenarios that most often caused civic leaders of various ideologies to call for what is referred to today as urban renewal were rare.

Second, while the Industrial Revolution had somewhat bypassed Beauvais, its potential as an industrial city had long been asserted (this was finally realized after the Second World War under the impetus of the national indus-trial decentralization policies, based on the locational advantages of the city).[44] Close to Paris and on the route to the French industrial north, England and the Low Countries, Beauvais' promise as an emerging economic center depended on both a sound local infrastructure and improved access to the outside,[45] therefore its surroundings, rather than the old city, were the logical focus of the planning efforts.[46] So just as before 1940 the *extension* aspect of the plan had been more important than its *embellissement*,[47] after 1940 the *aménagement* received more attention than the *reconstruction*.

BLOIS

Planning a new Vieux Blois in the 1940s

As noted earlier, Blois presented a number of similarities to Beauvais in June 1940 when both were devastated within ten days of each other. However, there were also important differences between the two cities, the most notable of which was that each had been built on a very different type of site. Historic Blois is on the north bank of the Loire river, and developed mostly on its steep and irregularly shaped embankment; this slope played a decisive role in giving it form, including its very tortuous street network. In contrast to Beauvais, there was also no ring road to act as a sharp containment device.[48]

There were also significant differences in the destruction and recon-struction of each city. As noted earlier, the destruction in Blois covered only a limited area, whereas in Beauvais almost the entire central district was destroyed. In addition, the street system in the destroyed zone of Blois, unlike in Beauvais, was radically changed, and contrasted sharply with the efforts to construct much of what was rebuilt in Beauvais in keeping with local character.

However, one particular difference between Beauvais and Blois is most rel-evant here, and corroborates the strong continuity in local planning priorities with the prewar period in both cities yet in diametrically distinct ways. It is clear that, among the urban concerns present in Blois in the decades pre-ceding the Second World War (since the nineteenth century, in fact), what dominated planning discussion was not how to encourage and manage the extension of the city but how to cut new means of communication within and across it. This was eventually reflected in the fact that, in the unevenly built areas *around* the city, only one new axis was proposed in the PRA in the 1940s (Fig. 6) and created afterwards: a short segment on the northeastern edge of town. This single new connection around Blois stands in contrast to the entire network of new roads that was envisioned for Greater Beauvais.

This inattention to Greater Blois was in contrast to the greater desire for cutting through and transforming the historic zones of the city. Indeed this

desire had been so pervasive that even conservationist personalities such as
Hubert Fillay, leader of the 'Friends of old Blois', were advocating significant
transformations in the city, including 'arteries that are as straight as possible
and open up so as to feature the ancient monuments for the tourists'.[49] To
understand the twentieth-century attitude towards the old city of Blois, it must
be placed within the long series, over centuries, of incisions in its fabric. And
to understand this lineage, it must be placed within the historical development
of the city's fortunes and consequently its demographic evolution.

Context: Centuries of planning a new Vieux Blois

Blois was a small Loire valley town until 1498, when it enjoyed a short-lived
golden period as a royal residence, a transformation which saw its population grow to 18,000 inhabitants.[50] But from 1530, the population gradually
declined, and few new buildings were erected, and when the population began
to grow again in the mid-1830s what little construction took place was mostly
situated outside the core. By 1940, Blois was therefore characterized by a

Figure 6. Detail of
zoning plan for greater
Blois, showing main built
area. Part of the package
of plans submitted for the
public hearing on the
PRA, 9.5.1942. Source:
A.N., CAC, 19800268 art.
22 (AFU 4954), folder
'Documents officiels sur le
Projet d'Aménagement du
20.1.1959,' 1942 zoning
plan

population that, relative to its low of 11,000 during the Revolution, had more than doubled (to 26,000 in 1936) but was living in a building stock that to a large extent dated back four centuries.[51] Moreover, the street system was characterized not only by its narrowness but even more so by the difficult connections between the lower town and upper town.

The step-by-step transformation of the street system can be understood within this context. It is first necessary to go back to the early eighteenth century, to 1724 when a new 300-meter bridge was built to the east of the former bridge that had been washed away by floods in 1716. The replacement structure was aligned with a secondary existing street rather than the main axis (*la Grande-Rue*) leading north towards Chartres and Paris.[52]

The exension of the secondary street into a major axis in line with the new bridge was envisaged soon after, but had to be abandoned largely because of the difficulties caused by the slope and particularly due to opposition from property owners.[53] This was actually only one element of an ambitious plan that was proposed in 1774 to widen most of the streets in the city and its immediate surroundings; quickly rejected, a more modest plan focused on widening just some of the commercial streets, especially the old *Grande-Rue*.[54] But even this limited plan was aborted.

From 1838, a number of particularly limited applications of piecemeal regulations (demolition of houses projecting into the street, changes in street cross-section, etc.) began to emerge. Nevertheless, this timid effort by the Municipality was met with strong resistance, including litigation. Therefore it was not until almost a century later, and simultaneously with the transformation of Paris by Baron Haussmann in the 1850s and 1860s, that a dynamic mayor, Eugène Riffault, created the many new streets through the city (Fig. 7). Riffault's projects, however, did not emerge in a vacuum. As Cospérec notes: 'All the big decisions were taken between 1820 and 1840,'[55] with many going back to alignments projected in 1774.

The most important new route of Riffault's era finally extended the axis of the bridge northwards.[56] In addition to improving northbound circulation, there was an undeniable visual consideration in the design of this route (Fig. 8).[57] Since the axis could not be continued indefinitely to the north because of an insurmountable hill, the vehicular street was deflected to the west and a monumental staircase (Denis-Papin) prolonged the alignment with the bridge. This type of axis had in fact long been an important feature of the other main cities along the Loire (especially Orléans and Tours), the legacy of the Absolutist period, and it was perhaps inevitable that such an axis would have been imposed on the historic fabric of Blois.

Until the post-1940 reconstruction, it was during the Riffault era (1850–70) that most of the changes in the city's urban fabric, since its Renaissance heyday, had taken place. However, a number of new streets and spaces had in fact been added to the old city over the years both before and after this period. For example, in 1767 a large avenue had been placed at the southern axis of the bridge as part of a new route leading to the Sologne region.[58] Place Louis XII, which was in the heart of the destroyed sector in 1940, had been erected around 1820, taking advantage of the demolition of a number of religious holdings during the Revolution.[59] And Porte-Côté and Gallois streets and Victor-Hugo square had been either created or enlarged in the 1880s.[60]

Prior to 1940, a number of other projects were considered for Blois but never realized. Notably the plan established to conform to the law of 1919. The *Plan d'extension, d'aménagement et d'embellissement de la ville de Blois* was prepared by Albert Renou and approved by the CM by 1925.[61] And this comprehensive plan also had antecedents. In particular, local architect A. Lafargue put forth, privately, a proposal in 1914 on the eve of the First World War (even before the 1919 law), which was written in the form of a rueful but prospective booklet, lamenting all that had not been done to improve the city, but clearly meant as a call for future action.[62] As in Beauvais, it is useful here to compare the plans for Blois in the 1940s to the 1925 plan, and in this case to its 1914 predecessor also.

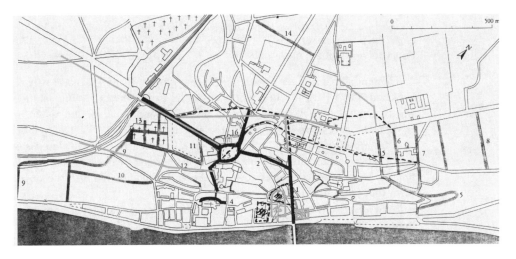

Figure 7. *Streets created or transformed on the right bank in Blois in the second half of the nineteenth century, primarily during the Eugène Riffault administration (1850–1870). Over these are shown some of the projects for new streets and public buildings proposed by Lafargue in 1914 (grey lines) and Renou in 1925 (broken lines). HV = New Hôtel de Ville (city hall). MP = New market place and post office.*
Source: Lines added by author on a drawing in Annie Cospérec, Blois, La forme d'une ville, Inventaire général des monuments et des richesses artistiques de la France, Région Centre, Cahiers du Patrimoine no. 35 (Paris: Imprimerie nationale éditions et Inventaire général, 1994), pp. 366–67

Figure 8. View from the Gabriel bridge of Denis-Papin street, named after the Blois-born inventor of the steam engine. The monumental Papin stairs close the Papin street axis.
Source: Photo by the author, 1994

Lafargue's first concern was for the tourist: 'Poor city of Blois, so well endowed, but where nothing has been showcased[63] properly!' His solution was to generate a well-studied overall plan, focusing on 'extending as far as possible the part reserved for the tourist and the bourgeois seeking a dwelling, who are inexhaustible sources for commerce'.[64] Similarly, Renou's plan designated various sectors for industry, workers' homes and gardens, and bourgeois houses, confirming the lower town as the site of commerce and the upper town that of administration.

Unlike in Beauvais, both the 1914 and 1925 plans called for a number of new and improved streets, both in the new zones and inside the historic settled part of the city, along with many institutional shifts, some of which were suggested for the heart of town (Fig. 7). Many of Lafargue and Renou's proposals were identical, and some of these matched those proposed in the plan of 1942.

Within the central area, some of the proposals that were to re-emerge during the reconstruction can be noted in both of the early plans. The axis of the bridge would be extended north beyond the Denis-Papin stairs until it met the main route to Paris. All the markets would be consolidated in one large (and controlled) space in the heart of the old city, which would include a new central postoffice. City Hall, on the north corner of the bridgehead, would be enlarged and set back on its site.[65] Finally, various localized demolitions within the historic city would make certain features more visible, especially the château. One important instance of this would be the *dégagement* of houses along the southern fortification to make this corner open, 'healthy and clean'. So the main consideration of the plans was the creation of perspectives; all of the streets proposed were straight and wide, with a major structure placed at one end at least.

It is true that, as local geographer Babonaux notes, the plan of 1925 was never applied.[66] However, the general ideas and the specific proposals contained within that plan, Lafargue's plan in 1914 and the others before that, dating back to Riffault and earlier, formed the conceptual layers on which the plan of 1942 was based, though again many of the ideas of this plan, as of those before it, were never realized.

A local planner of the new Vieux Blois

The reconstruction plans for Blois cannot be properly understood without the historical context provided by the long series of contemplated and implemented public-works intrusions. In Beauvais, this context included continuity in the players before and after 1940. In Blois, on the other hand, the principal planner was an outsider; nevertheless, here too local actors had an important function. One such player in particular held a crucial role, building on his pre-war vision of a transformed city center.

Within days of the city's destruction in June 1940, as in Beauvais the Municipality turned to a local architect, this time Paul Robert-Houdin.[67] The Mayor at the time, Dr Olivier, had placed the most urgent rubble-clearance under the direction of Robert-Houdin, so that teams of workers had already begun pulling down the most precarious walls on 24 June.[68] In the summer of 1940, Robert-Houdin was asked to prepare plans for rebuilding the devastated sector,[69] and was made a member of the commission for the city's *Plan d'aménagement* in August the same year. The task of establishing the topographic leveling was added to his assignments in October.

However, unlike in Beauvais, where the State took over the responsibility for all reconstruction in late 1940, in Blois the project was reassigned to Charles Nicod, a senior Parisian architect who, like Noël in Beauvais, had been a winner of the Premier Grand Prix de Rome.[70] At first Nicod was also chief architect, but this function was later split and conferred on a younger architect, André Aubert, a fellow winner of the Rome Prize.[71]

It is interesting to compare Nicod's plan with some of Robert-Houdin's earlier plans and with some of the plans that predated Nicod's involvement in the reconstruction. Building on the long line of those who had sought to transform the heart of Blois, Robert-Houdin had proposed as early as 1931 what can be labeled an urban renewal project for the area that was to be destroyed nine years later. The key feature of that proposal was a semicircular space; its dimensions were almost identical to that realized after the war (just under 60 meters/197 feet in diameter), though placed one block north of the bridgehead in this case. Beyond this pivotal space, Robert-Houdin envisaged widening numerous streets, as would be implemented in the destroyed zone eventually.

Later in the 1930s, in a competition to build a new *Hôtel de Ville* on its old site by the bridge,[72] Robert-Houdin proposed a redesign of the entire bridgehead area (Fig. 9). Once again, he conceived a semicircular space, this time opening up to the river and perfectly perpendicular to it, an even grander site and an 'architectural ensemble worthy of Blois' that would be created within the tradition of French squares, bringing to mind *places Royale, Vendôme, des Victoires* and *Stanislas*.

In the summer and autumn of 1940, Robert-Houdin would make numerous studies, by now not for renewing a district perceived as run-down, but for

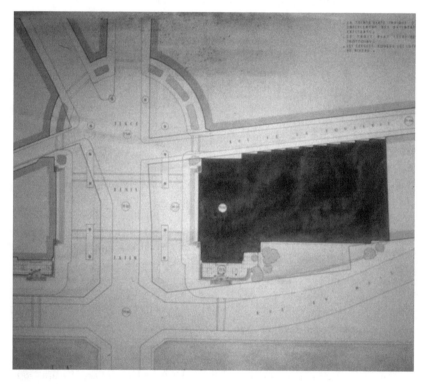

Figure 9. *Proposal by Robert-Houdin for a new city hall for Blois and a new Denis-Papin square at the bridgehead, 1930s.*
Source: Archives Municipales de Blois, Paul Robert-Houdin archive, untitled plan folder

rebuilding a ravaged city. His first postwar proposal in July 1940 featured no semicircle, however two streets did radiate from a rectangular space at the bridgehead towards the château and cathedral.[73] In his various studies he was trying out different schemes for two main architectural components of the historic city's plan: the shape of the space at the bridgehead and the streets that tied into it, and the area at the foot of the château. For the latter, several of Robert-Houdin's sketches featured substantial open space on this site, as would be implemented in the 1950s. Common to all of his studies for this particular zone was the total transformation and regularization of the space.

Robert-Houdin's studies for the reconstruction of the center of Blois were only some of those put forward during a period that experienced a flurry of rebuilding proposals. His 19 July scheme mentioned above was only one among close to three dozen designs that were prepared for a competition held locally seeking ideas on how to rebuild the city in the immediate aftermath of the destruction. Outside this competition, a number of prominent *blésois* also volunteered their own concepts of the key to the city's future reconstruction, often in the local press, and some of these featured what were to become principal features of Nicod's PRA, for example the hemicyclic space from which the streets would radiate.

The presentation and discussion of new plans for a new Blois continued right up until the end of 1940 when the reconstruction process was appropriated by the State and assigned solely to Nicod. For example, suggestions were sought in October from a regional architect, Léon Chesnay; his scheme was yet another bridgehead square (polygonal in this instance) with radiating diagonal streets, and an enlarged *place Louis XII* just below the château.[74] At the same time, a synthesis of the various plans that had been presented was being elaborated by the departmental commission (headed by the Prefect), of which Robert-Houdin was a member, in order to establish a definitive reconstruction plan.

When responsibility was transferred by the State to Nicod, the city and department had already gone through an extensive evaluation of the rebuilding of Blois and were on the verge of resolving the issue and settling on a final plan. This is most evident in one plan from autumn 1940 that shows streets, block outlines and the drainage system and is virtually indistinguishable from Nicod's PRA of the following year (Fig. 10). In fact, this crucial document resembles Nicod's later plan so perfectly that it verges on plagiarism and raises the question as to whether Nicod in fact made any contribution to the redesign of Blois' central district.[75]

Consequently, this pre-emption by the State meant both starting from square one and the continuation of a process that was well under way. Nicod's resulting plan, first presented in 1941 and later implemented with little

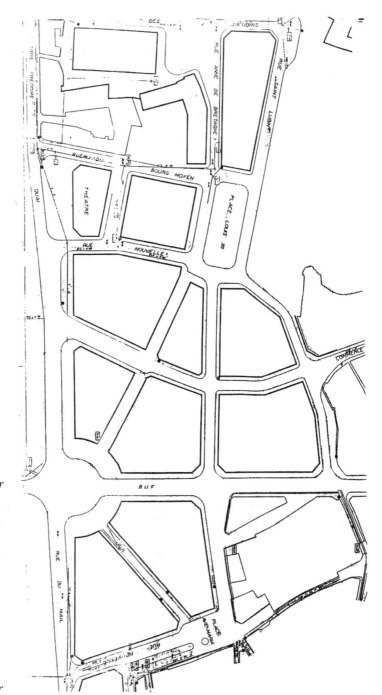

Figure 10. City of Blois, detail of plan for rebuilding the devastated sector, showing the street system, building blocks, drainage and sewage system, and street elevations. Prepared by Robert-Houdin, dated 8 September 1940. Source: Archives Municipales de Blois, Paul Robert-Houdin archive, untitled folder

modification, builds on the 1940 and other earlier proposals (Fig. 11). It is known that Nicod had consulted with local personalities, including Robert-Houdin, while preparing his plans.[76] So while the reconstruction in Blois, as in other French cities, was very much a top-down effort as both an evaluative and decision-making process, the design concepts of the lead urbanist (Nicod) were clearly permeated by pre-existing local ideas, which in turn were linked to enduring local concerns.[77]

Therefore, as in Beauvais the Blois PRA needed to take into account the concerns of the principal local actors and relate to the legacy of earlier plans based on these concerns. The difference between the plans for the two cities was that in Beauvais concerns focused on the *aménagement* outside the old city, whereas in Blois they focused on the *reconstruction* within it.

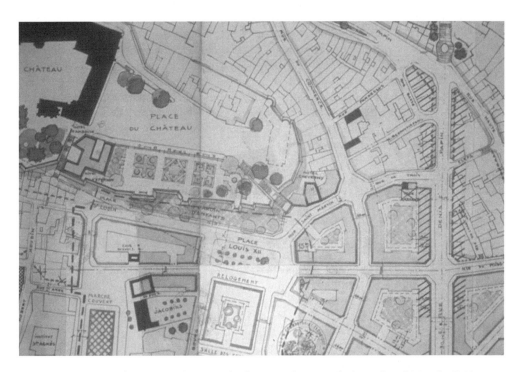

Figure 11. Detail of the PRA showing the historic district of Blois, dated March 1942, submitted by Charles Nicod for the public hearing of 9 May 1942. The area surrounded by a broken line has a lower height requirement than the rest of the sector, in order to keep a clear view to the Château. The frontage of Denis-Papin street (in diagonal hatching) has a special tolerance allowing higher buildings, due to the wider street. Surviving public buildings and registered historic buildings are in black.
Source: A.N., CAC, 19800268 art. 25 (AFU 4951), folder 'Dossier préparé pour l'enquête publique,' item no. 9

LOCAL ACTORS AND LOCAL CONCERNS AS CONTEXT FOR PLANNING

So what was the central concern that formed the essence of the plans for Beauvais and Blois, and how did this concern relate to previous concerns in the two cities? What continuities and changes in professional actors (especially the imposition of new actors by the national authorities) could be identified in each town, and what were the influences of each on the plans for rebuilding? In response to these questions, two main conclusions emerge in the course of the analysis of the PRAs and their development.

First, an essential factor behind the advances in Beauvais and Blois relative to other French cities in planning for their rebuilding was the integration of the reconstruction process with efforts to plan urban development that dated back several decades, and a receptiveness to the concept of planning.[78] These advances were based on a solidarity between the majority of the main local participants, and on a general accord between these local participants and the State-imposed actors, which meant that fierce controversies and endless quarrels were avoided. Indeed, the Director of Reconstruction Plans at the *Ministère de la Reconstruction et de l'Urbanisme* (MRU) declared that, in Beauvais, a 'perfect concordance with the local services, notably the road services' had been achieved.[79] We cannot confirm whether the agreement was truly perfect in respect of all services, local or other.[80] Nevertheless, discussions in Beauvais and Blois were rather calm in comparison to those in other rebuilt French cities such as Saint-Dié, where projects and counter-projects, architects and counter-architects were part of a particularly acrimonious debate,[81] or Dunkerque where conflicts between the chief urbanist and the chief architect were intense.[82] It was especially in these circumstances that national committees and officials had to step in to settle matters.

While local authorities could not avoid the lengthy planning process through which all French cities passed, they were however able to avert changes to the PRA that would have made the process even longer. Where there was harmony between the planner(s) put in charge by the State and the local authorities, there was a greater likelihood that planning and implementation would be swift, even though the local authorities had little decision-making capability. Therefore, although the national authorities had imposed a national decision-making process, the Beauvais and Blois PRAs overcame any hurdles with relative ease, in part because they matched local priorities, at least those of the most influential members of the community.

The State's takeover of urban and regional planning in the early 1940s, and the maintenance of this nationalization in the decades following the end of the war, meant that the national authorities provided a framework for all planning, set a new planning hierarchy, designated the actors within this hierarchy and established the general planning principles that these actors were to follow. As mentioned previously, there was also a common doctrine that governed both the wartime and postwar years: that beyond these general principles, the State would allow all the principal urbanistic and architectural tendencies of the time (from the 'modernist' to the 'regionalist') to be represented across the new French urban landscape.[83] Whatever the reasons for this pluralism of sorts may have been (whether pragmatic, ideological or other), it meant that as long as they remained within the general parameters set by the State, local priorities could be generally accommodated within the reconstruction plans. It appears that the margin of action of local actors, including those accountable to the central authorities, was sufficient to enable them to pick up the planning of their city from where they had left it before 1940, and in fact to use the wartime destruction and the new impetus and capacities for planning to empower them to embark on actions that many of these players had long called for but could only now bring about. This paper has thus shown how local professional actors, although stripped of many powers by the State, reacted by not only consenting to these changes but incorporating their aspirations into this new mold.

In addition, the choices made in the planning and design concepts in the various stages of the reconstruction period reflect a combination of local and national influences. The former can be seen in the continuity of planning concerns in Beauvais and Blois, as reflected in the precepts of the wartime PRAs despite the imposition of centralized management on the project. The latter is highlighted by the evolution of the projects during the 1940s and 1950s, reflecting national (and international) trends in urbanistic thinking.

In the case of France, the national-level origins of urban changes (that is, State intervention in the reconstruction process) during the so-called *trente glorieuses* ('thirty glorious' years) are now well understood. A contribution of this paper, then, is to add a dimension that has been largely missing from this knowledge: the influence of the 'local tradition' regarding planning. This refers to the debates on the future of the city that had been taking place locally for many decades, long before the appropriation of the process by the State. The planning by the State actors was therefore implanted into a discourse that was already established, and the French reconstruction combined the strong hand of the State's policies with the issues and ideas that had been circulating locally.[84]

In Beauvais, despite extensive devastation, the transformation in the street network was not radical. Of greatest importance in that city were questions relating to Greater Beauvais, including new routes to and around it. Meanwhile, in Blois, the main attention was devoted to thoroughly transforming the damaged area at the heart of the city, rather than to its periphery. In both of these contrasting cases, the transformations reflected issues often dating back to the nineteenth century, which were in fact the essence of earlier local proposals and plans.

NOTES

1. To mention just one citation: '. . . the work accomplished by these teams is unprecedented: in the span of a few years, most local administrative units – even those only lightly impacted by the war – are equipped with reconstruction plans. The chief planners have sketched a true national planning (*aménagement*) policy: the principles of the State's land interventions have been largely defined'. Jean Luquet (1991) 'Qui a reconstruit la France? ou la naissance d'une administration', in *Reconstructions et modernisation: La France après les ruines 1918 . . . 1945 . . .*, Paris: Archives Nationales, p. 87.

2. The varied roots include a range of interventions, both conceptual (such as Paris' so-called *plan des Artistes* in the mid-1790s), physical (such as breakthroughs like the rue de Rivoli and peripheral avenues like the Parisian *Grands Boulevards*) and administrative. In fact, despite various adjustments, the basic structure that distributed the power relations in a top-down hierarchy did not change in a fundamental way until the French Revolution. Thereafter the hierarchy was as follows: *Etat* (national authorities based in Paris), *département* (where the *Préfet* and other administrators were all appointed by and reported to the French president and the appropriate ministries), relatively weak *arrondissement* and *canton*, and finally the *commune*, the main local administration, where the authorities are chosen locally but whose powers are quite circumscribed by the national and departmental frameworks of laws and regulations. It is only starting in the 1960s (when a will to rebalance the national territory by strengthening the development of provincial cities and rural areas came to dominate State policy) and again in the 1980s (when the powers to make decisions and implement them on a range of public functions were delegated by the State to the *communes*, the *départements* and the newly created *régions*) that important reforms in this structure were implemented.

3. A law from 14 March of that year (the famous *Loi Cornudet*) sought not just to plan the rebuilding of cities destroyed in the First World War, but also to plan the beautification of cities that had escaped its ravages. Some additional laws, particularly one passed in July 1924, supplemented this fundamental law in the 1920s. For a history of the first years of modern urban and regional planning in France, see Jean-Pierre Gaudin (1985) *L'avenir en plan: Technique et politique dans la prévision urbaine, 1900–1930*, Seyssel: Editions du Champ Vallon.

4. Housing activity had collapsed with the onset of the First World War, remained considerably slow in the 1920s because of financial instability (inflation, depreciation and so on) and other postwar disincentives to construction (particularly rent control), and collapsed further in the 1930s. To this shortage was added in 1940–44 the loss of 460,000 buildings (269,000 of which were residential structures) across France as a result of the ravages of the Second World War. Marcel Roncayolo (1980) 'L'urbanisme, la guerre, la crise', in Maurice Agulhon (ed) *La ville de l'âge industriel, le cycle haussmannien*, vol. 4 of *Histoire de la France urbaine*, ed. Georges Duby, Paris: Seuil; and Anatole Kopp, Frédérique Boucher and Danièle Pauly (1982) *L'architecture de la reconstruction en France, 1945–1953*, Paris: Editions du Moniteur.

5. The rebuilding in France was very centralized, emanating from a national ministry (the *Ministère de la Reconstruction et de l'Urbanisme* (MRU), which replaced the *Commissariat à la Reconstruction Immobilière* (CRI) soon after Liberation), based on a national law (or rather a series of laws), and financed entirely by the

State through a normalized review of war damages. These were distributed with many conditions that were governed by State-appointed officials. The planners put in charge of the rebuilding (*urbanistes en chef*) and many other administrators and professionals were all selected in Paris. The new regulations gave to the State for the first time, or enhanced its existing powers for, either direct decision-making or administrative oversight over a wide range of activities. This covered everything from rubble clearance and historic preservation to plan-making and the definition of the reconstruction perimeters where special rules applied. See Danièle Voldman (1997) *La reconstruction des villes françaises de 1940 à 1954: Histoire d'une politique,* Paris: L'Harmattan; and Hélène Sanyas (1982) 'La politique architecturale et urbaine de la reconstruction: France: 1945–1955', doctoral thesis, Université de Paris VIII.

6.   As was mentioned above, the State had long governed the French localities, at least through the appointment of *préfets* and other local administrators. Still, many of the controls over the built environment in cities belonged to municipal authorities. Even when the Cornudet law was passed in 1919, it commanded the various *hôtels de ville* (city halls) to prepare plans – it did not have the national government do it for them. The extent to which each locality was proactive or passive in planning the lands within its territorial limits depended largely on the initiative of local authorities. This state of affairs changed abruptly when the State stepped in more forcefully in the early 1940s, due to the combination of the exigencies of war and the assumption by the 'Vichy government' of power.

7.   For the reconstruction in West German cities, see Jeffry Diefendorf (1993) *In the Wake of War: The Reconstruction of German Cities after World War II,* New York and Oxford: Oxford University Press. See in particular chapter 8 for an analysis of the total failure at establishing a nationally planned rebuilding effort, and the partial failure at controlling the rebuilding at the level of the provinces (*Länder*). For a comparison of the actual changes that resulted from the reconstruction of France, East Germany and West Germany, see Joe Nasr (1994) 'Continuité et changements dans les rues et parcellaires des centres-villes détruits en Allemagne et en France', in Patrick Dieudonné (ed.) *Villes reconstruites: Du dessin au destin*, vol. I, Paris: Editions de l'Harmattan, pp. 209–17.

8.   This term is only partially adequate here. It supposes the pre-existence of an entire planning process already in place that was taken over by the State. In fact, as mentioned earlier, the presence of an organized and comprehensive planning structure varied greatly between localities. Where only ad hoc and limited planning took place in the past, it may be more apt to talk of 'initiation' rather than 'appropriation'. One could state that the appropriation dates back to the institution of the republican hierarchical structure in the 1790s, with the dominance of the State and its intermediary, the *département*. On the other hand, this paper and other studies, such as Wakeman's history of the modernization of Toulouse, show that the further appropriation that took place during the Occupation period and was maintained after Liberation was far from total. Rosemary Wakeman (1997) *Modernizing the Provincial City: Toulouse, 1945–1975,* Cambridge and London: Cambridge University Press.

9.   A much more apt (and more gender-neutral) term is the French *édiles*.

10.   The purging of individuals, institutions, instruments and ideas were all equally difficult after Liberation. After Liberation, the new planning laws and organisms that replaced those of wartime – notably the new MRU, established in November 1944 – were largely based on the Vichy era precedents. Even Resistance hero and first Minister for Reconstruction and Urban Planning Raoul Dautry had to twist

historical facts to justify publicly the basing of his actions on legislation inherited from the wartime government. As a result, for reasons of efficiency, only a few amendments were deemed necessary to make the urban planning law of 15 June 1943 the touchstone for postwar reconstruction. Rémi Baudouï (1992) *Raoul Dautry, 1880–1951: Le technocrate de la République,* Paris: Editions Balland, p. 300.

11. Wrapped into the continuity-versus-break debate (but not identical to it) was the issue of modernity-versus-tradition (or in the case of France, 'regionalism'). Note that lying at the root of the emphasis on devastation-as-rupture thinking is a presumption that the devastation was total or near total in cities hit in the Second World War; however, even that assumption should be assessed more carefully. See Joe Nasr (1999) 'Destruction by Reconstruction: Perceptions of Devastation and Decisions of Preservation', paper presented at the 1999 ACSP (Association of Collegiate Schools of Planning) Conference, Chicago, IL, October.

12. In another paper I have shown that the rebuilding of even the best-known cases may not be what it appears: neither was Le Havre rebuilt based on a clean slate, nor was Saint-Malo a true instance of a *reconstruction à l'identique.* Joe Nasr (1997) '"La réalité de la perception": Changements morphologiques dans deux villes reconstruites (Saint-Malo et Le Havre)', in Rainer Hudemann and François Walter (eds) *Villes et guerres mondiales en Europe au XXe siècle,* Paris: Éditions L'Harmattan, pp. 177–91 and figures.

13. Several of these studies can be found in Patrick Dieudonné (ed.) (1994) *Villes reconstruites: Du dessin au destin,* Paris: Editions de L'Harmattan, 2 vols.

14. A major oral history project undertaken in the 1980s sought to chronicle the activities and thoughts of participants in the rebuilding of the country, however it concentrated on planners active within the national structure, including those appointed locally by the State to plan particular cities or oversee their planning. The activities (or for that matter, the presence) of pre-existing local planners was generally not recorded. Danièle Voldman (1990) 'Reconstructors' tales: An example of the use of oral sources in the history of reconstruction after the Second World War', in Jeffry M. Diefendorf (ed.) *Rebuilding Europe's Bombed Cities,* New York: St. Martins Press, pp. 16–30.

15. Voldman (1997), op. cit., p. 151. See also Sanyas, op. cit.

16. 'In the speeches of those in charge, the will to avoid the repetition of the mistakes committed by the elders recurs like a refrain.' Danièle Voldman (1987) 'Introduction: Les enjeux de la reconstruction', *Images, discours et enjeux de la reconstruction des villes françaises après 1945,* Cahiers de l'Institut d'Histoire du Temps Présent, Paris: Institut d'Histoire du Temps Présent, p. 5. For the 'first reconstruction' as an 'anti-model', see also Martine Morel, 'Reconstruire, dirent-ils. – Discours et doctrines de l'urbanisme', in ibid., pp. 34–35.

17. This matches Wakeman's talk of 'the sharp overtones of conquest, domination, and internal colonialism'. Wakeman, op. cit., p. 9.

18. The air attack on the bridgeheads in Blois was characteristic of the patterns of attack throughout the Loire valley, as the Germans sought to interrupt the movement of French armed forces to and from southern France; other cities in that central region received similar damage. On the other hand, the attack on Beauvais was part of selected attacks that aimed at terrorizing the French into a quick surrender – which is what transpired. The fire spread rapidly among the wooden constructions, quickly covering over 80 per cent of the old town.

19. The process for drawing up the PRAs was established in the law of 11 October 1940. This major law also set up the CRI as the organization in charge of guiding

the rebuilding of damaged cities across all of France, and fixed the responsibilities in this area.

20. In French, '*déclaré d'utilité publique*', or declared to be in the public interest.

21. The PRA of Beauvais was formally adopted on 16 May 1942, and Blois followed on 6 November of the same year. Jean Vincent (1943) 'La reconstruction des villes et des immeubles sinistrés après la Guerre de 1940', doctoral thesis, Université de Paris, Faculté de Droit, p. 98.

22. Beauvais and two other towns of the Oise (Senlis and Breteuil) were the first *communes* where the PRA was drawn up on the basis of what the law of October 1940 prescribed. Their approval thus marked the end of the application of the Cornudet law of 1919, which, despite whatever faults it may have been criticized for, had established the practice of modern city planning in France.

23. Maurice Brayet (1964) *Beauvais ville martyre . . .: ou trois mois de magistrature municipale (Juin-août 1940)*, Beauvais: privately published, pp. 116–17.

24. The decree of the Prefect Paul Vacquier demanded the setting up of 'a plan of alignment and leveling for the parts to be rebuilt as well as the summary study that the *plan d'urbanisme et d'aménagement* called for' by the law of 1919. Centre d'Archives Contemporaines (CAC), Fontainebleau, AFU 10191, folder 'PRA,' administrative item no. 1, 12 October 1940.

25. At the end of 1940, Laratte, one of the municipal councilors, demanded that the CM learn the details of the *projet d'aménagement* before 11 January 1941, the last day of the three-month deadline specified in the Prefect's decree. The three-month deadline had been prescribed by the 1919 law, but few *communes* had taken it into account. Archives Municipales de Beauvais (AMBe), Deliberations of the CM, 20 December 1940.

26. AMBe, Deliberations of the CM, 30 October 1940.

27. Simultaneously with Beauvais, Noël was also charged with preparing the PRA of Breteuil-sur-Noye, a small town to the north of Beauvais that was severely tested in 1940 with 1141 of its 2000 buildings totally destroyed. Vincent, op. cit., pp. 18 and 98. Later, two other cities were entrusted to Noël: Toul (Meurthe-et-Moselle *départment*) and Vitry-le-François (Marne). The latter's PRA, approved in 1943, was taken over by another architect after the Liberation, therefore Noël did not participate in the implementation of this plan. 'Toul' and 'Vitry-le-François', *Urbanisme* 45–48 (1956), pp. 198 and 206.

28. Gaston Bedaux (1942) 'La reconstruction dans le département de l'Oise', *Urbanisme* 77, April, p. 148.

29. CAC, AFU 10192, folder 'Désignation des hommes de l'art', letter of Bedaux, Chief Engineer of the *Ponts et Chaussées* (Public Works) for the Department, to Muffang, Reconstruction Commissioner, CRI, 22 January 1941. Bedaux explains that the law of 11 October 1940 defining the rules and responsibilities of the reconstruction, including the designation of the chief planners by the CRI rather than by the prefects and mayors, had 'appeared in the Official Journal of 25 October 1940, [but] was not known in Beauvais until beginning November'.

30. On 17 February 1941, Mayor Desgroux wrote to Commissioner Muffang that Parenty and Noël had already completed the draft of the PRA and had transmitted it to him. CAC, AFU 10192, folder 'Désignation des hommes de l'art'.

31. CAC, AFU 10191, folder 'PRA,' administrative item no. 2, letter of Muffang to the Prefect, 28 January 1941.

32. Ibid.

33. Within any designated perimeter, while the design of buildings was governed by general ordinances but otherwise left up to individual owners and their architects,

changes in the shape, area and location of parcels were administered through ASRs. These had to balance the demands of hundreds of individual plot owners while making sure that the complex reconfiguration yielded the same total of properties as before the war, either within the destroyed district or in new *terrains de compensation* zones outside it. As for the financing, it was drawn from the resources of the State, as the latter had taken charge fairly generously of indemnifying those who suffered war damages, whether regular citizens or municipalities. Danièle Voldman (1997) 'Les guerres mondiales et la planification des villes', in Rainer Hudemann and François Walter (eds) *Villes et guerres mondiales en Europe au XXe siècle*, Paris: Éditions L'Harmattan, p. 23. See also Joe Nasr (1999) 'Transformations in the lot patterns of France and Germany after World War II', in Jad Tabet (ed.) *Reconstruction of War-Torn Cities*, Proceedings of the UIA's International Conference, Beirut: Order of Engineers and Architects, November, pp. 133–41.

34. Brayet, op. cit., pp. 118–19.
35. For reasons that I did not manage to elucidate, Parenty pulled out from the replanning of Beauvais halfway through the process, leaving Noël alone as chief architect-planner. While a plan had been fully readied before Liberation, following the fall of the Vichy regime a plan had to be prepared and a step-by-step review gone through all over again. While some of the actors (especially the politically appointed ones at the top) were replaced, many were kept in place, foremost among them Noël. This process led to very limited changes in the original plan, most of them outside the ruined center. Despite these minimal deviations, the new planning process turned out to be lengthier than the original wartime one; the PRA of Beauvais was finally approved in 1948.
36. As Voldman and others have shown, this transformation was fairly general across French cities.
37. The Prefect was first requested to begin an annexation process on 25 November 1940. Charles Fauqueux (1965) *Beauvais: Son histoire de 1789 à l'après-guerre 1939–1945*, 2nd edn, Beauvais: Imprimerie Centrale Administrative, p. 200. It was not until the following November that the CRI contracted Noël and Parenty to establish an intercommunal *aménagement* project grouping the city and the suburban *communes*. AMBe, Deliberations of the CM, 21 November 1941. The fusion was decreed by the Minister of the Interior, after signature by the CRI, on 6 February 1943. CAC, AFU 10192, folder 'Renseignements d'ordre administratif et statistique'.

   The procedure used to bring about this *groupement régional d'urbanisme* had thus been conducted at the level of the *Préfecture* and the Ministry of the Interior, bypassing all the local authorities. Hearings in the four suburban *communes* had in fact shown a lack of support for the merger, but their leadership had mixed opinions on the matter. Since the merger had been imposed from above by the collaborationist government, an attempt was made at de-annexing the four suburban *communes* in 1945, but the majority of members of the new Municipal Council voted to maintain the grouping. André Thibault, 'Beauvais, une transformation, 1940–1985', manuscript, January 1993 pp. 3–7, deposited at the Archives Départementales de l'Oise, Beauvais.

   It is interesting to note that the year after the expansion was ratified, the MRU established a new and even larger *Groupement d'urbanisme* encompassing Beauvais and eight other *communes*, covering 12,305 hectares. CAC, AFU 10193, folder 'Création du Groupement d'Urbanisme de Beauvais'.
38. This plan is largely unmentioned in all the exchanges of ideas on the rebuilding of Beauvais, which is surprising, considering that Parenty had been one of the

two planners responsible for the PRA in 1940–41. Still, when comparing the two citywide plans, it becomes clear that the 1922 plan formed an important predecessor to the plans of the 1940s.

39. It planned for the development of 1800 hectares to be occupied by 50,000 residents. This population matches the level at which the population stabilized in the 1970s, after it had more than doubled within three decades.
40. Thibault, op. cit., p.6. Interestingly enough, the first undertaking, in 1929, was not an infrastructure project but a residential district for workers. This is one indication of the priority, elaborated below, given to the development of local industry.
41. Thibault, op. cit., pp. 3–5.
42. Beauvais has long been a junction of multiple main roads.
43. Ibid., pp. 3 and 6.
44. Note that the *rapporteur* for – and moving force behind – the special commission that was formed in December 1919 to devise a Plan for Beauvais was an industrialist, Lucien Lainé.
45. The strategic thinking of the local powers did not diminish after the Second World War. This is highlighted by the (unsuccessful) entry of the *département de l'Oise* into the 1958 competition for the new capital of Europe. A cluster of small towns closer to Paris (Chantilly, Senlis, Ermenonville) were proposed for a decentralized seat of European administration, but politicians from Beauvais with national contacts as well as local newspapers were essential to the promotion of the project. As Hein states, 'the special character of this design' was its regional planning dimension, centered on 'provisions made to link the capital to planned elements of European infrastructure: the highway between Paris and Brussels, the new international airport north of Paris, and railroad lines providing rapid transportation between Paris, London, and Brussels. Although decades passed before these elements were realized [and no European capital was located in the Oise], ultimately their presence had a positive effect on regional economy'. Carola Hein (1997) 'The network of European capitals: Steering the processes of concentration and decentralization', in Koos Bosma and Helma Hellinga (eds) *Mastering the City: North-European City Planning 1900–2000*, Rotterdam: NAI Publishers/ EFL Publications, p. 1:35. For further details see Carola Hein (1995), 'Hauptstadt Europa' PhD dissertation, Hochschule für bildende Künste Hamburg, pp. 135–37. It is interesting that, in 2002, the Beauvais airport is now functioning – at last – as a relief valve for some of Paris' European flights.
46. To exemplify this point, it is useful to note that the commissioner's representative at the very first official presentation of the initial draft of the PRA on 15 May 1941 remarked that: 'the special characteristics of this plan lie in the new paths of the National Roads across the urban area'. CAC, AFU 10191, folder 'PRA', administrative item no. 3, minutes, Sous-Commission départementale de la Reconstruction, 15 May 1941. Noël himself stated, in the main article in which he presented his work on Beauvais, that: 'to begin this study, it was necessary first to look with the greatest attention into the problem of road traffic and of the entrances to the agglomeration'. Georges Noël, 'Le Beauvais de demain', Circulaire Série A. No. 9, presented 14 April 1944, Paris: Centre d'études supérieures, Institut technique du bâtiment et des travaux publics, July 1945, p. 9.
47. Thibault, op. cit., p. 6.
48. Blois' fortifications had been removed by the eighteenth century and were not replaced by a circumferential boulevard, largely because of the intractability of the terrain.

49. For Fillay, the four principles that should guide the reconstruction were: '1) to substitute for the narrow and hard-to-access streets wide communication routes; 2) to thus provide the inhabitants with air, light, health; 3) to better display the most worthy monuments of our city; 4) to maintain a certain architectural unity in the part of the city to be rebuilt'. Archives Municipales de Blois (AMBl), Paul Robert-Houdin archive, press clippings file, Hubert Fillay, 'Plans de reconstruction', *La Dépêche du Centre*, July 1940. Fillay had in fact long been urging transformations in old Blois. He had already written a book in 1919 calling 'For a Renaissance of Blois'.
50. Yves Babonaux (1956) 'L'évolution contemporaine d'une ville de la Loire: Blois', *Information littéraire* 2, March–April, p. 45.
51. Ibid., pp. 45–48.
52. Annie Cospérec (1994) *Blois, la forme d'une ville*, Inventaire général des monuments et des richesses artistiques de la France, Région Centre, Cahiers du Patrimoine no. 35, Paris: Imprimerie nationale éditions et Inventaire général, p. 283. This is one of the most significant bridges in France. Designed by Jacques Gabriel, one of the best-known architects/engineers at the time, the bridge has a special place in history as the first structure to be erected by the national service of the *Ponts et Chaussées*, which for centuries was to play a crucial role in building and maintaining a countrywide system of roads and bridges.
53. Annie Cospérec (1986) 'Le pré-inventaire de la ville de Blois: Enquête préliminaire sur le secteur sauvegardé', in *Congrès du Blésois et Vendômois,* Paris, p. 128; and Cospérec (1994), op. cit., pp. 292–93.
54. Equipe départementale des professeurs d'histoire-géographie (1986), *'Le fait urbain'* – Blois: *L'exemple d'une ville moyenne*, Centre départemental de documentation pédagogique du Loir-et-Cher, Orléans: Centre Régional de Documentation Pédagogique, p. 40.
55. Cospérec (1994), op. cit., p. 322.
56. Ibid., pp. 360–68.
57. In the statement prepared for the creation of a company to build this street, the urgency of constructing it was justified as follows: 'This Project was born out of the need to give traffic, which has become much heavier, new outlets. It was also inspired by the necessity of beautifying the city, which had remained static with its narrow and tortuous streets, while most of the neighboring cities had already for many years not hesitated to undertake the greatest works towards this goal'. The project would also serve the public health as 'it would get rid of an entire neighborhood that is insalubrious to the highest degree'. A fourth reason given was the creation of jobs for unemployed construction workers. Bibliothèque Municipale de Blois (BMBl), Compagnie blésoise pour l'ouverture d'une rue à la suite et dans l'axe du pont, Public offering of shares, 15 June 1848.
58. Cospérec (1994), op. cit., p. 285.
59. Equipe départementale des professeurs d'histoire-géographie, p. 41.
60. BMBl, Ville de Blois, Expropriation pour cause d'utilité publique, Tableau des offres et demandes, 28 December 1886.
61. *Mémoires de la Société des Sciences et Lettres de Loir-et-Cher*, Vol. 16, Session of 10.5.1925, Blois: Grande Imprimerie de Blois, 1926 pp. 58–61.
62. A. Lafargue (1914) *Ce qu'on aurait pu faire à Blois depuis 50 ans*, Blois: Imprimerie R. Duguet.
63. The French phrase used here and which was to be used repeatedly in describing the handling of the main buildings in the reconstruction, *mettre en valeur*, cannot be translated adequately.

64. Lafargue, op. cit., p. 2.
65. It had been on this site since the Renaissance, having been rebuilt in 1777 following the new bridge alignment and demolition of walls along the Loire. Cospérec (1994), op. cit., pp. 288–89.
66. Babonaux, op. cit., p. 52.
67. Grandson of the internationally renowned magician and native of Blois who went by the same last name, Robert-Houdin was trained as an architect and specialized since 1927 in the preservation of the historical monuments of the Loire valley (particularly châteaux, including that at Blois). This interesting personality's own claim to fame was the invention of the *spectacles son et lumière* (lights and sounds show) in 1952 in the Château de Chambord, which he replicated over the next two decades in tourist venues around the globe. Beyond his regional role in the restoration of historic structures, his role in the history of modern tourism, notably the transformation of historic monuments into, literally, spectacles, is worth pursuing elsewhere. AMBl, Paul Robert-Houdin archive, for the rest of this paper (including the press clippings from *La Dépêche du Centre*), except where noted.
68. 'Le déblaiement des quartiers sinistrés se poursuit activement', *La Dépêche du Centre*, 22 August 1940.
69. His reconstruction plans were prepared for November.
70. CAC, AFU 4951, folder 'Périmètre de Reconstruction: Dossier officiel', administrative item no. 2, letter of Commissioner Muffang to Charles Nicod, 28 January 1941. Nicod, member of the Institut de France, chief architect for civic buildings, was also responsible for the plans of Bayonne and Toulouse, which were larger but undamaged cities. 'Le Plan de Reconstruction de Blois', *La Dépêche du Centre* (9–10 May 1942), p. 1.
71. Nicod later cut back on his involvement in the city after the initial round of the plan in 1941–43.
72. In August 1931 Robert-Houdin also participated in a competition to design a new post office at the location where it was eventually built after the war, on Victor-Hugo square.
73. Interestingly, Robert-Houdin's co-designer for this scheme was H. Lafargue, son of the author of the 1914 plan discussed earlier.
74. Léon Chesnay, 'La reconstruction de Blois', *La Dépêche du Centre*, 12 November 1940.
75. Unfortunately, the authorship and dating of this document could be substantiated only by a very faint handwriting on the side of the drawing, where I could make out 'P.R. Houdin' and '8 Sept. 40', but I could not ascertain this for sure. On the other hand, the fact that the plan is etched with 'Ville de Blois' and makes no reference to the CRI or any other national organism does corroborate that it is from 1940, before the involvement of the State.
76. See, for instance, letter from Nicod to Robert-Houdin, dated 28 February 1941.
77. A clarification is in order, though, differentiating design elements from their causation. We will use one such element to explain this. In both proposals by Robert-Houdin in the 1930s, the use of the circular element was not just decorative, but also a functional way of dealing with the problem of the very sharp angle that had been generated when the Haussmannian Denis-Papin street traversed the old rue du Commerce. When Nicod picked up that element in the 1940s, he pushed it against the river and eliminated completely the former location of the rue du Commerce. So the semicircle became an architectural device that outlived the circulatory difficulty that generated its conception.
78. However, the swiftness of the cities' planning process at the start was lost, especially as a result of the organization of a national structure for managing all

rebuilding. This appropriation by the State of the task resulted in a gradual diminution of the advances that the two cities had succeeded in gaining, so that in the end the rebuilding period for Beauvais and Blois matched those of other devastated cities.

79. Speech introducing 'Le Beauvais de demain', presented by Noël on 14 April 1944. Noël, op. cit., p. 2.

80. For example, there were conflicts between Noël and Boileau, the chief architect for Beauvais' Syndical Association for Reparceling, during the first amendment to the PRA. These conflicts led to the designation of a third person, Sirvin, as architect in chief for the city. CAC, AFU 10192, folder 'Affaires connexes aux études d'urbanisme', letter of P. Gibel to Randet, both with the MRU, Directorate for City Planning, 18 May 1945.

81. Vincent Bradel, 'Saint-Dié, sans Corbu, ni maître', in Dieudonné, Vol. I, op. cit., pp. 293–304.

82. Emmanuel Pouille, 'Dunkerque, genèse d'une reconstruction', in Dieudonné, Vol I, op. cit., pp. 7–18.

83. 'As much as the State had imposed its mark on the creation of the reconstruction plans, to a comparable extent was the style left to the prerogatives of the architects placed in charge of each of the devastated cities. The will to avoid favoring any artistic tendency and to entrust the entire profession with commissions enabled the public authorities to arbitrate between architects belonging to opposite streams, but also to act decisively where disagreements arose between the administration, the municipalities and the citizens of the devasted cities.' Danièle Voldman (1997) 'Les enjeux de la reconstruction', in Emmanuel Doutriaux and Frank Vermandel (eds) *Le Nord de la France, laboratoire de la Ville: Trois reconstructions: Amiens, Dunkerque, Maubeuge*, Lille, France: Espace Croisé.

84. Where one can detect a recurrence of certain urbanistic concepts, is it because these enter the collective memory and are passed on from planner to planner? Or because of the intrinsic power of the images as they impress themselves into that memory? Or perhaps because the concepts come up 'naturally' whenever a planner sits down in front of a map or walks around a city? In Blois, as in Beauvais, the evidence is not sufficient to elucidate which is the likelier explanation. I believe, though, that it is usually a combination of them all. When someone comes up with an idea, if it is 'natural' it will survive and re-emerge here and there. If not, or if the concept no longer makes sense as a result of a change in circumstances, it will probably not be heard of again.

PART IV

FOREIGN EXPERTS, LOCAL PROFESSIONALS

CHAPTER 11

FOREIGN HIRES: FRENCH EXPERTS AND THE URBANISM OF BUENOS AIRES, 1907–32

Alicia Novick
University of Buenos Aires

During the first decades of the twentieth century, numerous foreign urbanists visited Buenos Aires. These urbanists were initially called in by the successive city mayors for the purpose of drawing the first urban plans, and later invited by various local associations to deliver lectures on city-related matters.

The purpose of analyzing the activities of these experts is to shed some light on the problems experienced at the beginning of urbanism in Buenos Aires from a different angle. Traditional thinking on these origins, related to theories of dependency, looked upon foreign influence – manifested in the activities of these professionals – as cultural subordination. But re-examination of the work carried out by these experts reveals a series of interesting variations typical of this type of international cooperation, encouraged through the international circulation of papers, 'models' and official missions, and influenced by peripatetic experts who brought with them knowledge and experience derived from their personal involvement in projects in their own countries or elsewhere.

It should be noted that the profile of the technicians referred to here differs greatly from that of earlier professionals, hired as early as the first half of the nineteenth century, who stayed in the country to organize government technical departments and start university programs, and who were responsible for large public works, due to the absence of qualified local professionals who could meet such demands. They also differ from current municipal officials and independent professionals; they were 'experts' who were asked to apply their knowledge to the decision-making processes of public policies with which they were familiar, and being foreigners they could also establish a critical distance when addressing local issues – what Jean-Pierre Gaudin[1] describes as a distinct feature of the urban planning profession. The underlying hypothesis in this paper is, ultimately, that studies on the formation of such profiles are not complete if the intrinsically cosmopolitan character of the profession is not taken into account.

In a previous paper[2] we examined the role of these foreign experts in relation to 'demand', showing that their influence was modified as the expertise of local professionals became more relevant. Recent historiographic research has enabled us to go further in the study of European 'supply' of urbanistic solutions for Latin America, broadening this field of knowledge with new documents and new analytical perspectives. The evidence for these advances came from a wide range of literature focusing on exchanges between both continents[3] as well as from recent research meetings between Latin Americans and Europeans.[4]

This article will try to answer three questions:

1. What factors were decisive in the selection of hired professionals to act as experts or visiting lecturers? To answer this question we will examine the reasons for the local demand – the nature of the problems that the contracts intended to solve – and the circumstances of the international offer of services in each historical setting. This will allow us to contribute new insights *vis-à-vis* interpretations that bring to the forefront the local bourgeois fascination with the Parisian model,[5] or the political struggle between local groups of influence.[6]

2. How was cooperation established between people whose urban 'images' and 'representations' were so different? In other words, what were the characteristics of the interaction between foreign experts and their Argentinian counterparts? Recent research shows twin patterns: on one hand, foreign experts took a growing interest in local experience and applied it when designing solutions for the problems they were hired to solve. On the other hand, local professionals carried out 'transferences and translations' filtering these foreign contributions under the light of their own experience.[7] Once cooperation between both sides was achieved, original contributions were produced as a result of the foreign capability of redefining existing problems or proposing new ones.

3. In what ways did the experience of foreign urbanists in Buenos Aires influence their later professional careers? This aspect of international exchange has not been widely studied. It is a subject that Crasemann-Collins has recently called 'retro-transference'[8] in reference to the eventual influence of the experiences of these experts in the so-called New World on their doctrines as well as on their later careers. The subject has also been studied in relation to architecture,[9] and in this paper we will briefly address the issue for the first time.

We will begin by examining the activity of two French professionals – Bouvard and Forestier – who were hired by the Municipality of Buenos Aires.

We will then discuss the visits by Jaussely, Hegemann and Le Corbusier towards the end of the 1920s and beginning of the 1930s.[10]

BOUVARD AND THE *NUEVO PLANO* (1909)

In 1907, Carlos de Alvear, the mayor of Buenos Aires, summoned Joseph-Antoine Bouvard, head of public works for the city of Paris, and requested from him the elaboration of a plan for the transformation of Buenos Aires within the context of preparations for the celebrations of the Colonial Emancipation Centennial (1810–1910).

At the time of the centennial, the country's controversial modernization process, initiated in the second part of the nineteenth century, was in full swing, and the city was rapidly being transformed. The demographic growth due to European immigration increased the population of the capital from 400,000 inhabitants in 1880 to a million and a half in 1910. Works of infrastructure – ports, water supply, transport – as well as both public and private construction, were prompted by the accumulation of local capital within the increasingly agro-exporting country, and by foreign investment. At the same time, the increase in land values and the housing deficit, in addition to the lack of training in the professional body and the public administration, were leading to new problems for the city. The issues of hygiene and health, working-class housing, growth control and the construction of works symbolically representing the State dominated debates at the end of the century. The principal controversy was between the 'embellishment of the center' and the 'equipment of the extension', representing the two sides of nineteenth-century modernization. These issues were related to the 'atmosphere of the Argentinian Centennial', when official attempts at joining other nations as a modern country were articulated with a high degree of social discord.

After 1900, embellishment – justified by 'hygiene' and 'circulation' – came to the fore in the task of preparing the city for the centennial celebrations planned for 1910 (an exhibition that took its inspiration from Europe, though mainly from the Chicago Colombian Exhibition). A period of formulating innumerable projects to transform the city began, ranging from idealized proposals to small-scale reforms from a variety of specialists. This allowed the grid and urban form to be discussed in connection with the location of public buildings, parks and squares, as well as compositional instruments to enhance the grid (avenues and/or diagonals). Between 1905 and 1906, the Congress and the Municipal Council, placing within the scope of the debate the significance of 'expropriations', 'public interest' as well as the means of financing public works, analyzed the different proposals. Faced with the difficulties in selecting the projects and the urgency with which work on the centennial constructions needed to begin, the city's mayor hired French architect Joseph-Antoine Bouvard as an external consultant.

The contract

Bouvard's appointment has been described in the relevant literature[11] as yet another example of the fascination for the French of an elite that copied their housing and city models from Paris. However, many other factors were behind the mayor's decision to hire the Frenchman. Bouvard was a French official, and both countries, contemplating bilateral interests, endorsed his contract, which acquired the status of a diplomatic agreement.

Mayor Carlos de Alvear had previously been the Argentinian ambassador to France (1900–4), and during these years he had strengthened the solid network of personal and institutional relationships he had begun in 1887 during his family sojourns in Paris. His father, Torcuato de Alvear, had been mayor of Buenos Aires between 1880 and 1886, and due to the scale of his interventions became known as the local 'Haussmann'. His brother, Marcelo, later carried out diplomatic assignments in Paris (1919–22) before he became President of the Nation (1922–28).[12] The Alvears, as with many families of the Buenos Aires elite, maintained a vigorous exchange with Europe both during their private visits and when on government missions.

In particular, the Parisian City Hall was frequently consulted and was in fact the source of inspiration for the administrative organization of Buenos Aires. Paris also acted as a reference to a wide variety of management tools. In 1868 the landscape designer Edouard André carried out, from Paris, technical reports on behalf of Argentinian President Domingo Sarmiento. In 1880 preliminary information was requested in order to draw up the first building code (1887). In 1891 the same procedure was used to organize the city's *cadastre* (land registry), then in 1902 to establish municipal prizes for facade designs. Argentine demands were always answered with explicit interest from the Parisian administration, which was keen on exporting its know-how. In addition to all this was the influence of the French École des Beaux-Arts as a reference for architectural and city models.[13]

Contracts with foreign experts became commonplace, allowing a fluid circulation of professionals in charge of drawing both embellishment and extension plans. As expressed by Camillo Sitte, urban embellishment – 'a work of art' – could not be left in the hands of officials.[14] Competitions were required. The Competition of the New Guayaquil in 1906 shows the growing importance of the new countries in America as high-potential markets.

This interest became more keen in the years prior to the Great War, a period in which France started an aggressive campaign to enhance French presence in the 'new countries', challenging English hegemony and the growing influence of Germany. From this point of view, it is understandable that the final decision to hire the French official Bouvard was taken in 1906 when a municipal mission from Paris, headed by the Councillor Turot, came to Buenos Aires. On this occasion, Turot – helped by generous support from Alvear – gained interest from persons of influence in using the professional services of 'J.J. Bouvard, eminent director of architectural services for the Seine Prefecture'[15] to begin the transformation of the Argentine capital. That same envoy had also previously carried out missions in western and northern Africa, Indochina, the Philippines, Brazil and Istanbul in order to secure government contracts for his fellow countrymen.[16]

These international missions had been undertaken at the recommendation of commercial envoys traveling worldwide instructed to seek new markets for French products, financial investments and public works.[17] Thus while Bouvard was working in Buenos Aires, a consulting firm, with headquarters in Paris, was being formed with the aim of joining together influential European and Latin American shareholders who possessed information concerning potential public works business. The company's objectives were 'to attract French capital towards highly profitable businesses available in Argentina which suit our economic activities':[18] railways, tramways, mining, banking and public works enterprises. The role of urban technicians was therefore to secure investments in unstable markets like Argentina, and based on his performance in that country, Bouvard was named director of the new company.

The call for a mission in 1906 was in line with the mayor's need to import a technician to help with decisions concerning the works of embellishment to be carried out. Here, the usual request for competitions issued by the young professional associations was set aside, and a foreign consultant was brought in as arbiter to select from the numerous projects being considered. This arbiter, Bouvard, also weighed the scale in favor of his business friends.

Despite his position, though, Bouvard was not a well-known professional. He lacked written works and his municipal career was not visible compared to other contemporary figures such as Prost, Jaussely or Hénard who had studied at the École des Beaux-Arts and were highly successful in international competitions. Bouvard's main merits were his activities at the Paris Municipality and his participation as designer in international exhibitions.[19] He was the architect of the City of Paris pavilion at the Universal Exhibitions of 1878 and 1889, and collaborated in the world fairs in Brussels, Chicago (1893), Antwerp (1894) Melbourne and Saint Louis (1904), experience that was particularly valuable for Buenos Aires since it was preparing its own events for the centenary.[20]

Bouvard's activities in Buenos Aires have been studied in detail.[21] But let us here recall only briefly that in 1907 Bouvard traveled to Buenos Aires with two assistants – Delattre and Faure-Dujarric – and drew several projects: the layout for the exhibition, a hospital, a new neighborhood and some outlines of avenues and diagonals. His proposals were criticized in the local specialist newspapers, which pointed out his ignorance of local realities and the insufficient amount of time available for preliminary studies. This opposition, mainly from local architects, was aimed at recovering their role as decision-makers and directed against the mayor and his possible personal interests. The critics exposed the official attitude of ignoring the contributions of a technical body that had a solid background despite belonging to a 'new country'. On his first assignment, Bouvard acted as a project technician, resolving 'from scratch' all the projects, rather than as an expert. However, despite the criticism, Carlos de Alvear stepped up the pressure until the general plans were sanctioned by the City Council.[22]

Carlos de Alvear was succeeded in 1908 by a new mayor, Manuel Guiraldes, who took municipal policies in a new direction, actively supported by a group of professionals belonging to the ranks of social reformers. These ideas, in line with the emerging social unrest (like the tenants' strikes of 1907 and 1908) signaled, among others, the urgent need for workers' neighborhoods and the purchase of properties and land for municipal purposes.[23] In establishing these new priorities, the new authorities intended to call off the contracts signed by the previous mayor, yet the annulment of Bouvard's contract proved impossible due to diplomatic pressures.

Indeed, the activities of international consulting firms were directly supported by the French embassy, which backed them with local governments. In Argentina, diplomatic pressure was exercised to help French companies sign contracts for public works, ports,[24] artistic competitions,[25] and so on. This attitude was evident in 1908 when the French ambassador, M. Thibault, defended Bouvard's contract. Thibault reminded the local government that action such as this against foreign experts would tarnish Argentina's international reputation. In a letter, he reported: 'I reminded M. Zeballos [minister of internal affairs] that he had recently instructed his agents in Europe to reassure public opinion and businessmen as to the political and financial stability of Argentina, and that the mission for which M. Bouvard was hired had been a cause of celebration last year in Paris, government included. Was it not then a risk that this contract cancellation could be associated with the existence of a crisis in Argentina that M. Zeballos had taken the precaution of denying?'[26]

Faced with this situation, the mayor decided that M. Bouvard was to work with a commission composed of municipal officials and technicians experienced in the problems of the city. Bouvard's second and final project in Argentina reached a negotiated conclusion with his Argentinian colleagues. The document, published in 1909, reads: 'This Commission, after a long and thorough study of the plans already mentioned, has seen fit to uphold the general principles and resolutions thereof, while introducing some modifications in certain details based upon particular knowledge of the places, according to different circumstances and proven needs'.[27] Actually, the commission played a significant role in the project, since it adapted Bouvard's initial ideas of 1907, in line with its members' knowledge of the city.

THE NUEVO PLANO

The *Nuevo Plano* (New Plan) of 1909 confined itself to fixing the limits of streets and plazas according to the canons of 'civic art'. From then on, the construction of railway stations, infrastructures and housing for workers was beyond the scope of action and was debated in other spheres. Meanwhile, Bouvard passed on his experience in preparing the descriptive report, and in global decision-making, the tools that enabled him to present urban proposals in a new way. These contributions meant that the problems posed by the local technicians could be viewed in a different light.

First, Bouvard's descriptive report made significant conceptual contributions. The erudite references to Hénard (relating to circulation), Buls (relating to urban aesthetics) and Forestier (concerning park systems) lent a 'theoretical basis' to the entire proposal, with the intention (though only partially achieved) of going beyond fragmented projects towards a system for the city as a whole.

In addition, Bouvard signaled the need to open the city towards the river – one of the central ideas of his scheme. 'The decisions taken so far, particularly in relation to the denser parts of the city, have set aside the beautiful features of the incomparable river surrounding it'.[28] This idea surpassed the effects of an 1896 project proposing a circular avenue, part of which would run riverside, and aimed at alleviating the effects on the coast of the construction of port facilities. The proposal was inspired by Bouvard's own Parisian project to liberate the banks of the Seine after the Universal Exhibition of 1900. The innovation consisted of establishing a new relationship between the city and the river, an idea that would be repeated in future urban proposals.

The document was structured around a critical description of existing elements and a list of transformations to be carried out, with their respective justifications. The analysis of the city's problems was brief (no urban diagnostic had yet been made), and each of the problems identified was related to an element of urban design. Thus the lack of hygiene infrastructure and aesthetics was to be resolved by parks and plazas (Fig. 1), and the need for suitable communications and 'attractive and picturesque perspectives' was to be resolved via a 'system' of concentric streets, radiating obliquely or diagonally, decongesting the business center and improving the aesthetics of this city. The proposal was presented over a grid extending to the whole city, enhanced by avenues and green spaces. The superimposed system of Haussmannian seal was not Bouvard's contribution but the result of previous experiments in a variety of projects.

Indeed, the general directions of the proposal came from commission member Carlos M. Morales. In his capacity of city director of public works from 1891, Morales was one of the authors of the improvement plans of 1898–1904, in which Buenos Aires' own urban planning had been established.

The strong presence of the grid became the backbone of this new plan. Despite having been questioned under the ideas of urban art, and the subject of lengthy debates at the end of the century,[29] the grid structure was adopted for the 1904 'Alignment Plan' with the city's administrative control in mind. This structure, inherited from Spanish colonial roots, was reformulated under the engineers' ideas of regularity that prevailed during the nineteenth century. The adoption of the grid by the Bouvard Plan was the final consecration of the characteristic rigid urban morphology of Buenos Aires and became a filter through which various international models of the city would be passed.

To enhance the grid, a network of green spaces, plazas and other streets was superimposed over it. This solution, in various forms, was used in plans and projects throughout the nineteenth century[30] and was adopted for the *ex novo* project for the city of La Plata (1886). Evidently, the *Nuevo Plano*

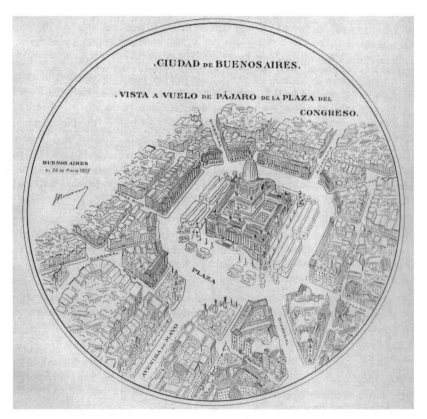

Figure 1. *Proposal by Bouvard for Plaza del Congreso, 1909*
(Source: Intendencia Municipal, Andrès, Bouvard, El Nuevo Plano de la Ciudad de Buenos Aires, Imprenta litografía y encuadernación Kraft, 1909)

adopted a solution that had already been in use in the region. In the design of the whole capital city, the local knowledge of the roads, the neighborhoods to be connected, and pieces of land that could be turned into open spaces was taken from the works of another Frenchman, Charles Thays, in charge of the municipal directorship for parks and promenades, and another member of the commission, Román Bravo, an expert in real estate development, took on the task of calculating the economic feasibility of the necessary expropriations. The 1909 plan was partially carried out. In 1912, the laws for the opening of avenues in the old district were approved and construction of the *Balneario* (bathing resort) commenced, resulting in a guide for the widening of roads and openings.

This plan, like those to follow, would largely use new instruments rather than present new ways of urban transformation. With the exception of the opening towards the river, there is a sort of synthesis of a process according to which many different projects for the city had been drawn. Within the new plan, these other projects formed part of a systematized scheme governing the changes taking place in the city. In this sense, the *Nuevo Plano*, with the assistance of Bouvard's know-how, conflated the modernization proposals for Buenos Aires at the turn of the century.

A business entrepreneur

After his work in Buenos Aires and until the beginning of the Great War, Bouvard acquired a reputation as an expert in urbanism and started a career as a business entrepreneur in Latin America. He designed the city plan, as well as several projects for plazas, for the city of Rosario (Argentina, 1911). In his capacity as director of the Sociedad Argentina de la Construcción, one of the branches of the Sociedad Franco-Argentina de Trabajos Públicos (French-Argentine Public Works Society), he directed the construction of a hospital and a network of schools across the country. Through his business connections, Bouvard drew up a *Plano de embellecimiento* (embellishment plan) for Montevideo (Uruguay, 1911). He also began a city plan for São Paulo (Brazil, 1911)[31] and carried out, together with Barry Parker, a project for garden neighborhoods in the same city.[32]

However, in his international career – mainly between 1907 and 1913 – Bouvard did not meet the expectations of his employers. In fact his performance was criticized in the professional circles of both Brazil and Argentina, and his work was not fully included as a guideline for public policies. Beyond his professional competence there existed a difficulty in establishing the scope of the task for a foreign expert hired for a limited period of time. These were times of transition between an urbanism of projects, as established in the nineteenth century, and an urbanism of plans, based on diagnostics, that was to emerge in the 1920s.

JEAN-CLAUDE FORESTIER AND THE *PROYECTO ORGANICO-PLAN REGULADOR DE LA COMISIÓN DE ESTÉTICA EDILICIA* (1925)

Like Bouvard previously, Jean-Claude Forestier was hired by the mayor of Buenos Aires to collaborate in the production of a city plan in 1923. However, both the context in which he acted and his professional profile were very different.

Between the centenary and the 1920s, the focus moved towards the subject of housing for workers. In 1912, the Saenz Peña law establishing the popular vote broadened participation of political parties which, after 1890, represented the new groups of immigrants. New projects concerning living conditions for those on lower incomes came into play together with many associations that exercised pressure on the authorities. After the projects and actions of the beginning of the century, a number of innovations heightened the significance of social and spatial problems in the city, and included the Comisión de Casas Baratas (Commission for Low-Price Houses, 1915), the debates at the Mutuality Congress (1918), the Cooperation Congress (1919) and the Housing Congress (1920), organized by the Museo Social Argentino (inaugurated in 1911, inspired by the Musée Social de Paris).[33]

Another issue that distinguished this plan from that of 1909 was the call for a comprehensive project that came from the technical associations and from the ranks of socialist and social reformers. The conclusions of the Housing Congress (1920) expressed the main concerns: the need to draft plans, put an end to the housing shortage and, in a more global sense, control and organize the production of urban space in a more rational way. These conclusions were drawn up during a period that was profoundly affected by the postwar crisis, mainly due to shortages in supplies.

Three years later, a better financial situation and a change of government brought new momentum to the great public works which, as for the centenary, required the drawing up of a coherent policy. In 1923 the mayor named a Comisión de Estética Edilicia (Civic Art Commission) for the design of the *Proyecto Orgánico, el Plano Regulador y de Reforma de la Capital Federal*, a plan for Buenos Aires that was to follow the principles of modern city-planning. According to the opening document: 'the most knowledgeable officials were summoned to supervise the construction of public works in the Federal Capital which must conform to the general plan . . .'.[34] The commission members were selected from the most important public institutions competent in these projects: René Karman, a French architect who had been assigned to the School of Architecture's workshop since 1912; Carlos Morra, president of the Central Society of Architects; Sebastian Ghigliazza, director of the Ministry of Public Works, representing the national institution in charge of the great building projects; the architect Martën Noil, president of the National Commission of Fine Arts; and the engineer Victor Spotta, director of the Municipal Public Works Department. Emilio Ravignani, a historian and secretary of finance of the city, was named secretary, in charge of writing the chapter on urban evolution. Jean-Claude Forestier was selected to carry out projects for parks and gardens, and to cooperate with the commission in the performance of its duties.

The contract

Forestier's contract shows differences and similarities in relation to Bouvard's. On one hand, diplomatic pressure had disappeared. On the other hand, Forestier was a well-established professional of international repute. Nevertheless, the same network of political relationships operated as had been the case for the centenary project. After the war, France abandoned its 'colonial' strategies, and a policy of exporting know-how in relation to the new 'scientific methods' for urbanism replaced the focus on seeking markets for goods and investments. The only official intervention was a note issued by the Ministry of Internal Affairs to the Seine Prefecture, requesting a license.[35]

Forestier was chosen as consultant by President Marcelo T. de Alvear, the brother – as noted earlier – of the Buenos Aires mayor who hired Bouvard in 1907. So in both cases the personal and institutional relationships of the Alvears with the Paris City Hall prevailed. These connections were shared by the Buenos Aires mayor Carlos Noël, who had taken his postgraduate course in philosophy at the École des Hautes Etudes in Paris, as well as by his brother, Martin Noël, who had studied in 1911 at the École Spéciale d'Architecture, one of the main institutions promoting the neocolonial movement in architecture. Martin Noël had met Forestier in Spain while both were working on the preparation of exhibitions.[36]

Since the beginning of the century, Forestier had been well known within the professional circles of Buenos Aires. The local magazines had published a series of his articles,[37] his theories had been included in the *Nuevo Plano* of 1909, and his treatise[38] was registered at the University Library and at the Architects' Society. Nevertheless, despite such a distinguished career, the payment of all the costs of his trip was severely criticized within the city council. Those who agreed with the mayor favored the presence of a foreign architect who would act as an advisor for the projects, but the majority of socialist council members objected for a variety of reasons. First they pointed out that the city had local specialists of great ability and experience regarding parks and gardens. They argued that the urban records needed to be prepared prior to the formulation of any urban plan, and in relation to this some council members favored the hiring of a North American architect, or instead Léon Jaussely, who was the director of the School of Urban Art of Paris and considered 'the right person to come from Paris to give advice and general directions'.[39]

As a background to the debate, we can see the ambiguity of the term 'expert'. What should be the role of an expert being brought in for a short period of time without being familiar with the site? Was his role that of a professor coming to the university to lecture? Or was he coming to prepare and direct the works? As at the time of the centenary preparations, the scope of work of a foreign expert when there were solid local professionals available was still uncertain. Despite the council members' questioning, the mayor confirmed the contract before the council had reached a decision.

The Proyecto Orgánico

The *Proyecto Orgánico* (Organic Project) was the first local document that tried to adopt the points of view of 'modern urbanism', addressing all the problems and including an up-to-date bibliography. It surveyed a wide variety of projects, as a preliminary step to forming an elaborated regulatory plan, the scope of which was detailed in the last chapter. Its introduction stated the major works and the problems to be resolved, followed by diagnostic studies and provisions (population, supplies, hospitals, etc.), while the last chapter proposed the need for a regulations committee to draw up a plan to ensure the overall coherence of the city (Fig. 2).

The central purpose of the Comisión de Estética Edilicia was to balance the urban structure of Buenos Aires, which had been transformed (and deformed) by its growth and size. It proceeded by selecting subjects that had already been debated (and partially agreed upon); for example it studied the relationship between the city and the river – as had been suggested by Bouvard in 1910 – as well as the total restructuring of the road network and open spaces. The 'civic centers' inspired by the Civic Art proposals and by the open and green spaces plan (where Forestier's interventions came in) were the instruments that led to the formation of an 'urban system'.

In contrast to the *Nuevo Plano*, the *Proyecto Orgánico* aimed at providing the necessary facilities to the more distant neighborhoods within the capital's boundaries. Considered during the nineteenth century as potential locations for industry and workers' housing, these neighborhoods became one of the strongholds of the socialist town councilors. The Comisión de Estética Edilicia also made equipping the 'workers' neighborhoods, gardens and suburban embellishment' one of the pillars of its proposals, which were to include the participation of neighborhood commissions (officially registered as of 1919). All this activity represented the municipality's first efforts to set up facilities and infrastructures for the city as a whole.

Launched during the centenary, the central embellishments versus suburban equipment debates persisted. The latter was argued for by the socialist town councilors and, evidently, was one of the main problems of urbanism they tried to resolve through, among other instruments, the 'parks system'. In fact, Forestier's role consisted of analyzing, from his particular field of knowledge, the projects attached to a loan sanctioned in 1923 to build the riverside avenue and walk (Costanera) (Fig. 3), enlarge the bathing resort and upgrade the plazas, parks for physical exercises and youth camps. The Directorate for Parks and Walks of the Buenos Aires Town Hall had already worked on these issues through both the aforementioned Frenchman Carlos Thays, as well as the Argentinean Benito Carrasco, who succeeded Thays in his post and had produced a notable plan for parks and plazas in 1921.[40] Carrasco received Forestier's contract with an ill-concealed displeasure, and became one the most hostile critics of the Organic Project.

Though his contributions to the system of urban green spaces were based on projects that had been formulated earlier, Forestier managed to articulate a comprehensive set of suggestions that his work colleagues found somewhat

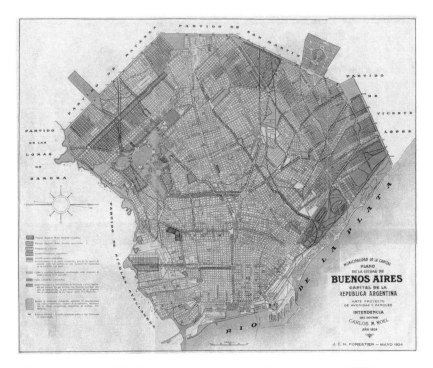

Figure 2. Proposal by Forestier for avenue and park system, 1924
Source: Intendencia Municipal, Comisión de Estética Edilicia, Proyecto orgánico para la urbanización del Municipio, Tallerers Peuser, Buenos Aires, 1925

excessive in terms of both dimensions and budget.[41] Nevertheless, his contribution went far beyond projects for the riverside avenue and a report on plazas and gardens.

To begin with, he brought with him an extensive knowledge of urban legislation. His proposals were linked with management procedures and legislation necessary for the projects to be carried out. Thus, he sent from Paris a complete set of laws and regulations concerning expropriations and city extension procedures, providing valuable information for the Comisión de Estética Edilicia.

Forestier's major innovation consisted of establishing the need to address the total agglomeration beyond its administrative boundaries. The question of extension had been one of his theoretical reflections, and he conceived of his system of green spaces as a metropolitan network that ignored administrative frontiers.[42] In 1906 he had stated the need for associating the city and its suburbs as one continuous agglomeration. He would later participate in the Extension Committee created by the Seine Prefecture (1913), the

VUE PERSPECTIVE DU BALNEARIO

PARIS. TEVRIER 1924
J.C.N. FORESTIER.

Figure 3. *Forestier's Perspective view of the Balneario*
(now Paseo Costanera)
Source: Jean-Nicolas Forestier, in Intendencia Municipal, Comisión de
Estética Edilicia, Proyecto orgánico para la urbanización del Municipio,
Tallerers Peuser, Buenos Aires, 1925

conclusions of which were used as a basis for the 1919 competition for the extension of Paris, and he applied these same ideas in Buenos Aires where: 'we look for, not only the embellishment of the better neighborhoods of the city, but also the future betterment of the peripheral neighborhoods, taking care of the hygiene and living conditions of the workers or the middle class living within them'. Further extending his ideas, he claimed: 'it would have been necessary to complement these projects, which could only be slowly applied, with a study of the industrial neighborhoods that stand outside the boundaries of the city . . . but the limits of my mission and the available documents did not allow me to go further'.[43]

The ability of a foreigner to observe as Forestier did was made possible by his previous experience. A document presented to the Rural and Urban Hygiene Committee of the Social Museum in Paris – in which he summarized his work experience in Buenos Aires – pointed out Forestier's dissonance with the local technicians: 'the considerable extension of the city, which could truly hold a population of three million inhabitants, had

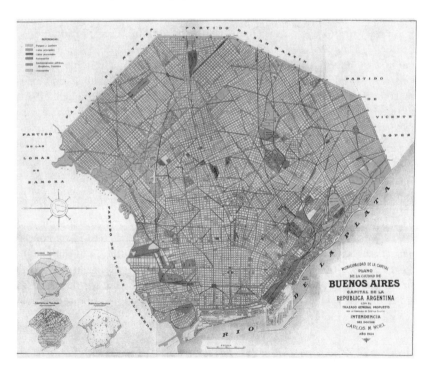

Figure 4. Proposal by Noël, 1924/1925
Source: *Intendencia Municipal, Comisión de Estética Edilicia, Proyecto orgánico para la urbanización del Municipio, Tallerers Peuser, Buenos Aires, 1925*

produced the notion that, in order to have good urban development, it was pointless to engage any efforts outside city boundaries (*enceintes*)'.[44] From the moment of his arrival Forestier battled against these ideas, arguing that the development of sectors outside the city limits was intricately and simultaneously linked to the population growth within.

The commission once again took Forestier's ideas and used them for the concluding document of the Organic Project (Fig. 4). But although the document included his proposals for rules, zoning and expropriation laws, there was nothing relating to areas outside the city limits, with the exception of his cemetery proposal. Despite this, Forestier did manage to establish the debate on extension in Buenos Aires, which was furthered in articles that engineer Carlos María Della Paolera sent from Paris, where he was studying at the time.[45] The 'Buenos Aires agglomeration', which includes the city and its surrounding territory, is a technical notion which Forestier helped establish and which influenced the new ways of looking at the city.[46]

An international career

In contrast to the French urbanists who preceded him, Forestier's influence transcended his role as an official. Rather, his career had been more international in nature since the beginning of the century, given his tasks as consultant and designer of parks and gardens in colonial countries (Marrakech and Rabat, 1913), as well as in Spain (Seville, Barcelona, 1914; Bilbao, 1918). But it was his work in Buenos Aires that opened the door to the Latin American market (for example 'El Malecón' in Havana, carried out in 1925, and a series of private gardens).

In this particular case, Forestier's concern for the environment, for indigenous vegetation as well as for management procedures, signals a period in urbanism that attempted to marry rational methods and techniques with characteristics peculiar to each place of intervention. His participation in the French urbanistic movement introduced him to the world of missions and consultants whose interest in 'new' countries was twofold: as potential markets for their projects, but also as a source of scientific information. In his texts, Forestier 'translated' many concepts related to English parks and the American 'City Beautiful' into a European setting. Indeed, the theories supporting his projects were based on a considerable amount of international experiences, which in turn nourished them.

MASTER CONFERENCES: JAUSSELY, HEGEMANN AND LE CORBUSIER

After the creation of the Comisión de Estética Edilicia (1923), three important debates in the Buenos Aires Municipal Council showed a shift towards urban planning. While the *Proyecto Orgánico* was still being elaborated in 1924, there were struggles over technical and hygienic components, including overt dissent over the excessively 'aesthetic' face of the plan. Then in 1929, a socialist took the lead on a request for the design of a *Plan Regulador* (Regulating Plan) that would put an end to social differences within the city. In 1930, a military coup interrupted the first period of governments elected by universal vote (1916–30). Upon the re-establishment of democracy in 1932, Councillor Rouco Oliva stated the urgent need to create a technical office for the elaboration of a plan, through an extended speech written by Della Paolera, who would become its director. The rapid setting up of a Municipal Urban Office, headed by an Argentinian professional – a graduate of the Institut d'Urbanisme de Paris – shows that the idea of a plan conducive to finding rational solutions for the city's problems was widely agreed upon. And the creation of a professorship of urbanism at Rosario University (1929), publications, urban planning exhibitions (1931 and 1932), the organizing of the First Argentinian Congress on Urbanism (1935) demonstrate the consensus.

After Forestier's contract, city mayors left urban matters in the hands of local professionals, while foreign experts participated as guest speakers in a series of lectures in Buenos Aires that had the purpose of lending international backing to different tendencies in disputes. In this sense, Buenos Aires, after 1925, took a different stance relative to other cities like Río de Janeiro where Agache[47] was in charge of producing the Regulating Plan, Santiago de Chile and Bogotá, the plans for which were designed by the Austrian Karl Brünner,[48] or Caracas, where Rotival[49] worked.

The first of this series of lectures was by Léon Jaussely, who in 1926 was invited by the Institute of the University of France in Argentina. The main purpose of the institute, which had been active since the centenary, was to organize the exchange of university professors. Men of influence, politically opposed to the *radicalismo*, who were testing their critical position towards the plan of the Comisión de Estética Edilicia, supported Jaussely's visit. He also had the support of the Asociación de Amigos de la Ciudad, founded in 1924 for the purpose of informing public opinion. This association organized events and published descriptive brochures such as: 'Do you know what a Regulatory Plan is?'[50]

The invitations for Jaussely's visit were granted by J.B. Hardoy and Della Paolera, both of whom had written their postgraduate thesis at the Institut d'Urbanisme in Paris. At the beginning of the decade, Della Paolera was one of the main promulgators of the ideas of the French Society of Urban Planners (Société Française des Urbanistes). Jaussely delivered nine lectures. His opinion on Buenos Aires – 'a friendly and beautiful city . . . that holds a leading position for its progress and sanitary development'[51] – was aimed at flattering the public, which was becoming acquainted with the economic and social dimensions of urbanism and its methods of diagnosis and intervention. The influence of his lectures could be found in various articles.[52] They corresponded to a demand for a city planning that considered itself 'scientific'.

In similar circumstances in 1931, Werner Hegemann visited Argentina, invited by the Instituto Cultural Argentino Germánico. His initial purpose was to present an exhibition on urbanism, shown at the premises of the Asociación de Amigos del Arte (Friends of the Arts Association), and to propagate the principles of urbanism.[53] The effects of Hegemann's visit have been studied in detail by Christiane Crasemann-Collins, focusing on the visitor's efforts to understand the local issues and to transmit them through the images and language of the city. Hegemann became a consultant for the plans in Rosario and Mar del Plata, and shared urbanistic perspectives with Della Paolera.

In contrast to other visitors, Hegemann rescued the importance of the grid and the 'house with patio' – a traditional Buenos Aires type – which he later used in his writings. The Argentinian experiences would be incorporated into his theoretical principles, which, like the other planners of his generation, helped to build his international reputation through events organized in different countries since 1909.

Le Corbusier visited Buenos Aires in 1929 and shared the same audience as Jaussely, who preceded him, and Hegemann after him. While he also had been sponsored by the Amigos del Arte, his main hosts were in fact the artistic avant-garde: a group of Latin American intellectuals, architects, painters and writers familiar with his texts and struggling to establish the ideas of the new art in Buenos Aires.[54] His lectures were later published in *Precisiones*.

Studies of Le Corbusier's visits to Buenos Aires and South America are exhaustive. But it is important to stress a central point: the influence of his Argentinian experience on the consideration of the landscape and the transition established between the *Cité Contemporaine* of 1922 and the *Ville Radieuse* of 1933. According to Liernur[55] and Montaner Monteys,[56] Le Corbusier's proposals for the city upon the river, illustrated in the well-known image of skyscrapers on the horizon, gave him new seminal ideas to develop his *Cité Radieuse* model. Upon the meeting line between the river and the Pampas – which he observed with interest from his first aeroplane flights – he placed *la cité des affaires,* like a leading nucleus that transformed his initial *Cité Contemporaine* concentric plan. So, among other contributions, his experience in Buenos Aires was reflected in his urban models.

Le Corbusier insisted on establishing contacts for future contracts, as his correspondence with Argentinians made clear. Finally, among other projects, he would produce in 1938 at his studio on the rue de Sèvres in Paris, together with the young architects Kurchan and Ferrari Hardoy, the *Plan Director de Buenos Aires*. This would be published in 1947 in the Spanish-language issue of *L'Architecture d'aujourd'hui* and later included in his complete works (Fig. 5).

The figure of Le Corbusier, selling ideas and selling himself, delivering lectures at all latitudes, and always alert to potential contracts, may very well be the 'paradigmatic figure' in relation to these foreign experts. Intent on applying his principles universally, Le Corbusier represents in a cruder way the profile of the modern professional. Nevertheless, though their concepts and methods may have differed, the professionals we have studied here shared at least two features: the search for new markets for their creations at a time when the European demand between the two world wars was diminishing, and a professional interest in studying new urban situations under the light of their own theories.

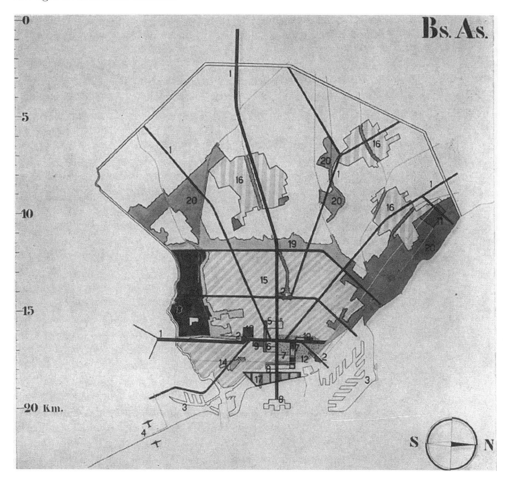

Figure 5. *Master Plan for Buenos Aires by Le Corbusier, 1937*
Source: Juan Kurchan and Jorge Ferrari Hardoy, Plan Director para Buenos Aires, off-print from L'Architecture d'Aujourd'hui, Spanish Edition, Buenos Aires, 1947

CONCLUSIONS: THE INTERNATIONAL EXPERT – A FIGURE AT THE ORIGIN OF MODERN URBANISM

In previous investigations we have showed that the influence of foreign urbanists who came to Buenos Aires at the beginning of the twentieth century diminished and gradually became indirect. This situation is connected with the establishment of the National University, the development of the Public Administration and the activities of a number of new associations that struggled towards the application of rational solutions in a city that was experiencing explosive growth. Furthermore, these elements created an encouraging environment for the accumulation of working experience in projects and urban management in the first batch of local professionals specializing in city matters.

At the beginning of the century, with the centenary imminent, numerous alternative projects were debated in Buenos Aires for the construction of a modern city. Thus the role Bouvard was called to play was that of an 'arbiter', a 'generalist' expert experienced in solving problems and capable of making the necessary choices. In the 1920s, Forestier was, in contrast, a 'peer', a specialist called upon to collaborate in his specific field of expertise – green spaces – with a team of Argentine professionals who were members of the Comisión de Estética Edilicia. At the beginning of the 1930s, the Oficina de Urbanizacion was created, directed by Della Paolera, the first professional urban planner in Argentina. And from that point onwards, foreign professionals began acting as 'validators', generally being invited to endorse the local competing tendencies.

In answering the questions posed at the beginning of this article, we are now able to add new conclusions to those already mentioned:

1. Until the 1920s, the radiation of the nineteenth-century Parisian model influenced the national authority's choice of foreign professionals. In that period, there were two determining factors: the network of personal links connecting the desires of Argentinian politicians to the sources of French urban 'expertise', the exportation of which was openly favored by the French, and the influence of the École des Beaux-Arts. After the 1920s there was an increase in the circulation of English, North American and German models ('Garden City', 'City Beautiful', 'Urban Art'), and in the international professional links through congresses, exhibitions and relationships between teachers and graduates from peripheral countries.

2. Plans and projects always took shape in the articulation between local experience and the know-how of international consultants, which helped give shape to the actions carried out, and opened new issues as a consequence of the external views of these foreigners. Bouvard's legacy was the idea of opening the city towards the river; Forestier's the joint consid-

eration of the city and its regions. Le Corbusier introduced the new models of architecture and city, while the main concerns of Hegemann and Jaussely leaned towards social and economic factors, housing and urban art. Considerations and the weight of local variables differed according to tendencies of each: Forestier, Jaussely and Hegemann took into account the existing city, focusing on understanding its characteristics and morphology; Bouvard and Le Corbusier – in rather different historical circumstances – applied their own models to a new reality without specifically taking the existing city into account. Nevertheless, in contrast with the long stays of European urbanists in Brazil, Chile, Colombia and Venezuela, foreign experts' visits in Argentina were short, and it is therefore difficult to think of them in terms of 'learning processes'. But in the proposals for Buenos Aires of these foreign visitors, we may see projections of their own preoccupations.

3.   Foreign experts 'bring' with them their know-how, but they also 'carry back' an experience that affects their thought – 'retro-transference' – and their later personal careers, eventually establishing them as international consultants and thus preparing the field for further contracts. The latter was illustrated with Bouvard and Forestier through their Latin American contracts. The former can be seen in the case of the influence of Hegemann's Latin American studies on his writings, and for Le Corbusier's intervention in the *Plan Director para Buenos Aires* in 1938.

However, the voyages of these experts were not exclusively aimed at the conquest of new markets. Their purpose was also to test their theories in new contexts. Indeed, the knowledge and the comparison of different urban realities and experiences, the propagation of what had been carried out, were some of the foundations of city planning as a discipline. From Cerdá onwards, knowledge of urbanism has been based on the critical analysis of both historical and current practices. Lavedan and Hegemann, to name just a few of the treatise writers of the time, analyzed the state of international art, marking the elements to be retained and those to be dropped. The French urbanists had their testing grounds in the colonial interventions in North Africa. In fact, the purpose of international meetings and exhibitions was to demonstrate and discuss different urban patterns.

The construction of modern urbanism was nourished by the propagation of doctrines and by the accumulation of all types of experiences. Beyond their differences, planners believed in the existence of rational solutions of universal worth. But to assume this does not mean we are implying that influences on peripheral countries have been in only one direction. Studying the professional careers of the traveling experts is, it seems, one possible road to constructing a vision acknowledging the complex formation – thinking and practice, global and local – of city planning in the early twentieth century.

NOTES

1. Jean-Pierre Gaudin (1987) 'Présentation' and 'Savoirs et savoir-faire dans l'ur-banisme français au début du siècle', in Gaudin, *Les premiers urbanistes français et l'art urbain, 1900–1930*, Paris: Ecole d'Architecture de Paris-Villemin, pp. 7–19 and 43–70.

2. Alicia Novick (1992) 'Técnicos locales y extranjeros en la génesis del urbanismo porteño', *AREA* Nª 1, *Revista de Investigaciones*, Facultad de Arquitectura, Diseño y Urbanismo-Escuela Politécnica de Lausanne.

3. Anahí Ballent (1995) *El diálogo de las antípodas: Los CIAM y América Latina*, Buenos Aires: Serie Difusión, SICYT-FADU-UBA; Sonia Berjman (1997) *Plazas y parques de Buenos Aires: La obra de los paisajistas franceses 1860–1930*, Buenos Aires: Fondo de Cultura Económica; Jorge Enrique Hardoy (1988) 'Teorías y prác-ticas urbanísticas en Europa entre 1850 y 1930: Su translado a América Latina', *Repensando la ciudad latinoamericana*, Buenos Aires: Grupo Editor de América Latina; Fernando Pérez Oyarzun (1991) *Le Corbusier y Sudamérica: Viajes y proyectos*, Santiago de Chile: Pontificia Universidad de Chile.

4. *Origens das Politicas Urbanas Modernas: Empréstimos e Traducoes* (1994), Seminaire org. IPPUR-UFRJ, ANPUR, CNPq, CSU-CNRS, Itamontes, Minas Gerais, Brazil, 29 August–2 September. *Programa Internacional de Investigaciones sobre el campo urbano* (1996), PIR-Villes-CNRS, IAA, CURDIUR, Vaquerías, Provincia de Córdoba, 17–20 October.

5. Ramón Gutiérrez (1992) *Buenos Aires: Evolución Histórica*, Bogotá: Fondo Editorial Escala Argentina.

6. Bénédicte Leclerc and Salvador Tarrago y Cid (1997) 'Une figure tutélaire de l'école française d'urbanisme', general introduction to new edn, in Jean-Claude Nicolas Forestier, *Grandes villes et systèmes de parcs*, Paris: Norma (1st edn 1906); Benedicte Leclerc (ed.) (1994) *Jean-Claude Forestier, 1861–1930: Du jardin au paysage urbain – Actes du colloque international sur J.C.N. Forestier, Paris, 1990*, Paris: Picard.

7. André Lortie (ed.) (1995) *Paris s'exporte: Architectures modèle ou modèles d'ar-chitecture*, Paris: Picard et Pavillon de l'Arsenal. See also Oligens, op. cit., and Proframa Internacional, op. cit.

8. Christiane Crasemann-Collins (1995) 'Intercambios urbanos en el cono sur: Le Corbusier (1929) y Werner Hegemann (1931) en Argentina', in *ARQ*, no. 31, Santiago de Chile.

9. Adrián Gorelik and Jorge Liernur (1992) *Hannes Meyer en México*, Buenos Aires: Proyecto Editorial; Jorge Liernur (1992) 'Un mundo nuevo para un espíritu nuevo', *Crítica*, no. 25, Buenos Aires: IAA.

10. As for the records used, we have examined municipal documents, articles in local specialized publications (*Revista de Arquitectura, Revista de Ingeniería, Revista Municipal*), as well as diplomatic letters kept in the French Ministry of Foreign Affairs and in the archives of the French Institute of Architecture, both in Paris.

11. Jorge Tartarini (1991) 'El Plan Bouvard para Buenos Aires (1907–1911) Algunos antecedentes', *ANALES*, no. 27–28, Buenos Aires: Universidad de Buenos Aires.

12. Félix Luna (1986) *Alvear*, Buenos Aires: Hyspamérica (1st edn 1958).

13. Werner Szambien (1995) 'La fortune des modèles', in Lortie, op. cit.

14. In 1889 Camillo Sitte published *The Art of Building Cities: City Building According to its Artistic Fundamentals* (translated into English for the first time in 1945 by Charles T. Stewart, former director of the Urban Land Institute for

Reinhold Publishing of New York). For a review of his ideas, see George R. Collins and Christiane Collins (1965) *Camillo Sitte and the Birth of Modern City Planning*, London: Random House.

15. *Bulletin municipal officiel de la ville de Paris* (1907), 4 January, p. 79.
16. Archives du Ministère des Affaires Etrangères (hereafter AMAE), Paris, Nouvelle Série, Sous-série: Argentine, Vol. 38, Série B, Carton 149. Centenaire de la République Argentine, 12 October 1909: Note remise par M. Turot candidat au Commissariat général de l'Exposition à Buenos Aires, folio 10.
17. Charles Wiener (1899) *La République Argentine*, Paris: Cerf; AMAE, Missions Commerciales (R-v). Maurice Rondet-Saint (1909) Rapport à M. le ministre de Commerce, Voyage de circumnavigation, 1908–1909: Italie, Egypte, Ceylan, Singapour, Extrême-Orient, Amérique du Nord, Amérique du Sud, Sénégal, Angleterre, Châteauroux, Badel, folio 14.
18. AMAE Nouvelle Série. Sous série: Argentine. Vol. 17. Industrie, travaux publics, mines. Mission dans l'Amérique latine. Direction des Affaires Politiques et Commerciales, A propos d'une Société française d'entreprises diverses dans l'Amérique du Sud, Lettre du Ministre Plénipotentiaire en Mission à son Excellence, le Ministre des Affaires Etrangères, 9 December 1909, folio 143, and appendix: *Note sur la Société Franco Argentine,* folios 144–47.
19. Anne-Marie Châtelet (1996) 'Joseph Antoine Bouvard (1840–1920)', in Vaquerias, op. cit.
20. For a review, see J. Allwood (1977) *The Great Exhibitions*, London: Studio Vista; Florence Pinot de Villechenon (2000) *Fêtes géantes: Les Expositions Universelles pour quoi faire?* Paris: Autrement; Linda Aimone and Carlo Olmo (1990) *Le Exposizioni Universali 1851–1900*, Rome: Humberto Allemandi & C.
21. Berjman, op. cit.; Tartarini, op. cit.
22. Concejo Deliberante de la Ciudad de Buenos Aires (1907) 'Se aprueba el plano general de apertura de Avenidas-Diagonales', *Versiones Taquigráficas*, Buenos Aires: Imprenta Litografía y Encuadernación Kraft. Sesión del 2 de junio.
23. Municipalidad de la Ciudad de Buenos Aires (hereafter MCBA) (1908) *Memoria de la Intendencia Municipal de Buenos Aires correspondiente a 1908, Presentada al H. Concejo Deliberante,* Buenos Aires: Imprenta Litografía y Encuadernación Kraft, p. 7.
24. German Adell (1994) 'Constituçao do hábitat popular em torno do porto de Mar del Plata, construido pela Sociedad Nacional de Obras Públicas' in Itamontes, op. cit.
25. Raúl Piccioni (1997) 'El monumento al Centenario: Un problema de estado', *Arte y recepción*, Buenos Aires: CAYA.
26. AMAE, Nouvelle série. Sous série: Argentine. Vol. 17. Industrie, travaux publics, mines. Légation de la République Française en Argentine. Direction des Affaires Politiques et Commerciales. Information réservée. Lettre de M. Thibault, Ministre de la République en Argentine à son Excellence M. Pichon, Ministre des Affaires Etrangères (dactylographié), 18 March 1908, folio 14.
27. Intendencia Municipal, Andrés Bouvard (1909) *El nuevo plano de la Ciudad de Buenos Aires,* Buenos Aires: Imprenta Litografía y Encuadernación Kraft.
28. Ibid., p. 17.
29. Adrián Gorelik (1998) *La grilla y el parque: Espacio público y cultura urbana en Buenos Aires, 1887–1936,* Quilmes: Universidad Nacional de Quilmes.
30. Alicia Novick (1996) 'Notas sobre planes y proyectos', *Territorio, Ciudad y Arquitectura: Buenos Aires, siglos XVIII-XIX,* Buenos Aires: SICYT.
31. Hugo Segawa (1995) '1911: Bouvard en Sao Paulo', *DANA,* no. 37–38, IAIHAU.

32. Barry Parker (1919) 'Two years in Brazil', *Garden Cities and Town Planning*, 9, no. 8, August; María Cristina Leme (1999) 'Os bairros-jardins em Sao Paulo' in María Cristina Leme, *Urbanismo no Brasil 1895–1965'*, Sao Paulo: Fupam. Studio Nobel.

33. Alicia Novick (1998) 'Le Musée Social et l'urbanisme en Argentine', in Colette Chambelland (ed.) *Le Musée social en son temps,* Paris: Presses de l'Ecole normale supérieure.

34. Intendencia Municipal, Comisión de Estética Edilicia (1925) *Proyecto Orgánico para la urbanización del Municipio,* Buenos Aires: Talleres Peuser.

35. AMAE, Industries et Travaux Publics, Vol. 72. (Pièces et affaires diverses 1918–1940), DOC. 85, Lettre du Préfet de la Seine au Ministre des Affaires Etrangères. (dactylographié). 20 September 1923, folio 52.

36. About the Spanish Noël works, see Ramón Gutiérrez, Margarita Gutman and Víctor Pérez Escolano (eds) (1995) *El arquitecto Martín Noel. Su tiempo y su obra*, Seville: Junta de Andalucía, Consejería de Cultura, Seville. About Forestier and his Spanish works see Salvador Tarragó y Cid (1994) 'Entre Le Nôtre et Le Corbusier', in Leclerc, op. cit.

37. Jean-Claude Forestier (1905) 'Los jardines obreros (reseña de la experiencia francesa)', *Revista Municipal,* no. 59, 6 March; Jean-Claude Forestier (1907) 'Los jardines modernos', *Caras y Caretas,* no. 165, Buenos Aires, 31 August.

38. Jean-Claude Nicolas Forestier (1906) op. cit.

39. Concejo Deliberante de la Ciudad de Buenos Aires (1923) 'Ingeniero Señor Forestier: Contratación de sus servicios', *Versiones Taquigráficas,* Buenos Aires: Imprenta Municipal, sesión del 9 de octubre, p. 2138.

40. Benito Carrasco (1921) 'Conveniencia de estudiar técnicamente la transformación de nuestras ciudades', *Segundo Congreso Nacional de Ingeniería celebrado desde el 11 al 22 de noviembre de 1922,* Buenos Aires: Centro Nacional de Ingenieros.

41. Berjman, op. cit.; Novick (1992), op. cit.

42. Jean-Louis Cohen (1994) 'L'Extension de Paris', in Leclerc, op. cit.

43. Intendencia Municipal, Comisión de Estética Edilicia (1925) *Proyecto orgánico para la urbanización del municipio: Buenos Aires*, Buenos Aires: Talleres Peuser, p. 423.

44. Musée Social de Paris (1928) 'Communication de Forestier: "Quelques travaux d'urbanisation à Buenos Aires: l'Avenida Costanera"', *Reproduction des procès-verbaux de séances de la Section d'Hygiène Urbaine et Rurale*, Séance du 15 juin, p. 302.

45. Carlos María Della Paolera (1925) 'Necesidad de un Plan Regulador para la Aglomeración Bonaerense', *La Razón,* 18 December.

46. Horacio Caride (1999) *Visiones de suburbio: Utopía y realidad en los alrededores de Buenos Aires durante el siglo XIX y principios del siglo XX, Documento de trabajo n° 13,* San Miguel: Universidad Nacional de General Sarmiento, Instituto del Conurbano.

47. Alfred Hubert Agache (1930) *Cidade do Rio de Janeiro, extensao, remodelacao e embelezamento,* Paris: Foyer Bresilien; Margareth Pereira (1994) 'Pensando a metropole moderna: Os planos de Agache e Le Corbusier', in Itamontes, op. cit.

48. Karl Brünner (1932) *Santiago de Chile: Su estado actual y su futuro,* Santiago de Chile: Imprenta la tracción; Humberto Eliah and Manuel Moreno (1989) *Arquitectura y modernidad en Chile, 1925–1965,* Santiago de Chile: Ediciones de la Universidad Católica.

49. Juan José Martín Frechilla (1992) *El Plan Rotival: La Caracas que no fue 1939–1989, Un plan urbano para Caracas,* Caracas: Ediciones Instituto de Urbanismo, Facultad de Arquitectura y Urbanismo, Universidad Central de Venezuela.
50. Benito Carrasco (1926) *Sabe Ud. que es un plan regulador,* Buenos Aires: Asociación Amigos de la Ciudad.
51. Horacio Cópppola (1926) 'Síntesis de nueve Conferencias Magistrales', *Revista de Arquitectura,* no. 411, November, p. 35.
52. Alfredo Coppola (1927) 'La salud de la América y la superación del pasado', *Revista de Arquitectura,* no. 422, October.
53. His visit may have been linked to the presence of Karl Brünner in Santiago de Chile, or perhaps he was sponsored by German constructing firms like Geope or Siemens, which had an important role in introducing the Modern Movement in Buenos Aires.
54. Oyarzun, op. cit.
55. J. Liernur and P. Psepiurca (1987) 'Precisiones sobre los proyectos de Le Corbusier en la Argentina. 1929/1949', *Summa,* November.
56. Xavier Monteys (1996) *La gran máquina: La ciudad en Le Corbusier,* Barcelona: Ediciones del Serbal.

CHAPTER 12

POLITICS, IDEOLOGY AND PROFESSIONAL INTERESTS: FOREIGN VERSUS LOCAL PLANNERS IN LEBANON UNDER PRESIDENT CHEHAB

Eric Verdeil

Institut français du Proche-Orient

President Chehab's administration (1958–64) appears in independent Lebanon as the major reference for the construction of a State inspired by Western legal norms, as well as the time of introduction of planned development and spatial management.[1] The word Chehabism has become shorthand for that era's strong will of reforms, and remains a very popular reference in the country. Social and developmental projects, particularly in the poorest regions of the country, were implemented. But during the years of Chehab's mandate, and in the years to follow, such a policy would also be strongly criticized by representatives of the old political class and the business community, called 'fromagistes' by General Chehab. The conservatives were confronted by the reformist side, which included, around Chehab and his political allies (the Kataeb[2] and the Progressive Socialist Party), young Lebanese technocrats as well as foreign experts who were his advisers, for example the Frenchmen Father Louis-Joseph Lebret and Michel Ecochard. The failures of the Chehabist reforms in the subsequent years are generally attributed to the incapacity of Chehab's followers to overcome the conservative pressures at a time when the international context (the Six Days War in 1967) caused a national economic crisis and ruined the Arab nationalism that represented one of the political planks of the Chehabist compromise.

Yet the unity of the reformist side was also not as solid as had been assumed. If most Lebanese economists welcomed Chehab's reforms as a whole, they sometimes disagreed with a particular set of measures or criticized the way the reforms had been implemented.[3] This chapter focuses on the field of spatial management where such controversies between local and foreign planners also occurred. Among the latter, the most famous were Father Lebret and his team from the Institute for Research and Education

Oriented toward Development (IRFED), who had worked in Latin America, and the town planner Michel Ecochard, who had already served in Syria and Lebanon before working in Morocco at the end of the French protectorate. Both belonged to the *tiers-mondiste* current that sought to develop solutions adapted to the situation of developing countries.

The purpose of the chapter is to look at how the Lebanese experts viewed these foreign experts and their propositions. The latter were some of the principal elements of the Chehabist policy. Two main issues that were discussed at the time will be elaborated here: the role of Beirut in Lebanon and the strategies for planning Beirut's suburbs. The debates reveal the resistance of some of the local experts to the ideas of the government and foreign consultants. This shows that in a postcolonial context, planning ideologies and technologies as instruments of reforms are not directly transferred from outside and roughly imposed on the developing country (even when backed by that country's leadership), but rather are screened and reconfigured by local experts. Among the motivations of these local professionals, particularly worth mentioning is the influence of professional or economic interests, which was sometimes greater than that of political or technical criteria.

IRFED, NATIONAL COMPREHENSIVE PLANNING AND TOWN PLANNING

The IRFED was founded in 1958 in Paris by Father Louis-Joseph Lebret, a Dominican priest. Lebret's itinerary in the twentieth century is very representative of the Social Catholicism movement and illustrates the change from a 'communitarian utopia' ideology to one of 'Catholic Third-Worldism'.[4] Social Catholicism was born at the end of the nineteenth century as a reaction to the new political and economic order set up by the French Revolution and the Industrial Revolution. It reflected the attempt of the Roman Catholic Church to formulate a political and social project to deal with modernity. Between capitalism and its society of individuals, and socialism and its collectivist society, the main idea of Social Catholicism consisted of preserving communities and the protective order they provide for individuals in a destructured world. This led the representatives of the movement to turn to a concern for the conditions of workers. After the Second World War, the originality of Father Lebret was his theory of 'harmonized development', which he put into practice in many countries of southern America. It included comprehensive national and regional planning and was intended to associate the poor with the development process. The creation of IRFED, an umbrella institution for experts sharing the same ideas and dedicated to development and education, sought to promote a better diffusion of such a theory and to implement it.[5]

The IRFED in Lebanon

When Chehab came to office in Lebanon in 1958, he quickly established a confident relationship with Lebret and the IRFED. It is a well established fact that the IRFED team enjoyed the full trust of the president:[6] they were the inspiration behind many investment decisions as well as the authors of many of the new laws the government adopted. They also contributed to what came to be known as the 450 million L£ (Lebanese pound) program (1961), which aimed to link every village of this mountainous country to the main arteries and to develop networks of potable water throughout the country, the Popular Housing Law (May 1962) and the law reorganizing the Ministry of Planning (June 1962).

National comprehensive planning was a key point of the IRFED doctrine, yet its various proposals were not brought together into a single master document. All of the proposals were based on observations of regional disparities in standards of living, but most of the proposed measures were sectoral or limited to economic planning. According to the IRFED, a comprehensive master document needed elaboration only in a second stage – as the summing up of local initiatives. This illustrates the IRFED's idea that development should be based on local communities, or at least that it should result from a bottom-top relationship; according to the organization's experts: 'the movement top-bottom/bottom-top is the condition of development'.[7]

The main purpose of the IRFED's proposals was the denunciation of the demographic and economic dominance of the capital over the country. This was expressed in terms that described the big city as chaotic, as a monster or as a cancer:

> The present polarization of Lebanon is excessively focused on the Beirut metropolitan area, which is all the more dangerous since, with no master plan having governed the capital's growth, Beirut gives the impression of a real cancer worsening incessantly through the construction of tall buildings along narrow and unorganized streets.[8]

This metaphor is not in itself very original since such a discourse was being conducted about many cities in the world, from Paris to Latin America. Evidently it also made reference to the well-known quotations of Le Corbusier on 'the street as donkeys' path' and 'the city as a cancer'. But the banality of this metaphor should not hide the originality of the IRFED, which prioritized rural lands (and peripheries) over cities.

Thus, the IRFED argued that the massive investments that were required for improving the capital would be out of proportion with the results they might produce, at least concerning the core of the city: 'Undoubtedly, a master plan whose implementation would be extremely burdensome may attenuate some of the shortcomings of the present city, but the situation may be resolved only through the transfer of some urban functions into a contiguous new town, planned, connected with the whole Beiruti agglomeration, with its harbor and its roads'.[9] This was why the IRFED emergency plan focused on the rural regions of the south, the Bekaa and the north, where the investments would immediately have positive economic as well as political impacts. As early as 1961, the government launched several infrastructure programs for roads, water and electricity, each of them known by the amount allocated in Lebanese pounds (L£), for example L£51 million and L£450 million (infrastructures), L£84 million (secondary roads), and L£10 million (Beirut's port silo).

Beyond these spectacular investments, the IRFED tried to promote what was known as 'harmonized development' by defining a 'polarization scheme' with four levels of places (the 'poles') (Fig. 1). Specific investments and services were listed for each level of this urban hierarchy in order to spread modernity throughout the whole country. But such a scheme remained mainly administrative (school, hospital, police, justice) and did not allow for coordination with private investments. Administrations such as the Social Development Office[10] failed to mobilize private actors while the private actors remained wary of governmental action.

Criticism of the IRFED by Lebanese Experts

Published in 1961, the first IRFED report[11] soon attracted much acclaim among the population and in academic or administrative spheres close to the government. But the reactions to subsequent IRFED initiatives are less known, particularly the debates dealing with non-financial aspects.[12] Indeed only very small circles within the government were aware of the further detailed proposals of 1961 to 1963, and the point of view of Lebanese experts has rarely been published. Some of these experts, along with a number of public administration managers, clearly supported the French team, and included Henri Naccache, president of the Executive Council for Great Projects, or Mitri Nammar, general director of the Directorate of Public Buildings,[13] both of whom collaborated closely with the IRFED in setting up the largest investment programs in roads and infrastructures of the Chehab mandate. However others were more reserved, if not hostile. Such is the case of experts like Georges Corm in his book *Planification et politique économique au Liban* (1964), or of specific institutions like the Council for Development and Planning.

Georges Corm, at the time a young graduate in economics from the French Institut d'Etudes Politiques, worked with the IRFED for several months,[14] and published his book at the end of the experience in 1964. The book was intended as an appraisal of the planning and development policy in Lebanon, delineating two periods. The first of these (1953–58) witnessed the initial attempts at planning. Although Corm's assessment of this time is very critical, stating its existence in a context where the IRFED was still active could be read, if not as a rehabilitation of the past, at least as an affirmation that the IRFED was not the absolute beginning either. As for the second part of the book, it consisted of a balanced appraisal of IRFED's propositions (1959–63), with great emphasis on economics.

Regarding some of the criticisms dealing with physical planning and spatial management, Corm found the IRFED's diagnosis excessively pessimistic as the survey's categories sometimes reflected ethnocentric biases. A number

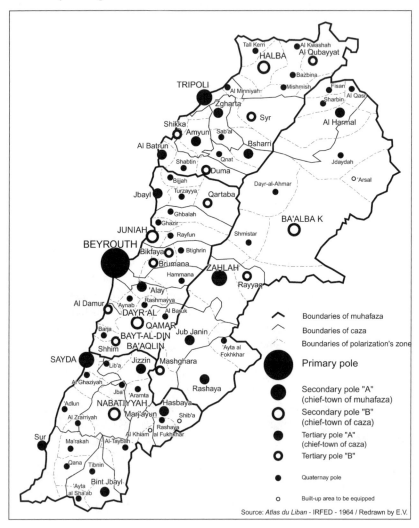

Figure 1. *The IRFED's Polarization Network for Lebanon.*
Source: *Atlas du Liban, Ministry of Planning, IRFED, 1964 (redrawn by the author)*

of them, such as criteria dealing with household electric appliances, were responsible for some very low development indices, which made the situation of rural places appear particularly bleak. Rather than underdevelopment, this was probably the sign, according to Corm, of 'a different civilization where the level of exchange remains very low and where the mechanisms of production and distribution are not the same as in the West'.[15]

As for the propositions, Corm first examined the new regional organization for development, which was a key point of the reform of the Ministry of Planning (Fig. 2). This included, at various devolved administrative levels (village, *caza* (sub-province), *muhafazat* (province)), services responsible for surveying and elaborating the needs of the Lebanese regions, and was, according to Corm, 'the greatest success of IRFED',[16] especially if compared with the central institution for development set up by the IRFED (the planning ministry itself), described by Corm as 'a real monster' because of its bureaucratic complexity (Fig. 3).[17] Yet the regional organization was still heavy and not very flexible, and was not adapted to the small size of Lebanon. Even if Corm did not say it explicitly, he probably censored this form of organization for not being adapted to small countries but praised by Father Lebret as a universal solution (Fig. 4).[18] The last critique concerned the priorities set up by the IRFED. In a large review of the financial planning for investments, in which Corm warned against the priority given to infrastructure projects over productive investments, the economist also called into question the priority given to rural land over cities. In another paper in the IRFED's archives, he was more precise, claiming that more than the proposed 0.9 per cent of the whole public investment should be for town planning.[19]

The relationship between the IRFED and the Council for Development and Planning bears scrutiny. The Council had been created in 1953 to advise the government on planning and development matters and to set up a first five-year plan, which it finished in 1958, just before the crisis that brought Fouad Chehab to power. Its members were to be recruited from various administrations, and some of them were appointed as independent professionals. Notable among these members was Joseph Naggear, who was present from the beginning. This French-educated engineer from the Ecole Polytechnique and the Ecole des Ponts et Chaussées was professor at the Ecole supérieure d'ingénieurs de Beyrouth, and the former head of the irrigation administration after working in both the land register and urban planning administration. He later became minister of planning in several cabinets after Chehab's mandate. Others worth mentioning here were Henri Eddé, an independent architect belonging to the family of a former president of the Republic, who was a member from 1959, and Assem Salam, another independent architect involved in town-planning matters and nephew of Saeb Salam, one of the most prominent politicians of the time. Beyond a specific competency that could not be denied, belonging to Beiruti leading families was another important criterion, and some of these families, such as the Eddés, became political opponents of Chehab.[20]

In 1962, the reform of the Ministry of Planning changed the function of the Council for Development and Planning, which assumed only a consultative role from then on. In fact, the former tasks of the council were now to be performed by the newly established Directorate of Studies. But given the inadequacy in the number and level of competence of Lebanese functionaries, the IRFED team had to substitute for this directorate. It had the double duty of setting up the five-year plan and training the future members of the ministry, who came from the ranks of collaborators of the IRFED or were graduates from the Institut de Formation au Développement, specially created in Beirut in 1963. The council was highly concerned with the IRFED's project and its advice was indispensable. However the IRFED believed that the council was unable to have a clear opinion on its proposals as its members were not full-time members, and were involved in many other activities.[21] The IRFED also called into question the competence of the council, considering its previous plan an 'academic dissertation'.[22] So, at the request of the IRFED, a Commission for Planning, with only two members representing the whole council, was established to provide the necessary advice.

For their part, the council and the commission seem to have had many reservations about the IRFED's projects. Unfortunately, the IRFED archives

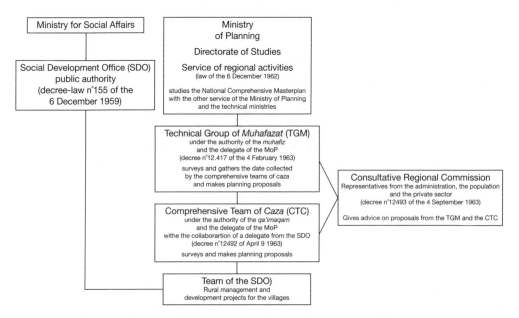

Figure 2. The IRFED's Regional Organization for Development in Lebanon.
Source: Synthesis by the author

are not rich in discussions of these projects, which can be explained by the fact that the commission met the French experts only twice.[23] Following is one concrete example of the divergence between them. The IRFED's team had proposed a project of twin tourist developments in Jbeil and Rmaileh, about 30 km (19 miles) respectively north and south of Beirut. The future seaside resorts were to become the starting points for excursions into the hinterland. Such a project, consistent with the overall project of developing Lebanese provincial districts, was based on the hope that the arrival of tourists from Europe would increase as in the models of Spain or Greece.[24] The Council for Planning and Development objected to such a project. The reason for such criticism is to be found in the previous five-year plan set up by this institution, which reveals an alternative vision of the future of Lebanon. The council believed in increasing tourist flows coming from Arab countries and therefore called for the development of the mountainous areas of Metn, Kisrwan and 'Aley – that is, the central Mount Lebanon, which was already much more developed than more peripheral areas and already

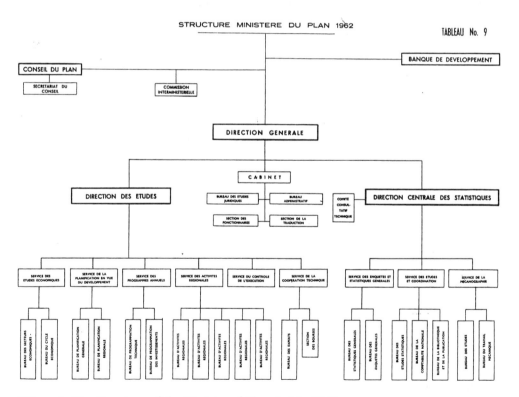

Figure 3. The Structure of the Ministry of Planning in 1962.
Source: Georges Corm, *Planification et politique économique au Liban, 1964*

popular with summer tourists.[25] Whichever of the projects was more appropriate, each implied a specific vision of the territory, suggesting that one difference between pro-Chehab circles and others was the tendency in the former to challenge Beirut's centrality in the country.

This example gains significance when compared to the objections raised by Henri Eddé against the spirit of the IRFED's proposals for spatial management, and especially its concept of a 'polarization scheme': 'If administrative decentralization has always been and still remains desirable, economic decentralization on the other hand has to be handled with greater care. It would have been particularly unfortunate to choose the wrong scale and to implement in Lebanon in an authoritarian way solutions which would be valid only in countries which are much larger and have more important and varied resources'.[26] The Lebanese expert set himself apart from the IRFED's state-control approach by being more prudent towards the centrality of Beirut. Conversely, it appears from the quotation above that he did not agree with the priority given to the needs of the countryside over Beirut, or with the quite authoritarian means of implementing such a policy.

Another factor may have played a role here. The IRFED's hostility to the Council for Development and Planning could also be explained by the fact that

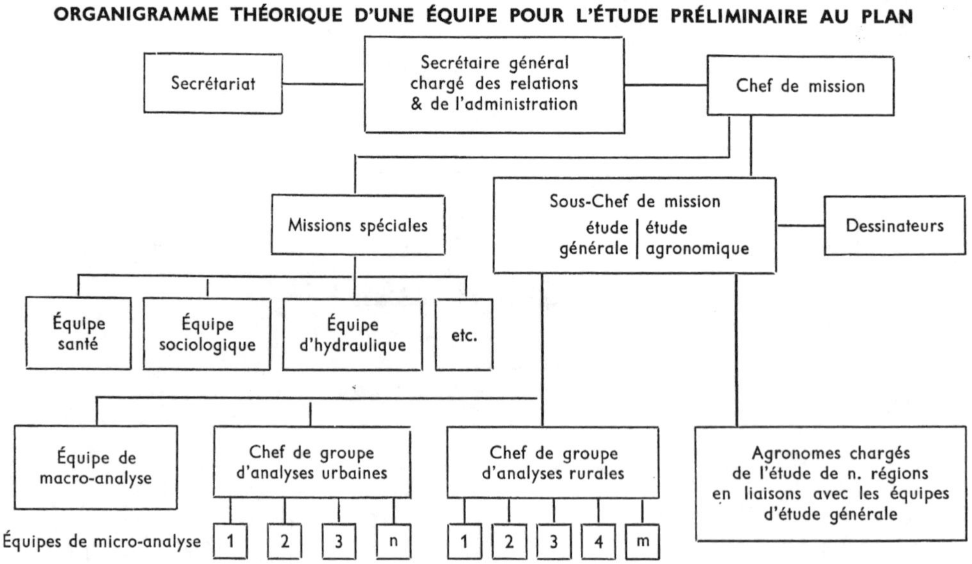

ORGANIGRAMME THÉORIQUE D'UNE ÉQUIPE POUR L'ÉTUDE PRÉLIMINAIRE AU PLAN

Figure 4. Father Lebret's Theoretical Organigram for a Central Service of Planning.
Source: L.J. Lebret, Développement et civilisations, Analyse des compétences nécessaires à l'établissement d'un programme de développement et à son exécution, 1962

some Lebanese experts criticized the incompetence of various members of the IRFED. In his memoirs, Henri Eddé recalls his 'reservations about the qualifications of some of the "experts"'.[27] Since similar misgivings seem to have been shared by other members of the council,[28] it is possible that they felt that foreigners whom they considered less competent, supported by Chehab, were putting them aside. Their opposition could then be explained by their belief that, as local experts, they would have a done a better job. The creation of an intermediate commission may have been more than a way of speeding up the work of the council: it may also have been a way of getting around its critics. The challenge to the competency of the IRFED may have relied on the opposition between engineers (like Henri Eddé or Joseph Naggear) and economists. Indeed, it is worth noting that the two members of the commission were economists: Elias Ganagé and Mohammad Atallah.[29] Thus professional, ideological and political grounds for opposition to the IRFED appear to have been highly intricate, and it is hard to judge which of these criteria was most important.

This example illustrates the disunity of the reformist side regarding the major orientations of spatial management. The withdrawal of the IRFED plan at the end of Chehab's mandate is often attributed to the political weakness of the newly elected president, Charles Helou. But the disagreements between the adherents of different development doctrines, competing for the same work, may also have been a reason for such a shift.

ECOCHARD'S SECOND MASTER PLAN FOR BEIRUT

Michel Ecochard and his projects were better received by local professionals than were those of the IRFED, perhaps due to the Frenchman's good knowledge of Lebanon and its professionals. As mentioned earlier, he was not unknown in Lebanon.[30] Having served in Syria, where he acquired his vocation for town planning, he was later commissioned as town planner in Beirut from 1941 to 1943. His attempts to reform the town-planning administration did not fully succeed, and his plan was never adopted because of opposition from the local business community.

Ecochard's Moroccan experience (1946–52) is of great significance here. He attempted to plan Casablanca according to functionalist criteria, putting in practice the CIAM (Congrès Internationaux d'Architecture Moderne) theories he had recently espoused. Once again, his action would be strongly opposed by the business community. On the one hand, he tried in his planning to develop what he called 'housing for the greater number', an attempt at social housing for Moroccans. Those reflections on the adaptation of functionalistic ideas contributed to his renowned as 'urbaniste tiers-mondiste'.[31] On the other hand, this episode is also considered a typical example of colonial exportation of the functionalist ideology, brutally implemented irrespective of the needs of the local population.[32] This is one of the most important reasons behind criticisms of Ecochard.

During the Chehabist mandate, there was no concern for planning Beirut's suburbs until 1961, when the IRFED report dedicated three pages out of more than a thousand to the strategy for Beirut, outlining the necessity of deconcentralizing the capital. The proposal focused first on the transfer of important public administrations and ministries from the city core to the suburbs. Among the priority tasks identified, metropolitan planning was ranked only seventh.[33]

In 1961, Ecochard was commissioned to draw up a master plan for the 'Governmental Cities', a new administrative district outside the core of the capital (Fig. 5). This was not really a new idea, since the minister Joseph Chader had suggested it in 1956,[34] as had been suggested the five-year plan by the Council for Development and Planning in 1958. The first report on the subject was in fact the work of the famous Greek planner Constantinos Doxiadis in 1959.[35] Ecochard's contribution was his insistence on including in that report a sketch of the master plan for the suburbs, going beyond the mandate for the Governmental Cities. The official launch of the preliminary studies for this master plan came only at the end of 1962, after renewed pressure from Ecochard. The final report subsequently covered an area much bigger than that initially designed by the government, once again apparently due to Ecochard's initiatives. This brief chronology demonstrates that, rather than broader planning for the metropolitan area as advocated by Ecochard, the objective was to set up a plan for Governmental Cities, for which an architectural competition was launched in 1963 and won by local architects. This was a consequence of the administrative reforms that were initiated by the government after 1958, and implied a spatial rationalization of the administration.[36] It also met a strategic military aim: to protect the government from troubles like those experienced in Lebanon in 1958 before Chehab came to power.[37] Lastly, this expressed a symbolic objective – the need to connect the country and its peripheries to the capital by cutting the links between the administration and the congested and politically hostile central business area.[38]

Therefore the spatial order of Greater Beirut had been a secondary concern for the Chehabist government, as both the agenda and the debates reveal, and whatever importance this issue had in the last years of Chehabism was due to Ecochard's influence. Parts of Ecochard's master plan were finally adopted in 1964, but without urban development projects such as the new cities to the south of the capital or the workers' city in Jdeideh to the north, which were to be developed by public-private real estate companies. The government included parts of them on the plan as the 'G' zone, which would be studied further but in fact would never been implemented. However, the road scheme was fully adopted, as was the zoning though with much higher floor-area ratios (FARs) than initially proposed, which apparently greatly angered Ecochard.[39]

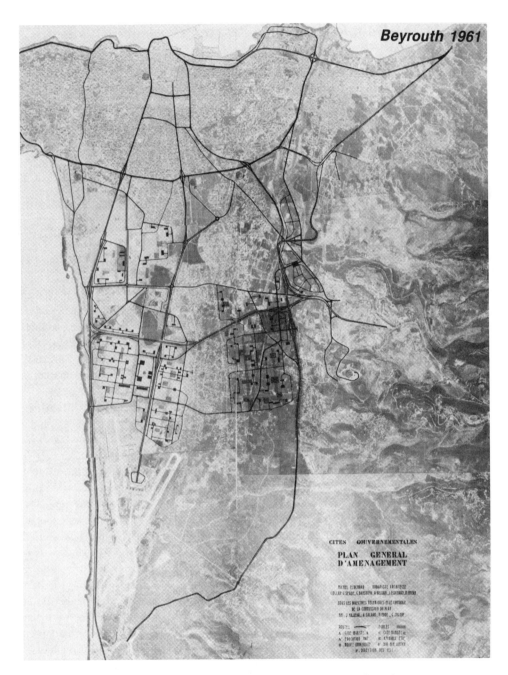

Figure 5. *Ecochard's Master Plan for the Governmental Cities (1961).*
Source: Urbanisme, 211, 1986

The Close Relationships Between Ecochard and the Lebanese Engineers

In contrast to the IRFED and its proposals, Ecochard and his plan were fully supported by most of the Lebanese experts. Ecochard had developed close links with Beirut and its local experts since the plan of 1943,[40] therefore his competence was broadly recognized, as Jean Eddé attested:

> By choosing the French town planner and architect Michel Ecochard, the Lebanese Government placed the fate of the capital in the hands of an experienced technician, renowned for his integrity and having to his credit, since 1934 [sic], a long practice of town planning in Lebanon: the master plan for Beirut (not adopted, but several main components of which became the spine of the actual one), master plans for Jounieh and Byblos (adopted), master plans for two new governmental cities at Bir Hassan and Chiah (adopted).[41]

His competence was probably not the only reason for the high regard in which Ecochard was held among the Lebanese engineers. The Frenchman also had forged numerous contacts in that milieu which certainly played in his favor. As town planner he had recruited and trained young engineers or architects.[42] As architect he had designed several projects including schools in Sidon, Baabda, Beirut and Tripoli. He was always associated, then, with local architects such as Amin Bizri, Fa'ez Ahdab and Henri Eddé. Therefore ties of friendship and of economic interest combined with his professional efficiency and prestige.

It is noticeable that some of the engineers and architects with whom Ecochard had worked, and to whom he remained close, were also members of the two independent administrative bodies that were supervising his work: the Higher Council for Town Planning and the Commission for Greater Beirut. They included representatives from different administrations, the president of the Order of Engineers of Beirut, as well as independent members.[43] Many of them were either members of the Council for Planning and Development, which was also in charge of evaluating the IRFED project, or at least belonged to the same circles. As members of the administration they had shared Ecochard's concern for town planning for as long as twenty years, so it is not surprising that they warmly welcomed most of his proposals, much more so than any of the IRFED proposals. While it is difficult to know whether some of the ideas in Ecochard's master plan were only inspired or the direct suggestions of members of these supervising committees,[44] it is certain that a number of the new measures meant to reform town planning were adopted as the result of the joint pressure exerted by Ecochard and local planners.

A good example of this are new land-reform instruments such as the real estate company. One of the problems for the Lebanese government in town-planning matters was its lack of land-management power. However, as early

as 1948 Joseph Naggear had proposed two new measures for land management: urban land pooling and reparceling, and mixed public-private real
estate companies.[45] Land pooling and reparceling had been adopted in 1954;
attempts were made in the Sands area, and after 1960 for Jounieh's new town
center based on Ecochard's master plan. Naggear's idea of a real estate
company deeply influenced Louis Fougères, a French state councilor close
to Ecochard, who had been invited by Chehab's government to draft the new
Town Planning Code in 1962 (article 19 of which dealt with such companies). Ecochard as well as all other local experts[46] had welcomed this proposal
with open arms.

In fact, the necessity of setting up a master plan for Beirut's suburbs was
undoubtedly one of the concerns shared by all of Lebanon's experts, and
pressure from these experts was certainly partly responsible for the launch
of the master plan. Those from the older generation, formerly in charge of
planning municipal Beirut, were concerned about the urban problems now
coming to prominence. They were aware that the master plan and zoning
they had set up in 1952 and 1954 had come too late and that these were
not strong enough to prevent urban sprawl: 'No real effort was made to issue
a zoning ordinance. [. . .] [The previously approved zoning ordinance] turned
out to be a consecration of a "de facto" status with a slight protection of the
small remaining unbuilt areas'. Georges Riachi, a reliable witness to this
process in his function as head of the municipal technical office, feared that
the lack of planning that had characterized the growth of Beirut proper was
now producing the same results in the capital's suburbs: 'So far, no serious
efforts have been made to include [the suburbs] in a Greater Beirut, at least
from the planning point of view'.[48] As a result he pressed for the creation of
an administration charged with urgently planning Greater Beirut, which
seemed to him to be the best way to avoid repeating past mistakes.

The call for the planning of Beirut had a more radical echo in the mouth
of younger planners such as Saba Shiber, whose chronicles in the *Daily Star*
were, for example, entitled: 'The Rescue of Beirut' and 'A Critical Glance at
Greater Beirut'.[47] Shiber frequently attacked government policies, comparing
them to those of other Arab countries like Kuwait, where he was also working.
The explicit references were to the Athens Charter or Le Corbusier. In this
respect, the choice of Ecochard was orthodox and could not be opposed.
Among local professionals, the idea that planning Beirut was an absolute
emergency seems to have been a consensus. Such a consensus also prevailed
in judging the master plan that was actually approved.

Indeed, the government's modifications of Ecochard's proposals bothered
the French planner more than they did the Lebanese experts. Although, as
mentioned above, he strongly rejected them, the plan was if not welcomed
then at least received with relief: 'Actually, the zoning approved on the
23 July appears as a compromise, maybe the best that could be reached

among all the surrounding difficulties. And one must have the courage to state it and to restate it in front of a public opinion more responsive to private interests than to the Public Good: this zoning is infinitely better than the previous void'.[49]

The concern of Lebanese experts regarding the implementation of the master plan was much greater than their concern with the raising of the FAR, which according to most of them was unavoidable. Commenting on Greater Beirut's plan, Henri Eddé noted that, although it was approved by the Higher Council for Town Planning (of which he was a member), the administration stopped its implementation because of a lack of staff. But many building permits had already been issued, 'blocking' that area: 'So, if such master plans are prepared, it is very good, but provided there is an administrative body able to receive them, to implement them immediately on the plans requested at the scale of 1/200 [sic], to get into the details, etc.'[50] More than the necessity of planning or the master plan itself, the Lebanese experts contested the ability of the planning administration and the government to implement the plans.

Disagreement and Competition

Despite this general consensus among Lebanese experts, a few points of debate or even disagreement on planning issues are also evident. Even if Ecochard was viewed as a kind of herald for a generation of Lebanese architects advocating urban reform, his master plan was nevertheless still subject to criticism. Two articles by Farid Trad in the journal of the Order of Engineers, *Al Mouhandess,* presented a very interesting counter-argument, the justification of which combined ideological, technical and professional interests. The first dealt with the highway network in Ecochard's master plan (Fig. 6). It recapitulated the prior attempts at planning such a network: Ecochard's 1944 plan and the master plan for the Beirut municipality in 1952. Adopting a tactic close to that of Corm mentioned earlier, Trad recalled their genesis. Ecochard's plan of 1944 included earlier ideas of Trad himself, from 1937, particularly a ring around the city core. As for the master plan of 1952, it was mainly a new version of the 1944 one. But once again, Trad emphasized the work of the Lebanese experts (and of himself) in the elaboration of the plan. The spirit of Ecochard's new master plan of 1963 differed very much from those previous attempts, which were the result of a common elaboration.

The master plan for the southern suburbs, approved after modifications in 1953 (Fig. 7), is of particular interest when compared to the proposal by Ecochard that was meant to replace it a decade later. One of Trad's critiques of Ecochard's plan focused on the twenty 'cloverleaf' interchanges he had proposed, which Trad described as mostly useless, wasting space and money.

The Lebanese engineer for his part praised roundabouts, which had given
the 1953 master plan the star junctions the design of which recalled Beirut's
city center and its Beaux-Arts conception, and this seems to have been a
point of contention in the elaboration of the plans. Ecochard strongly rejected
this concept in a letter to the director of town planning who was proposing
to modify such a roundabout in 'an area of the city still almost virgin', probably referring to the southern suburb: 'The new design has as its sole goal

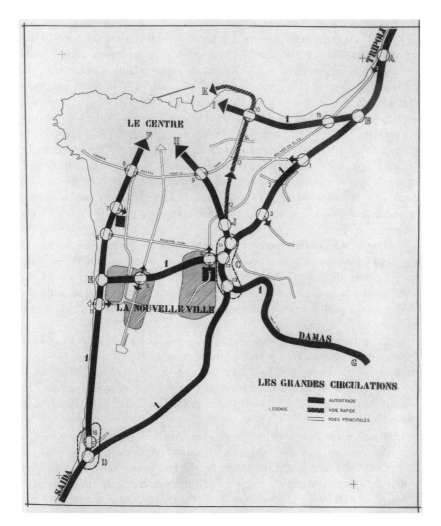

Figure 6. *Ecochard's Master Plan for Beirut and its Suburbs: The Traffic
Network (1963).*
Source: Institut français d'architecture, 61 IFA 36

to allow an alteration of this square into a star-shaped square, for which, as a modern town-planner, I can have no point of view other than to consider these forms as not only outdated, but also dangerous for automobile traffic'.[51] Moreover, they imposed on the surrounding neighborhoods, by extending the resulting radials, 'a complicated layout that would be difficult to organize and to ensure proper orientation for the housing'. Beyond the technical argument, this question of design is probably a sign that not all the engineers shared an affinity for modernist references, with a split lying between the older and the younger generation.

Farid Trad's opposition was not limited to this modernist reference. Many other critiques of the efficiency of Ecochard's proposals were raised in the articles. Another example is the zoning decreed in July 1964, where the density was very high, especially in the mountains. The chosen FARs, if applied, would have led to a far higher density than was needed according to the demographic indicators, and would have expanded urban sprawl into new regions: 'It is unfortunate that buildable zones and FARs accepted by Mr. Ecochard have been systematically extended without further thought. Some of the FARs, like those in sectors known as A1 or B1, which were already excessive in the previous zoning regulations, now pose an outright threat in a mountainous area [where] the population density will be allowed to reach and go beyond that of the most populous neighborhoods of the existing city'.[52]

Such criticism seems to be primarily directed at the government for having approved measures that were favorable to landowners, since the decree gave more value to their plots. But that argument may also be read as a criticism of Ecochard himself. Of course, the Frenchman did not agree with the governmental decree since the increase of the FARs reached values as high as one third. However, even in the initial draft of Ecochard's zoning ('the previous regulations'), this density was already very high. For instance, Trad would have preferred a FAR of 0.3 instead of 0.6 as had at first been proposed by Ecochard for the crests and the slopes. With 0.6, the FAR of the mountain areas would have been just below that of some parts of the immediate southern suburbs of Beirut, on flat land, where the lowest FAR was 0.75.[53]

Trad was in the best position to criticize Ecochard's project since he had been the developer of a subdivision at Ramlet el Baïda, in this southern district of Beirut, and one of the planners who had chosen such a low density in that suburb. According to observers of the time: 'Ecochard had to present a plan that could be considered as idealistic by landowners. If he had not done this, he would not have made it possible for the Higher Council of Town Planning to negotiate an acceptable position'.[54] But Farid Trad's view was that Ecochard had not been 'idealistic' enough, as if he had anticipated the raising of the density in order to make his master plan palatable, perhaps because

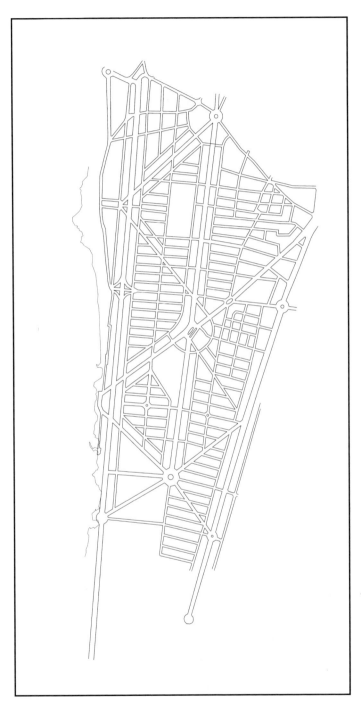

Figure 7. Master Plan
for Beirut and its
Southern Suburbs
(decree n°2616,
14 September 1953).
Source: General
Directorate of Town
Planning, Beirut redrawn
by the author

he was aware, after his first failure of 1943, of the importance of such a concession to landowners.

A further criticism of Ecochard's strategy can also be found in the first of Trad's articles. Commenting on the interaction between the Frenchman and the Higher Council of Town Planning discussing his proposals between 1961 and 1963, Trad stressed that the adopted network was the result of a gradual compromise between Ecochard's ideas and his own, a compromise that actually did not fully satisfy him: 'As it is, the plan called "Ecochard" still includes serious gaps'.[55] The meaning of this stance, 'called Ecochard', differed very much from that of Jean Eddé's stance cited (see note 38). It referred here to the fact that Ecochard had included several improvements suggested by his Lebanese counterpart, insinuating that the label 'plan Ecochard' inaccurately gives the Frenchman sole credit. Those improvements *vis-à-vis* Ecochard's first proposal in 1961 concerned, for instance, the adoption of a beltway independent of the existing road system, or the setting up of a freeway bordering Beirut's river and linking the harbor to the highway to Damascus (Fig. 8). With Trad denying the adequacy of the Frenchman's new solutions, the competition seems not to have been limited to technical or even ideological (modernist vs. Beaux-Arts) solutions.

It is interesting to note that, according to Trad, some of the highways proposed by Ecochard went through existing roads or subdivisions, which meant that the field survey was inaccurate. The field knowledge of the Frenchman and his team was attacked through Trad's critique, which implied that a Lebanese engineer (like Trad himself) would have been a better planner for this area. The competition, then, was between local and foreign planners.

This episode illustrates one of the main concerns of the Order of Engineers of Beirut, of which Trad was the president from 1958 to 1960. From its foundation in 1951, this organization tried to protect its members against unwelcome competition from foreign engineers as long as competent Lebanese were able to do the job. Hence it sought to contest the tendency of the government to hire foreign experts instead of giving projects to Lebanese engineers. The denunciation of this situation became at this time one of the slogans of the new generation at the head of the Order, which included Henri Eddé, Amin Bizri and their followers. Examples abound: in June 1964, a serious argument arose between Henri Eddé, then president of the Order, and the minister of public works, Georges Naccache, whom Eddé had accused of not applying the law restricting the work of foreign engineers.[56] The controversy surrounding Ecochard, a respected architect and town planner, was at least polite; however, other foreign experts, less recognized or less established in Lebanon than Ecochard, were victims of sharp and sometimes calumnious criticisms, among them the IRFED team and the architect Oscar Niemeyer and his project for a fair in Tripoli.[57]

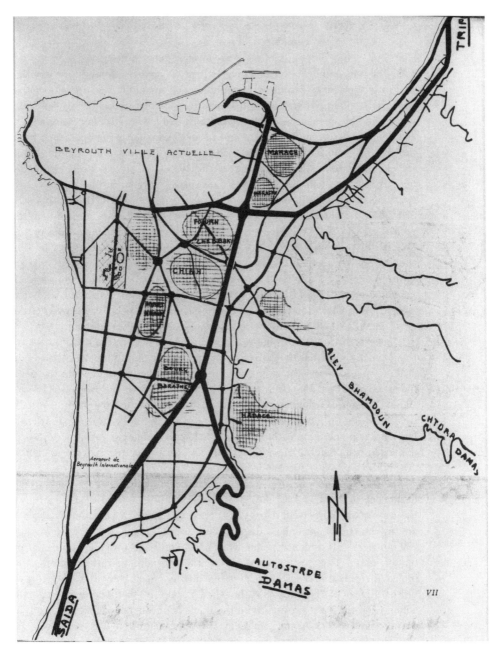

Figure 8. Trad's Traffic Network Proposal for the Master Plan of Beirut and its Suburbs (1963).
Source: Al Mouhandess, n°3, December 1964

CONCLUSION

The fate of the proposals of the two foreign experts discussed here would take different paths. Ecochard's master plan was partly adopted (but its original intentions were extensively modified) and his name remains associated with the setting up of urban regulations (even though he himself was not the author of the regulations). On the other hand, the IRFED's polarization scheme was never implemented, and its five-year plan was superseded by a much less ambitious one designed by the Council for Planning and Development in 1965. The name of the IRFED is still identified with its famous report but its proposals were essentially forgotten.

The contrasting attitudes of the Lebanese experts towards these proposals can surely be explained by the differences between the two foreign experts with regard to their theories as well as to the ways of implementing them. Ecochard's approach was rooted in a functionalist interpretation of the society. Beirut's problems related to traffic, housing, etc, therefore Ecochard's solution consisted mainly of physical design, setting up a hierarchical road network and sites for housing of different status and densities. Such an approach fits the vision and the means of action that Lebanese experts were used to, since their educational background was mainly technical.

Conversely, the IRFED's approach was concerned with the social needs of the population, seen as the gathering of weakened 'communities' (conceived of as cultural and geographical entities rather than religious ones).[58] In the field of urban planning, the IRFED found its inspiration in the work of Gaston Bardet,[59] a source which stood at the exact opposite of the Athens Charter that was the credo of Ecochard. The IRFED proposal did not meet with the same level of acceptance among the experts who had to evaluate it. Its priorities were contested, although the theory of growth poles on which they relied was 'orthodox' in the context of the 1960s, in France as well as elsewhere.

Yet the rejection of the IRFED proposal was not based on theoretical disagreement alone; it was also due to the attitude of the IRFED team and the way it was perceived. The IRFED tried to export to Lebanon its theory and methods of 'harmonized development', which happened to fit the political interests of President Chehab who subsequently bestowed his imprimatur on the team. This presupposed a new type of administrative action that included regional surveys by local teams and a central body, the newly organized Ministry of Planning, to gather data, set up the plan and coordinate all action. The IRFED team was to be the nucleus of this central administration during the years 1962–64, however this administration was perceived as authoritarian and led by foreigners (although it did include a number of Lebanese collaborators, albeit not at the top). Therefore, we can argue that the IRFED's failure is not only the failure of the political partisans of Chehab, but also that of the IRFED to find a common language with local experts and in making room for them in its projects. Many of them resisted and eventually were able to replace the IRFED's team when it left.

Ecochard's attitude was quite different. He knew Lebanon very well; to have his plan adopted, he made concessions (though such decisions can also be seen as responsible for the partial failure of the plan). After twenty years of practice in the country, his objectives and priorities were so closely shared by many local experts that it is hard to distinguish his ideas from their own. But this is the reason why Ecochard, though his ideas were largely supported, was also opposed. If his contributions were the same as those of local experts, the question inevitably arises as to why it was necessary to use him.

It is not surprising that the Chehabist era was the period when the Order of Engineers asserted itself, defending the place of Lebanese engineers in development policy. The confrontation between local and foreign experts also threw up a central question on the role of the foreign expert, revealing either a discrepancy between local and foreign ideas – which would justify local experts taking their country's future into their own hands – or a common view of the future, raising, then, the question of why foreign experts should be the dominant actors in the development field.

This shows that the idea of reformism in Lebanon in the 1960s (or in other contexts for that matter) must be handled carefully. Many reformers have been discussed here: Lebret, Chehab, Ecochard, engineers of the administration, young independent architects, economists and so on. They all were reformers, but of many different kinds and with strongly contrasted visions.

The distinctive fates of the IRFED and Ecochard schemes highlight the power of what might be called the cultures of planning. This is to be understood, according to the above examples, as articulating a set of ideas and practices, mixing international and local references as well as political and professional interests and networks. It delineates a new field of research that is especially useful for shedding light on the history of countries such as Lebanon, particularly in their renewed encounters with foreign planners.

NOTES

1. During the first months of 1958, civil riots took place in Lebanon between the pro-Western and mostly Christian faction of the president Camille Chamoun and his Arabist, pro-Nasser and mostly Muslim opponents. The end of the crisis was achieved by the landing of American troops and the election, in July, of Fuad Chehab, the chief of the Lebanese Army who had remained neutral. Being aware of the social and economic problems of the country, he promoted a policy of national unity. He first attempted to reform the administration by way of a confessional balance between Christians and Muslims, and to fight corruption by introducing new central and independent agencies in the administration. He then promoted a policy of social justice and of economic and regional development.

2. The Kataeb, the party of the Lebanese Phalange, had been founded by Pierre Gemayel in 1936 as a 'third-way party'. It was a nationalist party aimed at representing the Lebanese Christians, and was inspired by the Spanish and the Nazi experiences as well as the Czech one.

3. See Georges Corm (1964) *Planification et politique économique au Liban (1953–1964)*, Beirut: Imprimerie Universelle, and Kamal Salibi (1966) 'Lebanon under Fuad Chehab 1958–1964', *Middle Eastern Studies*, no. 2/3, pp. 213–22.

4. Denis Pelletier (1996) *Economie et humanisme: De l'utopie communautaire au combat pour le tiers monde. 1941–1966*, Paris: Cerf, p. 425.

5. As Father Lebret and his movement have had a great influence in Lebanon as well as in France, Latin America and some other countries like Senegal, Rwanda or Vietnam in the 1960s, but are now largely forgotten, it is worth giving some information about them. Influenced at the beginning of his priesthood by the ideas of Social Catholicism, Father Lebret attempted in 1929 to organize the defense of the fishermen's community in western France. He extentded this action in 1940 by seeking the help of the Vichy government before distancing himself from that regime. He then participated in the foundation of Economie et humanisme in 1941, a group with which he tried to broaden his social commitment. At the same time, he began to elaborate the theory of 'human economy', in which regional comprehensive planning was a key element, grounded on an innovative empirical survey methodology. These endeavors were recognized by the French Centre National de la Recherche Scientifique as early as 1944, ahead of the time when regional planning would become a priority for the French government facing the reconstruction of France. From 1947 onwards, the newly established relationship between Economie et humanisme and the Christian Democratic Movement formed the basis of a decade of close links between Father Lebret and Latin America. He directed several social surveys and development studies in Brazil (1952–56) and Colombia (1954). The success and popularity of these works motivated him to found the IRFED in 1958. The theory was then known as 'harmonized development'. Father Lebret, by now an international expert, greatly influenced the Pope as his economic adviser during the Vatican II council. See Georges Célestin (1981) 'L.J. Lebret et l'aménagement du territoire', *Les cahiers des Amis du père Lebret*, May, pp. 15–35, and Pelletier, op. cit.

6. Stéphane Malsagne (1997) *Les réformes économiques au Liban: 1959–1964*, DEA thesis, Paris IV University.

7. Archives of the IRFED mission, collected in the Fonds Delprat, have been consulted by permission of M. Raymond Delprat, former vice-director of the IRFED mission in Lebanon, at the Centre des Archives Contemporaines (hereafter the CAC) in Fontainebleau. IRFED, *Avant-projet de plan quinquennal (1964–68), Rapport du directeur,* Republic of Lebanon, Ministry of Planning (CAC, Fonds Delprat 87 AS, box 145).

8. Service A, GK/mm, *Avant-projet de plan sectoriel pour les investissements publics: l'urbanisation,* 15 July 1963 (CAC, Fonds Delprat 87 AS, box 124).

9. Ibid.

10. Created in 1959 as an autonomous agency linked to the Ministry of Social Affairs and the Ministry of Agriculture, it quickly became one of the main supporters of the IRFED's action. The IRFED team assigned it a major role in the implementation of its development policy.

11. Republic of Lebanon, Ministry of Planning, *Besoins et possibilités du Liban*, preliminary studies, 2 vols. plus 1 vol. of annexes, Mission IRFED Liban, 1960–1961.

12. Criticisms of the IRFED on financial and economic grounds are to be found in Salibi, op. cit. Raymond Delprat mentions some negative and positive opinions about IRFED's work: Raymond Delprat (1983) 'La mission IRFED au Liban', *Les Cahiers des Amis du Père Lebret*, March.

13. Raymond Delprat interview, 8 September 1999.

14. After his work with IRFED, Corm became an international consultant on Third World economics and finances. During the Lebanese war, he also wrote sociological and historical books about the geopolitics of the Middle East. After having been a virulent opponent of the reconstruction projects of Beirut, he became minister of finance in the first government of Emile Lahoud's mandate (1998–2000).

15. Corm, op. cit., pp. 39–40.

16. Ibid., p. 65.

17. Ibid., p. 46.

18. See Lebret, op. cit. The IRFED in Paris and its Lebanese branch, the Institut de Formation en vue du Développement, created in Beirut in 1963, were dedicated to the education of development specialists who were supposed to work in such regional institutions.

19. Note of the 15 December 1963 (CAC Fonds Delprat 87 AS, box 130).

20. Raymond Eddé, cousin of Henri Eddé, was a member of the first government of Chehab's mandate. But in the following years he became an opponent of the rise of what he perceived as a police state and corrupt elections. His opposition was also based on economic interests, as he represented the business class. His brother Pierre Eddé was a banker as well as a member of Parliament.

21. 'Are such abundant writings the testimony of the complexity of Lebanese problems or of the prolixity of the thoughts of the foreign experts?'(Corm, op. cit., p. 23). As Corm stated ironically, the IRFED produced such an abundance of documents that the government as well as the council might have found it difficult to read all of them.

22. Personal communication, Raymond Delprat (October 1999).

23. IRFED's five-year plan had actually been approved as the members of the commission were traveling in Belgium without having given their own final approval Stéphane Malsagne (1992) *Le chéhabisme sous la présidence du président Fouad Chéhab*, thesis, Paris IV University, p. 224.

24. Ministry of Planning (1963) *Dossier de base pour l'avant-projet de plan quinquenal. Troisième partie: les programmes d'orientation et d'incitation*, July (CAC, Fonds Delprat AN 87 AS, box 148).

25. *Note récapitulative sur le projet de plan 1958–1962* (CAC, Fonds Delprat 87 AS, box 129).

26. Henri Eddé (1997) *Le Liban d'où je viens*, Paris: Buchet Chastel, pp. 68–69.

27. Ibid., p. 67.

28. For example Joseph Naggear (interview, 21 October 1998) but not Assem Salam (interview, 6 November 1998).

29. Although it included only economists, the commission was also very hostile to the IRFED's plan. See *Réaction sur la note n°116 de la commission de planification*, note de Raymond Delprat, 23 April 1964 (87 AS, box 130) and a later document of the commission: Ministry of Planning, Commission for Planification, n°143 (EG/mm), *Principes directeurs pour l'établissement du plan quinquennal libanais (appréciation du projet présenté par la mission IRFED-Liban)*, p. 60, n.d. (CAC, Fonds Delprat 87, AS, box 130).

30. Marlène Ghorayeb (1998) 'The work and influence of Michel Ecochard in Lebanon', in P. Rowe and H. Sarkis (eds) *Projecting Beirut: Episodes in the Construction and Reconstruction of a Modern City*, Munich and New York: Prestel, pp. 106–21.

31. Samir Abdulac (1982) 'Damas: les années Ecochard (1932–1982)', *Les Cahiers de la recherche architecturale*, no. 10/11, p. 42.

32. Paul Rabinow (1989) *French Modern, Norms and Forms of the Social Environment*, Cambridge, Mass.: MIT Press, pp. 2–4; Jean-Louis Cohen and Monique Eleb (1999) *Casablanca: mythes et figures d'une aventure urbaine*, Paris: Hazan, pp. 289–313.

33. Mission IRFED-Liban (1961) *Besoins et possibilités de développement du Liban, Etude préliminaire, tome II, Problématique et orientation*, Beirut, Republic of Lebanon: Planning Ministry, pp. 269–71.

34. Joseph Chader (1956) 'Grands travaux et relèvement social', *Conférences du Cénacle*, X, pp. 7–12.

35. Hashim Sarkis (1998) 'Dances with Margaret Mead: Planning Beirut since 1958', in Peter Rowe and Sarkis (eds), op. cit., pp. 187–202.

36. Chehabist reforms by the administration created new institutions and amalgamated others. Rental of private buildings for some administrations was denounced as abusive, making it necessary to find new buildings. Besides, the will to develop the missions of the State increased the number of officials. It then became necessary to build additional offices.

37. During the riots mentioned in note 1, the president's palace had been located in a *sunni* neighbourhood, under the control of some of his political opponents.

38. Hashim Sarkis (1993) 'Territorial claims: Architectural and postwar attitudes toward the built-environment', in Samir Khalaf and Philip Khoury (eds) *Recovering Beirut, Urban Design and Post War Reconstruction,* Leiden, New York and Cologne: EJ Brill, pp. 101–27.

39. He was so angered that he refused to be held responsible for such a plan, as reported by Jean Eddé: 'Ecochard let it be known that he absolutely refused to associate himself with the approved plan – which therefore is still called Plan Ecochard'. Jean Eddé and Georges Attara (1965) 'Que faut-il penser du plan directeur des banlieues de Beyrouth?', *Horizons techniques du Moyen-Orient*, no. 5, January, p. 22.

40. See Jad Tabet (1998) 'From colonial style to regional revivalism: Modern architecture in Lebanon and the problem of cultural identity', in Rowe and Hashim, op. cit., pp. 94–104; and Ghorayeb, op. cit., pp. 118–20.

41. Eddé and Attara, op. cit., pp. 20–21. It is also worth mentioning Sidon's masterplan of 1956–58.

42. Including Grégoire Sérof or Rachid Bejjani. Jean Eddé, graduate of the Jesuits' Ecole supérieure d'ingénieurs de Beyrouth (ESIB) in 1947, worked in the administration of town planning and the municipalities before resigning and being recruited by Ecochard's team to collaborate on Jounieh's master plan.

43. Among the members of the Higher Council of Town Planning in 1962, it is worth mentioning Amine Bizri, representative of the General Directorate of Antiquities, Henri Eddé, then president of the Order of Engineers, Assem Salam and Joseph Naggear. As for the Commission for Beirut and its suburbs, it included in 1961 Joseph Naggear, Henri Eddé, Georges Riachi, Emile Yared, Henri Naccache, Fa'ez Ahdab and Assem Salam.

44. Assem Salam mentioned that the members of those commissions advised Ecochard regarding the economic or political opportunity provided by some measures, without being more precise (interview, 6 November 1998).

45. Joseph Naggear (1948) 'Equipement économique national et programme de grands travaux', in Gabriel Menassa (ed.) *Plan de reconstruction de l'économie libanaise et de réforme de l'Etat,* Beirut: Société Libanaise d'Economie Politique, pp. 296–98 and annex 17, pp. 575–86 (facsimile by the Order of Engineers of Beirut in 1998). Naggear's proposal was probably derived from the debates on the urbanization of the southern suburb that took place during Ecochard's study for Beirut's master plan in 1942–43.

46. For example Eddé, op. cit., p. 231.

47. Georges Riachi (1962) 'The structure and problems of Beirut', *Horizons Techniques du Moyen-Orient,* 1, p. 30. Georges Riachi was chief engineer at the Municipality of Beirut and as such head of the commission responsible for the zoning of Beirut in 1954. This article is the reprint of a paper prepared for the Arab Engineers Union conference held in Cairo in 1960: Georges Riachi (1963) 'The city of Beirut, its origin and its evolution', in Berger Morroe (ed.) *The New Metropolis of the Arab World,* New Delhi: Allied Publishers, pp. 82–100.

48. His chronicles are gathered in his later book, *Recent Arab City Growth* (Kuwait: Kuwait Planning Board, 1968). He was a Palestinian planner, educated in the US. He traveled back to Lebanon after the earthquake that struck the Jezzine area in 1956 to be employed in the Reconstruction Authority created at the time. Having co-founded ACE, the first regionwide Arab-based engineering partnership, he was later recruited at Dar al Handasah and then worked throughout the Arab world, mainly in Kuwait and Lebanon.

49. Eddé and Attara, op. cit., p. 22.

50. 'Une table ronde de l'Orient: Un urbaniste (anglais) et cinq architectes (libanais et français) discutent et diagnostiquent (William Holford, Henri Eddé, Assem Salam, Pierre el-Khoury, Raoul Verney, Jacques Liger-Belair)', *L'Orient,* 1 May 1964.

51. Letter from Michel Ecochard to the head of the Directorate of Town Planning, 30 August 1962 (Paris, Institut français d'architecture, Fonds Ecochard, box 32).

52. Farid Trad (1965) 'Observations sur le nouveau plan directeur d'urbanisme approuvé par le gouvernement', *Al Mouhandess,* no. 4, p. 17.

53. André Bricet provides a comparison between the zoning first proposed by Ecochard and that decreed; André Bricet (1965) 'Le plan directeur de Beyrouth et ses banlieues', *Horizons Techniques du Moyen-Orient,* 5, pp 8–9. The actual FAR of the zone A1 is 0.9, and the FAR of the zone I of the decree 2616 of 1953 for the southern suburb of Beirut is 0.75.

54. Eddé and Attara, op. cit., p. 21.

55. Farid Trad (1964) 'Réseau des grandes voies de circulation à Beyrouth et dans sa banlieue: Considérations critiques', *Al Mouhandess,* no. 3, p. 30.

56. See *L'Orient,* 2, 8, 11, 16 and 23 June 1964.

57. Raymond Delprat mentioned such sharp critiques (interview, 3 October 1998), also evident in the press. See for example the newspaper *Le Soir* during the year 1963. 'After Oscar Who?' is the significant title of an article by Saba Shiber complaining about the choice of the well-known Brazilian architect for Tripoli's fair (*Daily Star,* 29 July 1962).

58. Isabelle Astier and Jean-François Laé (1991) 'La notion de communauté dans les enquêtes sociales sur l'habitat en France', *Genèses,* no. 5, pp. 87–90.

59. Gaston Bardet (1945) *L'urbanisme,* Paris: Presses Universitaires de France.

CHAPTER 13

TOWARDS GLOBAL HUMAN SETTLEMENTS: CONSTANTINOS DOXIADIS AS ENTREPRENEUR, COALITION-BUILDER AND VISIONARY

Ray Bromley

University at Albany, State University of New York

From his first international consultancy projects in 1954 until his untimely death in June 1975, Constantinos A. Doxiadis[1] (1913–75) was a highly prolific analyst, designer and promoter of urban development. His engineering, architecture and planning firm Doxiadis Associates (DA) worked in more than forty countries designing some of the world's largest national housing programs and new city, urban expansion and urban renewal projects.[2] Doxiadis established and promoted a new academic discipline, which he called 'ekistics, the science of human settlements', and co-founded (with Jaqueline Tyrwhitt) the journal *Ekistics* as a discussion forum.[3] He authored or co-authored two-dozen books and hundreds of articles and planning reports, and organized twelve international conferences, known as the Delos Symposia, for many of the most creative intellectuals of the era.[4] In addition, in order to promote research and educational programs in ekistics and to support the development of a global network of scholars and practitioners, Doxiadis established the Athens Technological Organization (ATO) in 1958 and the World Society of Ekistics (WSE) was founded in 1965 at the initiative of various Delos participants. The ATO subsequently developed two branch organizations, the Athens Technical Institute (ATI), a vocational training school for support professionals in urban development, such as draftspeople and surveyors, and the Athens Centre of Ekistics (ACE), an international research, publishing and graduate education center.

Through his consultancy, teaching, writing, research and symposia, Doxiadis promoted the idea of 'human settlements' as a unifying concept enabling scholars and policymakers to link micro-, meso- and macro-scale processes throughout history and far into the future. He conceived of ekistics as a single spatial science extending from interior decoration and architecture to global spatial organization. His science of human settlements extended from the earliest forms of shelter in caves and huts, through the history of world urbanization and onward to what he called 'ecumenopolis, the inevitable global city of the future', an interconnected global urban network housing about 97 per cent of the world's population on 3 per cent of the world's land area. His prediction was that ecumenopolis would become a reality sometime between the years 2100 and 2200, and that the world's population would stabilize around that time at something between 15 and 50 billion.[5]

However questionable his assumptions and assertions, Doxiadis' efforts helped create the momentum for the United Nations (UN) Conference on Human Settlements (Habitat I) held in Vancouver in 1976, the establishment of the UN Centre for Human Settlements (UNCHS-Habitat) in Nairobi in 1978, and eventually for the Second UN Conference on Human Settlements (Habitat II) held in Istanbul in 1996.[6] These international events are linked with the creation of numerous national human settlements programs, agencies and secretariats, and a variety of university and non-governmental programs, centers, associations and journals advancing a human settlements agenda that embraces rural and urban areas and settlements of all types, shapes and sizes.

Doxiadis was one of many distinguished scholars, advocates, developers and consultants who sought to promote interest in global human settlements issues in the 1950s, 1960s and 1970s. Scholars such as Barbara Ward, Buckminster Fuller, Arnold Toynbee, Jean Gottmann, Jaqueline Tyrwhitt, Siegfried Giedion and Charles Abrams were good friends of Doxiadis and frequent participants in the Delos Symposia. In contrast, other important figures including Lewis Mumford, Le Corbusier, Lauchlin Currie, Father Louis-Joseph Lebret, Gaston Bardet, Kingsley Davis, José Luis Sert, Otto Koenigsberger, Jorge Hardoy, Walter Isard and John Turner were not closely associated with Doxiadis and either knew little of his work or held it in low esteem.

This chapter analyzes the career of Doxiadis and his rise to global prominence, focusing on how he used his background, nationality and social networks to build his firm, his research and training centers (the ATO, ATI and ACE), the study and practice of ekistics, the international network of public intellectuals associated with the Delos Symposia, and his influence on global human settlements scholarship and institutions. Three primary attributes are identified and discussed: his driving entrepreneurship in both business and scholarship; his global networking and coalition-building; and his ambitious vision, using futurology as a means to attract attention to his ideas and to influence global policy.

LIFE AND ACHIEVEMENTS

Constantinos Doxiadis (Fig. 1) was born in May 1913 in the Bulgarian town of Stenimachos.[7] At the beginning of the First World War his family moved to

Figure 1. *Doxiadis working on the roof of his Athens office, reviewing a design for Accra, Ghana. The Acropolis is in the background.*
Source: Life, vol. 61, no. 19, 7 October 1966, p. 55
© *David Lees/Timepix*

Athens. His father, Apostolos Th. Doxiadis, a pediatrician, fought for a time in the Greek underground seeking to 'liberate' the Stenimachos area, and later served in the Greek Government as Minister for the Resettlement of Refugees, Social Welfare and Health. The young Constantinos Doxiadis got his first degree in architectural engineering in 1935 from the Technical University of Athens where he was strongly influenced by the ideas and works of Dimitris Pikionis, an inspired teacher who combined a passionate interest in Greek art, history and culture with an imaginative comprehension of contemporary modernist architecture.[8] After his graduation, Doxiadis traveled to Germany for two years to complete a doctorate at the Berlin Institute of Technology, writing his dissertation on the scientific interpretation of urban design in ancient Greek ceremonial centers.[9] It was while he was in Germany that he was influenced by the work of Walter Christaller on central place systems,[10] Gottfried Feder on new towns and settlement strategies,[11] and Ernst Neufert on the standardization and mass production of buildings.[12] Returning to Greece he worked as chief town planning officer of Greater Athens and then as head of regional and town planning in the Ministry of Public Works.

However, Doxiadis' professional development was to be interrupted by the Second World War, during which he served as a corporal in the Greek Army and then as chief of a national resistance group against the German occupation of Greece, successfully collaborating with British military intelligence and directing sabotage operations against German military supply lines. In 1943 he began to draft a 20-year plan for the reconstruction of Greece that was eventually published in 1947.[13] At the end of the war he held the rank of captain in the Greek Army.

Soon after liberation in October 1944, Doxiadis was appointed undersecretary and director general of the Ministry of Housing and Reconstruction, and in 1948 coordinator of Marshall Plan aid for Greece's recovery program.[14] He represented Greece at the founding of the United Nations in San Francisco in 1945 and at the UN International Conference on Housing, Planning and Reconstruction in 1947, at which he presented his plans for reconstruction. He worked closely with the American administrators and technical specialists for postwar and Marshall Plan reconstruction, developing close personal friendships with several of them. Though Doxiadis tried to avoid petty politics by identifying himself as a planner, designer and manager, his record of resistance to the Nazi occupation combined with his disdain for communism identified him clearly as pro-Western and pro-capitalist. He saw the US as the vital superpower, and though later in life he wrote some affectionate criticisms of American ways,[15] he saw fluency in English and links with internationally oriented Americans as the keys to the reconstruction of Greece and his personal success. He built a reputation as an active, efficient, incorruptible person – the man who could make sure that reconstruction and development aid programs were successfully implemented in Greece, at the same time cultivating the image of a gracious Greek host, willing to entertain international visitors.

Despite his many loyal Greek colleagues, friends and subordinates who worked with him during the process of national reconstruction, Doxiadis had enemies in the political system. Greece had a tradition of corruption in construction contracting that Doxiadis frequently denounced, and his self-confidence, 'can-do' style and close relationships with American donors were viewed by some as arrogance towards Greeks, and by others as subservience to foreigners. Meanwhile, ideological and personal battles raged between communist and capitalist sympathizers, between those who had collaborated with the Nazi occupation and those who had fought against it, and between established political and regional factions. Despite this, Doxiadis survived in the postwar political system for over six years and through 21 changes of government, but in 1951, while hospitalized due to exhaustion and a perforated ulcer, his position in the Greek Government was abolished.[16] Disgusted at the way he had been treated, he traveled with his family to Australia where he spent two difficult years as a horticulturist growing tomatoes.

After his return to Athens in 1953, he gathered together some of his former colleagues from the reconstruction effort and established his consultancy firm,

DA. Making extensive use of the international network of contacts and friends he had built up over the years helped his firm obtain contracts for city and regional planning, settlement schemes, infrastructure projects and national housing plans. Some of these projects were in Greece, but most were in the Middle East, Pakistan and Africa. His old network of American friends from the Marshall Plan effort was particularly important in recommending Doxiadis and his firm, and in arranging a series of Ford Foundation consultancies. In 1958, after he had invested some of the profits from his firm in establishing the ATO as a non-profit institution, he began to receive major Ford Foundation research, training and technical assistance grants and contracts that eventually totaled over five million dollars.[17] Ford funding enabled him to conduct a major global study, 'The City of the Future', and provide extensive consultancy and training services to the Government of Pakistan, leading to his most famous contract – the plan for the new capital city of Islamabad (Fig. 2).[18]

DA expanded very rapidly in the 1950s and 1960s, becoming one of the world's largest housing, planning and infrastructure consulting firms. In the words of Philip Deane:

> By the time he was forty-nine (1962), in ten short years after he had returned penniless from Australia, Dinos Doxiadis had made himself the most important planner in the non-communist world, a planner whose ideas affect millions and millions of people, more people than are touched by the work of any of his colleagues . . . His projects were so spread out that he seemed to live in airplanes – not relaxing in his seat as he flew, but absorbing enormous quantities of information, answering letters, dictating endlessly into his portable tape-recorder.[19]

Similarly, Louis Winnick writes that, after Doxiadis established DA:

> The team's experience in large-scale redevelopment and as Marshall Plan administrators served them well at a time when the supply of such expertise was as scarce as its demand was high. DA scored one success after another. It burgeoned into a major architectural and engineering enterprise, with substantial contracts in more than a score of countries on four continents, hundreds of employees, and a number of branch offices, including one in Washington DC . . . DA lifted Doxiadis from penury to wealth. Yet, no matter how engrossed in commercial activities, he made time to refine the doctrines of Ekistics; the philosopher did not permit the entrepreneur to forsake the temple for the agora.[20]

Many of the plans DA prepared in the late 1950s and early 1960s were implemented, creating new cities and neighborhoods in the Middle East, Pakistan, Ghana, Zambia, Libya and other African countries. The firm also designed a large urban renewal project called Eastwick on the southwestern side of the City of Philadelphia, much of which was built,[21] and other smaller projects in US cities. In general, the DA housing projects were sensible and affordable, including congenial small public spaces in between low-rise housing structures. Housing was grouped into neighborhood units with community facilities, and these neighborhoods were separated from one another by wide,

Figure 2. *Standing on a mobile platform over a scale model of*
Islamabad, Doxiadis points out key features of his plan for the city.
Source: Life, vol. 61, no. 19, 7 October 1966, p. 56
© *David Lees/Timepix*

straight and visually unappealing transportation axes. Urban development projects provided the firm's main source of revenue, but Doxiadis was more excited by larger-scale projects and longer-term plans, even though they were never implemented, examples included his Trans-Asian Highway consultancy with the UN, River Plate basin development study with the Inter-American Development Bank, urban development plan for the State of Guanabara in Brazil, and his development study for the Mediterranean region of France.[22]

With the firm prospering, Doxiadis spent a great deal of time in the 1960s networking with leading scholars and public intellectuals around the world, and lobbying for increased global attention to the problems posed by rapid population growth and urbanization. His ATO and ACE training programs and summer schools in ekistics brought many young scholars to Athens from a wide range of countries, leading to the creation of a global network of ATO and ACE alumni. Meanwhile, he borrowed an idea from the International Congress of Modern Architecture (CIAM), which had held its 1933 Functional City Congress onboard a cruise ship in the Mediterranean, and had written its manifesto as the 'Charter of Athens'.[23] In summer 1963, less than four years after the final dissolution of CIAM, Doxiadis rented a cruise ship and held the first Delos Symposium, a 'by invitation only' event for distinguished scholars and friends including former CIAM secretary-general Siegfried Giedion and former CIAM committee member Jaqueline Tyrwhitt. Thus Doxiadis established the Delos Symposium format, which he repeated twelve times, and assumed some of the intellectual legacy of CIAM. In turn, after his death and until her own death in 1983, Jaqueline Tyrwhitt played a major role in continuing the ekistics movement.[24]

In the Delos Symposia, partly held aboard ship and partly on the Greek islands, Doxiadis developed a reputation for assembling a galaxy of talent, looking to the future, respecting and enjoying the treasures of Greek civilization and offering gracious hospitality. He made a special point of inviting leading architects and planners, for example Edmund Bacon, Buckminster Fuller, Colin Buchanan and Richard Llewellyn-Davies, as well as prominent scholars from across a wide range of disciplines, including such luminaries as historian Arnold Toynbee, anthropologist Margaret Mead, economist Barbara Ward, biologist C.H. Waddington, futurologist Herman Kahn, communication visionary Marshall McLuhan and sociologist Suzanne Keller (Fig. 3).

In the early 1970s, Doxiadis began to develop amyotrophic lateral sclerosis/motor neurone disease (ALS/MND), and this led to his death in June 1975 at the relatively young age of 62. As his medical condition worsened, he underwent periods of partial paralysis and difficulty in speaking, and yet he continued to work with great intensity to finish four books for presentation at the Habitat conference in Vancouver in 1976[25] and to continue the missions of the ATO, ATI, ACE, his firm, his journals and his Delos Symposia. His four books were formally presented to Habitat I by Barbara Ward and

Figure 3. *At Delos Two in July 1964, Doxiadis adds a dynamic element to Sir Richard Llewellyn-Davies' diagram, while Sir Richard (standing), Sir Robert Matthew (sitting) and Margaret Mead (back to camera) watch attentively.*
Source: Ekistics, vol. 18, no. 107, October 1964, p. 256

Buckminster Fuller, and Ward also wrote the principal theme book for the conference – *The Home of Man*. Enrique Peñalosa, secretary-general of the conference, concluded his preface to Ward's book: 'I would also like to join the author in paying tribute to the memory of the late planner and founder of the Ekistics movement, Constantinos Doxiadis, who must be acknowledged as the modern father of the science of human settlements'.[26]

Sadly, the intensity of Doxiadis' work combined with the unfortunate circumstances of his death created a situation in which he left no autobiography. His life, work and ideas can only be pieced together from his many publications, the projects undertaken by his firm, one brief and idiosyncratic biography published in 1965[27] and an enormous variety of correspondence, newspaper articles, archives and personal recollections. Since his death, one of Doxiadis' most loyal colleagues, Panayis Psomopoulos, has played the principal role in maintaining an ekistics office in Athens and in ensuring the continuation of the *Ekistics* journal and the WSE.[28]

DOXIADIS AS ENTREPRENEUR AND COALITION-BUILDER: FROM GREECE TO THE WORLD

Doxiadis was a global public intellectual who met a great number of leading politicians, businesspeople and scholars, and who was widely reported in the media – one of the only urban planners ever to have enjoyed such a remarkable celebrity status. In 1966, for example, the *Cleveland Plain-Dealer* headed an article on him 'Doxiadis is the World's Giant in Urban Planning', and went on to say: 'In music it's Beethoven. In baseball it's Ruth. But in city planning it's Doxiadis'.[29] In the same year, *Life* magazine profiled him as 'Busy Remodeler of the World'.[30] He showed great drive and ambition in his writing, in the expansion of his firm and in his global networking. The sheer volume of his work is quite extraordinary, greatly impressing the casual observer and overwhelming the serious scholar. Doxiadis wrote over twenty books and hundreds of articles, and coordinated two journals – the monthly *Ekistics* and the quarterly *DA Review*. His firm was responsible for planning projects in over forty countries, including planning the housing of over 10 million people. His research projects were global in scope, and his seminars and training courses brought hundreds of international participants to Athens for periods ranging from a week to two years.

Though his early academic training in Athens and Berlin might have prepared him for an academic career, the low salaries and lack of international prestige in Greek universities in the late 1930s, combined with the gathering storms of war in Europe, led him into professional practice, military resistance and postwar reconstruction. His regional vision of transportation and central place systems was framed both by Christaller's German scholarship and by the strategic visions of a resistance leader deciding which bridges should be blown up so as to best sabotage the German military machine.[31] His early writings on ekistics were published while he was engaged in postwar reconstruction work and were intended to support and orient those efforts.[32] Doxiadis' academic training and personal drive enabled him to develop a tremendous volume of publications and to mobilize others to write with and for him, but he was probably never tempted to seek a purely academic career. Instead, what he sought was the image of the scholar-planner-visionary, and he used this image very effectively to build his reputation, his international networks and his firm.

Doxiadis' conscious decision to establish ekistics as a new academic discipline rather than attempting to work within existing disciplines was a form of intellectual entrepreneurship. Ekistics studies the spatial distribution and organization of human activity as a single, integrated, pure and applied field. It embraces interior design, architecture, landscape architecture, urban design, civil and environmental engineering, planning, geography, regional science and all applied social and environmental fields concerned with activity patterns in space, and with how people use, organize and create spaces. It stretches in scale from the room to the whole world. Everything Doxiadis did in ekistics could indeed have been included within existing disciplines, but that would have meant dividing his work into separate portions. Instead he took the bold move of packaging his ideas and work as a unified new discipline, and giving that discipline a Greek name and some Greek terminology.

The new discipline of ekistics seemed to make academic sense. In the way it was packaged and presented, however, Doxiadis gave it a strong personal touch that increased its attractiveness during his lifetime but which has contributed to its relative obscurity since his death. The use of Greek words in books, articles and reports written in English was a distinctive Doxiadis brand image and also a way of saying that Greece had a longer tradition of urban analysis than any other nation on earth. Though primarily modern and futuristic in his approach to urbanism, and a corporate pioneer in mainframe computing in 1960s Greece, in his presentations Doxiadis also included frequent mentions of Greek archaeology and history. Greek words and traditions helped build his academic and corporate image, representing the continuity of history and civilization.

In building his reputation, his firm, his formative examplar discipline of ekistics and his global policy networks, Doxiadis was a brilliant exemplar of 'competitive advantage',[33] using his Greek nationality and location to the utmost. He managed to represent Greece as a font of ancient wisdom, science and urbanism, as a heroic and needy country worthy of support in its reconstruction, as a low-cost location to serve the Middle East, South Asia and Africa, a place of great hospitality and wonderful tourist opportunities.

During his doctoral studies in Berlin, Doxiadis gained attention because he studied Greece, often viewed as the main source of Western civilization, and developed new theories on the scientific planning of ancient Greek cities. During and after the Second World War, however, he downplayed his German connections and focused on speaking English and working through the Anglophone network of international development assistance. Working in Greece, he emphasized Anglo-American visions of efficiency while lavishly offering Greek hospitality and promoting Greek culture to his international visitors, which became DA's style. The firm was usually able to underbid Western European and North American competitors because professional wages were substantially lower in Greece. In almost all its international work, DA operated in English. Doxiadis' ekistic principles were presented as applicable throughout the world, and his lectures and project presentations were peppered with examples from a wide range of countries. For DA, the ATO, ATI and ACE, Greece was simultaneously a cradle of civilization, a tourist Mecca and a semi-peripheral capitalist nation that could offer cheap professional services on the global market. Few firms, research centers or universities around the world could rival the location of Doxiadis' offices on the side of Lycabettus Hill, with magnificent views of the Acropolis. For the many participants in ATO, ATI and ACE courses and seminars, Athens was a major attraction, and before or after the official events, international participants had abundant opportunities for low-cost tourism in Greece and Turkey.

The Doxiadis networks, established through his travels and friendships, through the work of DA, the ATO, ATI, ACE and WSE, through the circulation and contributions to the journal *Ekistics* and through the Delos Symposia, all contributed to building coalitions of interest for ekistics and global human settlements issues. Many colleagues, employees and students of Doxiadis were skeptical of some of his ekistic theories, prognoses and policy prescriptions, but most were sympathetic to his energy, commitment and drive, and almost all of them shared his fascination with human settlements. Especially in the 1960s and early 1970s, an informal international network of friendships and associations centered on his projects and institutions. In May and June 1976, many members of that network participated in the official Habitat I conference or in the parallel non-governmental Habitat Forum in Vancouver. In many senses, despite the death of Doxiadis a year before, the 1976 Habitat conference was the high point for the network, the moment when everyone involved could observe the global debates and feel part of a much larger human settlements community. Since then, of course, many members have died, others have lost contact and still others have moved on to new tasks and interests. Nevertheless, fragments of the network still survive, and the WSE continues to hold small annual congresses.[34]

As global theorist, futurologist and public intellectual, as practitioner of architecture, planning and engineering, and as self-styled 'ekistician', Doxiadis broke the bounds and norms of the Anglo-American academic world. He was unique, writing his own rules, inverting and transforming the 'center-periphery logic' of his era and demonstrating how sophisticated actors can 'play the system'. He strengthened the brand image of his firm and institutions by making his views known through abundant books, articles and speeches, and by closely identifying his firm and discipline of ekistics with those views.

Though Doxiadis' worldwide fame grew rapidly, it faded somewhat when his debilitating illness became apparent in the early 1970s, forcing him to reduce his traveling and public appearances, and it diminished quite rapidly after his death. His energy, charisma, personal history and ekistic discourse contributed to his appeal, but he was really projecting himself rather than building permanent institutions. His setting himself apart from other disciplines, with a proper identity as an ekistician, proved a problem after his passing as the mainstream architecture, planning and urban studies journals either gave him no obituary or granted him no more than a few lines, leaving only *Ekistics* and *DA Review* to produce major tributes, recirculating the message to a gradually waning population of converts rather than opening new horizons to a broader public. Doxiadis' Greek national identity created similar problems as few powerful Greeks shared his visionary internationalism. After his death, little official support was provided to continue the ATO, ATI and ACE, and there was no move to create a major global center for human settlements studies in Athens that might have permanently memorialized his life and work.

DOXIADIS AS VISIONARY: FROM ANTHROPOS TO ECUMENOPOLIS

Doxiadis' writing was characterized by extraordinarily ambitious long-term forecasting, often stretching two centuries into the future. Starting with his late 1950s 'City of the Future' study, funded by the Ford Foundation,[35] he became known for asking and answering the biggest long-term questions: What will be the world's total population in 50 years time, 100 years time and 200 years time? What percentage of that population will live in urban areas? Where will those urban areas be located? His style was to ambitiously increase scale in both space and time, always tending towards the global and the next century. This gave him tremendous international appeal because the issues he discussed were important to everyone, wherever in the world they were located, and because no one was able to prove him wrong as all his predictions were too far into the future. Overall his style was that of the global optimist, confident that policy changes and technological developments would help humanity avoid impending disasters and steer the world on a course towards greater prosperity and improving quality of life. Without specifying in detail how global changes would take place, he also implied that communism and the Cold War would somehow disappear, that the disparities in income and wealth between rich and poor nations would somehow diminish, and that the world would move towards a more multilateral international system culminating in some form of global federalism. When pressed as to how such changes would occur, he called on economists, sociologists and political scientists to find the necessary solutions.

In structuring ekistics, Doxiadis identified five elements of human settlements: anthropos (people as individuals), nature, society, shells (buildings) and networks (roads, utilities, transportation, communications and administrative boundaries). He saw settlements as rationally organized according to function, technology and scale, into a nested hierarchy of central places. On the global scale, he classified human settlements into a 15-level nested hierarchy of 'ekistic units' – man, room, dwelling, dwelling group, small neighborhood, neighborhood, small town, town, large city, metropolis, conurbation, megalopolis, urban region, urban continent and ecumenopolis. He described the highest levels of the hierarchy as still in process of formation as functional units.

Doxiadis sought to analyze all problems and topics both spatially and temporally, and whenever possible he conceptualized them in diagrammatic terms. His analyses always identified trends and projected them into the future, and defined a scale of concern and then sought to analyze problems at that scale, at the next smaller scale and at the next larger scale. He argued that economic development, population growth, urbanization, technological progress and globalization were inexorable forces in the world. He believed that global problems could be overcome by the concentrated effort and focused interaction of the most talented individuals from a wide range of disciplinary backgrounds. The task of the ekistician was to gather these individuals and to focus them on the problems and potentials of human settlements. Doxiadis used this multidisciplinary model in structuring the Delos Symposia, assuming the role of team leader and matchmaker.

Doxiadis offered a distinctive and principled vision of urbanism that opposed skyscrapers and automobile-dependent suburbanization (Fig. 4), arguing that modern cities should be dense and low rise with substantial provision of public transportation. They should be built with grid plans, a hierarchy of transportation and utility corridors, superblocks, and neighborhood units (Fig. 5). He believed that these principles guaranteed high levels of functional efficiency together with 'a human scale' at the local level – walkable, livable neighborhoods with public spaces and services to facilitate recreation and social interaction. He recommended that national governments prepare national urban development strategies and national housing programs so as to accommodate and canalize the inevitable processes of population growth and urbanization (Fig. 6). He argued that traditional urban growth was dysfunctional because the core areas of the city must be continually renewed as the periphery pushes outwards. Instead of expanding in all directions, cities should expand preferentially in one direction, creating a gradually widening linear city known as *dynametropolis* or *dynapolis*. Such cities, exemplified by Islamabad in Pakistan and Tema in Ghana, both planned by DA, were designed to facilitate continuing growth without the need to demolish and rebuild existing areas. Doxiadis advocated historic preservation and argued that historic settlements and sites should be preserved by channeling urban development elsewhere.

Doxiadis' roles as global optimist and believer in the power of capitalist economic development[36] were vital in the growth of his firm and his global reputation. He had many friends in big business and international organizations, including several who had worked on the postwar reconstruction of Europe. This provided a flow of public-speaking engagements and consultancy contracts, opportunities that would not have been available had he joined either of two opposing schools: the neo-Marxist theorists of imperialism who

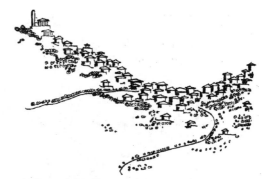

58. Anthropos has always created a social balance in his cities

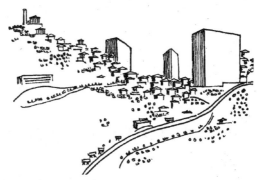

59. there is a loss of balance today in our cities

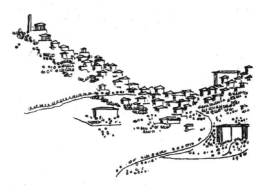

60. we must create a new balance

Figure 4. Doxiadis' rejection of skyscrapers.
Source: C.A. Doxiadis. Building Entopia. (New York: W.W. Norton, 1975),
p. 61

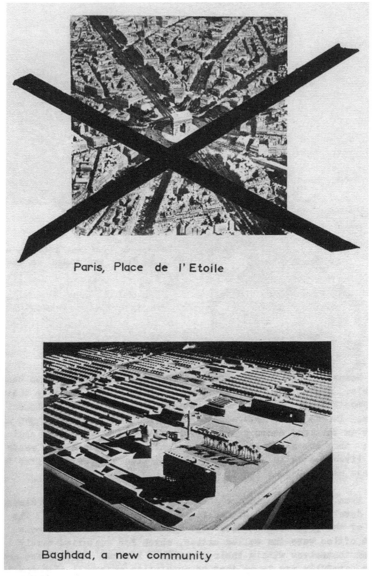

Paris, Place de l'Etoile

Baghdad, a new community

Figure 5. *Doxiadis' view that traditional urbanism such as the Étoile area of Paris is outmoded because of the associated congestion and need for urban renewal. Instead, he recommended the model of his superblock neighborhoods in Baghdad, with wide linear transit corridors and capacity for expansion by adding more superblocks.*
Source: C.A. Doxiadis. Dynapolis: The City of the Future (Athens: Doxiadis Associates, 1960), p. 5

believed that most poor countries were condemned by the prevailing global political economy to situations of poverty, growing indebtedness and cultural and technological dependency,[37] or the environmental pessimists who believed that population growth and economic development would consume the world's resources and lead to global warming, mass extinction of species and an eventual Malthusian crisis of population and food supply.[38] In his speeches, writings and symposia, Doxiadis was very successful in indicating that serious global problems needed attention, and that these problems could be solved by bringing together the best minds to work as a coordinated multi-disciplinary team. His 'can-do' approach and love of the distant future was shared by such visionaries as Buckminster Fuller, Herman Kahn and Marshall McLuhan,[39] and together they built networks of interaction and support for one another.

From the early 1960s onwards, the global optimists came under increasing attack. Books like those of Jane Jacobs, Rachel Carson and Robert Goodman,[40] combined with the growing movement in the US and Western Europe against the Vietnam War and the discrediting of Robert McNamara's technocratic vision of military victory, were subtly changing the climate of academic and policy discourse. The UN development decades did not seem to have worked for most of the world's poorer nations, the Cold War was

Figure 6. Doxiadis' delight in designing congenial human-scale neighborhood places – 'Gossip Square' in Mosul, Iraq.
Source: Philip Deane. Constantinos Doxiadis: Master Builder for Free Men (Dobbs Ferry, New York: Oceana Publications, 1965), p. 140

intensifying and the post-Second World War reconstruction mystique of planning was wearing thin.[41] Doxiadis responded in part by increasing the
discussion of historic preservation, community participation, ecological and
environmental issues in his symposia and journals. His final book, *Ecology
and Ekistics*, edited and completed posthumously by Gerald Dix, was
intended to continue this adjustment.[42]

The most influential dimension of Doxiadis' vision was in his analysis of
the emergence of metropolitan regions and the concept of megalopolis. This
inspired his friend and frequent Delos participant Jean Gottmann, and also
influenced the work of such geographers as Brian Berry and Peter Hall.[43] In
helping to create the vision of expanding and interlinking metropolitan
regions along such axes as Boston–Washington and Tokyo–Osaka, across
national frontiers in such areas as San Diego–Tijuana and Amsterdam-
Rotterdam–Antwerp–Brussels, and across the heart of Western Europe with
'the Blue Banana' axis from Birmingham to Milan,[44] Doxiadis expanded the
horizons of city and regional planning and created new spheres of action.

The most controversial element of his vision was probably his concept of
ecumenopolis, focused around a distant global future (Fig. 7). This was
discussed in many of his books and articles, and in the final version of these
prognoses, published in 1974 as a book, Doxiadis and his DA colleague and
associate John Papaioannou asserted that

> Ecumenopolis will come into being, binding together all the habitable areas of
> the globe as one interconnected network of settlements operating as one func-
> tional unit . . . The beginning of Ecumenopolis could actually take place at any
> time between 2100 and 2200. [p. 339] Its population may be of the order of 20
> billion, and . . . will remain stable for quite some time. [p. 342] In Ecumenopolis
> only 2.5 percent of the total land surface of the globe will be built up. [p. 344].
> The population of the world . . . may not necessarily become one state, but it
> must become some kind of a federation of equal people. [p. 344]. A real
> Ecumenopolis will need a unified global government of some sort. [p. 388] As
> traditional sources of energy are depleted, nuclear energy seems to promise to
> maintain this growth. [p. 209] There is good hope . . . [for] the coordination of
> all transportation, utility and communication networks, which might be termed
> 'coordinets'. [p. 333] The goal will eventually be reached when Anthropos can
> travel within the whole of Ecumenopolis in 40 to 50 minutes, traveling through
> tunnels or maybe a satellite for the longest distances between primary centers
> at 20,000 km [12,400 miles] per hour [p. 349].[45]

Such incredible visions of 12,400 miles-per-hour tunnel vehicles connecting Tokyo to Buenos Aires, Montreal to Sydney, and all other major cities to
one another, are more appropriate for science fiction novels than for the
discourse of planning practitioners. Characteristically, however, Doxiadis and
Papaioannou also included many statements that few would find objection-
able, for example:

Anthropos' only long-term hope is to establish a genuine partnership with Nature; his destiny is inextricably linked with that of the biosphere, that fragile and infinitely complex living system which forms the organic skin of the planet. [p. 340] If Anthropos continues to follow his present trends, then all local and national cultures will tend to be eliminated and a new global culture will develop based on the completely new systems of life that will then exist . . . We as citizens of the 20th century cannot fail to see the great dangers and threats involved in the disappearance of all the existing regional cultures. . . . As cultural diversity is surely desirable we expect that the majority of people are likely to realize this and therefore try and achieve it. [p. 389] We must set our goal as harmony between the five elements that make up human settlements – Anthropos, Nature, Society, Shells and Networks. Growth takes place naturally; harmony can be achieved through the conscious action of Anthropos. [p. 396]

The book *Ecumenopolis* was simply the most extreme example of Doxiadis' style, a captivating mixture of insight, futurology, prescription and preaching, but also a very personal style that could seem pedantic and patronizing. Nathan Silver, a reviewer of Doxiadis' mammoth textbook *Ekistics*, published in 1968, commented that: 'He so belabors the obvious, so claims credit for it, that even his siding with the angels at last seems sheer hubris'.[46] Silver went on to critique what many would consider Doxiadis' most questionable planning study, the lavish three-volume Doxiadis Plan for the Detroit Metropolitan

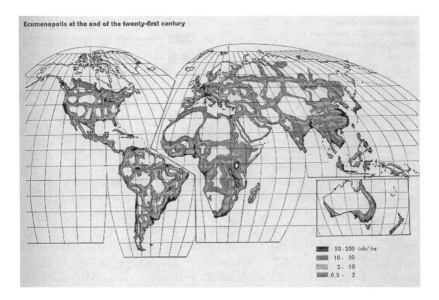

Figure 7. *Ecumenopolis at the end of the 21st Century – one of the many versions of Doxiadis' world map.*
Source: C.A. Doxiadis. Ekistics: An Introduction to the Science of Human Settlements (New York: Oxford University Press, 1968), p. 377

Region,[47] commissioned by Doxiadis' old friend and admirer Walker Cisler, chairman of the Detroit Edison Corporation, who had assisted Doxiadis in the postwar restoration and expansion of the Greek electric power system:[48]

> When the Ekistician gets finished taking account of nature, man, society, shells, networks; how they interrelate and also correlate with residence, commerce, industry, administration, defense; how these are affected by money, labor, materials, land, and so on, it's no surprise that 49 million alternatives appeared in a Doxiadis study of the urban Detroit area. So Doxiadis hit upon his IDEA method (Isolation of Dimensions and Elimination of Alternatives – no procedural explanation) augmented by his CID method. Fifteen arbitrary whacks later he's down to one 'alternative'. Logic wins again, as that character in 'L'il Abner' says when he socks somebody on the nose.[49]

In accordance with the one-in-49-million best development option, Doxiadis projected that between 1970 and the year 2000 the Metro Detroit area population, including portions of Ohio and Ontario, would rise from 8 to 15 million and that the expanded metropolis should form a 115-mile-long (185-kilometer-long) urban corridor running northeastward from Toledo, Ohio through downtown Detroit to Port Huron, Michigan, with a major new concentration of urban development to the northeast of the current city in the Richmond-St Clair area. In reality, the population in 2000 did not approach 10 million, linear development is mainly concentrated in the southern sections between Toledo and Detroit, and Richmond-St Clair is largely undeveloped. Meanwhile, in over 1,100 pages on the Metro Detroit area, Doxiadis had no analysis of the causes and consequences of the Detroit riots of June 1943 or July 1967, and no discussion of the race and class dimensions of suburbanization.[50] His visions of the distant future conveniently neglected the most pressing elements of the 1960s reality, and those same elements are still vital to understanding the Metro Detroit region.[51]

The assumption that poor nations could rapidly develop their economies and achieve prosperity enabled Doxiadis to prescribe the same urban development solutions throughout the world. In his 1966 book on *Urban Renewal and the Future of the American City*, for example, he recommended that US housing and urban redevelopment officials learn from his growth prescriptions for Khartoum, Islamabad, Greater Accra, Caracas, Karachi and Athens.[52] Amazingly, given the significance of the Civil Rights movement, the controversies over school desegregation and busing, and the race riots that had occurred in many US cities at the time,[53] he did not discuss race or segregation in the book, focusing exclusively on the physical growth, form and traffic flows of the American city.

Re-examining Doxiadis' linear urban expansion plans more than 30 years after they were written, there is little sign that his prescriptions guided urban development. He prescribed axial growth for Paris, Caracas, Copenhagen, Karachi, Beirut[54] and many other cities (Fig. 8), but in reality they seem to

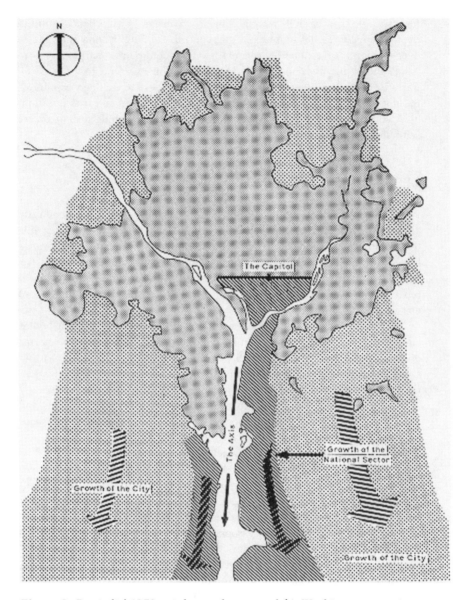

Figure 8. *Doxiadis' 1958 axial growth proposal for Washington, growing downriver along the Potomac axis. Since 1958 this proposal has been largely ignored, and the metro area has sprawled outward in all directions. The area with least development is south of the city and east of the Potomac River.*
Source: C.A. Doxiadis. Architecture in Transition (New York: Oxford University Press, 1963), p. 107

have sprawled out in all directions. Linear expansion in accordance with the *dynametropolis* model requires strong central planning, willing and able to override local governments, speculators and community participation to install infrastructure along planned transportation axes and to force developers to build in predetermined patterns along these axes. Such conditions did not exist in any of the cities where Doxiadis worked and it is questionable whether they will ever exist. Futurology and preaching do not create self-fulfilling prophecies.

LEGACIES AND LESSONS

Doxiadis' career is both an inspiration and a warning. He was a tremendously ambitious, optimistic and energetic figure who sought to broaden the agenda of planning. Many times, however, his ambition and penchant for long-range forecasting and global generalization led him to erroneous conclusions. His voluminous writings often educate, inspire and amuse, but they can also seem repetitive, pedantic and simplistic, full of typologies, banal illustrations and obscure terminology.

Though Doxiadis worked closely with Anglophone scholars, funding bodies and clients, he refused to subordinate himself to the Anglo-American norms of disciplinary identity and specialization. He tried to be a universal synthesizer, visionary and public intellectual in an era of increasing specialization. He was an obsessive systematizer and classifier of knowledge, constantly generating terms, typologies and theories. He reinvented many concepts and gave them new names in the process, but many considered his messages repetitive, inconsistent and full of clichés. He did so many things that it is difficult to make an overview of his achievements.

Doxiadis had a magnetic personality and a massive social network, yet was often considered a 'chieftain' or 'boss' – a personalistic leader who dominated his subordinates, sought pacts with other leaders and worked with public intellectuals and international celebrities keen to enjoy the surviving aura of Greek civilization. His association with the rich, famous, powerful and reputedly brilliant gave his work an elitist, top-down tone, and most of his real-world planning had no participation by local citizens. He often seemed politically, socially and environmentally insensitive, and was largely oblivious to the significance of race, class and gender. He was a late convert to environmentalism and public participation, preaching these virtues but not practicing them.

During his lifetime, Doxiadis was able to build a global network for ekistics and a major center of activity in Athens, but after his untimely death most of the activity faded away. Though there are still thousands of people around the world who participated in his projects, courses and symposia, and who remember his extraordinary energy, most contemporary planners have little idea of who he was or what ekistics is. The great enigma, of course, is to guess what impact he would have had if he had remained in good health throughout the 1970s and 1980s. Would he have significantly changed the history of Habitat I, the United Nations Habitat Secretariat and global human settlements policies? Would he have developed a secure network of academic and governmental institutions for his formative discipline of ekistics? Or would he have become an anachronism as more of his predictions were proved wrong and his most famous associates like Barbara Ward, Margaret Mead and Buckminster Fuller grew older and passed away?

Echoing the ancient Greek legend of Daedalus, who designed the labyrinth of Knossos to contain the Minotaur, a man-eating monster, Doxiadis also tried to contain a monster – a global *dystopia* that was based on rapid population growth, urbanization and environmental destruction. He designed a strategy for deliberate urbanization that would create a global *entopia* – excellent real cities that could facilitate economic, technological and social development while preserving the environment.[55] He created a grand vision and an international network, but his vision was flawed and rapidly fell into obscurity after his death. Nevertheless, Doxiadis' extraordinary career helps us understand six major aspects of planning: its many scales, and how they interrelate in both space and time; its disciplinary boundaries; its links with architecture, geography and regional science, and the distinctions between these disciplines; the significance and limitations of futurology and visioning; the importance of a global picture and agenda; and the many ways in which ideas can be diffused to a wider audience.

NOTES

1. For library research on Doxiadis, it is important to take into account various alternative spellings of his name. Constantinos is sometimes written Konstantinos, and in some of his early publications Doxiadis anglicized his first name as Constantine. Apostolos, his middle name and the first name of both his father and his son, may be omitted or written Apostolou. Doxiadis may also be written Doxiades. To his friends he was often known by the nickname 'Dinos'. The notes below use whatever spelling is used in the particular reference.
2. DA projects were extensively reported in Doxiadis' books, in hundreds of studies and reports delivered to clients, and in the firm's corporate journal, *DA Review*. After Doxiadis' death, DA was administered for a time by his son Apostolos, but it was eventually sold and now continues in name only, with no formal association with Doxiadis' intellectual tradition.
3. The journal began publication in 1955 and continues today. The most comprehensive overview of ekistics as a discipline is C.A. Doxiadis (1968) *Ekistics: An Introduction to the Science of Human Settlements*, New York: Oxford University Press.

4. The first Delos Symposium was held in 1963 and the meeting continued on an annual basis until the tenth symposium in 1972. There was no Delos Symposium in 1973, but instead Doxiadis convened a smaller conference called 'A City for Human Development'. The eleventh Delos Symposium was held in 1974, and the twelfth in July 1975 just two weeks after Doxiadis' death. Each of the symposia was reported in an issue of *Ekistics* shortly after the event.

5. C.A. Doxiadis (1966) *Urban Renewal and the Future of the American City*, Chicago: Public Administration Service, pp. 73–9; C.A. Doxiadis and J.G. Papaioannou (1974) *Ecumenopolis: The Inevitable City of the Future*, New York: W.W. Norton.

6. Graham Searle with Richard Hughes (1980) *The Habitat Handbook*, London: Earth Resources Research.

7. The principal biographical sources for Doxiadis are: Christopher Rand (1963), 'The Ekistic World', *New Yorker*, 11 May, pp. 49–87; Philip Deane (1965) *Constantinos Doxiadis: Master Builder for Free Men*, Dobbs Ferry, NY: Oceana Publications; *Ekistics*, vol. 41, no. 247 (June 1976), special issue entitled 'C.A. Doxiadis 1913–75: Pursuit of an attainable ideal'; *DA Review*, vol. 12, no. 97 (July 1976), special issue; *Ekistics*, vol. 62, no. 373/374/375 (July–December 1995), special issue entitled 'Forty Years of Ekistics on Persisting Priorities'.

8. Panayis Psomopoulos (1993) 'Dimitris Pikionis: An indelible presence in modern Greece', *Ekistics*, nos 362–363 (September–December), pp. 253–75.

9. Originally published in German in 1937 under the title *Raumordnung im griechis-chen Städtebau* (Heidelberg: Kurt Vowinckel Verlag), it was translated and edited by Jaqueline Tyrwhitt and published as Constantinos A. Doxiadis (1972) *Architectural Space in Ancient Greece*, Cambridge, MA: MIT Press.

10. Walter Christaller (1966) *Central Places in Southern Germany*, Englewood Cliffs, NJ: Prentice-Hall, first published in German in 1933 as *Die zentralen Orte in Süddeutschland* (Jena: Gustav Fischer).

11. This work was underway at the Berlin Charlottenburg University while Doxiadis was there, and was eventually published as Gottfried Feder (1939) *Die neue Stadt*, Berlin: Verlag von Julius Springer.

12. Ernst Neufert (1970) *Architects' Data*, London: Crosby Lockwood, first published in German as *Bauentwurfslehre* (Berlin: Bauwelt-Verlag, 1936).

13. Deane, op. cit., p. 34.

14. John J. Papaioannou (1976) 'Constantinos A. Doxiadis' early career and the birth of ekistics', *Ekistics*, vol. 41, no. 247 (June), pp. 313–19.

15. C.A. Doxiadis (1972) 'Three letters to an American', *Daedalus*, vol. 101 (Fall), pp. 163–83.

16. Louis Winnick (1989) 'The Athens Center of Ekistics: The urban world according to Doxiadis', unpublished manuscript, New York: Ford Foundation Archives (May), p. 9.

17. Winnick, op cit., p. 2.

18. Doxiadis Associates (1960) *The Federal Capital: Principles for a City of the Future*, Athens: Doxiadis Associates. See also Frank Spaulding, 'The politics of planning Islamabad: An anthropological reading of the Master Plan of a New Capital', unpublished paper presented to the seminar 'Imported and Exported Urbanism?', Beirut, December 1998.

19. Deane, op. cit., p. 55.

20. Winnick, op. cit., p. 11.

21. Albert M. Cole (1985) 'Eastwick revisited', *Ekistics*, no. 312 (May/June), pp. 239–46.

22. CEDUG and Doxiadis Associates (1972) 'Guanabara: A plan for urban development', *Ekistics*, vol. 34, no. 202 (September), pp. 209–10; Doxiadis Associates
(1972) 'The River Plate Basin: A methodological study for its integrated development', *Ekistics*, vol. 34, no. 202 (September), pp. 181–97.

23. Eric Mumford (2000) *The CIAM Discourse on Urbanism, 1928–1960*, Cambridge,
MA: MIT Press, p. 73.

24. See the special issue entitled 'Mary Jaqueline Tyrwhitt in Memoriam', *Ekistics*,
vol. 52, no. 314/315 (September–December 1985).

25. C.A. Doxiadis and J.G. Papaioannou, *Ecumenopolis*, op cit.; C.A. Doxiadis (1975)
Anthropopolis: City for Human Development, New York: W.W. Norton; C.A.
Doxiadis (1975) *Building Entopia*, New York: W.W. Norton; C.A. Doxiadis (1976)
Action for Human Settlements, New York: W.W. Norton.

26. Barbara Ward (1976) *The Home of Man*, Harmondsworth: Penguin Books, p. ix.

27. Deane, op. cit.

28. The ATO, ATI and ACE were closed down after Doxiadis' death but the WSE still
continues. Like the journal *Ekistics*, its continuation is based on the knowledge,
energy and talent of Panayis Psomopoulos, who continues to administer a small
Ekistics Office in Athens, and to serve as editor of the journal and as secretary-
general of the WSE.

29. 'Doxiadis is the World's Giant in Urban Planning', *Cleveland Plain-Dealer*, 21
October 1966.

30. Diana Lurie (1966) 'Busy remodeler of the world', *Life*, vol. 61, no. 15 (7 October),
pp. 55–60.

31. Rand, op. cit., p. 66.

32. C.A. Doxiadis, *Ekistic Analysis* (1946), *Destruction of Towns and Villages in
Greece* (1946), *A Plan for the Survival of the Greek People* (1947), *Ekistic Policies
for the Reconstruction of the Country with a 20-Year Programme* (1947), all
published in Greek; Constantine A. Doxiadis (1946) *Economic Policy for the
Reconstruction of the Settlements of Greece*, Athens: Undersecretary's Office for
Reconstruction; Constantine A. Doxiadis (1947) *Such Was the War in Greece*,
Athens: Department of Reconstruction.

33. Michael E. Porter (1985) *Competitive Advantage: Creating and Sustaining
Superior Performance*, New York: Free Press.

34. Most recently in Berlin (2001) and on the island of Tinos in Greece (2002).

35. Presented in C.A. Doxiadis, *Ekistics*, op. cit., pp. 81–199.

36. His positions were comparable to those of Walter W. Rostow (1962) *The Stages
of Economic Growth: A Non-Communist Manifesto*, Cambridge: Cambridge
University Press, and to those of the authors in Julian L. Simon and Herman Kahn
(1984) (eds) *The Resourceful Earth*, Oxford: Blackwell.

37. See, for example, Paul A. Baran (1957) *The Political Economy of Growth*, New
York: Monthly Review Press.

38. See Paul R. Ehrlich (1968) *The Population Bomb*, New York: Ballantine Books;
Paul R. Ehrlich and Anne H. Ehrlich (1974) *The End of Affluence*, New York:
Ballantine Books; and The Ecologist (1972) *A Blueprint for Survival*,
Harmondsworth: Penguin Books.

39. See, for example, Buckminster Fuller (1969) *Utopia or Oblivion: The Prospects
for Humanity*, Toronto: Bantam Books; Herman Kahn (1982) *The Coming Boom*,
New York: Simon & Schuster; Marshall McLuhan and Bruce R. Powers (1989) *The
Global Village: Transformations in World Life and Media in the 21st Century*,
New York: Oxford University Press.

40. Jane Jacobs (1961) *The Death and Life of Great American Cities*, New York: Vintage Books; Rachel Carson (1962) *Silent Spring*, Boston, MA: Houghton Mifflin; and Robert Goodman (1971) *After the Planners*, New York: Simon & Schuster.

41. See, for example, Mike Faber and Dudley Seers (eds) (1972) *The Crisis in Planning*, London: Chatto & Windus; Peter J. Boettke (ed.) (1994) *The Collapse of Development Planning*, New York: New York University Press.

42. C.A. Doxiadis (1977) *Ecology and Ekistics*, London: Elek Books, and Boulder, CO: Westview Press.

43. Jean Gottmann (1961) *Megalopolis: The Urbanized Northeastern Seaboard of the United States*, New York: Twentieth Century Fund; Brian J.L. Berry (1973) *The Human Consequences of Urbanization*, London: Macmillan; Brian J.L. Berry and Quentin Gillard (1977) *The Changing Shape of Metropolitan America*, Cambridge, MA: Ballinger; Manuel Castells and Peter Hall (1994) *Technopoles of the World*, London: Routledge.

44. 'The Blue Banana' is a name for Europe's core axis, including Birmingham, London, Paris, Brussels, Amsterdam, Cologne, Frankfurt, Munich, Turin and Milan; see, Peter Hall (1992) *Urban and Regional Planning*, London: Routledge, 3rd edn, pp. 159–87.

45. Doxiadis and Papaioannou, *Ecumenopolis*, op. cit.

46. Nathan Silver (1968) '$35 Worth of Hubris', *The Nation*, 23 December, pp. 695–97.

47. C.A. Doxiadis (1966, 1967 and 1970) *Emergence and Growth of an Urban Region: The Developing Urban Detroit Area*, Detroit: Detroit Edison Company, 3 vols.

48. See Walker Lee Cisler (1976) *A Measurable Difference,* Ann Arbor, MI: University of Michigan, Graduate School of Business Administration, pp. 103–4 and 136–48.

49. Nathan Silver, op. cit., p. 696.

50. In contrast, see Thomas J. Sugrue (1996) *The Origins of the Urban Crisis: Race and Inequality in Postwar Detroit,* Princeton, NJ: Princeton University Press.

51. See Reynolds Farley, Sheldon Danziger and Harry J. Holzer (2000) *Detroit Divided*, New York: Russell Sage Foundation.

52. C.A. Doxiadis, *Urban Renewal*, op. cit., pp. 61–68.

53. See, for example, Jon C. Teaford (1990) *The Rough Road to Renaissance: Urban Revitalization in America, 1940–1985*, Baltimore, MD: Johns Hopkins University Press.

54. On Beirut, see Hashim Sarkis (1998) 'Dances with Margaret Mead: Planning Beirut since 1968', in Peter G. Rowe and Hashim Sarkis (eds) *Projecting Beirut: Episodes in the Construction and Reconstruction of a Modern City*, Munich: Prestel, pp. 187–201; and Hashim Sarkis (2002) *Circa 1958: Lebanon in the Pictures and Plans of Constantinos Doxiadis*, Beirut: Dar An-Nahar Publishers.

55. C.A. Doxiadis (1966) *Between Dystopia and Utopia*, Hartford, CT: Trinity College Press. This book publishes three lectures, 'Towards Dystopia', 'Escape to Utopia' and 'Need of Entopia'.

CONTRIBUTORS' BIOGRAPHIES

Ray Bromley is Professor of Planning, Geography and Latin American Studies at the University at Albany, SUNY, where he directs the Graduate Planning Program. He has taught in Swansea and Syracuse, and researched in various Latin American countries. He has authored or edited six books, including *The Urban Informal Sector* (Pergamon, 1979), *Casual Work and Poverty in Third World Cities* (Wiley, 1979) and *Planning for Small Enterprises in Third World Cities* (Pergamon, 1985), and co-edited the Development and Underdevelopment series at Methuen/Routledge. His writings focus on city and regional planning, street and market trading, small enterprise promotion, and recently the history of ideas in planning and international development. His most recent publications are articles on the work of John Turner and Hernando de Soto.

May Davie is associate researcher at URBAMA (Urbanisation dans le Monde Arabe), University of Tours, France. She also teaches at the Institut d'Urbanisme of the University of Balamand, Lebanon. She has extensively published on the urban history and on heritage questions of the city of Beirut. Her publications include *Beyrouth et ses faubourgs (1840–1940): Une intégration inachevée* (Beirut: CERMOC, 1996) and *Beyrouth 1825–1975, 150 ans d'urbanisme* (Beirut: Order of Engineers and Architects of Beirut, 2001).

Alaa El-Habashi is a research fellow at the American Research Center in Egypt. A specialist on the historic preservation of the built heritage of Cairo and Alexandria, he has worked on the conservation of both ancient monuments and buildings dating from the nineteenth and early twentieth centuries. He completed his dissertation in architecture at the University of Pennsylvania in 2001.

Carola Hein is Assistant Professor at Bryn Mawr College (USA) in the Growth and Structure of Cities Program. Having studied in Brussels and Hamburg, she has published and lectured widely on topics of contemporary and historical architectural and urban planning. From 1995 to 1999, she was a Visiting Researcher at Tokyo Metropolitan University and Kogakuin University, studying the reconstruction of Japanese cities after the Second World War and the Western influence on Japanese urban planning. She is the main author of *Hauptstadt Berlin* (Gebr. Mann Verlag, 1991) and co-editor of the forthcoming *Rebuilding Urban Japan after 1945* (Macmillan, spring 2003).

Anthony D. King is Bartle Professor of Art History and of Sociology, State University of New York at Binghamton. With Professor Thomas A. Markus, he is co-editor of the Routledge series, ArchiTEXT, on architecture/urbanism and social and cultural theory, for which he is currently preparing *The Spaces of Global Culture*. Recent essays include contributions to R. Bishop, J. Phillips and W.W. Yeo (eds) *Postcolonial Urbanism: Southeast Asian Cities and Global Processes* (2003). Grant and J. Short (eds) *Globalization and the Margins* (2002) and G. Bridge and S. Watson (eds) *The Blackwell Companion to the City* (2000). His previous books include *Culture, Globalization and the World-System* (1997) and, as editor, *Urbanism, Colonialism and the World Economy* (1990).

Nora Lafi is the author of *Une ville du Maghreb entre Ancien Régime et réformes municipales* (Paris: L'Harmattan, 2002), based on her dissertation on Tripoli, Libya. She studies the evolution of the forms of urban government in North Africa and the Middle East between the eighteenth and the twentieth centuries. She is the editor of *Municipalités méditerranéennes* (Paris, 2003, forthcoming) and of the H-Mediterranean website (part of H-Net, based at Michigan State University) (http://www2.h-net.msu.edu/~mediter).

Joe Nasr is a USA-based independent researcher. He is currently Leverhulme Trust Visiting Fellow at the University of Central England in Birmingham. He will be spending 2004 in the Middle East as a Fulbright Scholar, exploring planning cultures in the Middle East. He has taught in the past at the University of Michigan at Ann Arbor, at Bryn Mawr College and at the American University of Beirut. Since 1997 he has been lecturer at the Institut d'Urbanisme de l'ALBA and associate researcher at the CERMOC research center, both in Beirut. In 1993 he co-founded the Urban Agriculture Network, a non-profit organization. The 1996 book he co-authored, *Urban Agriculture: Food, Jobs and Sustainable Cities*, will appear in a second edition in 2003, as will another book he is co-editing: *L'interface entre agriculture et urbanisation dans le bassin méditerranéen*. Other specialties include planning history, urban morphology and postwar reconstruction. He holds a doctorate in urban and regional planning from the University of Pennsylvania.

Alicia Novick is Professor of History of Architecture and of Urban Planning at the Facultad de Arquitectura, Diseño y Urbanismo of the Universidad de Buenos Aires, where she is a researcher at the Instituto de Arte Americano. She is the author of *La figura del técnico y la imagen del plan en los orígenes del urbanismo* (Buenos Aires, 2001), and of papers on urban planning history, including: 'Le Musée Social et l'urbanisme en Argentine' (in Colette Chambelland (ed.) *Le Musée social en son temps*, Paris: Presses de l'école Normale Supérieure, 1998); and 'La construction de la banlieue à Buenos Aires' (in Hélène Rivière d'Arc (ed.) *Nommer les nouveaux territoires urbains*, Paris: Edition UNESCO, Editions de la Maison des sciences de l'homme, 2001).

Roland Strobel is a planner and geographer based in Cincinnati, US. Building on his background in political science, development planning and German studies, his dissertation at the University of Southern California looked at the links between city planning and political ideology in postwar Berlin. His recent activities in Cincinnati include the planning for redevelopment of derelict sites in the city.

Eric Verdeil is a planner and geographer from the Institut Français d'Urbanisme. He recently completed his PhD in urban geography and planning history at the University of Paris I-Sorbonne on 'A City and its Planners: The Rebuilding of Beirut (1950–2000)'. In 2000, as head of the Urban Observatory at the Centre d'études et de recherche sur le Moyen-Orient contemporain (renamed Institut Francais du Proche-Orient in 2003) in Beirut, he launched an ongoing collective research project on the professional cultures of planning in the Middle East.

Mercedes Volait is a researcher of the Centre national de la recherche scientifique at URBAMA, François-Rabelais University of Tours, France. She is a specialist on the architectural and planning history of modern Egypt, and has also written on the invention of heritage in the Arab world. She is currently directing 'Patrimoines partagés' – a European program on modern heritage in the Mediterranean basin. Her most recent publications include editing *Le Caire-Alexandrie: architectures européennes, 1850–1950* (Cairo: IFAO, 2001) and a chapter on nineteenth- and twentieth-century Cairo in *The Glory of Cairo: An Illustrated History*, edited by André Raymond (Cairo: The American University in Cairo Press, 2002).

Stephen V. Ward is Professor of Planning History at Oxford Brookes University. He is the editor of the international journal *Planning Perspectives* and was President of the International Planning History Society from 1996 to 2002. He has written widely on the history of planning and related topics. His most recent book, *Planning the Twentieth-Century City: The Advanced Capitalist World,* was published by Wiley in 2002. Other books he has written or edited include: *The Garden City: Past, Present, and Future* (1992), *Planning and Urban Change* (1994) and *Selling Places: The Marketing and Promotion of Towns and Cities, 1850–2000* (1998).

Alexandra Yerolympos is Associate Professor of Urban Planning at the School of Architecture of the Aristotle University in Thessaloniki. An architect and planner, she has written widely on the history and planning of cities in Greece, the Balkans and the Eastern Mediterranean. Her bibliography includes *Urban Transformations in the Balkans* (Thessaloniki: University Studio Press, 1996); *Thessalonique 1913–1918: Les autochromes du musée Albert-Kahn* (Athens: Ed. Olkos, 1999); and *Ernest Hebrard 1875–1933: La vie illustrée d'un architecte, de la Grèce en Indochine* (Athens: Ed. Potamos, 2001).

INDEX OF NAMES

Names mentioned in the text and captions

INDEX OF PLACES

The index includes names of countries, ciies and neighbourhoods mentioned ion the text and in the captions.